Gun Crusaders

P9-EMH-302

DISCARD

Gun Crusaders

The NRA's Culture War

Scott Melzer

NEW YORK UNIVERSITY PRESS

New York and London

NEW YORK UNIVERSITY PRESS
New York and London
www.nyupress.org

© 2009 by New York University
All rights reserved

Library of Congress Cataloging-in-Publication Data

Melzer, Scott.
Gun crusaders : the NRA's culture war / Scott Melzer.
p. cm.
Includes bibliographical references and index.
ISBN-13: 978-0-8147-9550-7 (cl : alk. paper)
ISBN-10: 0-8147-9550-1 (cl : alk. paper)
1. National Rifle Association of America. 2. Gun control—
United States. 3. Firearms ownership—United States. I. Title.
HV7436.M45   2009
323.4'3—dc22   2009016276

New York University Press books are printed on acid-free paper,
and their binding materials are chosen for strength and durability.
We strive to use environmentally responsible suppliers and materials
to the greatest extent possible in publishing our books.

Manufactured in the United States of America
10 9 8 7 6 5 4 3 2 1

ACC LIBRARY SERVICES AUSTIN, TX

For Tina, Dan, and Mom,
my three pillars

Contents

Acknowledgments

This book would not have been possible without the many people who contributed in countless ways to its completion. Much of the data come directly from members of the National Rifle Association (NRA) who generously agreed to participate in this research. I thank them for providing me with (what I believe to be) their candid thoughts on a range of contentious social and political issues, and I trust they will feel accurately represented by this work.

I was fortunate to receive advice and feedback from many wonderful colleagues during this journey. Of special note, Scott Coltrane has left an imprint on my thinking and writing not just for this book but for all of my work. I am deeply appreciative of the positive impact Scott has made on me through his first-rate scholarship, editing, and mentoring. I am a better sociologist and a better person for knowing him. Ellen Reese also made invaluable contributions to this book and to my intellectual interests. Ellen proved to be not just a great scholar but a gifted editor, and, I note with humility, a champion of this book.

Many other colleagues offered suggestions along the way, notably Kirk Williams; Michael Kimmel, who helped sharpen my analysis of the NRA's masculinity; and Carolina Bank Muñoz. When I had an important decision to make, inevitably I consulted Richard Serpe and benefited from his sage advice. Many of my current colleagues at Albion College read parts of the manuscript, offering critiques from a range of disciplinary lenses. I especially thank Lars Fogelin, Hadley Renkin, Len Berkey, 'Dimeji Togundé, Geoff Cocks, Marcy Sacks, and Scott Hendrix.

Several institutions have also been of assistance, including the Graduate Division and Department of Sociology at the University of California-Riverside, the University of California-San Diego Social Sciences and Humanities Library, and Albion College's Student Research Partners Program. This work was supported by a grant from the Hewlett-Mellon Fund for Faculty Development at Albion College, Albion, Michigan. I also thank the students who contributed to this project: Janis Leodones, Mia Hall, and Becky Friedrick transcribed interviews and brought data and sources to light; and Noa Iacob, Hanna Robey, and Andrew Delaree read drafts of the manuscript and offered helpful comments.

Ilene Kalish at New York University Press enthusiastically supported this project since it arrived on her desk. She pushed me to think and write more clearly, ultimately improving the book. Ilene's assistant, Aiden Amos, has been particularly helpful negotiating the final stages of the process; my thanks to her and the rest of the staff at NYU Press. Several anonymous reviewers carefully read my manuscript at various stages, providing thoughtful and important critiques. I hope they see the enormous contributions they made within these pages. In the end, though, the work is my own; any shortcomings are the result of my own decisions.

I also appreciate the contributions of my social support network, as they were my foundation before and throughout this project. At Riverside, I am especially grateful for the support of Todd Migliaccio, Carolina Bank Muñoz, Tracy Hull, Pedro Payne, Davison Bideshi, Kay Pih, Wendy Lucas-Castro, Michelle Adams, and Anna Wire. At Albion, many friends and colleagues were generous with their time, interest, and good humor. Those in our carpools have probably listened to (and put up with) the most—special thanks to Lars, Hadley, and Helena Mesa.

Above all, I thank my family for their unwavering support. My mom, Hindy Melzer, has always been my biggest supporter, offering constant encouragement and confirmation. She is a great parent and friend, and I cannot express how appreciative I am for all that she has done for me. My brother, Dan Melzer, has been my mentor for as long as I can remember. Throughout the writing of this book he provided substantive and editorial suggestions, general advice, and, along with his partner, Toni Szot, welcome and needed distractions from work. My in-laws, Bonnie and Bill Fields, always express interest in and support for my work. My partner, Tina Fields, deserves much credit for this book. She read and edited one draft after another from beginning to end, improving the clarity of my writing. Her direct contributions to this book, however, are the least of all she shared with me, ultimately making this book possible. Tina, I am humbled by your patience, buoyed by your support, empowered by your encouragement, moved by your laughter, inspired by your passion, overwhelmed by your love.

Preface

I grew up in middle-class neighborhoods within South Florida's suburban sprawl, where guns had little impact on our lives. My family and friends neither participated in a rural gun culture nor had to deal with the high rates of gun violence so prevalent in urban areas at the time. Like so many boys, I shot BB guns as a kid. I'm sure some of our neighbors kept guns in their homes, and, as a teenager, I had friends and acquaintances who owned guns but they had little relevance in our world. Gun control and gun rights were not bitterly contested, and guns were not celebrated as symbols of freedom or derided as symbols of death. They existed much like a Florida alligator sunning itself by a golf course lake—appearing only occasionally and drawing lukewarm interest when doing so. If guns played virtually no role in my youth, then the political activities of the National Rifle Association probably crossed my mind about as often as those of the American Association of Retired Persons.

Masculinity, however, colors nearly every one of my childhood memories. From the role my athleticism played in making friends and avoiding being ostracized, to the endless rituals of questioning others' masculinity and having my own questioned, to the palpable daily fear of violence at the hands of bigger boys, masculinity mattered. Popularity and pecking orders were established largely based on athleticism and physicality. I earned enough cultural capital from sports and a quick mouth to prevent being a victim of boyhood violence, despite my small size. Even though my personal encounters with violence were as rare as my handling of guns, I almost never thought about guns but regularly feared getting hit by peers, often those whom I considered friendly acquaintances. Guns and masculinity are intricately linked in so many ways, but for my own childhood they only came together on television or in the movies. My friends and I could see the connections between guns and masculinity, but we didn't live these connections.

My interest in the NRA arises from my ongoing interest in masculinity. More specifically, I am interested in men's responses to actual and perceived threats to their status and identities. My earlier work includes an examination of the impact of men's jobs on their use of violence against women partners. Men working in women-dominated occupations, such as clerical support jobs, have the highest rates of violence against women partners among employed men. These men doing "women's work"—much like men who are unemployed or have women partners who earn most of the couple's income—may compensate for their diminished breadwinner status and masculine identities by using violence against women to reassert authority within the home.[1] When I began this project I conceptualized the NRA as a men's movement, or at least a movement centered on a particular form of masculinity. Only after analyzing NRA literature and speaking with NRA members did I fully come to understand the gun rights movement as a form of collective action in response to perceived challenges to conservative men's status and identities. At the individual level, some men use violence against their wives in response to perceived threats to their status and identity in intimate relationships. At the group level, some men join social movements that offer a masculinity politics promoting a similar, though more generalized fear of men's loss of status, identity, and power to other social groups (such as women).

When I began this study, little research on the NRA existed through the lens of gender or of social movements. My aim in this book is to show that the NRA incorporates both an explicit and subtle masculinity politics and that these political views and messages, and the responses to them, have fueled the NRA's extraordinary transformation into a potent conservative culture war force. Given the NRA's large membership and the singular political power it wields in Washington and across the country, the organization and its members are worthy of further study. In short, I want to know what makes them tick.

Introduction

"From my cold, dead hands!" shouted Charlton Heston. The audience roared its approval for their President and charismatic leader. Heston was the only person defiantly holding a rifle over his head, but, as I scanned the room, everyone appeared ready to take up arms in the gun wars. Forty thousand strong attended the 2002 National Rifle Association (NRA) annual meeting in Reno, Nevada. They came for the guns. To hold them, talk about them, celebrate them, and, most important, defend them.

Unlike millions of other gun owners, the NRA and its faithful members believe that "gun rights" are under attack. They are also distinct in their belief that threats to guns are threats to *all* individual rights and freedoms. Take away gun rights, they say, and all other rights are sure to follow. An unarmed population will be unable to defend itself against a tyrannical government. Committed NRA members support the organization, because they agree with the NRA's interpretation and defense of the Second Amendment to the Constitution. My conversations with committed NRA members reveal their profound love of the United States and their belief that gun rights are one of many that free citizens enjoy. But love is not the emotion that drives the NRA. Love is not what transformed this former group of gun enthusiasts into a four-million-member conservative social movement organization (SMO) and political lightning rod. Listening to NRA leaders and speaking with members, their most palpable emotion is *fear*.

They feel threatened by a gun culture on the decline, gun control organizations, "anti-gun" politicians, and any gun control legislation. They fear the government having the power to tell them how many and which kinds of guns they can own, if any, when and where they can shoot them or carry them, how and from whom they can buy them, and even under what circumstances they can be used for self-defense. They fear losing their guns, and they fear losing their freedoms.

Just beneath the surface of these fears lies the politics of gender and race. Freedoms and rights, after all, mean different things to different people. For the NRA and its supporters, overwhelmingly older, conservative white men, "freedom" means that the government is out of their lives. They believe that we should rely on ourselves, not the government, for basic needs like food, shelter, love, and protection. This, they argue, is how the country was founded and what made it great. Government involvement in citizens' lives—or, worse, control over their lives—is a threat to American values and freedoms. Others see it differently, as NRA members are quick to point out. They argue that gun control advocates want the government to protect you; feminists want the government to take care of your children; affirmative action groups want to give your jobs to unqualified minorities; and welfare proponents want the government to take your hard-earned tax dollars and give them to those who are too lazy to support themselves.

Today's NRA sees threats. Big government, or "nanny state," policies, NRA members warn, are part of a broader culture war threatening gun rights, individual rights and freedoms, the values of self-reliance and independence, and, ultimately, white men's status and power—all issues the NRA pushes and its members fear. To them, guns are the first line of defense. If lost, all other rights will be jeopardized and, ultimately, the political Left will have undermined American democracy and replaced it with a socialist, communist, or fascist government. NRA leaders portray themselves and their members as 21st-Century freedom fighters, fending off liberals instead of the British: *"From my cold, dead hands!"*

I'll Fight for Freedom

Upon landing at the airport in Reno, Nevada, to attend the 2002 National Rifle Association meeting, I and other NRA attendees were greeted with a sign welcoming us to the "Biggest Little City in the World." Billboards declaring "I'll Fight for Freedom!" had been peppered throughout the city by the NRA, announcing its presence and the theme of that year's meeting.

The next morning I turned on the television in my hotel room as I ate a quick breakfast before heading to the NRA's events. It was Friday, April 26, 2002, and something terrible had happened. A news anchor referred to that morning's tragic shootings as the "German Columbine." Seventeen people in Erfurt, Germany, were dead, including the shooter, a former student at the school where the carnage took place. Students were crying and hugging one another. Later that evening NRA President Charlton Heston would make the cable news rounds, politely but forcefully repeating the same line of reasoning the NRA has argued for decades: guns don't kill people, people kill people. Just three years earlier, nearly to the day, the American Columbine took place. That year the NRA annual meetings had not yet begun in nearby Denver, and the fifteen shooting deaths resulted in the NRA holding an abridged meeting schedule. Erfurt, Germany, is a long way from Reno, however, so no similar outcry to cancel the NRA meetings was heard. Rather than rhetorically jousting with the local media and mayor, as Heston had done after Columbine, NRA speakers did not mention the German shootings and Reno's mayor embraced the NRA at its welcoming ceremony.

The 2002 ceremony theme was "A Day for Heroes," as 9/11 had occurred less than a year ago and was on the minds of the NRA and its members. Groups of all political interests have honored the first-responders who risked their lives that tragic day. For the NRA, the task is effortless. Virtually all their ceremonies are awash in red, white, and blue. They see great overlap between the heroes of 9/11, the heroes throughout U.S. history, and the NRA-labeled heroes in the audience for the ceremony—all are American patriots fighting for freedom. The NRA's top officer, Executive Vice President (EVP) Wayne LaPierre, hosted the event. Despite having the unenviable task of regularly sharing the stage with the charismatic Heston and his salt-of-the-earth appeal, the stiff, bespectacled LaPierre generally receives enthusiastic standing ovations from NRA crowds. He was applauded because his long and steady leadership (along with Heston as figurehead) has helped the NRA reach its zenith. Four million members, serious political clout, and $200 million in annual revenue helps NRA members ignore whatever folksy charm LaPierre lacks.

I arrived at the ceremony as the doors were closing, a bit late because I'd spent some time furiously writing notes in the building's only discrete location: a bathroom stall. I managed to talk my way past a security guard, who was turning away all latecomers because the crowd far exceeded the room's seating and standing capacities. The ceremony began with the pledge of allegiance, soon followed by a mini Oak Ridge Boys concert. Between songs, one of the Oak Ridge Boys drew a roar from the crowd when he told us that, when asked to perform for NRA members, his only thought was "lock and load!" They began their set with "American Made" ("My Baby Is American Made, Born and Bred in the U.S.A.") and finished with some gospel music. As I looked around the room, I did not notice any non-Christian members walk out in anger or appear offended by the religious lyrics.

Soon the mood turned somber as LaPierre called out the names of 9/11 victims, family members, police officers, and rescue workers who were also NRA members. The ceremony was slow and emotional, as LaPierre greeted emergency responders and many of the victims' families on stage. With the terrorist attack still fresh in our minds, and public and political debates about balancing freedom and safety heating up, this tribute to the "heroes of 9/11" fit well with the overall theme of the meeting, "I'll Fight for Freedom." Later, singer Lee Greenwood took the stage and sang several patriotic songs, capped off by his hit song, "God Bless the U.S.A." With the crowd singing along, an NRA member walked from the back of the hall to the stage to shake Greenwood's hand. The member, a man in his seventies, wore a mesh NRA baseball cap and was decked out in red, white, and blue from head to toe. He was draped in a short-sleeve, button-down American flag shirt, shorts with U.S. stars on one leg and stripes on the other, and calf-high red-and-blue-striped socks with white sneakers. On the way back to his seat, an older woman stopped him to give him a hug. LaPierre ended the ceremony exclaiming, "Let's have a great weekend!"

Hotel shuttles, city busses, and a full parking lot of mostly trucks and RVs poured throngs of people into the Reno-Sparks Convention Center. A long row of well-staffed registration booths lined the wall of the main hallway, flanked on the left by an enormous gun show and on the right by meeting rooms for smaller weekend events. The main hallway ceiling was filled with ten-foot banners of famous NRA members and their guns, looming over us like watchful deities. Among those proud and famous members declaring "I'm the NRA" were Heston, fellow actor Tom Selleck, author Tom Clancy, and professional basketball player Karl Malone. Around the corner stood thirty-deep lines of admirers waiting to meet (or just buy books written by) Heston, LaPierre, and NRA Board Member/rock star/*Kill It & Grill It* author Ted Nugent. Another group lined up to purchase an incredible range of products emblazoned with the organization's image. Belt buckles and hats, mugs and bumper stickers, even earrings and infant bibs were gobbled up at the NRA store. The NRA is a brand that sells.

The crowd had a rural feel in Reno, with its profusion of NRA black-and-gold shooter's caps, jeans with suspenders, a lot of facial hair—and, if you never spoke to any of them or if you grew up in urban areas, perhaps a sense that all of the worst stereotypes of an NRA member are true. Trucks parked outside were covered with bumper stickers sharing members' views on guns, crime, and hunting: "If guns cause crime, then matches cause arson" and "I Love Animals: They Taste Great." T-shirts being sold and worn in the gun show hall displayed similar themes. One read "Nice Rack," with a picture of antlers splashed across the chest of a woman's spaghetti-strapped tank-top. A woman in her twenties passed by me wearing a T-shirt with the words "Feminine Protection" right above a picture of a semi-automatic handgun. Most members wore clothes that fit with stereotypes of poor or working-class rural gun owners: tight blue jeans, cowboy boots, big belt buckles or suspenders, and flannel shirts. But after speaking with dozens of them, it became clear that they are mostly middle class in terms of formal education, employment, and income. A year later when I attended the annual meeting in Orlando, suspenders and blue jeans were largely replaced by khaki pants and polo shirts. A handful of members were in full camouflage, including a seven-year-old boy in Reno who topped off his outfit with a military helmet. Others, virtually all staff and gun-show vendors, wore suits. A disproportionate number of young, blonde, attractive women worked the booths at the gun shows.

The attendees were largely men. Most striking was that over the course of the weekend I could count the number of people of color I saw on two hands—and I had walked by and sat next to thousands of people. The gathering was unquestionably white, and in that regard I fit right in. Though I was somewhat younger than most attendees, I was hardly noticeable in my usual unstylish graduate student outfit—a pair of dark blue jeans, hiking boots, and a plain T-shirt, just another bearded face in the crowd. A year later at the Orlando Board of Directors meeting, the incoming NRA President Kayne Robinson spoke about recruiting NASCAR fans, noting, "They're us and we're them." Knowing their supporters well, the NRA followed up the Oak Ridge Boys and Lee Greenwood in Reno with Toby Keith in Orlando.

On Saturday morning I headed back to the Reno-Sparks Convention Center. The official annual meeting of members session began with a brief prayer, followed by rock concert-like introductions of the NRA officers. President Charlton Heston received a thunderous standing ovation. Continuing an ongoing tradition, Wayne LaPierre located the youngest (age five) and oldest (age ninety-seven) lifetime NRA members in attendance. The oldest one grabbed the microphone and offered thoughts mirroring those of the NRA officer reports to come. He warned his fellow members about the importance of winning elections. If gun rights candidates lose, he cautioned, the cops will come to our homes and take away our guns. James Jay Baker, the NRA's chief lobbyist, earned a laugh when he told LaPierre that, after eight years of Clinton in office, Baker felt like the NRA's oldest member. This theme carried through the officer reports just as it comes up repeatedly in NRA speeches, mailings to members, and organizational magazines. Bill and Hillary Clinton, Al Gore, the media, gun control groups, and "anti-gun" academics and Democratic politicians (such as New York's Charles Schumer and California's Dianne Feinstein) are ridiculed and booed. They are the faces of gun control, the Left's cultural warriors threatening guns and freedom.

Then second Vice President (and later NRA President) Sandy Froman kicked things off by announcing, "I'm Sandy Froman and I'm proud to be part of the American gun culture." She attacked gun control advocate Josh Sugarmann of the Violence Policy Center as well as historian Michael Bellesiles, who wrote the controversial *Arming America*, which challenged the notion of a U.S. frontier gun culture.[1] Bellesiles was accused of scholarly misconduct by other academics and eventually chose to resign as professor of history at Emory University after an external committee of scholars raised serious concerns about his research. The Bellesiles controversy verified the NRA's suspicions and fears that academics are yet another arm of the anti-gun movement. Froman referred to the "intellectual terrorism" of these authors, and railed against colleges' and universities' "zero tolerance bigotry" against firearms, code for gun bans on campus grounds.

Executive Vice President LaPierre picked up where Froman left off. He accused gun control supporters of attacking freedom, referring to them as "political terrorists." Among those he accused were Americans for Gun Safety's billionaire founder Andrew McKelvey. LaPierre drew an analogy between McKelvey's well-financed attack on freedom through gun control advocacy and Osama bin Laden's well-financed attacks on freedom through terrorism:

> In fact, the way Andrew McKelvey's network operates sounds a lot like Osama bin Laden and [Al-Qaida]. A billionaire with an extremist political agenda, subverting honest diplomacy, using personal wealth to train and deploy activists, looking for vulnerabilities to attack, fomenting fear for political gain, funding an ongoing campaign to hijack your freedom and take a box cutter to the Constitution. That's political terrorism, a far greater threat to your freedom than any foreign force.[2]

For LaPierre the connections are clear: gun control supporters are no better than Al-Qaida, as both want to take away Americans' freedoms. The NRA warns that the Left's culture war is a greater threat to individual rights and freedoms than a real war. The crowd was engaged with LaPierre's strong words and surely looking forward to their President finishing the rhetorical disemboweling of the "anti-gunners." Heston, however, had begun to display the effects of what was later diagnosed as the early stages of Alzheimer's disease. Partly in lieu of a member-rallying speech, we were shown a Heston-narrated video tribute to Ronald Reagan, the first sitting U.S. President to attend the NRA's annual meeting and also the first presidential candidate the NRA endorsed, in 1980.

Show Us Your Gun

With free time before an afternoon session on the media, I headed to the gun show and exhibit hall. It was a shooter's paradise. The enormous hall was filled with row after row of guns and gear vendors, offering everything a hunter, sport shooter, collector, or self-defense practitioner desires. Gun enthusiasts wandered the building like kids in a toy store, admiring, touching, aiming, and talking about a vast array of firearms and accessories.

I hoped to speak with NRA members while flying under the organization's radar. I wanted to get a sense of members' backgrounds, their views on gun control and gun rights, how they feel about the NRA, and their broader social and political attitudes. Documenting the official positions of the NRA and its leaders through magazines and speeches is much easier. The NRA meetings attract a variety of members, though most are strongly committed to the organization. Some fly from all over the country to attend, and others only attend the meetings one time simply because it was held near their home. Some attend all gun rights sessions, whereas others only go to the gun show. The gatherings draw tens of thousands of members, but maybe 10% attend the official annual meeting where NRA business is discussed and sometimes voted on. Empty seats were plentiful in Reno and Orlando, suggesting a range of commitment among the attendees and therefore among those whom I spoke with and interviewed.

At the Reno meeting, I found a high foot-traffic area outside to solicit interviews. It was a typical spring day, sunny and mild. The combination of clear skies and a meticulously organized NRA gathering seemed to put everyone in a good mood. A steady flow of people filtered in and out of the convention center for the NRA gathering. Sign-up sheets in hand, I began obtaining contact information.

A couple in their sixties passed by and I asked if they would be interested in sharing their views on gun control. Big mistake. As they brusquely walked away, the woman turned to me and yelled, "What about people control?!" I refined my approach and avoided language that spoke to members' gun control fears, instead asking them to share their views on gun rights, the Constitution, and threats to both. I soon was filling my sheets with contact information for in-depth telephone interviews after the meetings.

I joined the NRA in 2001, when I began this research (see appendix for a discussion of research methods and data). By joining the NRA, attending some of its official events, reading countless NRA materials dating back several decades, and speaking at length with members, I can offer an insider's perspective along with an outsider's critique. Given the NRA's distrust of the media and academics, I had to convince many skeptical members that I would not misquote them or twist their words if they agreed to be interviewed. Flashing my membership card was undoubtedly a huge help in obtaining volunteers. Still, this was not enough for some. Three members who could have doubled as Hell's Angels bikers—big, stocky guys wearing jeans, boots, big belt buckles, leather jackets, and long facial hair—were not impressed. Before agreeing to share their contact information, they asked me to show them my gun. Ironically a sign on the convention center door made it clear that no personal weapons were allowed in the building. Sign or no sign, I assumed these guys could care less about the rules and carried a concealed weapon wherever they damn-well pleased. But I was not packing. Eventually I eased their fears and they warmed up to me, as we swapped stories about California's concealed carry laws. Complaining about the "Left Coast" poster child of "political correctness," where "all the Socialists are," is a favorite NRA pastime.[3] By lunchtime I obtained a long list of names that would later result in interviews, all without having to pull out a gun.

Liberals: Evil, Not Stupid

One of the defining characteristics and a key source of power for the contemporary NRA is its status as a top dog for the conservative movement. Gun politics have become increasingly partisan over time, and the NRA has explicitly picked a side by putting nearly all its eggs in the conservative/Republican basket. Today's NRA is a cultural warrior for the Right, so it is no surprise when fellow conservative cultural warriors are invited to speak at NRA gatherings about the perceived biases of the "liberal media," gun-related and otherwise.

At 1:30 on Sunday afternoon in Reno, a small NRA session on the media was standing-room only. "For The Record: Media Commentators Speak Out!" was moderated by former *Dallas* actress Susan Howard, an NRA Board member. The panel featured four participants: Kellyanne Conway, a regular conservative television commentator and President and CEO of the polling company inc.; Grover Norquist, conservative activist, President of Americans for Tax Reform, and NRA Board member; Debbie Schlussel, conservative political commentator and columnist; and Armstrong Williams, conservative columnist and radio and television host. No members of the "liberal media" would be speaking this day.

As expected at an NRA session of conservative media commentators, talk centered on the "anti-gun liberal media." Susan Howard set the tone for the session, casting conservative activists and media as victimized minorities waging a just battle against the omnipresent liberal media. She pleaded with her fellow members not to fear speaking up against the powerful majority. "When you stand before God, you'll know you did good." Grover Norquist, a major player in the conservative movement since at least the Reagan era, emphasized that gun owners and conservatives were not staring down well-meaning but wrongheaded opponents. Rather, the political Left is waging a culture war that threatens conservative values. "They're not stupid. They're evil" was Norquist's description of liberals and their agendas. He proudly pointed out that, despite the injustice at the hands of the media, "we're [conservatives] winning the elections."

Debbie Schlussel's interpretation was slightly different than Norquist's "evil, not stupid" theme. She tried to capture the NRA audience by arguing, "We're cool and they're the freaks." Schlussel was sick and tired of the "liberal media" repeatedly depicting NRA members as gap-toothed, suspender-wearing rednecks. NRA members, gun owners, and conservative rural Americans are the cool ones, she said. Liberals, or "weirdos" and "wackos," fell into the freak category. Gun control activists and "womb-envy" sensitive guys are "girly-men." They're the freaks. "But I'm a girl and I use a gun," Schlussel said.

The audience could barely stay seated, as one speaker after another told them what they already knew to be true and were happy to hear: they are the real Americans, the patriots, the ones who know what's best for this country. They must continue to fight, because liberals have gained too much power and influence, particularly over the media. America was losing its way, straying from its original values. Instead, the conservative panelists argued, the "liberal media elite," with their "chai teas and lattes," their "gated communities" and "private schools," are trying to push their own left-wing, anti-gun views and lifestyles onto the rest of the country. Using the not uncommon NRA practice of red-baiting, Kellyanne Conway argued that these "Bolsheviks" privately refer to one another as "comrade" and are conducting a culture war against gun owners. Conservative cultural warriors label anyone supporting some measure of gun control as a freedom-hating Communist.

Armstrong Williams, the only African American panelist, took the microphone and quickly had the nearly entirely white audience riveted. Few of them had likely seen an orator deliver a political sermon such as the one by this self-identified Pentecostal. Williams said that he had to let media members Bryant Gumbel and Ted Koppel know that "I'm American first" and Black second, so they shouldn't assume otherwise. As other conservative scholars as well as some liberal politicians and activists have done, Williams argued that gun laws are racist, as they prevent African Americans from obtaining concealed carry licenses. These critics point out that law-enforcement officers are less likely to sign off on African Americans' applications to carry a concealed weapon for protection. Though speaking to a nearly entirely white audience, Williams said that we need to "get minorities to understand that 'they' [whites] don't want 'you all' [African Americans] to own guns." In referencing the need for armed protection, Williams attacked single parents as the primary culprits raising criminals. Liberals and the liberal media are to blame for crime and the denial of the right to self-defense for African Americans, he argued.

Gun control was far from the panel members' only target, as this is only one of many culture war threats. Kellyanne Conway also attacked gays and lesbians, "pro-abortionists," and single parents. She told us that though it is "fun" to talk and e-mail gossip about gays and lesbians, in the end it is not an important issue. This followed her attack on "identity politics"—code for political divisions along gender, race, class, and sexuality lines. Do not pay attention to public polling suggesting otherwise, she admonished, because identity politics is unimportant. In one polling-related attack, Conway said that Americans have an easier time naming the Rice Krispies characters than Supreme Court Justices. Though she admitted that Snap, Crackle, and Pop get more face time on television, her point was that students do not take enough civics courses because they are too busy taking art, physical education, and other less worthwhile (often liberal) endeavors. Conway, half jokingly, expressed annoyance that Americans did so poorly on their Supreme Court quiz. "Come on, at least get the two chicks and the Black guy!" she scorned, as the room of listeners laughed. "Feminists probably didn't vote," she said, "because one of [the cereal character's] names was 'Pop'" and this was too "misogynistic." Identity politics does seem to matter for Conway, if only to serve as a source of contempt. She pursued her point in a description of a liberal counterpart who receives more air time than she does on CNN: "She's Black and has corn rows and the whole thing." For Conway, her African American colleague is a popular commentator for the liberal media because she represents identity politics.

At the conclusion of the final presentation, the audience rose in a standing ovation. Here were a couple hundred NRA members cheering on the conservative speakers' attacks on liberal figures and politics. It became clear to me that the NRA is not just fighting for guns. Committed NRA members' support for gun rights is about freedom, independence, self-reliance, and their American way of life. Though they rally behind and respond to these ideas, beneath all that is *fear*.

The driving force behind these gun rights activists is fear, and not just of gun control foes but also of feminists, criminals, terrorists, gays, and Communists. They perceive that liberals are plotting to take away their gun rights and give women, gays, and people of color not equal but "special" rights. The gun-owning, rural, conservative, straight, white man is the new victim of discrimination, the new minority, they believe. NRA members must fight back before it's too late. "We should have bombed Berkeley first, then Kandahar," one audience member said, wishing the culture war of the Right would produce as many casualties in liberal American cities as U.S. military strikes against the Taliban did in Afghanistan.

Playing Offense

The NRA is winning the gun battle. Despite their constant warnings about threats to guns and freedom, the NRA is a powerful social movement organization facing comparably weak gun control associations with modest agendas. The NRA typically errs on the side of fear tactics when deciding between talk of ominous threats and the likelihood of victory. Like many SMOs, they've discovered that fear generates more member support.[4] The reality, however, is that they have been dominating the gun wars for years, and nothing suggests that this will change soon.

At the modestly attended 2003 annual meeting session, "Women Aiming High," NRA 2nd Vice President Sandy Froman joined a discussion about Charlton Heston's positive impact on the NRA. Referring to the NRA's status, she told the audience: "We're at our peak . . . it's only gonna get better." Similarly, a video recognizing Heston's contributions rattled off NRA successes to a large crowd of Heston well-wishers. Heston ran for the NRA presidency in 1998 with the goal of quelling the NRA's internal fighting over financial problems and projecting a better image of the organization. He wanted to increase the membership and the war chest, steer the NRA back into the mainstream, and elect a pro-gun president by the end of the century. Three years later, at the 2000 Charlotte meetings, he reflected on his and the NRA's incredible accomplishments.[5] The organization had added one million members to reach four million, increased its budget and controlled spending, and was now in mainstream political debates and helped defeat Al Gore and elect George W. Bush. This was a rare moment when the NRA encouraged its members to focus on the organization's many victories and, at least momentarily, ignore any threats.

NRA leaders were more likely to share their joy and optimism in relative privacy at the two Board of Directors meetings I attended in Reno and Orlando, both beginning on the Monday after the annual meetings. The NRA's seventy-six person board far exceeded the number of regular NRA members attending the board meetings, many of whom appeared to be family members of officers and directors. I did not attend any board meetings that did not coincide with the annual meetings, but presumably even fewer regular NRA members would travel to attend just a board meeting. I imagine that NRA members' lack of attendance at board meetings reflects their satisfaction with the status and direction of the organization. NRA officers' gloating messages to the board contrasted sharply with their portrayal of threats to gun rights at the members' meetings. "The bottom line is, we're on the offense," Wayne LaPierre proudly announced at the Reno board meeting. By this he meant that the NRA was able to focus on lobbying *for* "pro-gun" legislation rather than *against* gun control legislation. In Orlando a year later he told the board that the NRA is "stronger and more widely accepted than ever."

Like many organizations, the NRA has a long history of bitter in-fighting that contributed to their varying degrees of effectiveness over time. No such bickering or factionalism was apparent in Reno or Orlando, only much self-congratulating and back-patting. Officers' reports were met with smiles and applause. Staff members and board members kidded one another. One board member, while nominating someone for a committee, joked, "Unfortunately, she used to be a Democrat." All leadership positions and committee nominations were unanimous. In Reno, Heston warmly referred to LaPierre as the "rock of the NRA." He then accepted what would be his final term as NRA President, saying, "If we can do what we've done over the past year . . . we're in deep clover."

God Gave Us Moses

I walked through the smoke-filled casino floor of my Reno hotel one night, finally escaping the onslaught of blinking and ringing slot machines when the elevator doors closed behind me. Heading up to their own room was a father with an "I'm the NRA" button and his young son. I struck up a conversation with the father, and he excitedly told me about shaking Charlton Heston's hand at the actor's book table. "What a great way to start the day!" the father beamed. The NRA has been around for more than a century and had three million members before Heston's arrival, but it is hard to overstate Heston's contribution to the NRA's success. His commitment to the organization brought it into the political mainstream and spurred a surge in membership and financial resources. NRA members both admire and identify with him, largely, of course, because of his leading role as a defender of gun rights. Beyond this, however, Heston embodies a masculinity born of the frontier. He (and many of the characters he played) reflects the NRA's ideology of individual rights and freedoms, independence, and a fight-for-your-rights attitude. When he enters or exits a room filled with NRA members, Charlton Heston always receives the loudest and longest standing ovation.

The NRA celebrated Heston's last year as President by making the 2003 annual meeting "A Tribute to Charlton Heston." NRA board member Susan Howard reflected upon the NRA's success at a small session on women and the NRA, saying it was "by the grace of God" that the NRA is doing so well and has been moved from out in left field to the mainstream. Panel member Susan LaPierre, the wife of the NRA's top officer, put it simply: "God gave us Moses." Heston, she continued, is the reason the NRA has moved into the mainstream, and they could not have been more fortunate than when he decided to dedicate himself to their cause.

No NRA references to Charlton Heston as Moses, in my experience, were offered tongue-in-cheek or metaphorically. Yes, Heston the actor played Moses in *The Ten Commandments*,[6] but Susan LaPierre sincerely referred to him as the leader of a people, sent by God to help them. In a tribute to Ronald Reagan, Heston spoke of freedom and faith: "[Reagan] believed in not just freedom of religion, but in the religion of freedom. He believed that's why God put us here. That fostering freedom is America's sacred purpose."[7] Like many NRA members, Heston believed that the Ten Commandments and Ten Amendments (to the U.S. Constitution) were handed down from God; they can almost see the divine intervention in the construction of the Bill of Rights.[8] In the minds of NRA members, God gave them two gifts: freedom and Charlton Heston to defend it. Or, as Susan Howard noted in her opening prayer before the 2003 annual meeting of members: "Lord, bless Charlton Heston, as Charlton Heston has blessed us."

A Friday night tribute to Heston was paired with a Toby Keith concert. After a rendition of the "Star-Spangled Banner," we watched a film montage of Charlton Heston's activities with the NRA, clips from his speeches, and even a segment showing him marching for civil rights with Martin Luther King Jr. Earlier in his life, Heston stumped for John F. Kennedy, but, the video's narrator explained, the Democratic Party had changed and was no longer maintaining its pro-gun roots. The video conveyed Heston's and the NRA's argument that it is a nonpartisan civil rights organization, saddened and upset by the Democratic Party's new gun control agenda.

When Bill Clinton's face appeared on screen resounding "booooooos" rose from the audience, as Clinton was regularly seen as the most anti-gun president ever. The video contained the usual heavy dose of NRA references to patriotism and freedom, dressed up in images of the American flag. The video and the rollercoaster of emotions it provoked as it followed Heston's life, his friends, and his enemies ended, and Charlton Heston and his wife ambled onstage. The crowd stood and cheered for a long time. Wayne LaPierre joined them and unveiled a statue of Heston as cowhand Will Penny, the actor's favorite role, from the similarly titled 1968 Western. LaPierre announced that the statue would be placed at the NRA Headquarters in Virginia as a symbol of Heston's contributions to freedom.[9]

Before the ceremony ended, we listened to a farewell speech Heston had taped before his health deteriorated. The crowd gave him a final standing ovation as he got up to leave. Members waved good-bye as Heston gestured his own farewell. Unlike a stadium-sized crowd collectively waving good-bye to a beloved retiring athlete, many audience members appeared to be sending their personal farewells to Heston. They leaned and stretched in their attempts to be singled out for his attention in this crowd of thousands. This scene was repeated the next day at the annual members meeting, where, again in a video, Heston officially handed the President's gavel to his successor onstage and said his final good-bye. NRA members again stood and cheered their outgoing leader. As Heston waved, I noticed a woman standing on her chair, waving enthusiastically. She was far away and hidden from Heston's view, but she stood and waved regardless, as though saying good-bye to a family member who was catching a plane. To many members, Charlton Heston is the NRA's icon, its cowboy hero, its Moses.

Heston's pre-taped messages at his farewell ceremony in Orlando only magnified how frail he appeared in person. Nevertheless, despite suffering from a debilitating disease, he mustered enough strength to lift that Model 1866 rifle over his head one last time before exiting stage left at the annual members meeting. He belted out five final words as an eternal reminder to both his admirers and his enemies that Heston, and four million NRA members, would rather die fighting than give up their guns: *"From my cold, dead hands!"* That was to be Heston's final appearance at an NRA event. He disappeared from the limelight until he succumbed to illness and died five years later in 2008 at the age of eighty-four.

The Gun Movement

Why do Heston's words resonate so strongly with NRA members? Why do four million Americans belong to the NRA? True, many perceive serious threats to their "gun rights," but, as Charlton Heston argues, the gun is just a *symbol*.[10] Former Director of the NRA-ILA (Institute for Legislative Action) Warren Cassidy once told an outsider, "You would get a far better understanding if you approached us as if you were approaching one of the great religions of the world." Indeed, this religion welcomes only true believers. "It was a religious war. You're either with them or against them," an aide to Arizona Senator Dennis DeConcini once said about the NRA, after DeConcini tarnished his perfect NRA rating and faced a backlash for supporting gun control legislation.[11]

NRA members, mostly conservative white men, cast themselves as heroic frontiersmen celebrating a version of American manhood from decades past. What drives them to join the movement is not pride or celebration, but a dedication to stem the tide eroding their religion of individual rights and freedoms, to defend what I call "frontier masculinity."[12] Characterized by rugged individualism, hard work, protecting and providing for families, and self-reliance, frontier masculinity is the mythologized dominant version of manhood from America's frontier past.[13] Think Gary Cooper in *High Noon*, Charlton Heston in *Will Penny*, or, more recently, Christian Bale in *3:10 to Yuma*.

The contentious debate over guns is provocative in itself, but the NRA uniquely interests me, as a sociologist, because it gained power and influence at the same time as did many other conservative, reactionary movements. The NRA and these other backlash movements are largely responding to earlier gains made by liberal movements of the 1960s and 1970s, and for all of them gender and race are often primary, if implicit, issues. The NRA has contributed to and benefited from a conservative shift in national politics. This swing to the Right has created opportunities for groups such as the Christian Right, the Promise Keepers, and movements pushing for "traditional" families to have enormous influence on national policy and public debates.[14]

The NRA, again like its conservative brethren, initially reacted to societal threats to its interests. Recently, however, its agenda has broadened beyond gun rights to conservative politics, and it has ridden the conservative wave to new heights of success. Internal stability and peaks in membership numbers and resources coincided with expanding political opportunities. Yet, the perceived (and often exaggerated) threat to gun rights and the NRA's idealistic frontier masculinity also persists, and thus the NRA can both enjoy its status as the most powerful single-issue lobbying group in Washington, D.C., while agitating its members into believing that gun rights are at death's door. The NRA frames threats to gun rights and frontier masculinity as coming from liberal culture war forces, knowing this message resonates with hundreds of thousands, even millions of conservative white men who feel they are under attack by various liberal causes, primarily gun control.

Threats to gun rights, even modest local ordinances, which in turn threaten freedom and frontier masculinity, puts at risk the fundamental beliefs and identities of devoted NRA members. Compromising on gun control is compromising oneself. They would rather die fighting than allow government authorities to confiscate their guns, which protect everything they hold dear. They are the Gun Crusaders.

Two groups comprise the Gun Crusaders: the "Critical Mass" includes the most committed NRA members and, not coincidentally, the most politically conservative; and the "Reserves," who are somewhat less committed to the NRA and conservative politics but remain largely loyal to both. Critical Mass members tend to have lifetime NRA memberships, are involved, as volunteers, in the NRA's political and educational activities, place gun rights as their first or second priority, and have far-right political and social views. The Reserves are less likely to be lifetime NRA members, do not volunteer to work for the organization, are much less likely to be single-issue gun rights voters, and hold more moderate conservative views.

A third group of weakly committed NRA members, the "Peripherals," is not included here. These members are less politicized and politically conservative who join the NRA because they enjoy hunting, competitive shooting, and collecting.[15] No data exist indicating the percentage of NRA members in these three categories. I assume that each group has hundreds of thousands of members, based on the organization's generally high membership levels, the fact that one-third of the members meet NRA voting eligibility requirements (lifetime or five-year consecutive members), and both large increases and large decreases in membership have occurred during contentious political moments in modern NRA history. The overall one-third NRA voting eligibility rate compares to a roughly two-thirds rate of eligibility among the members I interviewed.[16]

I include the Critical Mass and Reserves here but not the Peripherals, because the former two are the heart of the organization, aligning most closely with the leadership and the NRA's mission. Wayne LaPierre and Charlton Heston did not sign up to lead the organization because of a desire to spread the best technical firearms information possible or a deep passion for hunting. The NRA has staff to provide this information and support these less politicized commitments, thereby serving many satisfied Peripheral members. The top leaders and members who make a lifetime commitment to the NRA and are its grassroots army are the Gun Crusaders. If the NRA permanently de-prioritized gun rights, the Critical Mass and Reserves would join a different gun rights group. The NRA would be left with a large, politically weak group of gun enthusiasts and would no longer be the NRA. If the organization focused solely on gun rights politics, the Peripherals would join other hunting, collecting, and sport shooting organizations. But as the leading gun rights SMO and the largest advocate for the shooting sports, the NRA can both prioritize gun rights and retain and serve large numbers of Peripheral members.

Despite the closing of the frontier and the declining numbers of hunt-ers and gun owners,[17] NRA membership levels remain high. Threats to gun rights and frontier masculinity are met with a formidable backlash. Although gun rights are not so much at risk today as when the NRA first became an SMO and not just a gun enthusiasts' group, the NRA's recent fiery rhetoric still resonates with many gun owners, resulting in a mem-bership surge and unparalleled political power. Kayne Robinson, Heston's successor as NRA President, told his Board of Directors that gun owners respond to gun rights threats by joining or increasing their support for the organization. The NRA, he says, is a "motivational organization" that tries to get the millions of "free-riders" (gun owners and hunters who are not NRA members) to join the "gun movement," the "juggernaut" known as the NRA. Playing to members' fears is working. As top NRA officer Wayne LaPierre points out, the NRA is stronger than ever.[18]

The National Rifle Association, more than any other group or individ-ual, defines the terms of the gun debate. For better or worse, SMOs and politicians set the symbolic and legislative parameters of all culture war debates. Leaders of the NRA and those of the Brady Campaign to Prevent Gun Violence, of NARAL Pro-Choice America and the National Right-to-Life Committee, and of the Christian Right and the Human Rights Campaign are the voices in legislators' ears and the faces on television when the culture war topics of gun control, abortion, or same-sex mar-riage flare up. Culture war leaders engage in the highest-profile, media jousting matches and craft sound bites heard over and over again. True, ultimately the less polarized electorate gives thumbs up or thumbs down to culture war ballot initiatives, and politicians help craft and vote for leg-islation. Voters have little say, however, in what makes its way onto a state ballot or a congressional bill—the nuts and bolts of any gun, abortion, or marriage legislation. The activists do. And partly thanks to its enormous base of activist support, no other conservative culture war force has been as successful as the NRA.

Even skeptics of the culture war—who argue that most Americans are noncombatants—acknowledge that elites like major politicians and lead-ers of large social movements (as well as their base of activist supporters) are waging war on one another. The elites drive the cultural discourse and make policy. Those who do not participate in the culture war are still sub-ject to its outcomes. When the battles take place nearby—when mayors try to enact gun buy-back programs or local school boards paste stickers on biology textbooks warning that evolution is just a theory—the same rhetoric and debate parameters that elites create play out at the local level. With perhaps the weakest opposition for any culture war issue, the NRA and its broad base of Gun Crusaders are the primary determinant of U.S. gun policies. They are also the go-to single-issue group for conservatives and Republicans, waging the most successful battle in the culture wars.[19]

Outline of the Book

In the following chapters I explain why and how the National Rifle Association became a conservative social movement organization fighting the culture wars and drawing in millions of members. Part 1 discusses the historical and contemporary events that resulted in the NRA's defense of both gun rights and frontier masculinity. Chapter 1 examines the exaggerated history of a U.S. gun culture, connecting it to the similarly mythologized version of manhood that is frontier masculinity. The NRA was founded just as white men's pioneering on the frontier ended. It was only much later that the NRA relied upon culturally constructed images of frontier masculinity to support its political goals. As I discuss in this opening chapter, the NRA has had very different identities and missions since its inception in 1871, culminating in its transformation to the leader of the gun movement in the 1970s.

Chapter 2 places the NRA's emergence as an SMO in social and political context, analyzing the threats to gun control from liberal rights groups in the 1960s and 1970s. The NRA responded not just to threats to gun rights but also to challenges to frontier masculinity by civil rights, women's rights, gay and lesbian rights, and antiwar movements. This was a peak period for challenges to gender and racial arrangements, whereby many white men saw their status and identities at risk, sparking conservative reactive mobilization and today's culture wars. Gun rights are a key battle in this war for individual rights and freedoms.

Part 2 focuses on NRA's leaders' and members' rhetoric and politics on gun rights and the culture wars. Chapter 3 examines how the NRA has framed gun control and gun rights since the 1940s, focusing on NRA language during both heightened and relaxed periods of threats to gun rights. The NRA's recent warnings of impending threats to gun rights, even in the face of declining objective threats, resonates with members. Membership levels have increased with every newly framed threat. Further, the NRA has skillfully tapped into not only their members' gun control fears but also their concerns about declining individual rights and freedoms and attacks on frontier masculinity. Today the NRA calls its members "freedom fighters" and pleads with them to continue defending gun rights from the "gun-grabbing terrorists, liberals, and Communists" who threaten American freedom.

Chapter 4 shifts the focus to NRA members, examining how their views on gun rights and gun control threats compare to those of the organization. Most members perceive serious and impending threats to gun rights from liberal politicians, gun control groups, and the media. Like official NRA literature, members largely believe that the Second Amendment is the foundation of freedom: if gun rights are lost, all other individual rights and freedoms will soon follow. With few exceptions, NRA members lump together their opponents as Democrats, liberals, Communists, and socialists who seek to destroy the Constitution and the American ethos of self-reliance, hard work, and personal responsibility.

Chapter 5 delves deeper into NRA members' broader social and political views. Threats to gun rights, the most committed members argue, are part of a broader attack on their conservative political and moral beliefs. The most politically conservative members mobilize in response to a perceived culture war against white men. They believe that they are the victims of affirmative action policies, illegal immigration, and generous welfare programs, all of which, they point out, are part of a broad liberal culture war headlined by gun control efforts and threatening conservative values, white men, and frontier masculinity.

Part 3 analyzes the strong relationship between members' conservative politics and their commitment to the NRA, as well as the extent to which the NRA is embedded in the conservative movement. Members offer varying levels of support to the NRA. Chapter 6 examines the relationship between members' levels of commitment to the organization and their political orientations. The most committed members, the Critical Mass, are also the most socially and politically conservative. These are mostly older white men who perceive the strongest threat to gun rights, are more likely to hold positive views of the NRA, and donate the most time and money to the organization. The second category of members, the Reserves, though also committed to the NRA and generally conservative, are younger, have more women members, and are not as strongly aligned with the NRA or right-wing politics as Critical Mass members.

Chapter 7 reveals the views of the two categories of members on contemporary social and political issues. Those comprising the Critical Mass hold uncompromising right-wing political views on issues such as the war in Iraq, racial profiling, sexuality, and welfare. These highly committed members see the world in black and white, good and evil, just as they see the battle over gun rights. Reserve members offer more mixed and moderately conservative views on contentious social issues, reflecting their more moderate overall politics.

Chapter 8 explores the links between the NRA, the Republican Party, and the conservative movement. Millions of NRA dollars are donated to political candidates, overwhelmingly Republicans, who support gun rights. The NRA's lobby also spends millions of dollars but ultimately derives its status as one of the most powerful and effective lobbies in Washington because of the NRA's grassroots army of support. Over the past fifteen years, NRA staff and leadership have become increasingly connected to the conservative movement and the Republican Party. With the politics of NRA members and the organization shifting to the Right, the NRA is the Republican Party's most potent combination of financial and voter support.

PART I

Defending Guns, Defending Masculinity

1

Frontier Masculinity, America's Gun Culture, and the NRA

On Sunday morning in Reno I caught an early bus to attend the NRA Women's Breakfast. As we approached the convention center, we passed an adult cabaret eager to drum up some convention visitor business. Missing an apostrophe, a neon sign out front announced something I can neither confirm nor deny: "NRA Partys Here." After getting off the bus, I struck up a conversation with a member also on his way to the breakfast. Floyd is an affable Texan in his sixties, wearing dark-blue jeans, tan boots, a thin dark-striped white button-down shirt, and an NRA hat. A friendly Texas drawl spills from his white mustache-covered mouth. Floyd said he figured he would go to the breakfast because nothing else was going on at that time and he wanted to "check out what they're doing." As we walked to the breakfast and talked about the NRA, guns, and hunting, he excitedly recalled shooting his first spring turkey eleven years ago and shooting another not long before coming here to Reno.

Floyd and I found the right room and sat at a table full of women. Roughly one hundred people, about a quarter of them men, filtered through the breakfast buffet. Several corporate sponsors of guns and gear had banners hanging on the wall, and a portion of the video *Hunting with the Women of the NRA* played on a large screen, on mute, in the back of the room. At our table sat three women in their fifties, including Kathy, a lobbyist in Washington, D.C., and Tracy, a ranch owner from Texas. They were heavily involved in "Women in the NRA" programs, as both were panelists in the session that would follow on women, hunting, and shooting. In an attempt to break the ice, Floyd shared a joke about a caveman and cavewoman: "The cavewoman's dragging a kill by its tail and holding a big club. The caveman says, 'I'm supposed to be the hunter and you're supposed to be the gatherer.' The cavewoman replies, 'It was standing on something I wanted to gather.'" Everyone politely laughed, but as he broke eye contact with Tracy, I saw her face sour in disgust.

Floyd continued, undeterred, but only dug a deeper hole for himself. "In my experience," he said, "women are okay with the hunting, but they don't like to dress the kill." The women at the table, all experienced hunters, promptly disagreed. When Floyd asked if they have enough women instructors for women's hunts and training, Kathy said they never have enough *women* instructors. Floyd offered his services, though I began to sense that he was more interested in meeting single women than increasing women's interest in firearms. This was an NRA-sponsored event focused on building women's participation in the organization and in hunting and shooting, yet here was an older man reminding everyone just whose gun culture and gun group it is. With few exceptions and throughout their respective histories, the gun culture and the NRA have been led by conservative white men. True, a handful of women have played key roles in the gun culture and the NRA, and many more have been less celebrated participants, but full acceptance in either requires assimilation into frontier masculinity. Adopt the culture's values, beliefs, and in most cases hierarchical power divide between women and men, or expect to be marginalized by those men.

Event speakers informed us that this Women's Breakfast, only the second ever held, brought in $10,000 for the women's endowment, a tiny drop in the NRA bucket and evidence that even assimilation does not necessarily lead to enthusiastic acceptance. NRA leader Wayne LaPierre appeared toward the end of the breakfast to show his support, but clearly women are not the NRA's target audience. This is not surprising, as General Social Survey data reveal that women's gun-ownership rates have hovered at a consistently low rate of 9–11% ever since 1980.[1] The weekend meetings and gun show drew more than forty thousand people, and most of the sessions I attended in small rooms and large auditoriums were standing-room only. The Women's Breakfast, and the session that followed, "Hunting and Shooting with the Women of the NRA," however, did not enjoy strong turnouts. Some of the women from the breakfast, including Floyd, spilled over into this next session. There were only about sixty people, evenly divided between women and men.

This follow-up session presented the hunting video from the breakfast but with the volume turned on. After a woman shoots a pig, she and her hunting partner, Sue, head over to see if it's dead. Sue has her partner nudge the pig from behind with her foot, while Sue keeps the rifle on it.

She wants to make sure the pig is dead, because "you don't want a mad pig in your pocket." Later, during the question-and-answer period, audience members wanted to know how they could encourage more women to become involved in hunting and shooting. One woman said that the women she knows are more interested in firearms for self-defense. Several men offered their support for increasing women's involvement in shooting, with Floyd joking that he would be happy to help out but he's "just a man." Kathy, one of the session panelists, as well as our breakfast companion, responded that they needed men, too. To Floyd's delight, she told him it would be great if he helped out as an instructor.

All the women at this session referred to one another as "ladies" or sometimes "girls," which held true for the entire weekend. Kathy told a couple of entertaining "lady" stories during the session. She was not raised around hunting but was introduced to it when she met her husband. Before her first outing she bought a new outfit, not realizing "I'd be spending the day in a ditch picking up dead birds!" The audience laughed knowingly—a man would *never* wear new clothes to go hunting! Despite the session's focus on shattering myths about women and hunting, gendered roles were not seriously challenged.

Kathy related another story about a "lady" coming to her ranch to hunt. The woman had recently purchased a Glock pistol, and she telephoned Kathy and said: "I got a Glock, let's go kill something!" Kathy reeled in the new gun owner, starting her off with lessons using long guns. Another panel member, an editor for the NRA's *American Hunter* magazine, followed Kathy, offering his views on increasing women's presence in the magazine. He said that neither women nor men want to read articles "pandering" to women, such as "Jane likes to shoot and hunt. Jane hunts deer." His readers, he said, "are mostly good ol' boys" and they would stop reading the magazine if it included those kinds of stories. Instead, he incorporates women's presence into the magazine with pictures of women hunting or stories written by women who have technical advice to share.

Talking about gender in such a direct manner is not typical of the NRA. Although hunting, shooting, and gun rights activism are dominated by men, the NRA prefers to think of itself as a gender- (and race-) neutral organization. This attitude is consistent with their broader politics, which leans toward a libertarian approach to individual rights and responsibilities. When the *American Hunter* editor mentioned that several higher-ups in the magazine's chain of command were women, he didn't pause before explaining that they were hired not because of "quotas" but because they were "the most qualified applicants," the best available. Preferential treatment is an anathema to frontier masculinity, even when it is for individuals who have been historically marginalized or discriminated against. The philosophy of treating people differently, especially based on group affiliation, is the antithesis of the kind of freedom that NRA members fight for and revere as the bedrock of the American frontier—individual rights and responsibilities. At one point, Kathy told us that she had learned ten two-letter words from a politician: "If it is to be, it is up to me."

This do-it-yourself attitude is the basic philosophy of most NRA members. Need protection? Buy a gun and learn to shoot. Not earning enough money to make ends meet? Work harder. Can't afford child care or health care? Don't expect the government to bail you out. Freedom and self-reliance are indivisible. A country whose citizens have to rely on the government for personal safety or basic needs is a country that is lazy and apathetic, and ultimately undemocratic. This frontier masculinity ideology promoted by the NRA is rooted in a U.S. gun culture historically confined to white men. In many ways the gun culture has been exaggerated, but regardless of whether it was real or constructed afterward to sell stories and products, it continues to shape American culture and masculinity. Guns, masculinity, and freedom are intertwined and still resonate with Americans today, long after they were combined by Europeans and their descendents to take over, explore, and control the country. The NRA was founded and later attracted a large membership only after the frontier had closed and the gun culture became mythologized in popular media. More recently the previously apolitical NRA underwent a political revolution when the gun culture, gun rights, and frontier masculinity were threatened in the 1960s and 1970s. Today's NRA claims to defend not only gun rights but also frontier masculinity.

What Guns Mean

The Second Amendment to the U.S. Constitution reads, "A well regulated militia, being necessary to the security of a free state, the right of the people to keep and bear arms, shall not be infringed." NRA members, sharing their frontier masculinity philosophy, will confidently tell you that this wording clearly conveys that *individuals* have the right to bear arms. Gun control advocates, however, are convinced that *militias* are the centerpiece of the amendment, and that the federal government has every right to regulate guns. In 2008, a 5-4 Supreme Court decision sided with the NRA view, calling gun rights an individual right while still allowing some forms of gun control.[2] This book does not attempt to enter into this debate but instead focuses on what the NRA's interpretation of gun rights means to NRA members, how the organization's views on gun rights relate to their broader political views, and the connections the NRA stance on gun rights have to U.S. history and contemporary culture and politics.

Jeff Cooper, first elected to the NRA Board of Directors in 1985, mapped out some of these connections while holding a Colt .45 and thinking about its use on the frontier and by the U.S. Army. "'Just to hold [a Colt Model "P"] in your hand produces a feeling of kinship with our Western heritage—an appreciation of things like courage and honor and chivalry and the sanctity of a man's word.'"[3] NRA leader Wayne LaPierre then asks,

> What is the "gun culture"? The answer depends on your point of view. To millions of Americans, especially those who own firearms, the term refers to America's traditional bedrock values of self-reliance, self-defense, and self-determination. To others, most of whom dislike firearms and do not own them, the term is a pejorative. Participants think these outsiders use the term to distinguish themselves as the culturally elite, ruling the national media as moral superiors to the nation's gun owners.[4]

Regardless of one's position on the Second Amendment, guns are a visible part of American culture.

Even if you don't own and admire them like NRA members do, guns are part of our lives: those around us either own or use them, and news and entertainment media include them in their coverage. Moreover, there are countless gun metaphors in our everyday language: "Don't be gun shy"; "I'm calling the shots"; "Better stick to your guns"; and "Shoot first, ask questions later." These four gun metaphors relate to American manhood and may be interpreted to mean, respectively, "be fearless," "be in charge," "be independent," and "be aggressive." Psychologist Robert Brannon identified these as the four building blocks of American masculinity. First and foremost, "No Sissy Stuff" (boys and men must never do anything that appears weak or feminine); second, "Be a Big Wheel" (real men have power and control over others); third, "Be a Sturdy Oak" (be stoical and emotionless, relying only on oneself for strength); and, fourth, "Give 'em Hell" (men who are aggressive and take risks will be rewarded).[5]

It is not a coincidence that the language of guns and that of masculinity overlap. "At both symbolic and practical levels," sociologist R. W.

Connell says, "the defense of gun ownership is a defense of hegemonic masculinity."[6] Similarly, NRA members' devotion to guns and gun rights is intricately tied to a frontier version of masculinity. Their ideas about freedom and guns are rooted in a combination of mythologized gun culture and mythologized masculinity. Guns and masculinity have long been inseparable.

Frontier Masculinity and the Gun Culture

Guns are a part of U.S. culture, but is there a *gun culture*? For the first 250 years of their history on U.S. soil, European colonists and their descendants largely relied upon an agricultural economy, coupled in part by a continuous "frontier expansion."[7] Firearms, frontier expansion, and violence were common in 17th-, 18th-, and 19th-Century America, as whites clashed with indigenous populations.[8] Native Americans and African slaves were largely forbidden from possessing firearms in early colonial America. However, many indigenous groups obtained firearms through trade with competing European colonizers.[9] Whites relied on firearms to hunt for food and wage war. The mythologizing of firearms in U.S. history, however, soared with the Revolutionary War. "With the Revolution, the gun was virtually enshrined as our historic symbol of freedom."[10] Firearms, and especially stories regarding the citizen-militia, are fundamental building blocks of U.S. independence for many Americans. The Founding Fathers worried about standing armies leading to government tyranny, and though the militia had mixed success over the years, the Founders explicitly emphasized the militia's importance when writing the Second Amendment. But, like other freedoms solidified in the Bill of Rights, Second Amendment rights were originally only extended to white men.

American citizens dramatically increased their westward expansion during the 19th Century. Historians have noted that guns were decisive in whites' "winning of the West and the conquest" of Native Americans.[11] The frontiersmen who fought against Native Americans from the 1800s through the 1880s symbolize dominant culture narratives of the West— independent, brave, and virtuous white men fighting against the "savages."[12] While many men headed west in search of fortunes and a new life, others remained in rapidly growing cities.

The Industrial Revolution permanently changed the United States. As late as the mid-1850s, roughly 90% of white American men owned their own farm, shop, or small crafts workshop. However, industrialization and urbanization forced many of these men to sell their labor for pay. The term "breadwinner" was coined in the early part of the 19th Century, capturing men's new family responsibilities. Later the term would be tied to men's success in the new public sphere.[13] By mid-century another new term emerged, "self-made man," linking manhood and economic success, and providing an early cultural solidification of the American ethos. That ethos is a shorthand summary of everything the United States is supposed to represent and provide: opportunities and success for anyone willing to work hard. It was risky for men to navigate the new market-based economy, but a hard-working, self-made man did not fear the challenge of becoming a breadwinner.

Early on in this economic transformation, as industrialization created a need for workers, men initiated two separate spheres for men and women. This "separate spheres" doctrine, popularized by authors writing advice books for men, was clear-cut: men were in charge of the public (work) sphere, and women were confined to the domestic (home) sphere.[14] This helped white men deal with the insecurities of losing their status as self-employed artisans and fearless outdoorsmen, positions pushed aside by industrialization. Urbanization and technology reduced men's need to use their physical strength or skill to work in a field or labor as craftsmen.[15] When men's identities are threatened, a common reaction is to rely on religious doctrine or so-called scientific evidence to "prove" their superiority; in this case, they relied on the principle that women were incapable of performing adequately in the public sphere.[16] In this way, men gained status in the new labor market as the family breadwinner, living up to the long-valued work ethic that is woven into tales of American history. This "separate spheres" doctrine continues to heavily influence gender arrangements and Americans' beliefs today. It survives despite having been challenged by feminist politics, the sharp decline in jobs that pay sufficient salaries to support a family, and the high participation rates of women in the labor force.

The breadwinner legacy, like many glorified narratives, is not supported by the data. Indeed, it can aptly be described as the "male provider myth," perpetuated by ignoring family types that did not mirror the white, middle-class standard that is beyond the reach of many families. For example, because of racism and segregation, Black men could not earn a family wage and so Black families were excluded from the separate spheres doctrine. This is reflected in the fact that half of Black women were in the labor force in 1880, but 15% of white women, too, were in the labor force at this time. And these figures do not include women's other contributions to the household such as paid labor done within the home.[17]

Some self-made men battled to establish their masculine authority by creating a new urban, industrialized version of gender arrangements, and others simply took their guns and headed west. They literally escaped from women and the perceived feminizing influences of the city, including the urban disconnect from the land and the animals, as well as city dwellers' dependence on one another for basic needs.

The frontier is where firearms truly established their legend or, as many historians argue, where firearms have been mythologized as legendary. Research on gun violence today and an American gun culture of the past are controversial and contested, with biases on the part of both gun control advocates and opponents.[18] The cause of violence is complex and cannot be reduced to a single factor such as gun control laws or concealed-carry laws, as proponents and opponents of gun control often argue. Regarding a long-standing gun culture, the best research finds that 40–60% of late-17th and 18th-Century wealth holders owned a working gun, and that firearms were more prevalent among southern, rural, white, non-poor men. In sum, "gun ownership was neither rare nor universal" during this period.[19] Political scientist Robert Spitzer notes that not only is the supposed gun culture rooted in white Americans' earliest history and battle for independence, it is also intertwined with frontier history and the cultural mythology it spawned (and that continues today). He claims that the current gun culture is linked to the past by Americans' continued hunting and sporting ethos as well as a militia and frontier ethos, despite the lack of a contemporary frontier. These two philosophies "converge to produce a certain mythical elevation of the gun" that parallels and draws from "the broader mythologizing of the American frontier tradition."[20] In the view of historian Richard Slotkin, the gun culture narrative is actually a "Myth of the Frontier."[21]

Firearms were unquestionably part of white westward expansion, for hunting and for forcibly taking land from indigenous populations. But the role of firearms in this expansion has been exaggerated, as it took a great deal more than firearms to "settle" the West, notably ranchers and farmers.[22] In reality, many who traveled west found little use for firearms, especially after they reached their destination.[23] This revelation challenges our popular understanding of the roots of America's gun culture. Indeed, although this myth "originated in tales told by, for, and about rural [white]

'Anglo-Saxon' Protestant heroes," it has become widely accepted and valued beyond this group.[24] If history does not reveal a frontier gun culture, how was this myth created? Researchers find that the myth was largely concocted during the early part of the 20th Century, soon after the frontier was closed and white westward expansion was no longer possible.[25]

Pulp fiction magazines and novels of this period were a key ingredient. Zane Grey wrote *Riders of the Purple Sage* in 1912 and continued writing Westerns for many decades afterward. Louis L'Amour began writing Westerns in 1950, and many of his novels, such as *The Quick and the Dead*, became film adaptations. The tradition of the myth of the frontier has continued from television and movie Westerns to science fiction and detective stories. Gunfighter skills may be the most celebrated feature of the mythologized frontier gun culture, but they, too, exist as characteristics that were mostly constructed for post-frontier popular culture. In fact, the "gunfighter" Western only appeared in the mid-20th Century, when gunplay suddenly became a primary part of the myth of the frontier.[26] *The Gunfighter* (1950), *Gunfight at the O.K. Corral* (1957), and *The Magnificent Seven* (1960) helped establish a genre that continued into the 21st Century. Gun makers, pulp magazines, and dime novels were important contributors to the romanticizing of the gunfighter myth, and the producers of these goods benefited from its widespread acceptance.[27]

In some cases, frontier cities became infamous partly to serve as tourist attractions. For example, Dodge City, Kansas, despite a reputation to the contrary, had a mere five killings in 1878 at its peak of violence, revealing a distinct lack of duels and six-shooter pistols.[28] The men toting these Colt 45s (and other guns) and doling out justice, widely depicted as heroes of honorable frontiersmen in modern movies, were often not only the local sheriffs but were also criminals. Wyatt Earp and "Doc" Holiday, for instance, were thieves and murderers.[29] But these details, which detract from the commercial legend, quickly melt away. Also significant is that these mythical heroes all fall under the rubric of virtuous white male defenders of justice. African American cowboys, soldiers, and homesteaders, as well as many other groups comprising a sizable portion of the population in western states and territories, are nearly invisible.[30] The American gun culture was created and represented by, and largely benefits, white Americans.

Violence, including gun violence, generally decreased once displaced native groups were killed or removed and towns were established in the 1800s. Settlers then took steps to lessen violence. Quite the opposite of frontier individualism, new communities initiated forms of law and order that would encourage everyone to cooperate and benefit from mutual protection. Violence was largely the exception to the rule in these frontier towns. Gun control laws were even widespread by the late 1800s, when "most communities had laws dictating that firearms could not be carried publicly unless one was hunting, taking the weapon for repair, or going to or from a military muster."[31] Hollywood's mythmakers conveniently left out these laws in the plots of *Bonanza* and *Gunsmoke*.

Thus, although guns were a tangible part of white colonization and westward expansion, once people settled down they wanted safety. Depictions of loner gunfighters are mostly legend. Because firearms have been widely, though certainly not universally, used throughout white Americans' history, adding to the notion of a "national gun culture," this culture developed not simply out of the mass production of cheap guns but also through art, propaganda, and war.[32] And it is a culture that persists: "For millions of American boys, learning to shoot and above all graduating from toy guns and receiving the first real rifle of their own were milestones of life, veritable rites of passage that certified their arrival at manhood."[33]

The Civil War also played a part in the invented tradition of the gun culture, because it "transformed guns into symbols of freedom and masculinity."[34] Although the Civil War revolved around North–South disagreements regarding slavery, states' rights, and industrial capitalism versus agricultural slave-based economies, it was also a war over competing versions of masculinity. The new market-based, self-made men of the North squared off against the European patrician ties and chivalry of the agricultural South. The Union victory secured a standard of marketplace manhood—breadwinners must compete against and outperform other men to achieve success—that continues to be a measuring stick of masculinity to this day. This victory, along with increasing industrialization, the closing of the frontier, and, later, large numbers of women, free African Americans, and immigrants entering the labor force sparked a reactionary backlash by white men dealing with the perceived demise of frontier masculinity.[35] Black men contributed to slavery's end by participating in the war, and like other men before and after who found war to be a rite of passage into manhood, these marginalized men were no exception. Quickly, however, whites established "Black Codes" in the post-Civil War South, often denying African Americans the right to keep and bear arms.[36] As mentioned above, firearms were especially prevalent in the

South and Southwest, both because of the rural setting and the history of the South whereby owning a gun was a "white prerogative." White indentured servants were permitted (even occasionally encouraged) to have guns, whereas no African Americans could; guns were a symbol of white men's status.[37]

At the turn of the 20th Century the Union victory in the Civil War was one of many factors leading to "the unmaking of the self-made man," and a major contributor was the closing of the American frontier. Whereas in 1800 more than 80% of American men were farmers, by 1880 roughly half the labor force engaged in agricultural work. Reinforcing this pattern of urbanization and industrialization, about half the U.S. population lived in cities with populations exceeding eight thousand in 1910, compared to one in fifteen Americans in 1830. The frontier had been transformed into the more modest *outdoors*. The backdrop for a mythical era in America's gun culture was displaced by a new economy and fundamental transformation of American society. Frontier masculinity had lost its frontier, or, as sociologist Michael Kimmel puts it, "The Self-Made Man had tamed the wilderness, and so it could no longer be relied upon to make him wild."[38] Ironically the closing of the frontier overlapped with new rifle technologies that would reward highly skilled shooters with much greater accuracy. The United States, some military and political leaders argued, needed to find a way to transform gun owners into sharpshooters.

A Brief History of the NRA

Today's NRA relies on an image of the American frontier characterized by freedom, rugged individualism, and protection of the family. Though the NRA was founded just as the frontier was closing, it did not develop an interest in frontier masculinity or contentious politics for many decades. The culture war battering ram that defines today's NRA bears little resemblance to the NRA of yesteryear. The National Rifle Association of America was founded shortly after the Civil War, before white U.S. westward expansion peaked. The NRA truly was a National Rifle Association early in its history, as it began, in 1871, as a quasi-military organization with the aim of improving Americans' accuracy with rifles. Significant new developments in firearms enabled greater shooting precision, and the NRA founders wanted to ensure that the United States did not lag behind in marksmanship.[39] The organization got off to a slow start, however, with little initial support and an inability to maintain annual Board of Directors meetings until the new century. In 1905 President Theodore Roosevelt signed into law a huge benefit for the NRA, enabling the organization to purchase surplus military rifles at cost and sell them to members and civilian shooters.[40]

Roosevelt, who overcame a childhood illness and made a conscious effort to become, and be seen as, more manly, offers a fascinating case study of contradictions in masculinity at the turn of the 20th Century. He grew up on the East Coast but "journeyed west to stake a claim on his manhood."[41] He distanced himself from earlier meekness and elite roots, claiming to be the ultimate self-made man. Roosevelt's use of firearms, during cowboy and pioneer living, safari hunting expeditions, and military duty with the Rough Riders during the Spanish-American War, went hand-in-hand with his lifelong efforts to construct his image as a self-made man and reassert frontier masculinity as the foundation of his and all men's manhood. Roosevelt's perceived threats to his own and American manhood led him to embrace frontier masculinity. From a frail childhood that made him overly dependent on his mother to the social and economic shifts that were transforming the United States into an urban, capitalist country, native-born white men believed that their heritage and status were under attack.[42]

Teddy Roosevelt and successive administrations gave the NRA money for annual national shooting matches. Competitive shooting was the NRA's priority throughout much of the first half of the 20th Century.[43] The Great Depression temporarily halted government funding but only until 1936. The NRA maintained tight ties to the military since its inception, and many of its board members and presidents had a military background, including Ulysses S. Grant.

Soldiers returning from World War II had a newfound training and interest in firearms, leading NRA memberships to surge from 84,000 in 1945 to 155,000 the next year. These men were mostly interested in hunting, not competitive shooting. The NRA established a firearms safety program after World War II and pursued hunters as potential members, resulting in roughly half its membership identifying as hunters by 1950.[44] The NRA was moving away from its focus on competitive shooting and military history and becoming a more generic sportsmen's league.[45]

Membership reached 300,000 in 1956, and in 1958 the NRA had a new headquarters sporting a sign that read: "Firearms Safety Education, Marksmanship Training, Shooting for Recreation." The government again stopped paying for national shooting matches, this time permanently, and so the NRA bought land in New Mexico for the shooting competitions. General Franklin Orth, the NRA Executive Vice President at the time, along with other Old Guard leaders whose interest in firearms centered on being sportsmen, bought so much land that they had room not only for a world-class shooting range but also for camping, survival training, and educational programs on conservation and environmental awareness. Instead of calling it the "National Shooting Center," they named it the "National Outdoor Center," a decision seen as treasonous by a small but growing faction within the NRA who focused on preserving unrestricted gun rights. These "hard-liners" were Second Amendment fundamentalists who believed that any form of gun control was illegal under the Constitution. One such member was Harlon Carter, who attempted to engineer a leadership coup with similar-minded members. The Old Guard leadership caught word of this and, in a 1976 event dubbed the "weekend massacre," fired several dozen employees aligned with the hard-liners.[46] During this same period in the mid-1970s, the Old Guard considered moving the NRA headquarters to Colorado, partly to distance itself, literally and figuratively, from the political lobbying scene in Washington, D.C.

As examined in detail below, the NRA took center stage in the national storm that arose in the 1960s with the assassinations of President John F. Kennedy in 1963, and of Martin Luther King Jr. and presidential candidate Robert Kennedy in 1968. The man accused of killing JFK, Lee Harvey Oswald, purchased his rifle through a mail-order advertisement in the NRA magazine *The American Rifleman*.[47] While those in the Old Guard, primarily sportsmen, were trying to move the NRA away from gun control debates, hard-liners saw this as a turning point in history, a time when the NRA must step up and defend gun rights before they were permanently lost.

Prior to the 1977 annual meeting, the hard-liners organized and carried out the "Revolt at Cincinnati," effectively transforming the NRA into the primary defender of the Second Amendment.[48] This small, but well-organized group used walkie-talkies and parliamentary procedures to stage a political coup, ousting the entire Old Guard leadership and replacing it with hard-liners. The voting members at the meeting gave themselves greater power over the organization, halted plans to move headquarters to Colorado and build the National Outdoor Center, and voted out every top NRA official but one, replacing them with hard-liners known as the "Federation for NRA." Harlon Carter, who was voted Executive Vice President, declared: "Beginning in this place and at this hour, this period in NRA history is finished."[49] And so it was. The NRA had officially made its final transition: the organization was now primarily, if not solely, dedicated to preserving gun rights. Carter and others had redefined the NRA's mission in an effort to maintain their white gun heritage. "To the NRA faithful, Harlon Carter is Moses, George Washington, and John Wayne rolled into one," wrote journalist Osha Gray Davidson, adding that Carter, as an "Old West lawman, champion target shooter, [and] world-class hunter . . . was the embodiment of everything the NRA stood for."[50]

Following this coup the NRA experienced some setbacks, but the new leadership saw these difficulties as a purification process: only supporters of gun rights were now welcome. Between 1977 and 1984 membership tripled, as the new leadership ushered in a golden age for the NRA (see Figure 1.1).[51] A standing ovation greeted EVP Carter at the 1983 annual meeting, when President Ronald Reagan joined him on stage, symbolizing the epitome of the NRA's influence in gun control politics. Reflecting the dramatic organizational transformation from gun enthusiasts to hard-liners, the NRA headquarters now displayed a sign, in capital letters, stating: THE RIGHT OF THE PEOPLE TO KEEP AND BEAR ARMS SHALL NOT BE INFRINGED. Second Amendment language about militias was conspicuously absent. When Carter stepped down as Vice President because of illness in 1985, the NRA struggled to shape its leadership for many years afterward: it had no comparable hero linking the organization to white American's frontier past.

The NRA had faced firearms legislation before but nothing like the public outcry following the three assassinations in the 1960s. The threat to gun rights was never as serious and poignant as it was during this period. The NRA had received its initiation into gun control politics decades earlier in the state of New York. The 1911 Sullivan Law required a police permit for New Yorkers to obtain a firearm. Although the hard-liners would not influence the organization for many decades, the NRA's now famous mantra—"Guns don't kill people. People kill people"—appeared at this early stage as an argument against gun control.[52] The Sullivan Law was passed with the intent of combating juvenile delinquency. By the 1930s New York faced a more serious firearms crime issue—the mob. Along with the automobile, the submachine gun led to increased organized violent crime. The response was the National Firearms Act of 1934, which outlawed fully automatic firearms (those that can fire multiple rounds by simply holding down the trigger).[53] That same year the NRA launched its Legislative Division and began mailing alerts to its members. They had no official lobbyists until the 1970s, however, and so, through this division, they "merely provided the facts" and let NRA members act accordingly.[54]

FIGURE 1.1
NRA Membership Levels

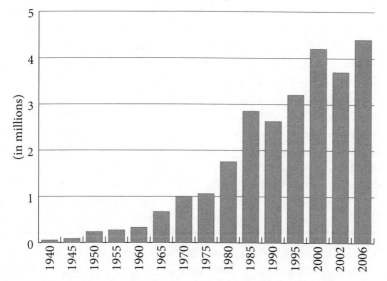

Data for 1940–1960: *American Rifleman* (January 1960): 19; Data for 1965: Anonymous,
"NRA is Shooting for a Million," *American Rifleman* (January 1965): 16–17; Data for 1970:
Anonymous, "99th Annual Meeting and Exhibits," *American Rifleman* (June 1970): Insert;
Data for 1975: *American Rifleman* (May 1976): 62; Data for 1980–2006: special thanks to Kelly
Patterson and Matthew Singer for sharing their NRA Membership Division and Institute for
Legislative Action data from their article, "Targeting Success: The Enduring Power of the NRA,"
Pp. 37–64 in *Interest Group Politics*, 7th ed.

After the 1930s, gun control was largely a non-issue until the assassination
of JFK, which helps explain why the Old Guard was able to run the NRA without internal hard-liner opposition. It took several years after JFK was killed,
and two more politically charged assassinations, for Congress to pass the Gun
Control Act of 1968 restricting firearms. The NRA sent mixed messages during this period, reflecting its competing Old Guard and hard-liner factions.
Top NRA officer Franklin Orth came out publicly in support of some form
of control in the wake of JFK's murder, arguing that no reasonable American
could take a different stance.[55] Harlon Carter and the other hard-liners thought
otherwise, eventually making their oppositional view the NRA's official position. The 1968 legislation was not as far-reaching as many wanted, including
President Lyndon Johnson. It imposed more restrictions (particularly on mail-
order firearms) and record-keeping requirements but no bans on guns.

The last time the NRA ever supported any form of restrictive firearms
legislation was in the early 1970s on a federal bill to ban "Saturday Night

Specials"—small, cheaply made handguns so labeled because of their reputation as criminals' tools.[56] Again, competing groups within the NRA were on different sides, with some forces supporting the bill and others working to undermine it. Ultimately the bill failed. In 1975 the NRA established its Institute for Legislative Action (NRA-ILA). Today the NRA-ILA is where most of the organization's energy is directed. Harlon Carter was its first director, enabling him to have a quasi-independent group to oppose gun control. However, he found that it lacked resources.[57]

After the Revolt at Cincinnati and the NRA transformation in 1977, the NRA did not face federal firearms legislation for many years. Instead, the organization was able to push a counter agenda through Congress. The 1986 Firearms Owners' Protection Act relaxed previous restrictions and increased punishment for offenders.[58] Harsher punishments for criminals and fewer gun restrictions bear out the NRA's frontier masculinity philosophy of individual responsibility: "There's no such thing as a bad gun, just bad people who use guns." The 1986 legislation was a significant victory for the NRA, but all was not well. Carter's replacements in the late 1980s proved inadequate, and the NRA suffered under poor leadership. Moreover, gun control threats emerged in the form of the Brady Bill (following the attempted assassination of President Reagan), as did fears about "cop-killer" bullets (able to penetrate police vests), the possibility of plastic guns (that could bypass metal detectors), and "assault rifles" (California banned semiautomatic assault weapons in 1989).[59]

In 1991 longtime NRA employee Wayne LaPierre took over as Executive Vice President, a position he continues to fill heading into 2009. Unlike Harlon Carter, LaPierre does not embody frontier masculinity; rather, he is a professional lobbyist.[60] He's not a physically imposing figure, nor does he command attention when he speaks. In fact, he is prone to erratic eye contact, sometimes looking at the ground instead of the person to whom he's speaking. On stage at NRA events, he sometimes appears wooden, straining to emcee an event or deliver a speech smoothly. But although LaPierre possesses no mythical stature, he managed to guide the organization through a bumpy period after ineffectual leadership, and he has recently risen to a lofty status in NRA history. During Bill Clinton's presidency, the NRA faced perhaps its stiffest White House opponent. Clinton, though despised by the NRA, proposed relatively modest gun control legislation, but gun rights proponents would disagree that Clinton's legislation was modest. They would argue, instead, that it was a slippery slope to more gun control legislation, and eventually registration and confiscation of all guns. In truth, Clinton certainly did not attempt to go as far as the original proposal for the Gun Control Act of 1968.

The NRA focused much of its energies at the state level during the Clinton era, successfully enacting numerous "right-to-carry" laws throughout the country, which provided individuals easier access to concealed weapons licenses. During the 1990s internal factional divisions occurred over the NRA's political purity and financial problems, but both were resolved before the new millennium. The NRA's only major public stumbling blocks during this period were the 1993 Brady Handgun Violence Prevention Act, which imposed waiting periods and background checks on purchasers of handguns, the 1994 Federal Assault Weapons Ban (now expired), and the organization's handling of the Oklahoma City bombing. The latter caused an enormous drop in NRA membership, not because the perpetrator Timothy McVeigh was a former NRA member, but because LaPierre sent out an unrelated fundraising letter shortly after the incident referring to federal law enforcement agents as "jack-booted thugs," a term commonly associated with fascism and Nazi SS soldiers.[61]

This led the former president George H. W. Bush and many others to resign their lifetime NRA memberships. LaPierre soon backtracked from the comment, but this only created more trouble, as he was criticized by fellow NRA leadership even more fervent against gun control than he was. LaPierre's original statement was accurate, they argued, and he should not have distanced himself or the organization from its intent. One of these hard-liners, and LaPierre's main opponent, Neal Knox, was the former protégé of Harlon Carter (although he lost that status temporarily after attacking Carter for perceived gun rights compromises). The NRA faced a possible tipping point, only to be saved by a new icon of frontier masculinity, Charlton Heston, possibly the only living man able to challenge Ronald Reagan's image as a symbolic pioneer and frontiersman. During the 1992 California voter mobilization campaign, Heston established his pro-gun chops by drawing an analogy to the state symbol, the Golden Bear, which had been killed off in California by frontier settlers in the 1920s. "Today gun owners," he argued, "are the endangered species."[62]

In 1997 Heston joined LaPierre in pushing for a mainstream image for the NRA, leading a "stop Knox" campaign.[63] Heston and LaPierre won, with Heston replacing Knox as NRA 1st Vice President and then taking over the NRA presidency the following year. Breaking the recent NRA practice of two-year terms, he continued as President through the annual meeting in 2003, when, as noted, he had to step down for health reasons.

As a renowned actor, Heston brought with him a mainstream legitimacy, and his image as a frontiersman, a truly self-made man, made him the perfect antidote to the NRA's public image problems. Yet, as NRA President, he still could speak on behalf of, and satisfy, most members' gun control concerns. Heston's successors (Kayne Robinson, Sandy Froman, and John Sigler) are unknowns outside the gun debate, and even among many NRA members. As illustrated in Figure 1.1, Heston's presence sparked the NRA's resurgence, leading it to unprecedented membership levels, followed, in turn, by more resources and influence. The NRA currently has about four million members, numerous advocates in Congress, and few opponents or rivals that threaten the organization's agenda.

Heston was the unchallenged and unequaled leader of the NRA not just because he supported an uncompromising view of the Second Amendment, but also because he defended frontier masculinity which many members perceived as under attack. NRA member and supporter Edward Leddy represented an ideal NRA member type, namely, everything Charlton Heston and the NRA want to project. Leddy says,

> If the [NRA] were to portray itself as a symbolic person, he would be a pioneer heading west with a rifle. He is self-reliant, morally strong, and competent. He is also peaceful by preference, but ready to defend himself from attack. He believes in personal rather than collective responsibility. He is not against government but sees its role as subordinate and supplementary to individual personal efforts. He opposes the arbitrary abuse of government power but is openly patriotic.[64]

Clearly the symbolic NRA person is a self-made *man*. Can this model continue as a standard for manhood in a country with no frontier, increasing urbanization, and social forces that prevent many men from being able to translate individual effort into success? Conversely, will these mounting threats to frontier masculinity compel its supporters to defend and reassert this version of manhood?

Post-Frontier Masculinity

One might think that the images projected by Charlton Heston, the gun culture, and frontier masculinity would decline as that part of U.S. history fades into the more distant past. Certainly who could imagine that this version of masculinity would be the standard to which American men are held today? However, updated versions of the same core characteristics of frontier masculinity continue to resonate and play an important role in Americana, and in national politics as well. In 1960 John F. Kennedy spoke of the "New Frontier" at the Democratic National Convention, attempting to steal some of the rugged individualist populism that Republicans had effectively controlled up until now. Historian Richard Slotkin points out the long-standing political benefits of projecting an image of frontier masculinity:

> The history of the frontier did not "give" Roosevelt or Kennedy or Reagan the political script they followed. What they did—what any user of cultural mythology does—was to selectively read and rewrite the myth according to their own needs, desires, and political projects.[65]

By erasing the presence of anyone but white Americans on the frontier or exaggerating the existence of loner gunfighters dispensing justice, today's political actors craft images of themselves that mirror their own selectively constructed images of frontier masculinity.

The election of action movie star Arnold Schwarzenegger as governor of the state of California speaks to the ongoing relevance of widely valued masculine traits such as independence, self-reliance, strength, and the ability to settle problems with violence, if needed (especially using overwhelming firepower). Former president George W. Bush appropriated some of these characteristics to further his popularity. Even though he does not possess Schwarzenegger's physical strength or the pull-yourself-up-by-the-bootstraps immigrant background (indeed, quite the opposite), Bush conveyed an "everyman" image through his frequently noted mispronunciations, Texas charm, and straightforward dichotomous view of how the world works. One of the most famous old West figures, John Wayne (born Marion Morrison), shared a similar worldview: "They tell me everything isn't black and white. Well, I say why the hell not?"[66] Many Americans agree that there are no gray areas. "You're either with us or against us," Bush argued after 9/11, warning Osama bin Laden that he was wanted "dead or alive." The President had all but nailed a "Wanted" poster to every wood pole in America. Of course, today's digital images of bin Laden on our TV screens have replaced the frontier's weathered parchment paper reward notices for Billy the Kid or Jesse James. Frontier masculinity remains a pervasive force in today's U.S. culture and politics, but the challenges it confronts from myriad social and cultural forces have resulted in today's culture wars.

2

Why a Gun Movement?

"Cultural war is fought without bullets, bloodshed or armored tanks, but liberty is lost just the same. If we lose this cultural war," NRA President Charlton Heston warned, "you and your country will be less free."[1] Heston, the self-anointed leader of the conservative cultural warriors, was crusading for more than just gun rights. He viewed gun rights as the most important freedom of all but only one of many under attack by liberal cultural warriors. In the view of Heston and like-minded conservatives, frontier masculinity is the blueprint for the United States, undeservedly and dangerously challenged by group-rights movements of the 1960s. "None of us really wants to fight this war. We didn't pick this fight," Heston lamented.[2]

Charlton Heston saw the culture wars as an urban versus rural issue.

On one side we have a rural society based on farming with a belief in independent self-determination, individual initiative, and mutual trust. On the other side stands an urban culture in which the individual is subordinate to the group, where transience and congestion alienate man from the land and from his fellow man, where upheaval and social decay give way to crime and a climate of fear, and where many are satisfied to sacrifice essential liberty for the illusion of safety. So who started the cultural war, and why? For the answer, meet me at the city limits.[3]

The growth of U.S. cities and the declining number of rural Americans has little to do with culture or masculinity and much to do with technological developments that led to industrialization and mass production. Despite the apolitical roots of this urban/rural split, it has contributed to a cultural divide. "The firearm stands as a symbol dividing these two worlds," Heston stated, "because it gives the common man or woman the most uncommon personal freedoms."[4] Heston casts the ideological differences as night and day: rural vs. urban, freedom vs. dependence, gun owners vs.

anti-gunners, frontier masculinity vs. the "nanny state," conservatives vs. liberals. These ideological battles—real, perceived, exaggerated, or a combination of all three—drives the Gun Crusaders.

Heston and the NRA offer a seemingly contradictory message. On the one hand, theirs is a defensive masculinity. They fear changes and challenges to frontier masculinity, labeling themselves victims. Addressing "Raging Revisionism" from the "storm troops" of the Left, Heston wrote, "Increasingly we are becoming victims of the cultural war's Big Lie."[5] And he warned,

> The message from the cultural warlords is everywhere, delivered with the arrogant swagger of absolute confidence. Summarized, it is this: Heaven help the God-fearing, law-abiding, Caucasian, middle class, Protestant (or even worse *evangelical*) Christian, the midwestern or southern (or even worse *rural*) hunter, apparently straight or admitted heterosexual gun-owning (or even worse *NRA-card-carrying*) average working stiff, or even worse still *male* working stiff, because not only do you not count, you're a downright obstacle to social progress. Your tax dollars may be just as welcome and green as you hand them over, but your voice deserves no hearing, your opinion is not enlightened, your media access is virtually nil, and frankly mister, you need to wake up, wise up, and learn a little something about your new America. *And until you do, why don't you just sit down and shut up!*[6]

Many find it difficult to be a straight, white, middle-class, conservative, rural man in America today. They worry that frontier masculinity is on the verge of becoming another corpse buried in history's grave of manhood.

Yet Gun Crusaders also cast themselves as heroes and warriors, courageously fending off the demise of frontier masculinity and protecting American freedom. In Heston's words:

> It's time to say, "Enough!" Are you a black Republican who speaks good English? . . . Are you a soldier who shudders at the thought that a woman may someday take a bayonet in the belly and die beside you on some distant battlefield? Are you a Christian who believes that Southern Baptist is not a synonym for redneck hillbilly? Do you wish that homosexuals would keep their lifestyle a matter of personal conviction, not constant controversy? Do you own a firearm and wish it were once again an honorable responsibility? Do you realize that each one of these demands courage to be truly free?[7]

Heston's book, *The Courage to Be Free*, sympathizes with fellow embittered Gun Crusaders and conservatives who feel marginalized and threatened by liberals, feminism, secular-driven urbanism, gay rights, and gun control. He encourages conservatives to fight the culture war and save America. The other side started the culture war and is prepared to finish it, Heston warns in his book, so rural gun owners better mount up and enter the battle.

And so they have. The NRA and the Gun Crusaders are winning their battle, if not the culture war. The opposition generated by other liberal causes such as abortion rights or same-sex marriage is as deep as that spurred by gun control, but conservative movements fighting against abortion or same-sex marriage face powerful countermovements. Public support for gun control does not translate into the same level of commitment as does support for abortion rights. If the pro-life movement introduces a state ballot initiative that threatens *Roe vs. Wade*, as happened in South Dakota in 2006 and 2008, a powerful pro-choice movement, even in such a conservative state, quickly organizes to fight back. Gun rights groups trying to gut gun control laws face no such opposition.[8] After Al Gore's loss to George W. Bush in 2004, the Democratic Party seemed to view gun control as a losing issue, and it has the battle scars to prove it. But although neither gun control groups nor politicians seriously threaten gun rights, the culture wars still fuel the NRA even as, unlike other conservative culture war groups, it repeatedly wins its battles.

The Perfect Storm

The NRA Revolt occurred during a second peak period of dramatic social change that profoundly altered U.S. race and gender arrangements. The first period, which occurred much earlier, followed the expansion of capitalism in the 1800s and resulted in a marketplace manhood whereby (some) men had the opportunity to achieve individual success based on their economic autonomy. The American Ethos, which asserted that *anyone* determined to work hard would get ahead, was simply a code word established in the early part of the 19th Century. "Anyone," of course, meant white men, as women and men of color were not afforded the same protections and rights under the Constitution.[9] Men continue to be held to this do-it-yourself breadwinner standard today, despite an economy that makes it difficult for most to achieve.

Challenges to gender and racial arrangements hit a second high point beginning in the 1960s, highlighted by deindustrialization and declining working-class incomes, a failed war in Vietnam, and movements for civil rights, women's rights, and gay and lesbian rights. The uncertainties, challenges, and threats brought upon white men by capitalism and industrialization in the first period, and by de-industrialization and group-rights movements in the second, resulted in patterned responses during both periods. These group-rights movements challenged white men's privilege, sparking a conservative backlash and leading to today's culture wars. Some label these two periods "masculinity crises."[10] The NRA's political transformation to the Gun Crusaders, I argue, is another form of backlash to this second masculinity crisis.

Many working- and middle-class white men have felt threatened by these massive social changes, as Charlton Heston suggested. Perceiving that they are the targeted victims, they feel a loss of status and power, a decline in the rights and privileges they enjoy as individuals but are able to obtain partly because they belong to a dominant social group. When groups that were historically marginalized and discriminated against fought for equal rights and opportunities, when the United States lost a war to a tiny and poor communist country on the other side of the planet, and when the economy began its steady march toward greater inequality between the haves and have-nots, conservative white men felt threatened. When bullets took the life of a president, and later his brother and a civil rights leader as well, much of the country called for gun restrictions. Civil rights, women's rights, the Vietnam War, and gun control were key events pushing die-hard gun owners onto the front line of the culture war.

A perfect storm of threats to conservative white American men's identities, beliefs, and status, which emerged in the 1960s and continues today, sparked many conservative movements including those against feminism, affirmative action, and same-sex marriage. The culture wars have also drawn in dedicated combatants who engage in angry debates over abortion, separation of church and state, and "family values." Committed NRA members and other Gun Crusaders see gun rights as the only factor standing between traditional American values and a culture war victory for the political Left. Some may question my use of sweeping labels such as "conservative" or "liberal." Admittedly few of us fit neatly into these categories, and most of us cannot agree on precisely what they mean, but these labels are popularly understood and are used in the scholarly literature on social movements.[11] The NRA and its Critical Mass and Reserve members are conservative, I argue, because their goal is to "preserve long-standing institutions and values through minimizing reforms."[12] The distinct political beliefs and agendas of self-identified liberals and conservatives shape the political environment within which gun rights and gun control organizations and leaders operate. As noted, conservatives, men, and whites are the groups most opposed to stricter gun control laws.[13]

Historically many conservative movements in the United States have responded to perceived threats to their status and prestige.[14] Conservative movements appeal to individualism, patriotism, and moral "absolutism," to "basic American values of God and family," and to "self-control, industriousness, and impulse renunciation."[15] Those who conform to these ideals are "model citizens," but those who fail to live up to or, worse, actively oppose these moral standards are the source of fear and moral indignation; they are the "nightmare citizens."[16] According to these standards, feminists, gays and lesbians, and poor people all qualify as nightmare citizens.[17]

In examining the politics of individual NRA members in the chapters that follow, I discuss different forms of conservatism and types of conservatives (throughout my research no committed NRA members were liberals). I contend that the NRA offers a conservative politics that fears not only gun control but also a broad liberal agenda that deeply committed NRA members perceive as a culture war against conservatives.

Social Forces Threaten Frontier Masculinity

By the time the NRA was founded in 1871, the U.S. economy and culture were undergoing rapid change; the first of two peak periods challenging American manhood, discussed above, was under way. New threats to white men's manhood included modernization, industrialization, urbanization, alienating bureaucracies, massive immigration, an end to slavery, and women's movements.[18] Before industrialization took hold, white men had lived a more stable existence working as artisans and farmers, just as their fathers had. Before the forces of capitalism turned most of them into paid laborers, these breadwinners enjoyed few challenges to their status or identities.

Once the nation became industrialized, however, in order to support their families these men were forced either to sell their labor or head west in search of an easy fortune. Becoming a laborer meant competing with other men for the dangerous, difficult, and low-paying work available.

Escaping this situation proved no less difficult. As time passed, opportunities for white men to "conquer" the West were deteriorating. White settlements took hold across the region, and with the end of the frontier, some men felt powerless. Many thought that the shift toward more urban and less rugged lifestyles was causing an outbreak of effeminacy among men. Teddy Roosevelt was one of the most visible and vocal advocates for getting boys and men out of the eastern cities and into the western woods. The frontier, Roosevelt argued, "brings out manly virtues—mutuality, honor, self-respect—not the 'emasculated milk-and-water moralities' of the eastern elite."[19] Today, well over a century later, many rural Americans continue to believe that urban settings and lifestyles poison and threaten manhood. The accusations and fears of effeminacy remain not just a theme of contemporary masculinity but, arguably, its core feature.

The dominant standard of U.S. masculinity is constructed largely in opposition to femininity. To be a man, in other words, is about *not* being a woman—or feminine or gay. Men must avoid anything our culture associates with femininity or else face the consequences. It is no different for boys, and even perhaps more important, because they are too young to establish masculine identities through work or fatherhood. Boys are expected to create an identity that is distant from, even oppositional to, girls. There are exceptions, of course, to these unwritten rules. Some families or communities may create an environment whereby boys are allowed and even encouraged to break out of their gendered box. However, as most boys and men can tell you, there are usually tremendous negative consequences for violating social norms of masculinity. This is one key reason why parents, particularly fathers, fear that their boys will not quickly and completely carve out a masculine identity.

Industrialization had indirect effects on boys fashioning masculine identities. Men and older boys were less likely to be working at home, so younger boys spent most of their time around sisters and mothers. Further, the number of women teachers of young children increased dramatically at the beginning of the 20th Century. These factors, coupled with the era's perceived challenges to men's identities and status, contributed to men's fear of boys' feminization, which led them to respond in similar ways.[20]

According to sociologist Michael Kimmel, men's reactions to these widespread societal shifts fell into three categories: antifeminist backlash, pro-male backlash, and pro-feminist support.[21] In their antifeminist response, men used religion, science, and politics to justify their emphasis on the "natural" differences between women and men. Antifeminist forces opposed the efforts of the Women's movement to achieve suffrage, claiming that women were neither built for nor capable of making important, rational decisions about politics. They also argued that it was unnatural for boys to be socialized under women's feminizing influence, for doing so might make them into "sissies." Similar explanations centering on so-called "natural" racial differences were also promoted during this period of heavy American immigration. The category "white" was challenged during the late 1800s and early 1900s with the arrival of Jews, Irish, and Southern Europeans. Although these groups are labeled "white" today, the pseudo-science of the early 20th Century argued otherwise. By the 1940s, the courts and U.S. culture drew a color line around the *outside* of Europe rather than within to determine whiteness and the privileges it accorded.[22] These new "other" whites assimilated, thereby helping whites deal with the abolition of slavery by clearly demarcating racial groups, segregating them, and maintaining a racial order.[23] Still, white men were threatened by challenges to both gender and racial arrangements at this time. Clear evidence of this is the surge in the Ku Klux Klan's (KKK) membership, which peaked at close to five million in 1926.[24]

Men's second response to the heightened threats to white manhood, pro-male backlash, offered a "vigorous reassertion of traditional masculinity."[25] This backlash countered feminist goals but not women as individuals or a group. Frontier masculinity needed to be celebrated and practiced with vigor, supporters argued, a view epitomized by Teddy Roosevelt and his Rough Riders. This response also ties into a fear of boys' feminization, as seen, for example, in the founding of the Boy Scouts of America in 1910. The Boy Scouts were established to make big men out of little boys. Scouts were introduced to the American Ethos, receiving a mentor on the path to their achievement of independent manhood. The organization's leaders mourned the loss of the frontier and acted to ensure that boys would not become effeminate in the new urbanized and industrialized America. *Scouting* author Daniel Beard expressed this sentiment in 1914:

> Wilderness is gone, the Buckskin man is gone, the painted Indian has hit the trail over the Great Divide, the hardships and privations of pioneer life which did so much to develop sterling manhood are now but a legend in history, and we must depend upon the Boy Scout Movement to produce the MEN of the future.[26]

Adult men also benefited by serving as Scoutmasters, thereby validating their own frontier masculinity.[27]

In an attempt to escape from women and their perceived feminizing influences, men created other homosocial, masculine spaces during this period, for example, organized sports, fraternal orders and lodges such as the Elks and the Sons of the American Revolution, and additional college fraternities.[28] The intersection of gender and race is significant here. Obviously the KKK was comprised of white men responding to racial and gender changes, but white men also tended to dominate organized sport, college fraternities, and fraternal organizations; indeed, these were often exclusive to white men.

Undoubtedly the smallest and least influential response by men to these sweeping challenges to gender and race was to support women's gains. These early pro-feminist men founded women's colleges and became involved in the women's suffrage movement. Welcoming and promoting change rather than fearing it was, of course, the exception. Overall, many white working- and middle-class men found ways to remove themselves and their boys from women's presence at this time, creating sites where both adult men and young boys attempting to enter manhood could establish their masculinity.[29]

The first crisis declined around 1920. By this time, the massive wave of immigration was winding down, women had gained the right to vote, and World War I was under way.[30] War had always provided men and boys with a homosocial outlet to prove their manhood through guns and violence, and it also isolated them from women's feminizing influences.[31] Racial segregation within the military, moreover, allowed white men to assert their masculinity in a racially homogeneous setting, reducing the threat to white men's traditional privileges.

New Challenges to Frontier Masculinity

American manhood appeared strong after World War II, the war having served as a masculine proving ground, turning boys into men according to dominant cultural perceptions. The United States had won a moral war against the genocidal practices of the Nazis, and soldiers were rewarded with a booming 1950s economy.[32] But these trends did not last. Another period of rapid social change and shifts in work and family relations in the second half of the 20th Century again challenged gender and racial arrangements. Multiple social movements emerged, including second-wave feminism and civil rights, threatening the gendered separation of spheres, racial segregation, and other forms of white men's grip on dominant status and power. At the same time, women's paid employment enjoyed enormous growth; the economy took a downturn; manufacturing jobs for working-class men were transferred regionally and eventually shifted overseas, replaced largely by service jobs filled by women and immigrants; and homosexuality became a visible alternative to the heterosexual order.[33] On top of all these changes the United States was enmeshed in an unsuccessful and culturally divisive war in Vietnam. By the 1970s, when the NRA's political transformation took place, few if any outlets existed for men to assert their frontier masculinity.[34] Many white men felt they were losing their grasp on society, and in some ways they were right—men of color, women, and a shift to the Left in national politics was eroding white men's cultural and institutional power.[35]

Similar to their predecessors, many men at this time responded with antifeminist criticism, pro-male backlash, or pro-feminism. The 1950s ushered in the modern signs of a forthcoming antifeminist reaction. The most visible arrival was *Playboy* magazine, whose first issue included a feature article attacking the concept of alimony and, more broadly, "Gold-Digger" wives.[36] These precursors to the men's rights movement encouraged bachelorhood as a way to reclaim the home as masculine, and also promoted "one-night stands." "Playboys" welcomed women to their home as sexual partners, not potential life partners. Author Barbara Ehrenreich argues that, although the magazine was selling sex,

> *Playboy* was not the voice of the sexual revolution, which began, at least overtly, in the sixties, but of the male rebellion, which had begun in the fifties. The real message was not eroticism, but escape—literal escape, from the bondage of breadwinning.[37]

Playboy's rhetoric, and later that of the men's rights movement, centered on the notion that women had pulled a fast one by living off men's labors while enjoying a leisurely life at home. Betty Friedan's *The Feminine Mystique* (1963) countered this notion, pointing out that many women are unhappy and unfulfilled at home.[38] The solution for these discontented women was to enter the paid labor force.

Men, however, were not about to rescind their breadwinner status so easily, wrapped up as it was in their masculine authority and identity. Blurring the gendered spheres would erase a piece of their manhood.

Men's antifeminist backlash grew more overt as second-wave feminism was increasingly perceived as threatening "traditional roles," that is, challenging women's deference to men's status and power. In 1982 the Equal Rights Amendment (ERA) was defeated and, ironically, hailed as a "victory for women" by conservatives such as Phyllis Schlafly, who sounded the death knell for everything from heterosexual marriages to gender differences had the ERA succeeded. The ERA would have erased women's "freedom" to be housewives, they argued, demanding instead that women work which, in turn, would free men from their breadwinning responsibilities. Thus, within the same argument, they revealed their distrust of men and their contempt for feminists.[39]

Along with feminist victories such as no-fault divorce laws and the 1973 pro-choice *Roe V. Wade* Supreme Court decision, antifeminist backlash grew and spread, with conservatives at the forefront of the attacks. Clear links could be drawn between the campaign against the ERA, Phyllis Schlafly's Eagle Forum organization, and the far-right anticommunist John Birch Society, which declared that "[the] ERA threatens women's freedom" two years before the ERA became a national issue.[40] The New Right equated feminists with Communists because some feminists were pushing for government-sponsored day care. This red-baiting tapped into the long-standing conviction among conservatives that citizens should work hard and provide their own way. To them, feminism meant dependence on others, especially the government. Antifeminists ultimately fought for the underlying characteristics of frontier masculinity.

Authors and groups supporting conservative men's rights added to the antifeminist backlash, focusing on the costs of contemporary masculinity: fighting and dying in wars, having a shorter life span than women do, and suffering the stress that goes along with being the breadwinner. They ignored (or sometimes questioned) the costs of societal gender arrangements for women: widespread domestic violence and rape, glass ceilings at work, and working a "second shift" at home taking care of their children and doing the housework. These conservative men, unlike antifeminist proponents such as Schlafly and the Christian Right, do not support a return to separate gendered spheres and patriarchal hegemony. Rather, they believe that gender relations are destructive to men, as they place unrealistic expectations on men to be breadwinners and sacrifice their mental and physical health to masculine expectations. Dying in wars, sustaining injuries in contact sports, and suffering from poor communication skills and distant relationships are commonly cited as negative consequences for men who conform to gendered social norms. Similar to feminists, these men imagine a "more healthful, peaceful, and nurturing" version of masculinity, but they dismiss feminist counterarguments that men do not share equally in the oppression caused by contemporary gender arrangements.[41]

In fact, men's rights advocates generally dismiss women's oppression altogether on some of the most well-documented structural inequalities that exist, such as sexual harassment, negative media depictions, intimate partner violence, post-divorce financial inequality, and so on. Instead, they claim that men are the true victims of gender inequality because of the changes resulting from second-wave feminism. Richard Doyle, author of *The Rape of the Male* and *Save the Males*, argues, "In the past many prejudices favored men over women. Today, that situation is reversed."[42] Writing about men and divorce, Doyle says, "A man is like a solitary pawn, face-to-face with the queen on a chess board. Like a black man in the South competing for a job 50 years ago, he must be superior just to be considered equal."[43]

Shifting his attention to rape, Doyle blames women's dress and behavior, making the unfortunate claims that men's sexual violence is beyond their control and of mild consequence:

> Some women seem to have a rape wish. If one is curiously attired, or un-attired, it follows that one is going to be the object of curiosity. For that reason, flirtatious women who go about in public only partially clothed, whether or not in "style," have little cause to complain about unwanted sexual advances, even vigorous ones, or [troublemakers] leering after them. Even though rape is a natural act, the prehistoric means of perpetuating the species, it is uncivilized in modern times, and must be severely punished—*when proven*. As with adultery, the urge is natural but succumbing to it is unacceptable behavior. Without in any way condoning actual rape, it must be said that it usually involves no physical harm and far less mental harm than that suffered by many men in divorce.[44]

Author Warren Farrell shifted his allegiance to the men's rights movement after being an early model for men's participation in the feminist movement. The author of *The Myth of Male Power*, which he described as a "500-page debunking of the myth of men as a privileged class," Farrell finds no gender discrimination in the pay gap and calls "statistics that men batter women more than women batter men" lies. His book, he says, "looks at men as 'nigger': all the ways that men are treated as second-class people." Farrell's men-as-victims argument knows no bounds: "In America and in most of the industrialized world, men are coming to be thought of by feminists in very much the same way that Jews were thought of by early Nazis."[45]

Antifeminist backlash generally aims to restore "traditional masculinity" where men are at the top of the hierarchy—or, in the Christian Right version, they are above women and just beneath God. Feminist gains of this period explicitly threatened the worldview and practices of fundamentalist religions, as did gay liberation and the sexual revolution. In response, right-wing Christians, in the 1970s, mobilized to reverse the gains made by the liberal Left. A recent example, built on earlier Christian Right activism, is the men's movement known as the Promise Keepers. Founded in 1990, these evangelical Christian men seek to revive the kind of "Muscular Christianity" seen at the turn of the century.[46] They challenge men to take back control of their families, and they worry that women have taken on too much responsibility, while "sissified" men fail to fulfill their Christian obligation to be leaders of the family. Speaking to Christian men, Tony Evans, the leading voice of the Promise Keepers, insists,

> I'm not suggesting that you *ask* for your role back, I'm urging you to *take it back* . . . There can be no compromise here. If you're going to lead, you must lead. Be sensitive. Listen. Treat the lady gently and lovingly. But *lead!*[47]

Conservative religious leaders believe that men's failures leave the entire family weak, feminized, and without a moral compass. This movement relies on a biblical essentialism that declares men and women different and assigns men as heads of families. At its peak in the 1990s, the Promise Keepers packed football stadiums with men and allowed no women to enter these gatherings. Although the organization only denied entry based on sex, its events largely drew white, middle-class men. Not surprisingly, antifeminist backlash, whether by John Birchers, men's rights advocates, or Christian Promise Keepers, was led by and resonated strongest with those who stood to lose the most if gender and racial arrangements were threatened—conservative, white, middle-class men,[48] the same demographic of most NRA members.

The second reaction to late-20th-Century societal shifts, like that which occurred decades earlier, was pro-male backlash. When their masculinity is threatened, many men go to great lengths to reclaim their status. The unsuccessful U.S. war in Vietnam represented failed American masculinity in at least three ways: American soldiers fighting the war had lost; many soldiers were unable to fight in what they saw as the war's inhumane conditions, as documented by the discovery of numerous unfired weapons; and many men at home protested the fighting.[49]

A far cry from their father's generation—the celebrated heroes who bravely fought against and defeated fascism, saved the world, and secured American freedom—the men of this later generation found that the Vietnam War had left deep scars on the American male psyche, as well as the entire nation.[50] According to sociologist James William Gibson, many men responded to the failures of Vietnam and the challenges of a changing society by slipping into "warrior dreams" by means of *Soldier of Fortune* magazines and meetings, paintball battles, elite combat shooting schools, action adventure books and movies, and, later, fantasy sports leagues and violent video games. For Gibson, the popularity of Sylvester Stallone's *Rambo* movies, along with these other celebratory versions of violent masculinity, reveals a growing paramilitary culture.[51]

Not all men were drawn to this paramilitary culture, however; it resonated most strongly with lower-middle-class working men, particularly those who were white and conservative. A large percentage of soldiers in Vietnam were of the working class, so the many impacts of the war fell disproportionately onto this group. White, working-class men, in particular, felt that their welfare was threatened—by immigrants of color, civil rights advocates, and the loss of manufacturing jobs. Previously combat had provided men with a ritual transition from boyhood to manhood, an event otherwise unmarked in much of American culture. But, to many men, the failures of Vietnam translated to failed masculinity. Some chose to blame "effeminate" liberals for failing to unleash the full force of America's warriors, and others perceived shortcomings within themselves.[52]

The third, and again the smallest response to a peak in challenges to gender and racial arrangements were the attacks on the prevailing models of masculinity by pro-feminist men. This highly critical perspective is mostly isolated within academia. Radical pro-feminist men recognized that they benefited as a group from gender arrangements, and chose to focus on issues like rape and violence against women and other negative outcomes of patriarchy. Socialist pro-feminist men took on a more structural view, pointing out how gender arrangements cause and reinforce gendered behaviors that lead to negative outcomes for women and men.

Because our society is patriarchal, they argued, women as a group suffer more from gendered expectations and arrangements than men do.

This perspective went beyond a simplistic binary breakdown by incorporating the intersection of race, ethnicity, class, and sexuality with gender. Although men as a group benefit from patriarchy, many lose these privileges because of racial or class inequality, leaving some men rather powerless compared to other men and some women.[53] In sum, structural patterns and tendencies of unequal relations exist between women and men, but these are based on social constructions and thus are not absolutes. Both socialism and popular caricatures of feminism are marginalized and attacked by conservative and even mainstream America. Any views hostile to the American Ethos and frontier masculinity, the notion that everyone has equal opportunities and only themselves to blame or thank for their life circumstances, are likely to be pushed to the margins. These critical views challenge the values and status of the culturally ascendant version of U.S. masculinity.

Similar to men at the turn of the 20th Century, most of these contemporary (also mostly white) counterparts in the second half of the century found ways to escape from women and attempted to create new rites of passage and rituals to display their manhood. It is not a coincidence that during this period the NRA shifted from being primarily a hunting and sport-shooting organization to a social movement organization aggressively defending a fundamentalist interpretation of the Second Amendment and, more generally, shielding frontier masculinity from the onslaught of threats posed by structural and cultural shifts.

The Culture Wars

Conservative white men's reaction to the massive social changes they saw as threatening their manhood began "a 'chain reaction' . . . whereby issues of race, group rights movements and reform, and taxes collided at the same time as a conservative upswing in national politics that altered party affiliations for many whites."[54] Liberal social movements challenged the country's institutionalized inequality, seeking rights for groups that had always been treated as second-class citizens. They also tested the core values of American culture. Supporters of civil rights, women's rights, and gay and lesbian rights exposed the contradiction between America's *message* of rights and freedoms for all and its *practice* of segregation and discrimination.

These liberal activists fought to secure the same rights and freedoms as their white, male, and straight counterparts. Though they hoped to enjoy individual rights and freedoms eventually, they organized as group-rights movements because people of color, women, and lesbians and gays were denied rights based on their group affiliations. They created grassroots movements outside the government, hoping to influence the government to make the structural changes needed to institutionalize their agenda. Leaving aside the question of exactly how effective these movements have been, they inarguably contributed to social changes that many viewed as threats to conservative values.

These cultural clashes continue to color the political landscape of the United States, visible not only in ongoing SMOs but also in legislative debates. The federal government, liberals passionately argue, was needed to end racist school segregation practices and sexist laws denying women's right to choose what to do with their bodies. The federal government, conservatives fervently argue, enforces discrimination against white men through affirmative action programs and coddles non-native, English-speaking immigrants through multi-language voting ballots and multi-cultural education. The atrocities and discrimination that liberals point to in America's dominant culture are directed against virtually all social groups except white men. Conservatives argue that any atrocities committed by white men are ancient history, and continued attempts to address them merely perpetuate new group-based discrimination against white men. People who self-identify as conservatives, vote for conservatives, or hold views labeled as conservative are much more likely to believe that movements and policies promoting group rights are anathema to frontier masculinity and U.S. culture. On the other hand, people who identify with and support liberals are much more likely to think that conservative claims of "equal opportunities for all" glosses over ongoing racism, sexism, and group-based inequality.

Do group-rights movements and laws ensure that everyone has equal rights and freedoms, or do they attempt to give *special* rights to some groups over others? Is the federal government a force for social justice and fairness, upholding the values promised for all but historically denied to so many? Or is the U.S. a freedom and rights-grabbing "nanny state" that threatens frontier masculinity values such as independence and hard work that made our country great in the first place? "At the heart of the culture war," says sociologist James Davison Hunter, "is a conflict to define the meaning of America."[55]

As linguist George Lakoff argues, "Perhaps no idea has mattered more in American history than the idea of freedom."[56] For the many gun-owning conservatives and hardcore NRA members who fight the culture wars, nothing matters more than defending an individual right to own and use guns. Nothing cuts to the heart of their fight against group rights and big-government, nanny-state politics like the battle against gun control. In their minds, the loss of gun rights will lead to the loss of all other individual rights and freedoms. This is why the NRA labels any form of gun control legislation, however modest or limited in its goals or jurisdiction, as a threat to all gun rights and, ultimately, all individual rights and freedoms. They link gun control to frontier masculinity and identify threats to both by pro-gun control, anti-freedom, pro-tax, pro-(special) group rights, and big government, nanny-state liberals who think they know what's best for us all.

The Gun Crusaders' mission is clear: Defend gun rights. Win the culture war. Save America. This message resonates with NRA members and other gun owners, and brings them to gun rights organizations, voting booths, and politicians' offices. This is why the NRA usually wins.

The culture wars go well beyond the issue of gun rights for many conservative (and liberal) combatants. Multiple conservative reactive movements formed in response to the second peak period of cultural and social structural changes to gender and racial arrangements. The thread connecting them is their sense of victimization at the hands of a liberal culture run amok. In their eyes, immigrants, gays, women, the poor, and other groups are (undeservedly) granted special rights and privileges.[57] These conservative white men feel as though they are an endangered species, victims of "reverse discrimination" liberal policies that chip away at their individual rights, spoil America's do-it-yourself culture, and even steal their jobs.

In response to their frustrations with the liberal culture war agenda, they join conservative movements. These include self-identified "pro-family" movements that critics label anti-feminist and anti-gay rights, as well as pro-life, anti-evolution, anti-affirmative action, anti-immigration, English-Only, and anti-tax movements, to name a few. Collectively they comprise the supply lines for a conservative movement decades in the making. The movement has been bolstered by objective and perceived threats posed by liberal politics. Though the NRA has been winning battles over gun control, American culture has largely veered to the Left since the 1960s, even as U.S. politics has veered to the Right. Conservatives' inability to translate election victories into rollbacks in abortion rights, the teaching of evolution, and wider acceptance of gays and lesbians "creates among [hardcore conservatives] a perpetual outrage machine."[58]

As I discuss in chapter 8, the NRA is deeply intertwined with the well-organized conservative movement. For the NRA and its Critical Mass and Reserve members, however, gun rights are *America's First Freedom*, as the NRA magazine title boldly states. Opposition to taxes, welfare, illegal immigration, and other causes of the conservative movement are secondary or tertiary. Even the First Amendment to the Constitution takes a backseat to the Second.

The NRA's politics is an exercise in competing if not contradictory masculinities. NRA members self-identify as both victims and heroes. Part of their politics is defensive, reflecting threats to gun rights as well as a broader conservative reaction to challenges to frontier masculinity. They feel their status and power eroding, their identities damaged. They are victims.

Yet, they also offer a competing narrative. To stem the liberal tide, the NRA casts gun rights activists as contemporary freedom fighters, exemplary patriots and exemplary men. They are 21st-Century Paul Reveres warning the nation about impending threats from oppressive big-government forces. They are modern-day James Madisons mobilizing against federal power. They are symbolic frontiersmen relying on their guns, work ethic, and frontier masculinity values to achieve the American Dream without government interference. They are heroes.

NRA members simultaneously claim victim status, as endangered conservative, gun-owning white men, and hero status, as virtuous patriots protecting gun rights and thereby preventing U.S. citizens from losing all other rights and freedoms. They are victims of the culture war. They are heroes winning the culture war.[59]

Is There a Culture War?

Stepping back for a moment from NRA members' and conservative white men's claims about their status, the culture war metaphor itself generates controversy and is worth examining separately. In all the supposed culture war battles, violent acts are far and away the exception—one reason why many scholars argue that the metaphor is a misnomer at best.[60] There have been cases of anti-abortion activists shooting doctors and bombing clinics since the landmark *Roe vs. Wade* decision. Timothy McVeigh, convicted and executed for killing 168 people in the 1995 Oklahoma City bombing, committed what was then the worst act of terrorism on U.S. soil based on his belief that the government was waging a secret war that involved violating citizens' rights. He cited government actions at Waco and Ruby Ridge, both motivated partly by gun control law violations and involving the longtime nemesis of gun rights proponents, the Bureau of Alcohol, Tobacco, and Firearms (BATF). McVeigh and many others concerned about government power have cited Waco and Ruby Ridge as examples of oppressive government forces stomping out citizens' gun rights, freedoms, and even their lives. It would be inaccurate to label McVeigh's terrorist act a sole product of the gun rights battle, but his politics reflect an extremist position of conservatives' anti-big government, culture war position.

It is noteworthy that only pro-life and gun rights supporters regularly argue that they are prepared to lay down their lives for what they see as transcendent causes worth dying for, whereas English-Only advocates and immigration foes do not pepper their rhetoric with self-sacrifice in the name of their cause against multilingual education, multiculturalism, or undocumented immigrants.

Another reason why some may discount the notion of a culture war is that, historically, political scholars have paid more attention to class and economics than culture. James Carville, President Bill Clinton's adviser, offered the now famous mantra "It's the economy, stupid," which epitomizes this economics-based approach to understanding voter behavior. Other scholars note that the majority of Americans hold centrist political views or liberal views on some issues and conservative views on others, and that no cleanly defined, two-sided battle exists. Critics such as political scientist Morris Fiorina argue that most Americans do not participate in or perceive that a culture war is raging.

> The simple truth is that there is no culture war in the United States—no battle for the soul of America rages, at least none that most Americans are aware of. Certainly, one can find a few warriors who engage in noisy skirmishes. Many of the activists in the political parties and the various cause groups do, in fact, hate each other and regard themselves as combatants in a war.[61]

Those who dismiss the idea of a culture war tend to focus on all Americans, researching their political affiliations and attitudes; war, however, tends to be a "minority affair."[62] Those who argue that the culture war exists often focus on the activists who claim to be the combatants. Even those who question whether a systematic culture war exists admit, as do Fiorina and colleagues, that "the activists are several times more polarized than everyone else," and "within the political class . . . something that might be called a culture war does exist."[63]

The two major political parties and many social movements continue to organize around and fight over class issues. Debates about tax cuts, minimum wage hikes, and privatizing Social Security are sure to rile up voters of all stripes. But today culture war battle lines are drawn based on labels and values such as conservative and liberal or traditionalist and modernist. The politicians and activists waging the culture war are prone to label their opponents un-American. The war, therefore, is ideological rather than materially driven.[64] Even materialist issues are easily transformed into culture war battles; arguments about taxing the rich at higher rates, for instance, often result in debates about socialism.

Because movement activists are driven by ideological differences, they tend to be more involved politically compared to centrists and those with mixed political views. Politicians have also become more polarized. These patterns speak to the existence of a culture war. Although these highly polarized actors are, statistically, a minority in the United States, they are also the ones controlling public discourse on the issues by creating and defining the battles, as well as crafting legislation. The less politically active centrists are often stuck with the decision of voting on positions that do not align closely with their views. They are faced with voting for or against the politicians and policies brought to them, both so often born of the culture war.

Voters electing politicians based on the candidates' gun views are voting on politicians who have been supported, vetted, lobbied, or attacked by supporters of gun control and gun rights. Given that the gun rights movement dominates the debate, these politicians are more likely to have enjoyed the support or incurred the wrath of dedicated NRA members than of members of gun control organizations. The lack of highly restrictive, federal gun control legislation in the United States today testifies to the power and influence of gun rights activists and organizations. Politicians who have crafted or supported gun control policies and have borne the brunt of angry letters from gun rights activists and the NRA's political machine would likely argue that the culture war is no myth. Most Americans do not get too involved in gun politics, but the hundreds of thousands and perhaps millions who do are driving the debate and aligning it with a broader culture war.[65]

The NRA Revolution

The culture wars were only just beginning when a group of NRA gun rights hard-liners took over the organization in a 1977 political coup. The Revolt at Cincinnati was a culmination of many events and social forces. First and foremost, gun control threats drove the NRA's 1970s emergence as the primary defender of the Second Amendment. Although group-rights movements threatened frontier masculinity during the organization's political conversion, early NRA references to these were much more the exception than the rule. The NRA had only recently rhetorically expanded its mission to defending frontier masculinity when it began to consistently connect threats to gun rights with threats to all individual rights and freedoms in the late 1990s. These Gun Crusaders had slightly less political savvy than their counterparts today. To explain why and how the NRA has become the dominant force in today's gun control/gun rights debate, I first examine the NRA's transformation from a group of gun enthusiasts to a gun rights group.

My account addresses the emergence of both the gun rights movement and the NRA as the primary social movement organization within the movement.[66] Several direct threats to gun rights, some internal to the organization and others external, help explain why gun rights hard-liners took over the organization. The most visible events and the ones that generated the most external pressure on the NRA were the assassinations of the Kennedy brothers and Martin Luther King Jr. Critical events are often unexpected and focus public attention on a particular issue, spurring increased movement and countermovement activity.[67] For gun rights supporters, the assassinations and subsequent calls for gun control legislation were considerable threats. For gun control advocates, an important window of opportunity had opened.[68] Inside the NRA another critical event took place when the Old Guard laid off dozens of NRA staff sympathetic to the hard-liners. After this "weekend massacre" in 1976, the more fundamentalist gun rights advocates set up the coup the following year.

The hard-liners were able to wrestle control of the NRA from the Old Guard primarily because the former were more committed to their cause. The hard-liners were politically motivated, and they believed that any compromises on gun control legislation meant compromising one's moral or religious beliefs. Sociologist Kristin Luker, writing a few years after the Revolt took place, suggests that one reason the NRA and similar organizations can be so effective despite their small numbers is that they hold "strong opinions" on a matter that is not of central concern to most people.[69] To hard-liners, the Constitution is the Bible for freedom, and the Second Amendment is nothing less than the foundation of America's Ten Commandments (the Bill of Rights). On the other hand, the Old Guard was comprised of firearms and outdoors enthusiasts who largely supported the NRA's defense of Second Amendment rights but did not view this as the NRA's central purpose.

Political threats or opportunities, even when they appear as critical events, often are not enough to spark collective action unless a movement has sufficient numbers and some form of organization. For example, Civil Rights groups used churches for their source of organization, where a sympathetic audience could quickly be mobilized.[70] The hard-liners in the NRA had an even easier source of organization and numbers. Instead of creating a new gun rights group, they simply took over the million-member NRA. Gun control supporters also had roots in other organizations, including religious, labor, and nonprofit groups.[71] So both sides of the emerging debate grew out of and built on earlier relevant organizations.

The New Gun Crusaders

Social movement theory sheds light on why the Gun Crusaders took over the NRA and then took it to new heights. The NRA became one of many emerging conservative organizations responding to the liberal threat posed by gun rights movements. When the conservative movement gained traction in the 1980s, the NRA and other individual-rights proponents benefited not from threats but from political opportunities that included a sympathetic Reagan administration and a Congress willing to roll back gun control laws. As political parties gain and lose influence and control of the branches of government, social movements challenge threats or welcome opportunities. Similarly, changes in American culture—a series of mass shootings generating support for gun control or the conservative movement helping to promote individual rights as opposed to group rights—may cause threats or opportunities to ebb and flow.

As social movement scholars have argued, threats become relevant only when individuals perceive them as threats.[72] Rather than assuming that threats exist, social movement activity may increase simply because individuals *believe* that threats or opportunities exist. Conservative organizations like the NRA have responded to the liberal movements of the 1960s and 1970s by casting them as threats to individual rights and freedoms.

NRA hard-liners were able to successfully oust the Old Guard partly because they raised culturally resonant concerns. Although they did not center their defense of gun rights around frontier masculinity, as the NRA does today, they occasionally connected guns with broader freedoms and individual rights. NRA members and other gun owners perceived threats to gun rights and responded accordingly.

By the 1980s U.S. politics had turned sharply to the Right. The Reagan Revolution and a conservative movement created over decades pushed back against earlier liberal gains. With white men's masculinity challenged by structural and cultural shifts, it was inevitable that many would react harshly to defend their power. A predictable conservative backlash responded to progressive gains by feminists and Civil Rights movements; an example is the new Christian Right.[73] The NRA contributed to and benefited from the political opportunities available to conservatives, as evidenced by their membership surging to nearly three million in 1985. The culture wars were well under way. As gun control became increasingly affiliated with the Democratic Party, and gun rights with the Republican Party, the NRA shifted its rhetoric and appealed to conservatives.

Unlike the NRA's dramatic transformation of the late 1970s, this new Right-leaning strategy buttressed rather than replaced NRA ideology. Instead of drumming up support by merely framing gun rights as a key constitutional right, the new approach cast the NRA as freedom-fighters bravely defending all individual rights and freedoms, or frontier masculinity. Pointing out the cliché of guns as penis symbols, gender scholar R. W. Connell has argued that "the gun lobby hardly has to labour the inference that politicians trying to take away our guns are emasculating us."[74]

As pointed out in chapter 1, and illustrated in Figure 1.1, NRA membership slowly increased until the 1977 Revolt, after which membership exploded, peaking after the new millennium. The NRA built its membership in response to widespread threats, but it recently extended this early success by taking advantage of both expanding political opportunities provided by a national shift toward more conservative politics and by framing threats to gun rights in exaggerated terms. By any measure, threats to gun rights have declined considerably since the 1960s and 1970s. Along with a dramatic increase in membership came a similar increase in resources, as the organization has, historically, been financially dependent on membership dues. In 1954 the NRA's income was $1.7 million. It moderately increased to $4.5 million in 1964. By 1986, a golden age for the NRA after the Revolt, partly because of a conservative swing in national politics and relative internal stability, organizational income surged to $80 million. By 1990 it edged up to $88 million, and in 2001, in the middle of a second stretch of unparalleled success, NRA income rose to a staggering $200 million.[75] These incredible numbers have certainly contributed to the NRA's effectiveness. Although I emphasize the importance of social forces and NRA rhetoric to explain the NRA's success, the organization's vast resources clearly have also contributed.

Perhaps most impressive about the NRA's membership surge during the last thirty years is that it has come during a period of not only declining gun control threats but also a significant decline in gun ownership and hunting. With increasing urbanization and suburbanization, declining space for hunting and shooting, and an aging gun-owner population, one would think that NRA membership would be declining.[76] In 2006 less than 35% of General Social Survey respondents reported they had a gun in their home, down from over 43% in 1996 and nearly 50% in 1976.[77] Rather than wilting and fading, however, the NRA has flourished. It has done this by becoming a key conservative culture war force defending frontier masculinity, framing threats to gun rights as threats to all individual rights and freedoms, and hitching its wagon to the conservative movement. This strategy has literally paid dividends, drawing in strongly committed gun rights activists who talk loudly *and* carry big guns.

The NRA as a Social Movement Organization

Because of its agenda and powerful lobbying wing, the NRA is often referred to as a single-interest group. However, it is best described as a social movement organization,[78] a formal, organized group that aligns its goals with a social movement or countermovement in order to implement these goals.[79] Despite its primary focus on institutionalized politics, the NRA uses multiple tactics and has several strategies, making it much more than a special-interest lobbying group. I consider the NRA to be an SMO, because it promotes its goals through less institutionalized tactics such as consciousness raising and local rallies and protests, particularly during election seasons.[80] The NRA also has many active state associations, involves members through its grassroots Election Volunteer Coordinators and workshops, and mobilizes members for letter-writing campaigns. It raises money from hundreds of local Friends of NRA Banquets, publishes magazines, provides grants, distributes literature, its top officers give lectures and speeches, and it provides education in firearms training and gun safety to adults and children, teaches self-defense courses, and holds an annual meeting that draws tens of thousands of members.[81]

The NRA is part of a larger gun rights movement, including Gun Owners of America, Citizens Committee for the Right to Keep and Bear Arms, the Second Amendment Foundation, Second Amendment Sisters, Jews for the Preservation of Firearms, and, arguably, less formalized groups such as militias. The NRA is not the most fundamentalist of these groups in terms of its gun politics, but it is the most powerful and institutionalized. Some of the other organizations have attacked the NRA for compromising on gun legislation, and they often use language that makes the NRA's language appear measured. Charlton Heston's views on defending gun rights to the death reflect those of the organization and its Critical Mass and Reserve members. But their fear of government abuses of power pales compared to militia groups that train for their perceived impending battles against the communist and fascist "one-world government."

In general, though, the rhetoric is the same across gun rights groups. For example, most gun rights organizations would argue that, "If you outlaw guns, only outlaws will have guns"; "Guns don't kill people, people kill people"; and "Enforce the gun laws that already exist, do not create new ones." They aim not only to fend off gun control legislation at local and national levels but also to repeal older, restrictive laws and pass new pro-gun legislation.[82] These groups spend a great deal of time and money attempting to counter the argument that more guns equals more crime and support the reverse, as John Lott's highly contested book, *More Guns, Less Crime*, proclaims.[83]

Certainly, however, the NRA's focus is on conventional forms of political participation through lobbying and elections, which makes it a somewhat unique case.[84] I interpret the NRA as a unique SMO promoting not simply individual gun rights but rather a specific frontier version of masculinity politics. This helps explain the NRA's 1977 emergence as a gun rights defender and its continued dominance in the gun rights debate, because it allows for a connection between threats to gun rights and broader social structural changes and cultural representations linked to gender and race relations. Social movements scholar Doug McAdam notes that the threat is at least as important, if not more so, than opportunity when studying contentious politics. Furthermore, both threat and opportunity are socially constructed and not objectively measurable conditions. If people perceive that their rights, status, and identity are threatened, they will be motivated to act.[85]

Defending gun rights is an act of patriotism, according to NRA leaders. "The Second Amendment is, in order of importance, the first amendment. The Second Amendment is Americans' first freedom," Charlton Heston declared, "because it is the one right that protects all the others. Among the freedoms of speech, of the press, of religion, of assembly, of redress of grievances, it is the first among equals. The right to keep and bear arms is the one right that permits 'rights' to exist at all."[86] NRA leaders often speak about the Second Amendment as the foundation upon which the Constitution and Bill of Rights rest. Accordingly, the NRA implores supporters of gun rights to defend the Second Amendment from gun control advocates in government just as the Founding Fathers fended off British colonialists. The Founding Fathers are to be revered as near immortals, the Bill of Rights was (free white men's) covenant with God, and freedom itself can only exist through a no-compromise defense of its foundation—the Second Amendment. According to NRA literature, current members' defense of the Second Amendment mirrors the historical significance of the Founding Fathers fighting off the British monarchy.

NRA strategies to frame the gun control movement as the "gun-grabbers" often appear apocalyptic and excessive to outsiders, given that legislation to ban guns is virtually nonexistent in the United States. The perceived threat is real enough to NRA members, however, particularly the most dedicated supporters of the group whose political views reflect those of the organization. This may help explain why the NRA has successfully fended off gun control legislation and helped place and keep pro-gun candidates in office. Their success is particularly impressive given that each year there are roughly thirty thousand firearms-related deaths (homicides, suicides, and accidents), national polls reveal strong support for various kinds of gun control legislation, and only recently have the courts held up an individual right to keep and bear arms.

In addition to the gendered and racial shifts that pressed the NRA's politicization, and its later use of highly resonant gendered framing strategies, this group's increasingly reactionary politics has led to a large majority of conservative members and expanding connections to conservative politics in general. This makes the NRA a prime example of the convergence of gender, race, and contentious politics in the United States. NRA leaders have become increasingly affiliated with other conservative culture war causes and groups, along with the Republican Party, and these changes have led to changes in NRA framing strategies.

The extent to which the NRA and its rhetoric have moved to the Right reflects a similar move in the Republican Party. Political scientist Alan Wolfe, a skeptic of the culture wars, nonetheless argues, "Since the 1980s liberals and Democrats have not moved nearly as far to the left as Republicans and conservatives have moved to the right. . . . The culture war being fought by partisans and ideologues continued because conservatives and Republicans want to see it continue." Why do they want to fan the flames of the culture wars? Wolfe concludes, "The astonishing political success of Republicans is premised upon mobilizing high levels of anger within the electorate—one reason why conservatives tend so often to see themselves as victims of liberal elitists, even when liberals have relatively little political power."[87]

Charlton Heston's culture war discourse embodies the new NRA's recruitment strategy of not wasting time and resources appealing merely to gun owners. Instead, they wisely chose to rally conservative cultural warriors who are deeply committed to the idea that gun rights and freedom go hand-in-hand, and that the Left is trying to eliminate individual rights and freedoms. If the NRA doesn't fight back, Heston warned, liberal cultural warriors will impose government dependence and write frontier masculinity out of American history. Heston cautioned,

> Among the cultural revisionists and contemporary thought police, guns are the symbol of evil most often invoked against an old-fashioned traditional, constitutional American culture. Firearms personify the struggle between traditional and New Age political reckoning, between the Constitution and contemporary revisionist theory that seeks to rewrite both history and the Bill of Rights.[88]

PART II

Talking Guns, Talking Culture War

3

Framing Threats to Gun Rights

One of the starkest differences between the NRA's more tranquil past and its current status as a highly politicized SMO is how the NRA talks about guns, gun control, and itself. Though the NRA became a political force after its 1977 internal coup, two decades passed before it embraced the culture wars and adopted its Gun Crusader identity. In 1996 the NRA produced a recruitment video narrated by Charlton Heston, who had not yet joined the NRA leadership, in which he warned that Americans could easily lose their Second Amendment gun rights, and, if that happened, the torch of freedom would lose its flame. Wayne LaPierre concluded the video in now typical NRA fashion, pitching the fight in grand terms: "You can join or recommit yourself to our crusade to save the Second Amendment."[1]

The NRA soon brought Heston aboard and officially began its crusade to defend gun rights and frontier masculinity, battling gun control advocates and liberal culture war foes. As soon as Heston joined, the NRA cranked up the volume, casting gun rights as a religious and moral imperative. "I remember when European Jews feared to admit their faith. The Nazis forced them to wear yellow stars as identity badges. So," Heston questioned, "what color star will they pin on gun owners' chests?"[2]

Many would find this analogy offensive; there is no impending Holocaust against gun owners. But Heston's metaphor resonates with Gun Crusaders and reveals their intensely passionate gun rights ideology. Like Jews, Heston argued, gun owners should not have to fear who they are or what they believe in; the gun rights faith should not be surrendered in the face of a threat.

Heston's Nazi comparison is regrettable, but equating gun owners with a religion and identity is prescient. In theory, a gun owner could become a non-owner by just giving up his or her guns. In reality, Gun Crusaders are unlikely to abandon their guns and gun rights, just as Orthodox Jews are unlikely to abandon their faith and identity. For both, it is who they are. When your group's status and identity are threatened (or you perceive them to be), you're going to fight back. Heston and the NRA knew this, so they adjusted their messages, appealing to gun owners who feel gun rights, frontier masculinity, and conservative white men are under attack by liberals.

As social movement research reveals,

> Social conditions become social problems when groups label them as such and make claims about them. Such claims crystallize discontent and identify causes and solutions to social problems. Whether such claims gain public support partly depends on their ability to tap into broadly resonant values, beliefs, sentiments, symbols, myths, and experiences.[3]

Recent history demonstrates that large numbers of U.S. citizens, particularly conservative white men, will take action when their status, practices, or beliefs are threatened. People will mobilize in response to obvious threats, as when, for example, rising gun control support in the 1960s sparked a gun rights movement.[4] Often, however, merely the *perception* of a threat leads to reactive mobilization. Social movement organizations like the NRA can generate support by influencing people's perceptions, even if these perceptions do not match reality. Few of us know the average number of shark attacks each summer, but many of us will stay on the beach after seeing shark attack stories repeatedly plastered across the top of newspapers. Perception matters.[5]

As political scientist Murray Edelman argues, words or phrases such as "gun control" can become symbolically linked to broader threats, leading to reactionary mobilization that far exceeds the actual threat. This symbolic use of politics reflects Edelman's claim that "mass publics respond to currently conspicuous political symbols: not to 'facts.'"[6]

The gun rights movement is one of many conservative social movements trying to prevent social change and "maintain structures of order, status, honor, or traditional social differences or values."[7] Some recent men's movements, such as the Promise Keepers, have mobilized hundreds of thousands of men partly in response to what they perceive as men's loss of authority and status. A sizable research literature also documents how groups and institutions can "mobilize fear and shape social groups' interpretations of, and responses to, threats."[8] The growth of these and other conservative reactive movements over the last forty years suggests that there is a "mobilizing effect of threat."[9] As discussed below, conservative movements have not captured the market on this style of discourse. However, the cultural and political changes of the last several decades, largely pushed along by several liberal group-rights movements, has made it easier for conservatives to connect with audiences that believe their status and identities are threatened.

Framing the Message

Sociologist Erving Goffman used the term "frames" to describe how individuals attempt to understand "what it is that is going on here" through observation and interaction.[10] Like a picture frame, linguistic frames tell audiences what to focus on and what to ignore. Framing is a dynamic, interactive process used by SMOs to target their messages toward current and potential participants, and elite decision makers such as politicians and the media.[11] SMOs offer competing frames to gain the most support. For example, the rhetoric of SMOs on both sides of the abortion debate guides and limits how their audiences think about the issue. Even the names of their respective movements frame the debate as pro-choice versus pro-life. The former raises the question: Do you support the freedom of Americans to choose what to do with their own bodies, or do you think the government can remove people's freedom to choose? The latter group frames the debate as a life issue. Do you support protecting innocent lives, or do you think mothers can choose to terminate a pregnancy whenever they please? Each side frames the issue so that their target audiences have tunnel-vision. After all, who wants to be labeled anti-choice or anti-life?

Three main factors affect framing processes and the characteristics and content of frames: (1) the structure of political opportunity (is the political environment in your favor?); (2) cultural opportunities and constraints (is the cultural environment in your favor?); and (3) audience effects, or the intended audience of the framing process. Social movements construct collective action frames (CAFs), or "action-oriented sets of beliefs and meanings that inspire and legitimate the activities and campaigns of [SMOs]," to maximize their support.[12] Collective action frames comprise diagnostic, prognostic, and motivational frames.[13]

Diagnostic frames involve identifying a particular problem as well as attributing blame or causality to a specific source. Movement participants point out and harp on "victims" of specific injustices, because direct action often requires a source of blame.[14] Returning to the abortion debate, a pro-life diagnostic frame would argue that the fetus is an innocent victim of careless or selfish mothers. Prognostic frames suggest solutions and identify various strategies, tactics, and targets. The solution for pro-life supporters is to outlaw abortion.

The third and final component of collective action frames, motivational frames, offer rationales or justifications for action that go beyond diagnostic and prognostic framing. Though many people are sympathetic to social movements, only a fraction will act on these feelings. Pro-life motivational frames include the argument that activists are doing God's work by fighting to save innocent lives, even helping to bring an end to what they sometimes label as genocide. By framing the issue as both a horrible injustice that can be fixed and a cause that is central to people's belief systems, SMO framing strategies can motivate people to commit time and money or to increase their current commitment.

I examine NRA rhetoric and framing strategies over roughly a sixty-year period, beginning in 1945, by analyzing NRA publications, fundraising letters, and leaders' speeches. I focus on how the NRA socially constructs gun rights threats within a context of broader culture war threats to conservative white men's status and identity—a strategy that produces a large membership and an active Critical Mass. NRA appeals to frontier masculinity are apparent throughout the last six decades, becoming more evident recently. In several important ways, however, the NRA has adjusted its discourse since the 1977 Revolt. Since the late 1990s in particular, the NRA has been exaggerating gun control threats, shifting to the political Right to connect gun threats to liberal culture war threats, and portraying threats to gun rights as threats to all individual rights and freedoms. The NRA frames defenders of gun rights as patriots and freedom fighters, and labels gun control supporters as freedom-haters and terrorists.

Implicit Appeals to Frontier Masculinity

Any membership-dependent organization will do its best to appeal to audiences with the same interests. The AARP does not use a lot of pop culture references in its membership pitches to older Americans. Labor union magazines do not show many pictures of their members vacationing at summer homes. Similarly NRA literature is produced mainly by and for the biggest group of gun owners, conservative white men, and reflects current and potential members' demographics and interests. Recent NRA framings more explicitly appeal to conservative white men by citing a lib-eral culture war and threats to group rights, but NRA membership prior to the 1977 Revolt most likely had the same lack of racial and ethnic diver-sity as today, with an even smaller proportion of women decades ago.

Official current and historical data do not reveal the race, ethnicity, or sex of NRA members. However, no evidence suggests that yesterday's members are any more diverse than the members at today's annual meet-ings. Looking at roughly a thirty-year period before the 1977 Revolt, all signs point to the group's long-standing appeal to mostly white men. Pe-riodic listings of NRA board members reveal even fewer women than the 2008 figure of less than 14%.[15]

NRA magazine pictures reveal few women and almost no one of color, whether leaders or members. Advertisements overwhelmingly picture white men as well. Despite the NRA's claims of nonpartisanship and hav-ing no gender or racial preferences during this earlier period, the organi-zation appears to be dominated by white men, especially those affiliated with the military.

Reflecting both NRA and 1940s politics, the association's magazine, *American Rifleman* (hereafter, *Rifleman*), hinted at the gendered nature of shooting sports. Yet race and gender were rarely mentioned explicitly. Even though NRA members supported World War II unquestioningly, 1940s *Rifleman* issues generally avoided war and politics and focused instead on the technical merits of various firearms. Much of the leader-ship had left their organizational posts to return to overseas service in the armed forces; yet key World War II dates pass without mention in the *Rifleman*. However, some racist Japanese depictions appear at this time, including a cartoon with a buck-toothed Japanese man saying "prease" [*sic*] and "so sorry."[16]

As the McCarthy and Cold War eras unfolded, the NRA increasingly used "red-baiting" to paint gun control advocates as anti-American Com-munists and, occasionally, as fascists like Hitler. One NRA article com-pared the politics of gun control proponent Ted Kennedy to the Commu-nist Party in the United States and abroad.[17] An editorial, "Communism versus Gun Ownership" (warning about the dangers of "big government") serves as a prelude to the now constant NRA theme linking American freedoms and gun rights.[18] Conservatives have long been the most out-spoken opponents of communism and expanding the federal govern-ment (even if their leaders sometimes fail them), viewing any govern-ment encroachment as an attack on their freedom and independence.

Communism meant dependence, and dependence is and was, according to the spirit of frontier masculinity, the antithesis of what it means to be a man in the United States.

A 1961 NRA recruitment advertisement refers to "wives or other dependents of NRA Annual and Life Members," thus revealing that the NRA expected only to recruit male members.[19] It also assumes a separation of spheres for women and men, with wives economically dependent on their husbands. A July 1962 editorial conveys the spirit of frontier masculinity—independence—stating, "It will take a new appreciation of the basic principles of freedom for our people to get back to pioneering individualism and to maintain the solidarity of our nation."[20] An article on the history of firearms use further reveals the author's, and presumably readers', makeup when it celebrates the storied defeat of "1,000 painted savages," not needing to clarify that the article is about white men's gun history.[21]

In response to urban riots in the late 1960s, armed self-defense for women became a recurring theme. As one *Rifleman* author wrote: "There's a certain awesome responsibility in placing a gun in a woman's unskilled hands," and unless negative attitudes about guns and taking a life in self-defense are overcome, "the woman should forget firearms and rely on screaming for the police."[22] The author assumes that all women are inherently unskilled with firearms and must overcome their "natural" tendency to avoid killing another human being, whereas men apparently have no such biological barriers to killing. Early 1960s NRA President John M. Schooley implied that gun control would negate the NRA's gendered agenda: "I am concerned that our entire program might be emasculated by restrictive firearms legislation."[23] The NRA of this era was comprised of and for white men, who viewed the realm of firearms as a masculine domain threatened by gun control advocates, portrayed either as women or effeminate men.

Challenges to U.S. racial inequality did not go unnoticed by the NRA in the 1960s, as the organization distanced itself from the Black Panthers' appeal to gun rights laws. Pointing out the differences between the NRA and the Black Panthers, Ashley Halsey Jr., a hard-line gun rights supporter and editor of *Rifleman*, wrote, "[The Black Panthers have a] strong partisan slant while NRA is 'non-political and non-partisan,'" and, furthermore, "the Black Panthers are, as their name connotes, primarily racist."[24] He contended that the NRA makes no racial distinction in its membership. The earlier NRA rarely engaged in direct discussion of race or gender, while still signaling its white, frontier masculine perspective to its readers.

Explicit Appeals to Frontier Masculinity

The new emphasis on gun rights after the 1977 Revolt likely drew in a more conservative membership, which increased further since the late 1990s when the NRA began using culture war discourse and embedded itself in the conservative movement. The NRA's lack of gender diversity clearly persisted after the Revolt: one year later only four out of fifty nominees to the Board of Directors were women.[25]

Though not pitched in explicit racial or gendered terms, Confederate-related apparel has occasionally appeared in the *Rifleman* throughout its history, indicating that at least a portion of the members respond to these southern conservative white symbols, which outsiders criticize as celebrations of slavery. In NRA magazines, the symbols usually appear in advertisements for products bearing the Confederate flag (knives or belt buckles) or, in one case, a 1991 ad soliciting funds to save the "Confederate Embassy" mansion in Washington, D.C.[26] Confederate appeals clearly target conservative whites, sending African Americans (and liberals) elsewhere.

At times, magazine material has not resonated well with women, either. A woman NRA member from California wrote a letter to the editor about the cover of a *Rifleman* issue done in "poor taste."[27] The October 1994 issue in question is titled "Stop the Rape of Liberty"; the cover depicts a man emerging from behind the Statue of Liberty, which has become a live woman, covering her mouth and grabbing at her clothing. The lack of non-conservatives and women participating in the NRA at all levels influences not simply advertisements in the association's magazines but also the NRA's framing strategies.

More recently, the NRA has tried to improve its appeal to women, including establishing a self-defense course ("Refuse to Be a Victim") and an official magazine for women members, *Woman's Outlook*, which was later eliminated in 2006. Despite NRA hopes for making significant inroads into a new membership source, gun rights and gun control are highly gendered issues. Even with women's high participation in the paid labor force, they are still considered to be children's primary safeguards and thus are more likely than men to be drawn to the appeals of gun control groups to reduce violence against children.

The Million Mom March (MMM) in Washington, D.C., in 2000, was organized in response to the number of firearms-related deaths of children. The MMM called for "sensible" gun control, attempting to appeal to mothers' expectations to protect their children. Casting MMM supporters as easily swayed soccer moms, NRA Executive Vice President Wayne LaPierre labeled the event the "Misled Moms March" and claimed these women were a tool of Al Gore's presidential campaign.[28] LaPierre recognized that attacking concerned moms was a politically dangerous move, so he used bridge-building language now almost unheard of in the NRA. He described moms who supported gun control as well-meaning but misinformed as to what actually reduces children's firearms-related deaths. The NRA and MMM engaged in a battle over a "motherist frame," whereby both groups appealed to expectations placed on women to be the protectors of their children.[29] The NRA argues that an armed mother is a good mother, as this is the only way she can protect herself and her children. The MMM contends that the easy availability of dangerous firearms is the cause of violence, and good mothers will act to reduce the hazardous presence of guns.

Recently, NRA leaders have delved into the cauldron of the culture war's identity politics with rhetoric that reveals how threatened they feel by challenges to the racial and gender status quo. Noting his support for what amounts to conservatives' version of affirmative action, NRA President Charlton Heston said, "And I also believe it should be color-blind. I've fought against racism all my life. So why would I tolerate racism in reverse?"[30]

LaPierre, however, regularly echoing Heston's claims of anti-racist sentiments, creates an inaccurate and racist generalization of terrorist threats:

> I guess it's okay to wand-rape someone's daughter in public, but no pro-filing! No, we don't want to risk offending an Islamic ex-con with two aliases and no job, paying cash for a one-way airline ticket with no luggage whose shoes are packed with plastic explosives. Who're we fooling? Terrorists fit into fairly narrow categories of gender, age, nationality and religion.[31]

Heston repeatedly attempted to make his conservative commentary on race widely acceptable by pointing out his involvement in the Civil Rights movement of the 1960s. He argued that our current "cultural war" is basically another "great civil war," and wonders why, "when I told an audience last year that white pride is just as valid as black pride or red pride or anyone else's pride, they called me a racist."[32] Sociologist Mitch Berbrier's research on contemporary right-wing conservative groups such as "New Racist White Supremacists" (NRWSs) shows how they transform their rhetoric from the explicit race-based vitriol of the past to a focus on loving one's own heritage, or white pride, today.[33] Berbrier's work reveals other parallels between Heston's rhetoric and that of the NRWSs. Both frame whites as an endangered group facing similar levels of discrimination as racial/ethnic minorities; or, as Heston put it when he took a stance similar to that of the NRWSs against affirmative action, he opposes "reverse racism."[34]

The NRA perceives that its heritage is under siege by liberals trying to silence conservatives. On presumed attempts by liberal politicians to ban gun shows, LaPierre stated, "It's about suppressing our culture, our heritage, and our freedom."[35] And, in Heston's words, this "Political Correctness is just tyranny with manners."[36] Though the organization's gendered and racial messages have increased in number and complexity, a thread is apparent throughout the last sixty years: defending gun rights is primarily a (conservative) white men's cause. This despite long-standing NRA claims that they comprise "millions of Americans representing a diverse contrast of age, sex, race and religion."[37]

Gun Control Threats since the 1960s

Although the NRA has alerted members about gun control threats throughout its history, the Heston-era NRA alone purposely exaggerated the extent of threats to gun rights as a strategy to mobilize members. During most of the NRA's modern history, membership levels fluctuated with changes in the political environment. When threats of federal gun control legislation increased, NRA membership levels increased. When gun control threats faded, membership also declined. In short, more threats equal more resources for the NRA. An organization that strongly depends on its membership dues, the NRA must find ways to maintain its membership levels or it will lose some of its power and influence. In fact, today's Gun Crusaders frame threats to gun rights as more serious than they actually are (by any objective measure), and this strategy, combined with the NRA linking gun control to culture war threats, has helped them reach their historic peak despite declining gun control threats.

Identifying what counts as a serious threat to gun rights is not a precise scientific undertaking. The same piece of gun control legislation—say, businesses being able to decide whether they allow firearms in employee vehicles parked on company property—may be a good idea to some people, insignificant to others, and to still others a sign that gun rights are being eliminated by liberal culture war forces and confiscation is imminent. All these parties could be gun owners, even NRA members.

Surely, however, ways can be found to minimize our personal opinions about guns and weigh the extent of particular gun control threats more objectively. I believe this can be achieved by focusing primarily on federal gun legislation. Political assassinations, gun violence, negative media coverage of guns, strong public support for gun control, court decisions in favor of gun control, and the size and strength of gun control groups also serve as threats to gun rights. Each of these threats, however, is best measured by its contribution to federal gun legislation. The severity of gun control legislation will depend on how restrictive it is (bans, licensing and registration, usage restrictions, waiting periods, background checks), what or who is controlled (all guns, certain kinds of guns, gun features, ammunition, all or some owners and sellers), and the scope of its application (federal, state, or local legislation).

A handful of major *federal* gun control laws have been passed in the United States. (1) the 1934 National Firearms Act, which regulates machine guns, short barrel (or "sawed off") shotguns and rifles, and silencers, as well as the licensing of dealers; (2) the Gun Control Act of 1968, which created age, citizenship, mental health, and criminal-history restrictions, as well as dealer licensing requirements and the prohibition of mail ordering of all but antique guns; (3) the 1986 Firearms Owners' Protection Act, actually a gun rights law that rolled back some of the 1968 restrictions, limited dealer inspections, and prohibited the federal government from keeping records of registered firearms owners but also banned the future ownership and transfer of fully automatic machine guns; (4) the 1993 Brady Handgun Violence Prevention Act, requiring waiting periods for purchases and background checks on dealer sales to private purchasers (the waiting period was subject to patchwork exceptions by local jurisdictions and was replaced in 1998 by a National Instant Criminal Background Check System); and (5) the Federal Assault Weapons Ban, which prohibited the sale of certain kinds of semi-automatic firearms based on model and features such as high-capacity magazines, which proponents argued had no sporting purpose. This law expired after ten years because of a sunset provision and a 2004 Republican-led Congress that chose not to renew the legislation.[38]

Evaluating this list, one gun control scholar concluded, "Much of the national gun control legislation that has been passed has, not surprisingly, had little effect on gun owning or crime. The legislation can generally be described as tinkering at the edges."[39] The modest federal legislation speaks volumes about Gun Crusaders' influence, even dating back to the 1960s when the NRA had not fully committed to gun politics but many of its members lobbied Congress. Gun control *laws* certainly do not paint a complete picture of threats to gun rights. Many of the laws began as more restrictive bills that were rejected or altered, and many more bills were voted down or never were voted on at all (which calls into question how serious a threat they were).

The peak threat to gun rights arguably occurred before the 1977 NRA Revolt, during the 1960s and 1970s when the most restrictive legislation was seriously considered, and when the political and cultural climate was the strongest for such action. What would later become the 1968 gun control law was introduced in 1963. Though gun registration was on the national agenda in 1963, "none of the registration bills came close to passage."[40]

NRA membership increased to about seven hundred thousand in 1965 and one million in 1968 in response to the threat of federal gun control.[41] The possibility of restrictive gun legislation continued even after the 1968 law was passed. In 1975, two years before the NRA Revolt, Senator Ted Kennedy, brother of gun-assassination victims John F. Kennedy and Robert F. Kennedy, introduced a bill that he announced would "[ban] the manufacture and possession of over 99.9 percent of all handguns."[42] Kennedy's actions legitimately heightened the fears of hard-line NRA gun rights activists. During this period, another congressional bill was proposed to ban handguns for everyone except police and organized competitive shooters, as well as a bill aimed at *revoking* the 1968 restrictions on gun rights. Neither bill became law. Still, these were unsure times for gun owners.

Here was the hard-liners' view within the NRA in 1975: more politicians have been shot and two assassination attempts were made on President Ford; gun crimes are increasing; public support for gun control (including registration) is strong; the Gun Control Act of 1968 passed and many increasingly restrictive bills continue to be presented in Congress; the Republican administration is proposing some gun control; a Bureau of Alcohol, Tobacco, and Firearms was created in 1972, and it is expanding and threatening gun rights, and engaging in questionable legal behavior against gun owners; gun control groups seeking bans or strict controls have formed; some Democrats are pursuing what amounts to virtual handgun bans; and the Old Guard is trying to move the NRA out West and get out of politics, as evidenced in part by their firing of gun rights hard-liner staff.[43] The NRA's earlier Gun Crusaders responded by forming the Institute for Legislative Action in 1975 and successfully revolting two years later. During the early 1970s some fifty federal gun control bills were introduced, but they all failed. This period represented the best chance for a legitimate and effective gun control movement to emerge.[44]

From 1972 to 1988 no federal gun control legislation was voted on by Congress.[45] No gun control laws were passed until the 1993 Brady Act, a quarter-century after the 1968 law. Gun violence and legislation continued to be an issue in the 1980s, but not nearly as much as they were the decade before. In 1982 Californians rejected a state proposition that would prevent future handgun purchases. State-level, gun control laws were rare in the 1970s, remaining in single digits until the early 1990s ushered in a brief period of regulation.[46] A 1981 assassination attempt on President Reagan led to the federal Brady bill, but it failed to win approval in Congress during his presidency.[47] The 1986 Firearms Owners' Protection Act was a significant victory for gun rights advocates and an indication that they did not just weather the gun control storm but had obtained repeals in an anti-control political environment. The NRA curbed its framing of the threat to gun rights in proportion to the reduced gun control threats of this period. As the threats declined, so did both the framing of threats and NRA membership.

Federal gun control legislation reappeared early in Bill Clinton's presidency, and the Brady bill finally made it into law a dozen years after the attempt on Reagan's life that left his press secretary, James Brady, wheelchair-bound. To prevent a Republican filibuster and send the bill to Clinton's desk, compromises were made, including the passage of a sunset provision on the five-day waiting period that eventually was replaced with an instant checks system. As a leading scholar on gun control pointed out, the Brady Act, "the modern gun control forces' most far-reaching achievement in twenty-five years . . . did little more than plug part of an existing loophole by requiring criminal background checks on a limited category of gun buyers."[48] The legislation did chip away at the NRA's perceived invincibility, if not significantly at gun rights.

The late 1980s and early 1990s were marked by high rates of gun violence, owing largely to wars between crack-cocaine dealers. Like the history of the Brady Act, another earlier episode of gun violence led to federal gun control legislation under Clinton, the 1994 Federal Assault Weapons Ban. Five years earlier, in 1989, a shooter in Stockton, California, had killed five schoolchildren, wounding many more, with a semi-automatic rifle. As mentioned, however, the ban expired in 2004. Clinton continued to press for more gun control, but the 1994 law helped mobilize NRA members and gun owners and contributed to the huge 1994 Republican congressional victory. With a Republican-controlled Congress, Clinton failed in his efforts to pass legislation mandating safety locks and ensuring background checks for more types of gun purchases. Even the 1999 Columbine massacre did not provide enough pressure to make gun rights supporters in Congress waver.

Bill Clinton's efforts actually turned out to be helpful for the NRA. In obtaining gun control legislation, his modest success and ongoing threats mobilized gun owners and increased NRA resources. "People respond when there's a threat," the NRA's Wayne LaPierre noted, and "Clinton is mobilizing gun owners at record rates."[49] NRA membership peaked at the time at nearly 3.5 million in response to Clinton and the two federal gun laws he signed. After Democrats lost badly to Republicans in 1994, the Clinton threat was neutralized. However, a short-term decline in membership was seen as a result of an increase in dues, financial and factional problems, and LaPierre's reference to federal law enforcement agents as "jackbooted thugs."

In the late 1990s the NRA bounced back and began the ascent to its unprecedented membership levels and political power. Gun control bills abounded in Congress at the time, even if they typically had little chance of becoming law.[50] Clinton and his vice president and 2000 Democratic presidential candidate Al Gore continued to support the same modest measures regarding background checks and trigger locks. When Gore lost the 2000 election, federal gun control was viewed as not just a dead issue but a losing one for Democrats. The only federal gun control laws from the last four decades that remain in effect today do not confiscate, ban, license, or register firearms. The Gun Crusaders are winning the war.

Local gun control efforts were also failing. By 2005 forty-five states had passed full or partial preemption laws limiting the opportunities for localized bans or licensing. The NRA's primary opposition, gun control groups, still posed a weak threat. These groups combined have about 7% of the NRA's roughly 4 million members. Only one of the major gun control groups, the Violence Policy Center, even goes so far as to "[endorse] a ban on civilian possession of handguns."[51] Federal gun control threats have declined since 1994 and, since 2000, have evaporated. If history repeated itself, the NRA would have seen a big dip in membership levels as the threat lessened. Instead, the NRA recruited and retained members by highlighting non-legislative threats such as media and scholarly attacks on gun culture and gun rights; lawsuits against gun manufacturers, framed as a backdoor attempt to impose gun control by bankrupting the industry and limiting the availability of guns; campaign finance reform, framed as an effort to silence the NRA; law enforcement's illegal and overzealous actions, seen most recently in temporary gun confiscations in New Orleans after Hurricane Katrina; and gun control and violence in countries around the world.

Although I argue that gun control threats peaked during the pre-1977 Revolt period, it is not a given that gun owners will flock to the NRA without prompting. "The traditional equation is that NRA membership rises in direct proportion to anti-gun threats. That rise," according to former NRA public affairs director Johnny Aquilino, "presupposes that the NRA leadership can astutely tie a sense of urgency due to the anti-gun threats to its membership pleas."[52] In the past, the NRA boosted its membership and influence by framing the NRA as the voice of gun owners against objective threats to gun rights.

The NRA's recent all-time peak in membership levels, resources, and political influence has a different cause. True, political threats and opportunities as well as an existing organization affect the NRA's power and resources. But I believe that the NRA reached its peak because of its ability to mobilize members by framing threats to gun rights in ways that resonate deeply with gun owners. Three such changes in rhetoric appeared around the 1977 Revolt, but they reached a high point beginning with Heston's presidency.

First, the NRA moved from suggesting that threats to gun rights are rare and are supported by only a minority of the population to a position of repeated and exaggerated warnings of the impending registration and confiscation of all firearms. Second, as support for gun rights became more aligned with conservative politics, the NRA diagnosed liberals and Democrats as the source of gun control threats, accusing them of engaging in a culture war against individual rights and freedoms. Third, the NRA transformed its rhetoric regarding people who support gun rights, now labeling them as "patriots" and "freedom fighters" because, the organization argues, the Second Amendment is the foundation upon which freedom stands.

Threat Coverage before the Revolt

NRA ideology in the mid-20th Century reflected the organization's sporting interests.[53] The *Rifleman* was dominated by articles on sport shooting and hunting, usually about technical aspects of firearms in relation to their sporting uses. Before 1960, threats to the right to keep and bear arms only occasionally were referred to in print. For example, a November 1945 editorial protests the "latest register-all-firearms-and-eliminate-crime campaign" as a backdoor approach to the confiscation of firearms.[54] Similar themes periodically appear in columns of the 1950 *Rifleman*, where the "Legislative Bulletin" points out the "dangerous minority" intent on registering firearms.[55] Writings in 1955 on the right to bear arms are mixed. For example, one article suggests that all gun control legislation should not be opposed; each should be assessed on its merits.[56]

The NRA Executive Vice President at the time said that gun legislation is "largely supported by well-meaning individuals" who are misinformed about how to reduce crime and violence.[57] Further, a recruitment advertisement read, "give [your friends] applications so that they may join our campaign for sensible gun legislation."[58] Today the NRA would view as "sensible" only legislation that expands or protects gun rights, whereas the ad refers to compromise and avoiding *excessive* restrictions. Prior to the 1960s assassinations, threats to gun rights were not serious and neither was the level of rhetorical response by the NRA. A July 1961 editorial placed the Second Amendment on a par with the other amendments to the Constitution.[59] The 1960 annual report demonstrated that only a small component of the *Rifleman* represented firearms legislation—only 26 pages of 1,328 dealt with this topic in 1959.[60] Instead, the magazine focused on firearms performance, competitive shooting, and hunting issues.

The tone of gun control discussions began to shift quickly, however; the same editor the following year asserted that gun control arguments were not logical, because "the problem lies with the criminal, not the firearm."[61] An early 1960s brochure is titled "The Gun Law Problem," and in this spirit the NRA sent twenty-six gun rights legislative alerts to more than two hundred thousand members in 1961.[62] President John M. Schooley's retirement speech to the organization demonstrates an explicit threat to the Second Amendment: "If we lose our right to keep and bear arms, the very reason for our Association has fallen."[63] After President Kennedy's assassination, gun control sentiment rose and the media looked to the NRA to respond to calls for more restrictive firearms legislation.

"Never before," the NRA noted, "has there been such a wave of anti-firearm feeling or such vocal and almost universal demand for tighter controls over the mail-order sale of guns."[64] An official NRA statement announced that the organization opposed any governmental licensing or registration. In 1965 separate articles revealed that the NRA continued to have mixed emotions about gun control; one piece referred to the problem of "overly" restrictive firearms legislation and another discussed the "vital part" that concealed firearms play in some areas not in self-defense but in crime.[65]

By the mid-1960s the Dodd bill (later, the Gun Control Act of 1968) was gaining momentum, as was gun rights coverage in the *Rifleman*. Supporters of gun control in Congress and budding gun control groups argued that more restrictive firearms legislation was needed to prevent further killings. The NRA offered a new counterargument to gun control that they still use today: enforce the current laws instead of creating new ones.[66] Legislative coverage increased dramatically, partly a result of mass killings at the University of Texas-Austin, a wider debate on the Dodd bill, and a new *Rifleman* editor, Ashley Halsey Jr., who was aligned with the NRA's growing hard-line faction. Harlon Carter concluded a brief term as NRA President at this time, a full ten years before the Revolt resulted in his becoming the NRA EVP. This speaks to the long-standing factionalism and gradual transformation of the NRA into a social movement organization. Carter likely influenced the decision to hire Halsey Jr., who repeatedly editorialized on gun control threats, contributing to the politicization of members and the NRA's eventual political transformation.

After the political assassinations of Martin Luther King Jr. and Robert F. Kennedy, a version of the Dodd bill gained enough support to become law. The Gun Control Act of 1968, however, was not as far-reaching as gun control proponents had hoped, because it did not require any form of registration. Internal leadership disagreements were common and often visible in the *Rifleman* during this period. Old Guard EVP Franklin Orth, feeling pushed into the role as gun rights defender, lamented,

> Never before has the NRA or any other *sportsmen's organization* been more assailed and misrepresented. . . . Circumstances have propelled us into the position of serving the American public as the prime defender of one constitutional right in particular—the right to bear arms.[67]

Meanwhile, Halsey Jr.'s editorials against gun control were titled "The Latest Twist in Anti-Gun Propaganda" and (again previewing a common NRA framing strategy to come) "Can Three Assassins Kill a Civil Right?"[68]

After the Gun Control Act of 1968 passed, the *Rifleman* reduced its coverage of gun rights issues. Old Guard EVP Orth died, and a February

1970 *Rifleman* article mentions Orth receiving angry letters from gun owners "in remote places," upset about NRA gun control compromises in 1968. But the article argued that "compromise is the essence of Washington politics," and it was a "near miracle" to stave off confiscation after the assassinations.[69] In keeping with its factional interests, though, hard-liners remained focused on gun control threats and continued to write articles addressing this topic. They also convinced the NRA to register a representative under the Federal Lobbying Act to keep abreast of D.C. legislative issues. However, the Old Guard still retained control of the organization. Overall, from 1945 to 1977, the *Rifleman* was overwhelmingly dominated by articles on sport shooting and hunting. As threats to gun control expanded, so did coverage of these threats. Similarly, as these threats concluded or waned, the NRA gave less attention to these issues.

Post-Revolt Threat Framing: Not Crying Wolf

NRA hard-liners took over the organization and officially altered its mission and ideology at the 1977 annual meeting. Harlon Carter took over as EVP and immediately spoke to the meeting attendees and assured, if not demanded, "Beginning in this place and at this hour, this period in NRA history is finished. There will be no more Civil War in the National Rifle Association."[70]

The first *Rifleman* issue after the Revolt contained the following new second paragraph under "What NRA Is":

> The NRA, the foremost guardian of the traditional American right to "keep and bear arms," believes that every law-abiding citizen is entitled to the ownership and legal use of firearms, and that every reputable gun owner should be an NRA member.[71]

The NRA had made the full transformation to a conservative social movement organization leading the fight for gun rights.

Despite publicly declaring themselves targets for gun control attacks, the new leaders of the gun rights movement, according to the *Rifleman*, faced fewer threats than they had a decade earlier. New NRA leaders were aware of and concerned about gun rights threats but calmly addressed them as they arose. By the early 1980s, as Reagan took office, threats to gun rights diminished and so did NRA coverage of them.[72] Though it had undergone a political makeover and established an uncompromising stance on gun control, NRA rhetoric remained as muted as gun control forces.

EVP Carter described the NRA's reactive posture, writing,

> We don't come to you [for donations] except when there is a real need, and it has now been nearly a year since we have done so. . . . During that same period, other organizations, through professional fundraisers, have been milking you regularly, writing strident and "cry wolf" letters about gun legislation that is not moving in the Congress and not likely to move.[73]

As Carter pointed out, introducing a bill in Congress does not make it a legitimate threat. He assured members that the NRA would inform them when gun control legislation was impending. He also maintained that the NRA was about honesty and integrity, and was not trying to create a problem simply to perpetuate fundraising, something today's LaPierre-led NRA has been accused of by a former insider.[74]

When a threat did emerge, the NRA and its members quickly mobilized. The Bureau of Alcohol, Tobacco, and Firearms is a long-standing source of NRA angst.[75] A 1978 NRA-ILA report, titled "Carter White House Gets Taste of Gun Lobby Might," proudly noted that the BATF received more than 175,000 letters opposing any form of gun registration.[76] Calls for gun control were sporadic and largely ineffectual during this period. The NRA emerged as an unmatched force in the gun rights debate, and Presidents Reagan and Bush Sr. took office as fellow NRA members.[77]

The 1980 *Rifleman* was almost astonishingly apolitical, signaling a reduced threat to gun rights. BATF enforcement abuses of the 1968 Gun Control Act helped spark Senator James McClure, a longtime NRA supporter, to initiate legislation reforming this act. Gun rights advocates had gained momentum through a growing NRA and a sympathetic White House, leading to expanding political opportunities and reduced threat. In turn, the NRA diminished its framing of threats. Stepping down as EVP in the beginning of 1984, Harlan Carter reflected on his successful tenure: "During the years of my responsibility for the NRA, no restrictive firearms legislation passed . . . and very important rollbacks have been made in the Gun Control Act of 1968."[78] The only gun control development of note was an article addressing Handgun Control, Inc., which, the NRA said, had launched an "anti-gun media blitz."[79] Otherwise, threats were virtually nonexistent, as was NRA rhetoric about perceived threats. The NRA continued to mobilize its constituents whenever a threat emerged, and organizational ideologies and framings were generally unwavering throughout the 1980s. Recently, however, the NRA has been soliciting member donations to fight a number of less severe threats to gun rights, most of which have little chance of producing serious, if any, gun restrictions.

Now, More Than Ever! New Threat Framing Strategies

Shortly after Wayne LaPierre took over as the new EVP in 1991, a *Rifleman* article commented on the Brady bill, which finally was gaining momentum at the time: "At stake is nothing else than your ownership and use of all firearms."[80] James Jay Baker, succeeding LaPierre as head of the NRA-ILA, framed the threat as a last stand against fascists: "Clearly we are engaged in an all-out fight against a *dictatorship of ideas*, and the stakes are American's guns and Americans' rights—for today, forever."[81] LaPierre, introducing an argument he had used repeatedly, warned, "Never before have I seen such a massive, coordinated assault on our American hunting tradition."[82] By any objective measure, namely, the Brady bill's narrow and mildly restrictive goals of background checks and waiting periods, this was hardly an assault on all gun rights.

The strategy of framing any legislation as the end of gun rights was the exception, not the rule, even during a period of impending gun control legislation in the early 1990s. The NRA had mixed success by 1995, with some victories (the 1994 Republican takeover in Congress, for example) and various threats and concerns (such as the Federal Assault Weapons Ban and more BATF abuses). Bill Clinton was cast as the NRA's primary nemesis, and rhetorical exaggerations about the threat he posed to gun rights appeared in conjunction with legislation regarding assault weapons and the Justice Department's mishandling of its confrontations at Waco and Ruby Ridge with groups alleged to own illegal weapons.

Although the NRA regularly (and accurately) called Clinton the most anti-gun president in U.S. history, and Clinton clearly disliked the NRA, this president did not portray himself as anti-gun. In fact, he sometimes claimed his Arkansas roots through hunting photo-ops. The NRA interpreted this moment (and similar ones by other gun control supporters) as public relations stunts, though Clinton (and later Al Gore and John Kerry) argued that they would never ban guns typically used for sporting or self-defense. Regardless, the NRA constructed Clinton, and later Gore and Kerry, as serious threats to gun rights because they incorporated gun control legislation into their agendas and actively opposed the NRA's un-compromising stance. At the 2003 Orlando Board of Directors meeting, incoming NRA President Kayne Robinson thanked Clinton and Gore for having been a threat and thus contributing to NRA's membership growth.[83]

Numerous signs are evident that the NRA has recently rededicated it-self to fighting against gun control as well as other causes that threaten conservatives. In the late 1990s the NRA began publishing the *American Guardian*, directed at covering Second Amendment politics. Renamed *America's First Freedom* (hereafter, *Freedom*) shortly before the 2000 pres-idential elections, its articles and NRA fundraising letters convey a greater sense of threat to gun rights and freedom than at any moment in NRA history. One article warned,

> In just one term as President, Al Gore could appoint two, three, four or more gun-hating Supreme Court Justices whose constitutional interpreta-tion would saturate our society for a lifetime, unraveling the fragile free-doms guaranteed by the Second Amendment.[84]

Even after Al Gore was defeated and prospects for federal gun con-trol had vanished, the NRA amplified and continued to frame the threat. The old NRA would have reduced its framing and coverage of gun control threats in response to the reduction of objective threats, but this may be difficult to do today with a new magazine focused almost solely on this issue.

Freedom covers from 2001 to 2003 have the appearance of a "threat-of-the-month" in the form of "anti-gun" media, politicians, celebrities, orga-nizations, lawyers, doctors, and so on. The NRA claims to have many po-tent enemies, among them the Violence Policy Center (VPC), perhaps the most aggressive gun control organization based on its support for banning handguns.[85] The horror-show image in Figure 3.1, including bullet-like teeth, depicts the VPC as a dangerous menace to gun rights, and contrasts with *Freedom's* red, white, and blue flag-like logo. The message is clear: whereas the NRA celebrates gun rights and freedom, the menacing (Big-Brother) VPC thinks it knows what is best—NRA members and American citizens cannot be trusted with guns, and so their individual rights and freedoms should be eliminated under the guise of anti-violence programs.

Another in a string of threatening monthly covers dealt with the 2002 law on campaign finance. The NRA (and organizations across the

Figure 3.1. An NRA cover story on the Violence Policy Center depicts the NRA's view of how this gun-control group sees gun owners. *America's First Freedom,* February 2002, 38.

political spectrum) argued that the law would silence them as elections approached, leaving them unable to express either support for or opposition to candidates. The NRA saw the law not only as an attack on freedom of speech but also on gun rights and the group itself. The image on the July 2003 *Freedom* cover (Figure 3.2) evokes similar themes to the VPC cover months earlier: gun owners be warned—powerful (read: big government) forces are "muzzling" the NRA's and your individual rights and freedoms, namely, free speech; if gun rights advocates are silenced during elections, gun control politicians will be elected.

As part of the efforts of this new politically focused magazine to ratchet up warnings to gun owners, *Freedom* offers a monthly "BAN-DE-MONIUM" award to individuals perceived as threats to gun rights. It also displays a monthly "Freedom Index" that rises or falls based on threats to gun rights and other issues of concern to the NRA. Figure 3.3 shows a summer 2004 index of 39, despite Vice President Cheney's recent address

Figure 3.2. Gun owners are silenced by officials in this NRA magazine cover depicting the threat of campaign finance reform laws. *America's First Freedom*, July 2003.

THE LATEST FROM WWW.NRANEWS.COM

NRA NEWS

FREEDOM INDEX:

0   50   100

39

THE FREEDOM INDEX rose three points this month on news of gun owner victories in several states. Recognizing the failure of the federal "assault weapons" ban, the Maryland Senate killed its own version of the bill. To settle a state Supreme Court snag in Right-to-Carry implementation, the Missouri Senate gave local sheriffs expanded powers to pay for the program. And finally, the Florida Senate sent a bill to Governor Jeb Bush prohibiting any kind of permanent recordkeeping on gun purchases.

FREEDOM TOOK A HIT WHEN:
Illinois Governor Rod Blagojevich threatened to veto a bill that would allow retired police officers with at least 10 years of service to carry concealed firearms. The governor's senseless opposition to what amounts to increased police presence in crime-stricken neighborhoods comes at a time when Chicago leads the nation in the number of murders.

Following Sweden's lead, the European Union is moving to ban all lead in all ammunition. On the surface, the measure appears motivated by environmental concerns. But its real purpose is to march Western nations one step closer to the day when all shooting sports and all firearms are permanently eliminated.

FREEDOM GOT A LIFT WHEN:
Vice President Dick Cheney addressed NRA members at our 133rd Members' Banquet, held recently in Pittsburgh. Cheney drew wild applause from NRA members when he reaffirmed the Bush Administration's firmly held belief that the Second Amendment guarantees an individual's right to keep and bear arms.

NRA announced the launch of a new and very important member service. NRANews.com will battle the campaign finance reform gag law by providing members, via live daily Web casts, with high-speed, information-age tools critical to the defense of the Second Amendment.

Keitt's attorneys questioned "the outrageous conduct" of Queens District Attorney Richard A. Brown, whose office granted the clerk, Edwin Marte, immunity in exchange for grand jury testimony against Keitt on March 30.

"We believe that the district attorney's conduct is unethical and potentially illegal," defense attorney Scott Brettschneider said in the letter.

Prosecutors contend Marte was defending himself when he shot Keitt in the head after Keitt showed a gun and tried to rob the Ramon Food Market. Marte was originally charged with misdemeanor criminal possession of a firearm—an unlicensed .38 caliber revolver—and would have faced up to a year in jail if convicted.

Keitt had been conditionally released by parole officials last September after serving more than three years for possession of stolen property.

Michigan Woman Chases Off Churl, Changes Chief's Mind
WHEN A MICHIGAN woman called only "Angela" to retain anonymity drew her concealed firearm and scared off a potential armed robber, she did more than just save her own life—she also helped change the mind of one police chief who was initially against passage of the state Right-to-Carry law.

When Angela, a married mother of two, was arriving at the office where she has worked for six years, she saw a man get out of a nearby car and walk toward her. When he passed the entrance to the building, continued toward her and came within 10 feet of her, she knew she had to act.

"I didn't get a chance to get in the office," she told *The Daily Oakland Press.* "He had his hands in his pocket with his hood pulled up. I opened my purse and pulled my gun out. I felt my life was in trouble. The first instinct was to pull out my gun."

The man quickly turned and walked away, and the car pulled up

Figure 3.3. The NRA adjusts its monthly "Freedom Index" up or down based on perceived threat levels to gun rights. *America's First Freedom,* June 2004, 20.

at the NRA annual meeting to demonstrate the Bush administration's strong support for gun rights. Gun control threats at home and abroad are included in the index as reasons why "freedom took a hit," including the slippery slope argument that the European Union's efforts to ban lead in ammunition is ultimately about banning guns rather than environmental safety. The NRA constructs any perceived legislative threat to firearms (or ammunition) as the first step toward the removal of all gun rights. As the 2004 elections approached, the Freedom Index remained low as a reminder to NRA members of legislative threats to gun rights.

The by-line to a September 2002 article stated that, if the Democrats take over the U.S. House of Representatives, "the most anti-gun Congressmen in history would be running the committees dealing with firearms legislation."[86] In an article on the American Medical Association president's depiction of gun violence as a public health epidemic, *Freedom* linked the group to another NRA nemesis—the United Nations, referring to the UN as "the massive sovereignty-busting, worldwide gun-ban" organization.[87]

In the May 2002 issue of *Freedom* (Figure 3.4), UN Secretary-General Kofi Annan is depicted as a Rambo-like character with super-muscular arms, headband, torn shirt, cartridge belts across his chest, and an enormous machine gun still smoking from spent rounds, his finger defiantly poised on the weapon's trigger. Here the NRA is calling attention to the fact that Annan's armed security guards are free to bear weapons in New York City that American citizens cannot. Apparently, the NRA argument goes, the UN wants to ban firearms around the world—except for U.N. leaders. Also suggested is that Annan is not unlike a military dictator or perhaps a drug kingpin like Scarface (the "little friend" reference). Once again, the implication is clear: the goal of world leaders is to remove individual rights and freedoms, in this case by controlling guns and gun rights and possibly enforcing martial law.

Clearly the gun rights coverage and rhetoric is overwhelmingly greater than that of older versions of the NRA, as evidenced by the new magazine (*Freedom*) dedicated solely to the right to bear arms in contrast to the sporadic attention paid to gun rights in earlier volumes of the *Rifleman*. Further, literally, *any* type of gun control legislation is always cast as the slippery slope toward registration and confiscation of *all* firearms.

LaPierre offered the following slippery slope argument in one of his books, which, like Heston's culture war tome, generated huge sales at both NRA meetings I attended:

Figure 3.4. An NRA story suggests that UN officials do not hold themselves to the same gun-control beliefs and laws they support, thus revealing their anti-democratic agenda. *America's 1st Freedom,* May 2002, 16.

The anti-gunner's formula for surrendering our Second Amendment freedoms is clear: first, enact a nationwide firearms waiting period; second, after the waiting period fails to reduce crime, enact a nationwide licensing and registration law; and the final step, confiscate all registered firearms.[88]

By LaPierre's logic, a waiting period is merely a short step away from gun confiscation. The rhetoric, however, does not match the reality. As one scholar argued, "NRA leaders have consistently employed a Chicken Little ('the sky is falling') rhetorical style, with constant prophesies of imminent doom."[89] This approach reduces the legitimacy of the organization, except for the true believers, the Gun Crusaders.

Over the years the NRA has faced backlash for its rhetoric from outside and within but, from the late 1990s on, the NRA has heightened its framing of threats, knowing it helps recruit and maintain an army of cultural warriors far more valuable than less committed and quieter gun owners or a sympathetic public.

The social construction of threats to gun rights was probably at its peak in fundraising letters sent to the membership. EVP LaPierre, trying to raise funds for a television show about gun owners fending off attackers, wrote, "nothing can make a bigger difference in the next chapter of Second Amendment history than for you and me to put 'The Armed Citizen' on TV."[90] A month later he argued that the war on terrorism is now targeting firearms, and that "the Second Amendment and your NRA are under attack in the media like never before in our 130-year history," adding, "this may be the toughest battle we have ever faced together."[91] LaPierre's hyperbole is matched by mailings from then NRA-ILA Executive Director James Jay Baker. Two years after NRA ally George W. Bush became president and federal gun control threats all but vanished, Baker asked for more funds; in his words, "there has never been a more important time to recommit yourself to the defense of the Second Amendment."[92]

In 2002 Baker mailed out a "Truth about Gun ownership" (TAG) poll, with the envelope reading, "MOST IMPORTANT TRUTH ABOUT GUN OWNERS POLL EVER!" Included in the letter was a sidebar that said, "this TAG Poll may be the single most important document I have ever mailed to you and other NRA-ILA supporters."[93] Baker's replacement, Chris Cox, continued this fundraising tactic of invoking threats when he contended that lawsuits against gun manufacturers "have the power to drive a stake through the heart of the Second Amendment."[94] Without members' financial support, the Second Amendment could be eliminated. Baker summarized, "The lessons of history prove that taking guns away from law-abiding citizens is the single most effective way to give the enemies of freedom an infinite advantage over those who love freedom."[95]

Several inconsistencies reveal the socially constructed nature of the NRA's recent claims of unparalleled threats to gun rights. In a letter to members, the NRA acknowledged that it has been labeled the most effective lobbying organization in Washington.[96] With no gun control organization to mount a serious, consistent threat to the NRA's power, claims of impending gun registration or confiscation are dubious. The day after the conclusion of another profitable and successful annual meeting in Reno, LaPierre's report to the Board of Directors included his cheerful and satisfied assessment of the gun rights battle—"We're winning."[97] A year later LaPierre offered a similar message, boasting that the NRA was more widely accepted and stronger than ever.[98] Speaking at the 2000 Conservative Political Action Committee meeting, LaPierre declared, "Our agenda is moving forward. Our membership is growing by hundreds of thousands, our war chest is brimming, and our army of grassroots activists is ready for this election year."[99]

The recent organizational harmony and unity, an NRA rarity in the last four decades, speaks to their success. Only a month after mailing out a fundraising letter to members describing a "life-or-death" battle for gun rights, Baker reflected on his and the NRA's recent achievements in his resignation letter to the membership: "Although victory for the Second Amendment will never be completely won, I believe that our well-fought battles have brought us to a point where our rights are as secure as at any time in recent history." But as NRA spokesman Andrew Arulanandam noted of the NRA's success, "It's a double-edged sword because people are not as focused when they don't feel threatened."[100]

Eventually the framing of exaggerated threats to gun rights will become so commonplace that they will lose their ability to alarm the target audience. As people grow increasingly accustomed to these so-called threats, they will be seen to exceed the objective reality and the public's attention will wane. Indeed, research on social movements in general suggests that this is so.[101] Some Reserve NRA members I interviewed complained about the NRA's rhetoric used in fundraising letters, suggesting that the NRA would be wise to curb its threat framing. Like other movement activists tirelessly dedicated to their cause, even NRA Critical Mass members will grow weary if the NRA continues to "cry wolf." A few years after defeating

Gore and peaking in its political power, however, the NRA tested its limits, continuing to frame white-hot threats to gun rights.

Shifting Right

Recent NRA framings constructing imminent threats to gun rights go hand-in-hand with partisan and culture war politics. With gun control becoming increasingly aligned with Democrats, the NRA focused its attention on casting Democrats as the primary threats to the Second Amendment. The NRA officially abandoned non-partisanship in 1980 when, for the very first time, it endorsed a presidential candidate—Republican Ronald Reagan. Even then the overlapping interests of gun rights, freedom, and conservative politics were wrapped in a neat package: "The combination of a belief in the people's right to keep and bear arms, and in the right of citizens to be free from the bondage of an oppressive government will be for us a new beginning."[102]

As noted, a few months before the 2000 elections the *American Guardian* was renamed *America's First Freedom* because,

> Now more than ever, the forces of oppression are allied against America's gun owners, poised for an effort to ban guns. That's right. It's not about trigger locks or "smart" guns or licensing or registration. It's about using those issues as a prelude to eventually outlaw private firearms ownership.[103]

The first *Freedom* cover was a morphing of outgoing President Bill Clinton's face and that of his vice president and 2000 Democratic presidential candidate Al Gore, with the title: "He's Clinton to the Gore: The Face of Gun Hatred in America." As the election approached, a *Freedom* cover showed a donkey in a politician's suit chewing on a Constitution with crumpled Second Amendment language (Figure 3.5). Leading Democrats are portrayed as out-of-touch politicians, "Gun Haters" who have spent too much time in Washington and not enough time in rural America. The cover is a reminder to the probably large number of NRA members who belong to unions and may therefore be inclined to vote for Democrats that Al Gore, accompanied by liberal Democratic members of Congress from California and the East Coast, will strip you of your gun rights.

Fighting for gun rights is a key to "Winning the Cultural War," declared Charlton Heston. He accused liberals of influencing America's universities

Figure 3.5. An NRA cover story shortly before the 2000 elections frames Democrats as becoming increasingly opposed to gun rights and Constitutional rights. *America's First Freedom*, September 2000.

to serve as "incubators for this rampant epidemic of new McCarthy-ism" that "stifles and stigmatizes personal freedom."[104] Heston continued his cultural war theme in a speech at Brandeis University, listing liberal menaces:

> More and more we are fueled by anger, a fury fed by those who profit from it. Democrats hate Republicans. Gays hate straights. Women hate men. Liberals hate conservatives. Vegetarians hate meat eaters. Gun ban-ners hate gun owners.[105]

Each example cites Left-leaning groups who hate Right-leaning counter-parts, stressing that conservatives are the victims forced to defend them-selves against the culture war of the Left.

In 2000 Heston published *The Courage to Be Free* to coincide with his multi-year lecture tour railing against the Left. In a section titled, "Di-vide, Conquer, Then Pour an Iced Mocha"—an often repeated conserva-tive jab against Democrats for being 'latte-sipping liberal elites'—Heston complained,

> The entrance fee to the elite class is at an all-time low, requiring only that a person agree to the general tenets, for example, that white males are disposable, corporate America is inherently evil, southern Christians are somewhat dumb and misguided, guns are dangerously prevalent, and les-bian Islamic rainforest biologists (or name any other interest group you like) have more worthwhile views than other people."[106]

Not only are guns and gun rights targets of the Left's culture war, Heston argued, but so, too, are conservative white men and their frontier mascu-linity politics.

Incoming NRA President Kayne Robinson continued his predecessor's cultural war theme, directing his ire toward the social elitist, "politically-correct speech Nazis."[107] Shortly before 9/11, LaPierre mailed out a fund-raising letter for the new "Madison Brigade," composed of "American Patriots" willing to stand up to the revisionist historians attempting to remove the Founding Fathers from U.S. history texts (and replace them with "politically correct" accounts of these white men's racism and acts of violence). In the following, LaPierre shares his conservative agenda and the NRA's politics by lumping together gun control advocates and groups with various liberal leanings and agendas:

Today we face an enemy perhaps more powerful than Bill Clinton was in the last eight years. An enemy made up of revisionist historians, the anti-gun media, the trial lawyers, the American Bar Association, the American Medical Association, Handgun Control, Inc., and the self-proclaimed new heroes of political correctness—[Democrats] Hillary Rodham Clinton, Ted Kennedy, Charles Schumer, Dianne Feinstein, and Barbara Boxer.[108]

In a common social movement framing strategy, a Heston-narrated NRA recruitment video pitches gun rights supporters as "us against the world," underdogs fighting the good fight. In it Heston talks about the status of the Second Amendment, bemoaning that "textbooks ignore it, schools teach against it, clergy preach against it, politicians legislate against it, media ridicule it, movies perverse it, courts avoid it . . . too many gun owners permit [all this to happen]."[109]

Late-20th-Century challenges to frontier masculinity by group-rights activists put conservatives on their heels. To mobilize a response, a range of conservative social movements, including gun rights, anti-immigration, and anti-affirmative action, appealed to their constituents by warning of threats to their resources, status, values, and identities. Heston helped the NRA launch a culture war response, with an implicit anti-feminist and explicit pro-male backlash in his speeches. He and many other gun own-ers felt that their voices and interests were being drowned out by "lesbian Islamic rainforest biologists" and other left-wing special interest groups. Heston and the NRA encouraged members to be "politically incorrect" and fight for gun rights and individual rights by reasserting traditional frontier masculinity.

I contend, however, that "conservative movements are not alone in mobilizing moral indignation, fear, and 'status anxiety.'"[110] Progressive movements make similar emotional appeals, criticizing sources of power and privilege that they believe marginalize them. A conservative political turn that began in the 1980s also led liberal movements such as welfare rights and immigrant rights to offer threat frames that appeal to target au-diences' sense of moral injustice, as well as their fears and anxieties. Im-migrant rights activists, for example, "have recently mobilized immigrants against proposed legislation that would make undocumented immigrants and those who assist them into felons, appealing to immigrants' desire for greater social acceptance and respect."[111]

Current NRA leaders are mostly forthcoming about their status as conservatives fighting liberal "anti-gunners." LaPierre, annually speaking on behalf of the NRA at the Conservative Political Action Conference, marks his in-group status by referring to "we conservatives." He offers an NRA staple—gripes about liberal media biases against conservatives— noting, "Almost all media people admit a liberal leaning."[112] Heston, pos- sibly reflecting on his earlier decision to switch political party affiliations, mourned, "Liberal used to mean discussing issues objectively, on their own merits, with intellectual honesty and—above all—an openness to any viewpoint. But liberals like [gun control advocate Rosie] O'Donnell today aren't liberal—they're militant."[113]

Patriots and Freedom Fighters Protecting Civil Rights

> But as I tell my colleagues, the gun itself is just a symbol. It's individual freedom we're fighting for.
>
> —Charlton Heston, 2000

At a session of the 2003 NRA annual meeting, then 2nd Vice President Sandy Froman related a story about a workshop she once attended on constitutional issues. When the attendees were divided up into groups to decide which of the ten amendments they would keep if they could only choose one, every group except her own chose the First Amendment. Hers was led by an old, gruff police sergeant who told the group, "We're gonna keep the 2nd and take back the rest."[114]

Linking the defense of gun rights to defending freedom has been a central collective action frame of the NRA since the late 1990s, but it is also apparent at times in earlier organizational rhetoric. For example, in 1995, LaPierre made the following statement on fending off gun control: "But mark my words: What we have done is still not enough, nor will it ever be. Constant vigilance, the Founding Fathers remind us, is the price that free people must pay."[115]

More recently, touting himself as a champion of the oppressed, Char- lton Heston told a Yale University audience that, "supporting civil rights [in 1963] was about as popular as supporting gun rights is now."[116] Equat- ing gun rights with other Civil Rights, referred to as "frame appropria- tion,"[117] is a strategy the NRA uses repeatedly to legitimize its cause, its leaders often boasting that their SMO is the biggest and oldest Civil Rights organization in the country.[118] Heston took the Civil Rights comparisons furthest. To win the culture war, he told a conservative audience, you have to be willing to engage in civil disobedience, to "have the courage to put yourself at risk. Dr. King stood on lots of balconies. You must be willing to be humiliated . . . to endure the modern-day equivalent of the police dogs at Montgomery and the water cannons at Selma."[119]

Neutral observers may well question what sacrifices gun owners can possibly make compared to Civil Rights activists risking their well-being, and frequently their lives, for their cause. Heston also borrowed language from movements fighting hate crimes. In a speech to the Young Republicans Association Convention in Cincinnati, he complained, "hate speech against gun owners is now not just accepted, but encouraged as a catalyst for positive social change."[120]

Just as Civil Rights leaders made new connections between their movement and political and religious values, the NRA's frame appropriation of Civil Rights for gun rights is an example of what political scientist Thomas Rochon calls a "value connection," which "involves forging a conceptual link between phenomena previously thought to be unconnected."[121] The gun rights as Civil Rights framing strategy is key for conservatives. Although the Second Amendment refers to "the right to keep and bear arms," the militia versus individual rights debate was unsettled when the NRA began using Civil Rights language for guns. Further, the rights movements of the 20th Century fought against primarily conservative opponents.

Gun rights was the first "rights" issue for the Right, used occasionally by the NRA even before the liberal rights movements of the 1960s. The emergence of a powerful gun rights movement in the 1970s helped take back some control of the highly resonant "rights" frame from liberals. The very term "gun rights" is symbolically significant, as it promotes individual rights instead of the group rights of liberal movements.[122] Other conservative movements use a group-rights approach, including men's rights and white rights activists. For example, proponents of "white pride" (a term Heston used) argue that affirmative action discriminates against their racial group. These right-wing groups "appropriate the language of civil rights activists to counter those activists' characterization of white supremacists as racial oppressors and to define themselves as a minority group."[123]

As far as the NRA is concerned, all other Civil Rights take second place to the Second Amendment. The NRA believes it is the foundation upon which freedom exists. Immediately after launching *America's First Freedom*, Heston wrote that the magazine's goal is to be "the nation's first journal of news, opinion, in-depth analysis and undiluted, unflinching, unapologetic defense of the one right that safeguards all our freedoms as Americans: The Second Amendment right to keep and bear arms."[124] The NRA, the foremost guardian of gun rights, claims to be comprised of the nation's freedom fighters, charged with fending off "disgusting freedom-haters"—gun control advocates.[125] The NRA casts its members' financial commitment to the organization as parallel to the sacrifices made by America's first freedom fighters—the Founding Fathers. One of LaPierre's fundraising letters states:

> [The Founding Fathers] took a risk—and made a sacrifice—that you and I still reap the benefits of 225 years later. I'm asking for your sacrifice today . . . that our descendents can reap the benefits of 225 years from now.[126]

LaPierre's message is clear: today we can reflect upon and appreciate the Founding Fathers' contributions to freedom. These individuals, the earliest examples of virtuous white frontier masculinity, fended off the "savages" and then won the Revolutionary War. In the 23rd Century, Americans will reflect upon and appreciate NRA members' financial contributions to the organization and note that by fending off threats to gun rights, this new generation of virtuous white men defended the right to keep and bear arms, and thus freedom itself, and won the culture war. Both groups will be remembered as freedom fighters and true American patriots who relied on firearms and the Second Amendment to win their wars, whether against Native Americans or the British Monarchy, or, more symbolically, against revisionist historians, liberals, and socialists. Regardless who they are and when they appear, these defeated enemies are incapable of American democracy and freedom.

The American patriot analogy was not lost on Charlton Heston as he accepted a third term as NRA President:

> George Washington hung around until the Revolutionary War was won. Roosevelt hung around until World War II was won. Reagan hung around until the Cold War was won. If you want, I'll hang around until we win this one, too.[127]

The late 20th Century saw a "chain reaction," whereby issues of race, group rights movements and reforms, and taxes collided at the same time as a conservative upswing in national politics that altered party affiliations for a large number of whites.[128] The NRA aligns itself with this upswing by emphasizing its anti-big government stance (against gun control). This position is consistent with other concerns (high taxes, "special benefits" to women and people of color) that resonate with these new conservatives opposing increased government influence in their lives. Although Heston's cultural war, and arguably even the battle over gun rights, remains largely symbolic, the NRA can construct links to more tangible forms of threats to freedom to boost its argument that freedom is making its last stand.

No recent threat to the United States has been more tangible than that of terrorism. After 9/11, the Bush administration declared that the terrorists hate America because of its freedoms. The NRA borrows this language and applies it to gun control supporters. Following the Gun Crusaders' argument, gun rights groups defend freedom and therefore anyone whittling away gun rights is actually attacking freedom. Seven months after 9/11, Wayne LaPierre equated all "anti-gunners" with terrorists—"They're attacking freedom . . . they're terrorists . . . they're political terrorists."[129] This is a significant departure from past mainstream NRA views on freedom and gun rights.

Before the NRA became politicized, it merely acknowledged the Second Amendment as one of many important components of the Constitution. Today, however, the NRA has transformed this organizational ideology into a collective action frame asserting that the Second Amendment is the foundation upon which all other constitutional amendments, rights, and thus freedom itself rests. By equating gun control advocates with terrorists, the NRA implies that participants in the Million Mom March are simply a less violent version of the 9/11 hijackers. Wondering who opposes freedom (namely, gun rights), LaPierre comes to a single post-9/11 conclusion—terrorists. And because the NRA argues that the Second Amendment is the foundation upon which freedom stands, anyone attempting to restrict these constitutional rights through gun control must oppose freedom, and therefore they must be terrorists.

Like red-baiting during the McCarthy era and the Cold War, terrorist-baiting is frequently used in NRA materials. NRA-ILA director Chris Cox referred to the "Clinton-Gore gun-ban regime,"[130] and LaPierre called them the "the Clinton-Gore axis."[131] Once again, NRA rhetoric piggybacks on the rhetoric of then president G. W. Bush, this time borrowing from his phrase "axis of evil." LaPierre continued, "[Gun-hating politicians] have vowed to hold Congress hostage." Here he uses terrorist-related language to implicitly link gun control with terrorism. The analogy is less subtle in a LaPierre letter flatly stating that, "like the terrorists, the gun-ban crowd will try to mask their true intentions. They will use guerilla attacks to conceal their legislative agenda in Homeland Security bills."[132]

NRA's 1st Vice President Kayne Robinson also linked the gun control battle to freedom fights at home and overseas: "We're at war today, against disguised, deceitful, stealthy, all-but-invisible enemies of freedom. We're at war at home and abroad. We're at war for no less than our very freedom as Americans."[133] Robinson's comments returned to the path of Heston's culture war framings. Indeed, Heston used this rhetoric even before 9/11, referring, on separate occasions, to "animal rights terrorists," the "gang of cultural terrorists" (media/entertainment elite and academics), and "religious tyrants" (left-wing culture warriors who harass religious fundamentalists and evangelicals).[134]

The Gun Crusaders have referred to campaign finance reform as a "senatorial jihad against the NRA."[135] And just as they cast threats to gun rights as terrorist attacks on freedom, the NRA also works the links in reverse: "I am enlisting you in freedom's fight against these terrorist killers—whoever and wherever they are—who want to destroy our Constitution, destroy our Bill of Rights, destroy our economy, and disarm and silence all Americans."[136] Of course, the NRA is not the only entity adopting terrorist discourse post-9/11. Given the impact of those attacks, the ability of SMOs to connect threats to their favorite issues to terrorism is probably an effective way to mobilize resources.

Like rights frames, terror frames resonate with cultural beliefs, experiences, or fears, and can therefore be used by many social movements, even competing ones. The NRA has successfully used freedom and rights frames to represent gun rights as a battle for all constitutional rights and American freedoms.

How Much Does the Message Matter?

As the multi-billion dollar advertising business reveals, the message matters. SMOs often boost their status by increasing the polarization between themselves and countermovement organizations.[137] They want people to take sides. Former NRA employee Richard Feldman saw "a profitable them-and-us division" between gun control groups and the NRA. "Let them collect their funds and sign up members; we'd do the same—in spades."[138]

According to sociologist Aldon Morris, "A crucial feature of hegemonic consciousness is that it always presents itself as a set of values and beliefs that serves the general welfare."[139] This may be seen in the way the NRA frames its culture war politics as the source of America's freedoms and rights. Many NRA members may have been drawn into the organization because of tangible incentives such as magazines, courses, and clubs, as well as the group's political strength and success.[140] But many other individuals, predominantly white men and especially conservatives, who may have never picked up a gun in their lives, will also agree with or support the group in some manner because of the culturally ascendant viewpoints it espouses. These ties may help explain why the NRA has an enormous membership base and yet probably a smaller critical mass that does most of the work and contributes the most money to the NRA.[141]

To help answer the question "Does the new NRA rhetoric work?" the next several chapters examine NRA members' views on gun control and gun rights, their politics, and their commitment to the organization.

4

Under Attack

"An armed resident is a citizen; an unarmed resident is a serf," Quincy, an NRA lifetime member tells me, repeating one of many phrases widely used by gun rights proponents.[1] "Tell that to a liberal, and they think it's about taking over the country," he adds and, without pause, corrects his hypothetical liberal critic by insisting that gun ownership is actually about "preventing government tyranny." Quincy is a white, married father of two and is in his mid-forties. He is a college graduate, a lifelong Republican, ex-military, an NRA-certified instructor, and lives in an upper-middle-class community in the Southeast. Like most NRA members, his first memories of picking up a gun are tied to his dad. He reads the NRA's political magazine, *America's First Freedom*, "cover to cover" each month and describes it as "excellent." Quincy joined the NRA for political reasons: "If the Democratic Party had their way, they'd ban guns tomorrow. What part of 'shall not be infringed' don't people understand?" he asks me, both rhetorically and incredulously. He supports instant background checks on gun purchases to keep guns out of the wrong hands, and self-identifies as usually a single-issue voter for gun rights.

Quincy is satisfied with the NRA's leadership, pointing out the group's large membership. The truth is, he tells me, "People against the Second Amendment do more for our membership than our leadership does." Quincy believes that his fellow members perceive threats to gun rights just as he does and that Democrats pose the primary threat. He worries that the Democrats and the UN are working together to subjugate countries and their citizens to treaties that include gun control and confiscation. To help inform his voting decisions and keep his congressional representatives tuned into his concerns about gun rights, Quincy discusses gun issues with them. He "never misses a chance to vote," and only votes Republican in national elections so that he can help prevent federal gun control legislation. In short, Quincy is a Gun Crusader.

By framing threats to gun rights and individual rights and freedoms, the NRA stokes its members' fears and motivates them to mobilize. The power of the NRA's rhetoric is evident by their peak membership levels at a time when conservatives controlled all three branches of government and the threat of restrictive gun control was nonexistent. Perhaps even more impressive, the NRA exceeded four million members several years into the new millennium, despite an ongoing decline in the number of U.S. hunters and gun owners.

Because of the reputation of the NRA's lobbying wing and the media attention it receives, the true source of the NRA's power—the millions of members and activists—has largely been overlooked. The NRA can spark its highly motivated Gun Crusaders to pressure politicians at key moments.[2] When NRA lobbyists and leaders remind legislators to consider how NRA members might respond to gun-related proposals or even the politician's next run for office, the threat is real.

Like any organization with a large support base, the NRA's members are not always in agreement, even concerning the issue that initially brought them together, guns. However, similar to the NRA leadership, members are overwhelmingly conservative, and so they support the organization not only because it opposes gun control but also because broader threats to their values and beliefs mesh with NRA rhetoric. Those I interviewed represent the more committed members, and, as I discuss in detail in chapters 6 and 7, the Reserve and Critical Mass members, nearly without exception, range from moderately to extremely conservative.

Most Gun Crusaders perceive serious threats to gun rights. Further, they connect threats to gun rights to threats to broader freedoms and frontier masculinity. What makes them uniquely fascinating is that they believe gun rights are the backbone of all rights and freedoms. They think the same people who attack gun rights—gun control groups, liberals, and the media—are basically Communists, socialists, and fascists, whose agenda to confiscate guns is the prelude to an across-the-board culture war victory for the Left.

Threats to Gun Rights, Freedom, and Frontier Masculinity

Many NRA members are old enough to remember when gun control was not part of the national dialogue, and certainly not part of a culture war. Zach, in his seventies, observes, "We went through that era where the

Kennedy's were shot and that really brought a lot of support for these gun control people, and of course it got them votes."

Although the threat of federal gun control legislation has diminished since the 1960s, some areas of the country have more restrictions than others. Walter had to transfer some of his firearms to relatives in a state with weaker gun control laws. Another member, Andrew, told me, "[A couple of decades ago] I wasn't as politically active or as politically knowledgeable that there was even a threat to the Second Amendment. I was just oblivious to it. I never thought that the Constitution was in jeopardy in any way." Members point to leading Democratic senators whom they see as a vocal and dangerous threat to gun rights.

Andrew says, "I definitely see [gun rights] under threat, and I think they are under threat by misguided Americans." His language mirrors that of 1960s Old Guard NRA leaders, who viewed gun control supporters as well-meaning but misinformed. Most members view gun control advocates as anything but well-meaning. Ernie says, resentfully, "Every time we compromise, they stick it to us." His opinion is shared by members who view gun control advocates, quite literally, as enemies of the country, as illustrated in the following NRA Madison Brigade posting:

> [The media and some politicians] are unscrupulous and they want your guns and they won't stop until they get every last one! [They] are among the domestic terrorists who damage our Nation more than any foreign terrorist ever could. It's our job to stop them and to maintain our American heritage. (Chris Jackson)[3]

A few members I interviewed do not see serious impending threats to gun control but, instead, view significant losses of gun rights as a long-term issue. According to Mark,

> But would I consider that there's a boogie man right around the corner that's going to try to take over the United States tomorrow or try and get rid of the Second Amendment? No. I don't think that the population is that complacent yet. Maybe it is sometime in the future, but not right now . . . it's an incremental threat. You know, nothing happens overnight.

Only two members brushed off the likelihood of serious threats to gun rights, generally offering the caveat that it was not a concern for them *right now*. Critical Mass and Reserve NRA members perceive threats to gun rights, whether short-term or long-term, and they respond to NRA framings of these threats by becoming active Gun Crusaders.

Americans who do not own guns are obviously more supportive of gun control and less likely to fear threats to gun rights than NRA members. But what makes NRA members unique is the extreme disparity between their opposition to gun control and that of the general gun-owning population. Nearly 90% of *non*-owners and nearly two-thirds of gun owners favor requiring a police permit before buying a gun. Committed NRA members could not disagree more. To them, registration is the last step before confiscation. Unlike NRA members, half of gun owners also believe that "there should be more legal restrictions on handguns."[4]

A recurring theme in members' thoughts on gun control is that these are tied to broader threats. For example, they often link the 9/11 terrorist acts to attacks on gun rights. Madison Brigade member Jim Frenzen writes, "09/11/01, has brought renewed attacks on the 2nd Amendment by liberals, revisionists, historians and politicians. A strong NRA serves as a guardian of our freedom[s]." A pervasive belief throughout the organization is that, because gun rights are under attack, the future of America is in doubt. Similar to NRA frames, many members argue that the Second Amendment is the foundation upon which freedom stands. Member Bobby Holmes adds, "We as a people cannot allow this most important Amendment to be [whittled] away at or even completely destroyed and taken away. For if we do, 'How much longer would it be before the First Amendment and the rest of the Constitution would follow?'" Raising gun rights to this lofty status is a fundamental reason why Gun Crusaders exist and why they are so motivated to fight against any gun control measures. For, "if the Second Amendment isn't about granting the individual a fundamental right to own a gun, then the gun owner is only a hunter, or a target shooter, or someone who needs a form of personal protection. In the end, he is only a gun owner. But with the Second Amendment, he is a 'freedom fighter.'"[5]

Freedom and independence are inseparable, in the view of NRA members, so any form of dependence on the government is a restriction on freedom. They frequently cite socialism as a prime example of the loss of independence, and many members see links between this ideology and attacks on gun rights. When asked who poses the greatest threat to gun rights, Craig responds, "Socialists, because they know it's important [to restrict gun rights to prop up their movement]." A fellow member agrees: "Our government has gradually become a socialist leviathan, continuously stealing more and more of our political rights, and now it has a bull's eye painted on the Second Amendment" (Victor Phipps). These members, of course, do not actually identify Socialist Party members but rather Democrats promoting programs that redistribute wealth and expand the government's size or authority.

Whereas some members may see nuances among gun control supporters or government programs aimed at reducing poverty or inequality, the most committed NRA members see everything in black and white. The belief that any government effort to pass any form of gun control forebodes the end of gun rights mobilizes members. The NRA fans the flames as its members catch fire.

Ed Schultz, CEO of the gun manufacturer Smith & Wesson, entered into negotiations to determine the concessions his company could make, such as installing trigger locks, to end the lawsuits against the gun industry. The NRA called the British-owned gun maker "a foreign-owned company that does not care for the Bill of Rights," provoking some Gun Crusaders to send Schultz tea bags as a reminder of the American Revolution; he also received death threats.[6]

The Second Amendment as the Foundation of Freedom

If supporting the NRA and gun rights is tantamount to supporting freedom, then, according to most NRA members, promoting gun control is the same as opposing freedom and the Constitution. "We are not a special interest group . . . we are a constitutional rights issue group" (Albert). And what will happen if these constitutional rights are revoked? One Madison Brigade poster states, "Believe this, your firearms and your freedoms are dependent on one another. You will not have one for long without the other being intact" (Chris Jackson). Not only is the defense of the Second Amendment a central issue in maintaining freedoms, it is literally the sole or primary issue for the most committed NRA members.

As expressed in the title of the organization's political magazine, *America's First Freedom*, members see gun rights as the very backbone of freedom in America. The Second Amendment is "the armed guard of the rest of [the amendments]" (Mark) and is "by far the most important of all the amendments" (Bobby Holmes). Or, as NRA member Nicole put it, "You know there's the famous saying that my Second Amendment protects your First [Amendment]." Pete shares his thoughts on the relationship between freedom and gun rights:

And the Founding Fathers, I think, put [the Second Amendment] in the Constitution so that the government, if it ever got to the point, couldn't put the finger on the people. Because if you remember that was what all these dictators have done in the past. Hitler . . . took the guns away from the population and that happened in Italy also . . . in this day and time people need to [have firearms].

The loss of gun rights means the loss of freedoms, which, in the minds of many NRA members, means fascism.

Although all members do not necessarily see impending fascism, they do point out several modern examples of countries that lost their freedoms along with gun rights. "I don't really think it's going to happen," Ernie told me, "but neither did the Nazis, the Czechs, or the Russians . . . That is why the Second Amendment is put in there." Nor do all members view the Second Amendment as the foremost guardian of freedom. Quincy believes that gun rights come second based on the order in which the Founders thought freedoms should be protected. Madison Brigade member Henry Vassalo expresses a similar view: "The wisdom of our Founding Fathers was proven when they selected freedom of speech as the only right more important than Americans bearing arms." Though these members prioritize First Amendment rights, they would not belong to the American Civil Liberties Union (ACLU), an organization the NRA sees as liberal because of its position that gun rights are not an individual right or a civil liberty. Though members holding this stance are not as adamant as others who believe that the Second Amendment is the foundation of American freedom, still they are asserting that the right to bear arms is the second most important factor in keeping the United States free.

A small percentage of members do not see gun rights as a key source of freedom. Ernie, for example, has mixed feelings. His views of the Second Amendment are tempered by his lack of fear that gun rights and freedoms are under threat. Although he warns of the histories of gun control in relation to the "Nazis, Czechs, and Russians," as quoted above, he backs away from the perspective that guns protect freedoms: "I'm not convinced that if they take away our rights to own firearms that the government is going to trample it like the Nazis are. I'm not that much of a rabid gun owner."

Overall, however, concerns about the government's imposition on individual rights are a consistent theme in the NRA. Members use analogies ranging from socialist Sweden to Nazi Germany. In both cases, threats to gun rights and freedom are internal: members perceive a far greater threat at the hands of left-wing Americans than they do from foreign invaders. "Nowhere," James Sawyer wrote, "is the threat to our freedoms greater than here at home." The dismantling of the Soviet Union may have reduced fears of a military-based communist takeover of the United States, but some members see the possibility of communism emerging out of an increasingly controlling U.S. government. Gerry warns, "[Freedom] gets taken away if you're not paying attention," and Raymond Byrd picks up on Gerry's concern, cautioning, "A little sleep, a little folding of the hands . . . and the enemy within will attempt to legislate your constitutional rights out of existence. Fight for freedom or die without it!"

The threat of anti-gun politicians stealthily hacking away at gun rights year after year motivates NRA members to oppose each and every piece of gun control legislation. If they respond to a local county ordinance restricting the location of gun ranges as the first volley in a broader anti-freedom liberal assault, compromises on any gun control legislation means not only failing to defend gun rights but also endangering the Constitution and frontier masculinity. Deeply committed members certainly perceive those who oppose gun rights not as well-meaning or misinformed but rather as anti-freedom conspirators. One Madison Brigade member asks,

> Why has the Second Amendment moved to the top of its list? There can be little doubt that the right to bear arms is a serious thorn in the side of those who desire greater government control over our society and our individual lives. These same people have little or no respect for true freedom, liberty, and natural rights as defined under the original intent of the Constitution (Victor Phipps).

Members repeatedly share the sentiment that "freedom is not free." "The NRA and its members are freedom fighters," says Will Tansky, and they must be vigilant in their battle against gun control proponents or else the enemies of gun rights will gladly take away all other freedoms once they remove the Second Amendment. Ongoing legislative battles over gun control—whether big or small, whether the legislation is likely to become law or not—keep members active and feed their sense of peril. Members and fellow gun owners are urged to act now, or "soon there will not be enough freedom left even to attempt to stop or reverse this [attack on freedom by Democratic Socialists]" (Louise Dunfee).

Voting

Unlike some militia members who oppose gun control, NRA members take part in the political process by electing government representatives who share their beliefs. For Critical Mass and many Reserve NRA members, gun rights is either the primary or sole issue determining who gets their vote. During interviews, I asked members if they are single-issue gun rights voters. Donald told me,

> [Gun rights candidates] seem to think the right way in other matters too, you know—individually instead of the state. Anti-big government . . . Less government, the people govern it, not the state. I'm all for that. More individual freedoms.

Quincy said that his vote is largely based on guns, but it is important that the candidate is a Republican. He would vote for non-Republican, pro-gun candidates only in local elections, but Congress, he believes, needs to be controlled by Republicans.

Many members hesitated to align themselves with the stereotype of a single-issue voter. Bob, like others, stated that the Second Amendment is his primary litmus test but not the only issue he uses when voting. Typically conservative politics come into play, because, in most cases, Republicans are far more likely to support gun rights and Democrats more likely to support gun control.

Mark, a highly committed NRA member, does not consider that he is a single-issue voter, but he finds that the gun issue takes care of itself thanks to his broader politics:

> I would say more often than not I would be a conservative Republican, which would basically put me on the side of most either neutral or pro-gun people, just due to my politics to start with . . . Less government is better government.

Usually a "myriad of things" determines his vote, he told me, and it is generally based on candidates' conservative versus liberal positions.

Irene uses the NRA voter guide when casting ballots, making her a single-issue voter. "They're in the magazine that we get from the NRA. We get information as far as who to support, things like that. They're pretty much all on the Republican ticket, so that takes care of it." As a loyal Republican, she finds that she can vote for (NRA-determined) gun rights defenders without worrying much about casting a ballot for Democrats. Andrew also prioritizes gun rights when deciding whom to vote for, explaining,

> Yeah, I'm like a lot of people. I mean, I think most Americans have a single primary issue, political primary issue . . . And I think I'm not different in that I'm a single-issue voter as well, and my single issue is the Second Amendment rights. Although I, you know, I do take other things into consideration, [but] that's my primary.

Ian puts "freedom as my primary means for anything." Firearms rights are inherently part of his voting philosophy, but it is not the sole determinant. Walter struggles with the question and, with a sigh, tells me: "It is an important issue but it is not the primary issue in my life." "But," he adds, "I can honestly say I have voted for some people that either had a neutral view or had not expressed a view because it was the type of election I didn't think it was important enough to skew things in one direction or another." For Walter, gun rights are not always threatened, and so he feels comfortable at times prioritizing other issues.

Helen also thinks that gun control is only one of many important issues, for example, the abortion debate. Frank clarifies his own position on this issue: "I think the Second Amendment rights are one factor that would help me . . . to consider a person in a favorable way, but if [a candidate] was only strong on that one issue, then I don't think that would be a determining factor." Some less committed NRA members go even further. Pete, in response to my question as to whether gun rights alone determines his vote, told me, "No, certainly not. Certainly not . . . I determine the best candidate by his past record, and what he says he's gonna do."

Freedom as Individual Rights and Responsibilities

Individual rights and responsibilities go hand-in-hand with personal freedoms, according to NRA members. Our country is free because we have individual rights and responsibilities, they argue, and we have individual rights and responsibilities because our country is free. As NRA member Ben told me, "That's what the Founding Fathers did. All the people came here to be pioneers. They worked hard, they saved their money, and they built this country . . . on freedom." These *self-made men*, NRA members argue, picked themselves up by the bootstraps via their work ethic and a Constitution that allows anyone to achieve the American Dream.

If freedom is based on self-sufficiency, then dependence on government is a form of imprisonment. Ben put it bluntly: "This country was founded for every person for themselves." Walter agreed, asserting, "I think everybody needs to stand on their own merit or fall on their face." These worldviews reflect long-standing American values tied to capitalism and frontier history. Craig reflected on the unique perspective of self-reliance, Americans, and freedom: "[The Swedes] want to be taken care of [cradle-to-grave]. And that's appealing to a lot of people. To Americans it's not . . . we're a country that grew up on the frontier." Economic libertarianism's strict view of individual success based on the free market is a central element of conservatism.[7] The history of rugged individualism by contemporary white Americans' European ancestors is a constant reminder that freedom is inseparable from personal responsibility and individual rights. Remaining independent from government, communities, and even sometimes family for economic support is intrinsic to American freedom.

Ben shared his thoughts on this topic:

> Typically [NRA members] believe you should work for what you get. Everybody should work hard, save money, don't expect things from the government . . . You should do it all on [your] own . . . The government [was] out of [early Americans'] lives and out of their head and out of everything. The government wasn't involved with people back then . . . Over the years . . . the government [is] just taking over.

Government power, dependence on others, and group rights and responsibilities are liberal toxins to freedom for these members. "The battle lines in [the debate over gun control] mark the divide in American culture between individualistic and collectivistic values," with the former correlating with gun ownership and the latter to gun registration.[8]

"The problem," says lifetime NRA member Harry, is that "we're taking personal responsibility away from citizens and giving it to someone else." This Ethos of personal responsibility was spawned on the frontier, where government control was minimal. Today, however, Harry thinks,

> The people in the big cities look upon the federal government as a benevolent entity that will take care of you and be there. [Whereas] people

out in the country, in jobs where I am, the kind of stuff that I do, look upon the federal government as a very powerful force that is trying to, well, keep me from doing what I want to do.

Harry worries about our country's future if we continue to lose the frontier spirit. He says that government assistance is a form of dependence, and labels this as an assault on individual rights. "For me," he adds, "the federal government is so involved in my life, in my recreation, in my jobs, in my personal desires, and my personal freedoms."

Harry would prefer the government to be less involved in his life, but he does not think that most Americans feel that way: "[People] want somebody else to take care of them." But he worries that "maybe the country can't survive, we're going to go down the road to socialism, and eventually end up with a dictatorship again." He sees the first two amendments to the Constitution as the most important ones, combining to serve as the foundation of freedom. For Harry and fellow NRA members, as the United States moves further away from its frontier history, and as the number of gun owners declines because of urbanization, fewer Americans will defend gun rights, individual rights, and the ethos of self-reliance. Freedom will be lost.

There are realistic threats to freedom, Harry told me, especially "some of the liberal left. They have the most to gain [by] getting rid of guns [from] our society. If you look throughout history, people who have taken over government, that's their first concern is to disarm the population." Thus Harry's thoughts, like those of other Critical Mass and Reserve NRA members, come full circle: defending gun rights is a defense of freedom, and freedom's roots lie in personal rights and responsibilities; therefore, defending the American Ethos—and ultimately frontier masculinity—is important to fend off those who would like to implement greater government control, the very same people who champion gun control.

Religion and the Gun Crusade

Many NRA members are devout Christians and believe that the Founding Fathers and the Constitution were, in one way or another, inspired by God, and that the right to keep and bear arms is a divine right. Religion was a pervasive theme in Madison Brigade postings. The Brigade originally centered on defending against revisionist attacks on the Founding Fathers and Constitution, but when the events of 9/11 occurred, its postings incorporated items related to the attacks. If, as these NRA members argue, defending gun rights is the same as defending freedom, and if the documents that represent American freedom come from a higher power, than anyone attacking the Second Amendment and gun rights is open to the charge of blasphemy.

"The Constitution is a document inspired [by] God," Madison Brigade member Adam Leskin asserted, and, if that is so, then, according to Tony Riggs, members can argue that "freedom is a gift from God." Many Madison Brigade members are defiant about gun rights, insisting that no human-made laws can eclipse those handed down by a higher power. Drawing out the links between religion, freedom, and individual rights, Chris Jackson stated that "our nation's Constitution enumerates and explains your freedoms and your rights, but they are granted by God, not by government." The religious language is more than symbolic metaphors. Even the metaphors contain an uncompromising tone, such as this one from member Dan Townsend on the Bill of Rights: "These are the commandments of the USA and not subject to change." Fellow Madison Brigade member Roy Dawes summarized the attitudes of many of his peers when he argued,

> A government that is solely accountable to God is the only government that can ensure Liberty. Our Constitution and Bill of Rights are based on God's law. We must therefore defend and regard them, as we would also defend and regard the holy name of our Lord Jesus Christ.

The NRA created the Madison Brigade to help fend off "revisionist historians" who demean the Founding Fathers and the Constitution, especially the Second Amendment. This campaign dovetails with the Christian Right's battle against secular humanism. Revisionists endanger "Dominion Theology," which claims that America was founded on biblical principles and Christians must occupy secular institutions until Christ returns.[9] Some Gun Crusaders equate the Bill of Rights to the Ten Commandments, and argue that defending the former is their Christian duty. NRA member Matt Stidman summed up this perspective: "As Jesus Christ gives us eternal life by his sacrifice, the NRA gives us eternal freedom by fighting for our 2nd Amendment rights." Gun Crusaders must defend God's laws, including gun rights, even if it means sacrificing their lives to do so—"*From my cold, dead hands!*"

If defending the Second Amendment is a Godly duty, then those attacking gun rights and the Founding Fathers—who were brought together by God to pen American freedoms—are not only anti-gun freedom-haters opposing their country's heritage, but they are also blasphemous revisionists. Incorporating the ideology of frontier masculinity, Drew Ariola put it succinctly, "GOD, GUNS, and GUTS MADE AMERICA FREE!"[10] Even nonreligious NRA members sometimes draw religious analogies when referring to the Constitution. During our conversation, Harry told me, "As a matter of fact right here next to my chair I have a copy of the Declaration of Independence of the Constitution, and I carry a copy of it with me in my day planner. I mean, I'm not a religious person, but to me, that's kind of like my Bible." Nicole, who shares this commitment, observed, "[The two posters hanging in my room] are the copy of the Bill of Rights . . . and then also the Declaration of Independence. I carry a copy of the Constitution around in my purse all the time." Whether devout Christians or Constitutionalists, Gun Crusaders draw links between defending gun rights and what they believe to be other fundamental individual rights and freedoms that no one will take away from them.[11]

Fighting Communists and Socialists

In all my conversations with NRA members, no one ever explicitly spoke of feeling emasculated by gun control laws. However, they did speak about threats to gun rights and frontier masculinity values, the groups behind these threats, and other political agendas these groups support. Gun Crusaders point to feminists, socialists, and Communists as groups wanting to eliminate America's freedoms. These left-wing groups, they argue, are waging a culture war in their efforts to impose a "nanny state" by removing gun rights, increasing taxes, expanding welfare, and enforcing multiculturalism and affirmative action. Conservatives' vilification of the "nanny state" "[conveys] the view that people should be 'real men' and take care of themselves. [They construct] a set of dichotomies: welfare state, socialism, femininity, dependence, and indulgence versus the [free] market, laissez-faire values, masculinity, independence, and austerity."[12]

NRA members cite several targets who threaten to expand government control over citizens' lives, largely by threatening the right to keep and bear arms. The most obvious are gun control groups. Though members toss around the term "anti-gunners" rather broadly, it is most frequently used for gun control organizations. But like the NRA leadership, members agree that the lines between gun control groups, the media, and politicians are blurred. In Ernie's view, "the anti-gunners are mostly people that didn't grow up with guns and couldn't care less one way or the other." These people, he adds, are willing to please the media, which NRA members assume is both liberal and in favor of gun control. One member suggested,

[The] media and the anti-gunners are one [and] the same . . . They are ultra-liberals. Left-wing liberals is what they are . . . If you were to do an interview with them you would see that they were all socialist for sure. And they are pro-communist. (Ben)

Positions on gun control increasingly divide along partisan lines.

Today gun control is aligned with the "liberal Left," identified by NRA members as the media, revisionist historians, and, depending on the member's level of conservatism, politicians interchangeably labeled as Democrats, Communists, socialists, terrorists, and fascists. The range of political views and strategies among these groups is, of course, hardly debatable, but most NRA members do not look for shades of gray. Like many people, they tend to focus on the similarities and minimize the differences between outsider groups they believe are threatening them.

To Albert, the mainstream news media is responsible for the gun control problem, because "they are in total lockstep, joined at the hip with the Socialist Party in this country." Even though Albert does not believe that many Americans are socialists, he maintains that those who are hold "the most powerful positions, like in Congress, in the Senate . . . and that's who we're fighting." This comment typifies the culture war mentality of many NRA members: the fear that powerful socialists, by controlling and confiscating guns, are scheming to remake America and eliminate individual rights and responsibilities, independence, and freedom.

Andrew, though he considers gun control advocates a threat, has a more moderate view compared to most NRA members I interviewed. He told me, "I don't think that the anti-gun people are people to be hated. I don't think that they are people to be feared. I think they are people who need to be educated." Though he views them as a legitimate threat to gun rights, he does not believe that their intention is to dismantle the Constitution and hijack freedom. He accepts that their "cause is to help prevent people from dying [from gun violence], and we need to respect [that]," but at the same time offer a different outlet for grief and pain that comes from such violence such as harsher sentences for the perpetrators. Some members agree, though they are in the minority, that the views of "anti-gunners" are more a result of ignorance than a desire to wage a cultural war against conservative values and freedoms. Highly committed NRA members typically view "anti-gunners" as anything but well-meaning. Madison Brigade member Pat Linkhart warned, "Against the modern day Bolsheviks of the Political Left, who wish to rewrite History, we face the ultimate challenge."

After 9/11, NRA leaders and members compared violent terrorists to revisionists and other liberals threatening America's freedom from within. Chris Jackson, a Madison Brigade participant, warned that we should not let these people "infiltrate our hearts":

> [These] other terrorists [destroy] the social fabric of our nation and, more insidiously, they attack us from within the trusted confines of our own families by misleading our children from within their schools. These social activists threaten our freedoms at their very core by kicking God out of our schools and allowing in the worst social deviancies of our day.

The label "domestic terrorists" is, to date, the most radical in a long list members use to describe those who threaten gun rights, freedom, and the United States.

"If the Democratic Party had their way," Quincy pointed out, "they'd ban guns tomorrow." Pete agreed: "I think there are some people in our government that would like to [register and possibly confiscate firearms]. Hillary Clinton, Bill Clinton, and a lot of the Democrats. Yeah, the liberals." Although Pete admitted never having known anyone who was anti-gun, he said that he'd seen them on television, and "they don't know which end of the gun the bullet comes out of." Frank and some fellow members effortlessly ticked off a list of other Democrats threatening the Second Amendment, including party leaders in the Senate. Donald, laughing, called them, "Bad, bad people." Like most Critical Mass members, Donald sees no difference between U.S. Democrats who support gun control and admirers of Fidel Castro. "They all want a communistic type government," he concluded. And Albert agreed:

> We're not fighting Democrats man, we're fighting socialists. Dianne Feinstein, [Charles] Schumer, and of course in the House of Representatives you've got fifty-five people who have actually outright declared themselves to be socialists. And guess who they are? They represent the biggest part of the Black Caucus. You know, and I'm not prejudiced, don't

misunderstand me. But, uh, they are really pushing that stuff, you know? They will not even talk to [conservative Black Congressperson and NRA Board member] J.C. Watts.

I asked Albert why Hispanics or Blacks are not joining the organization in even modest numbers, and he responded that "the Democratic Party has a real strong influence on these people," and they are being taught in school to hate guns, presumably by liberal educators.

NRA members mostly avoid raising issues of race and ethnicity, preferring instead to use political labels to describe threats to gun rights, freedom, and the status quo. These members, of course, are well aware that their organization's membership is overwhelmingly comprised of white men, and so they likely recognize that they are joined by fellow conservatives in pushing for gun rights. The most conservative members paint their political opponents as extremists and believe that the Democratic Party, in Ben's words, "might as well be communist." And, as Ben told me,

> Communism has failed and socialism doesn't work. Our country, it's unbelievable, is going down that road . . . Been turning that way for a while, especially when the Clintons were in the White House. We almost turned into a communist country during [those] eight years.

Wilson Kieffer warns, "If you value America and your freedoms, be constantly vigilant in resistance to the fascists and socialists like Feinstein, [Schumer], Klinton [*sic*], and their ilk."

The United Nations

Occasionally members see internal threats to freedom and external threats to U.S. sovereignty as overlapping. Although members' use of the term "social terrorist" is metaphorical, their concern about the Democratic Party's relationship with the UN extends beyond symbolism. Some NRA members assume that Democrats and the UN hope to disarm the United States and strip it of its individual beliefs and practices. Al Gore had an idea to limit gun violence by only allowing single-shot firearms, NRA member Rick told me, and then asked: "Have you heard of the one-world order?" He described it as one police department for the whole world and believes its primary purpose would be to disarm people. He said that

John F. Kennedy was the last president not involved in pushing for this global force, and that every Democratic and Republican president since Kennedy has been involved. Rick's bipartisan, anti-gun global conspiracy is, however, an exception.

Most members view the UN as a left-leaning body more likely to be "lock and step" with the Democrats, as Quincy put it. They worry about relinquishing U.S. rights and freedoms to an international body that many feel is trying to disarm countries and individual rights around the world. Albert offered the following example:

> Haiti was somewhat of a free country. Most of the citizen's there owned firearms before the UN went in . . . Now any gun ownership in that country is totally prohibited and anybody that owns a gun now is [doing so] illegally. So they literally turn free countries into socialist countries after they leave there.

Forgetting about tax rates, economic policies, social welfare programs, and virtually anything that might distinguish socialist countries from nonsocialist countries, this member believes that free countries allow citizens to own firearms and socialist countries do not. Giving into UN rule, NRA members fear, will transform independent, free nations and peoples—in short, gun owners—into unarmed dependents of the "nanny state." Thus the United Nations serves as another threat to gun rights, independence, and American freedoms.

Frontier Masculinity and Gun Crusader Ideology

In an influential analysis of the different ways that liberals and conservatives think about the world, cognitive linguist George Lakoff uses a sweeping, two-pronged "Nation as Family" metaphor. According to Lakoff, we tend to conceptualize and refer to the nation as a family. For example, we speak of the Founding Fathers and Uncle Sam, talk about brotherhood among citizens, send our sons and daughters off to war, and sometimes worry that Big Brother is watching us.[13] If the nation is a family, then government leaders are its parents, and citizens its children. Lakoff argues that both liberal and conservative worldviews are linked to family-based moral views and practices. Liberals adhere to a "Nurturant Parent Morality" and conservatives to a "Strict Father Morality." Liberals' Nurturant Parent Morality emphasizes egalitarianism, compassion, and fulfilling all people's needs and desires, partly by protecting them from pollution, pesticides, corporate greed, and other dangers. Conservatives' Strict Father Morality sees the world as a dangerous place that requires authority figures (fathers/presidents) to discipline, protect, and promote their children's (citizens) self-reliance. For both camps, good politics mirrors good families.

The moral politics of Lakoff's Strict Father Morality and my conceptualization of frontier masculinity overlap. Both highlight such conservative values as self-reliance, hard work, individual rights and responsibilities, protection of self and family, and opposition to government interference in citizens' lives. Both models also produce conservative attitudes and behaviors. But, in my view, there are two fundamental differences between Lakoff's perspective and that of NRA members.[14] According to Lakoff, people's moral politics are a matter of internal processes, rooted in metaphors and psychology. Strict Father Morality arises from the conservative version of the metaphor. "It is the common, unconscious, and automatic metaphor of the Nation-as-Family," Lakoff contends, "that produces contemporary conservatism from Strict Father morality and contemporary liberalism from Nurturant Parent morality."[15]

In contrast, I use the term "frontier masculinity" to emphasize the effects of *outside social forces* on the NRA's new politics and NRA members' support for gun rights and other conservative culture war issues. I argue that U.S. frontier history and cultural and political threats to white men's status and identity are the driving force behind their political views. Fear of change and of loss pushes NRA members to become ever more committed to opposing gun control and a left-wing culture war. For Lakoff, *internal psychological processes* lead people to conservative (or liberal) attitudes and behaviors.[16] Although individual actors clearly hold particular worldviews and use these to guide their politics, even more important are the social, cultural, and political arrangements and shifts that lead NRA members to perceive threats to frontier masculinity. NRA framings of these threats are effective recruitment tools, resonating with members who fear the demise of frontier masculinity and gun rights. "The acceleration of the NRA's political agenda, dating to the 1960s, is both a cause and a reflection of member concerns—concerns that the NRA fans in its numerous strident communications with its members."[17]

Another difference between Lakoff's model and mine is that his seeks to explain how *all* conservatives (and liberals) think, whereas mine only tries to explain the unique moral politics of Gun Crusaders. And clearly they are unique. Gun Crusaders, unlike conservatives committed to other single issues, believe that losing their battle would mean the death of all rights and freedoms. Frontier masculinity values would be eliminated and replaced by "nanny state" socialism, or worse. Or, mapping this onto Lakoff's model, losing gun rights would lead to the end of Strict Father Morality and the cultural takeover of Nurturant Parent Morality.

Conservative activists might frame a loss on some other single issue as a signal of the culture's demise, but they do not frame any other single issue as the last line of defense against the culture war of the left. Many pro-life advocates oppose abortion as fervently as NRA members oppose gun control, but the pro-life movement does not frame *Roe v. Wade* as the end of personal responsibility and the beginning of a slippery slope that will inevitably lead to affirmative action programs or weaker punishments for criminals. Most pro-life activists probably support gun rights, as both are aligned with conservatism, but only gun rights activists believe they are protecting all other conservative causes. Welfare opponents do not claim that increasing welfare spending will lead to same-sex marriage. Anti-immigration groups do not argue that more immigration will result in more gun control. But Gun Crusaders view themselves and gun rights as the line in the sand, the final barrier separating frontier masculinity from the "nanny state." Lose this battle, and everything else they believe in will also soon be lost. The fears of Gun Crusaders help explain why the NRA has such a large and committed membership, including a core group of Critical Mass and Reserve members that prioritize gun rights when voting.

Why did Charlton Heston join the NRA leadership to speak nationwide against what he saw as a liberal culture war against conservatives? He could have chosen other culture war battles—abortion, evolution, same-sex marriage, affirmative action, or multiculturalism—but he chose gun rights because, in his view and that of the NRA and other Gun Crusaders, gun rights are America's "first freedom," the armed guard of all others. Gun Crusaders believe that gun rights protect the right to assemble, to practice any religion or none, to obtain wealth, and to do as one wishes with one's private property. But none of these other rights guarantees your right to bear arms. Following this argument, Lakoff's Strict Father Morality will cease to exist soon after gun rights are taken away. Conservative citizens will be unable to stand up and fight against government power or protect themselves against attackers. Legitimate moral authority will be undermined. Competition will be eliminated. Self-discipline and self-reliance will be unnecessary. And all this will occur because gun rights will have been lost. No other single-issue movement, conservative or liberal, has claimed to be the backbone of an entire ideology and been validated as such by the extent and intensity of support enjoyed by the NRA.

Consequently, no other issue generates as much fear among its supporters by highlighting the across-the-board implications of losing. The NRA's efforts to link their pet issue with something more far-reaching is nothing new. It is a basic framing strategy used by many social movements. Liberal advocates for the working poor argue that minimum wage raises are needed to prevent poverty and homelessness, and to ensure social justice. Similarly, many conservatives argue that same-sex marriage threatens the institution of marriage and the moral fabric of our society. These messages may very well resonate with citizens who despise what they perceive to be unjust or immoral, leading them to vote for or against related ballot propositions or the candidates that support them.

But how many of us would support a party or candidate based only on a single issue such as raising the minimum wage, opposing same-sex marriage, universal and affordable health care, or a flat tax? Would we threaten to fight to the death to defend the right to strike or allow evolution to be taught in schools? How many of us would commit to a social movement organization by subscribing to a lifetime membership—or even annual dues for many years or even a single year? The NRA, with its four million members, is unique. As NRA member Bob cautions, to no one in particular, "God forbid the government ever tries to take away our guns," warning that such an act would be met with an armed uprising.

I do not doubt the sincerity and depth of emotion felt by supporters of other single issues, such as anti-war or anti-abortion activists. The passionate commitment for these respective issues, however, tends to be short-term for the former and part of a broader set of religious-based concerns for the latter. No other single-issue SMO of any political persuasion approaches the NRA's broad, passionate, and committed base of support. Indeed, many of the non-gun issues discussed here, according to public opinion polls, probably have widespread support. But few of these poll respondents are sufficiently committed to the causes they claim to support to do anything other than cast votes for it, let alone make it their political priority and define it as the cornerstone of their beliefs. Perhaps the only similar movement that dwarfs gun rights is the Christian Right. This movement, however, is not a single-issue movement, as it supports prayer in school and teaching intelligent design, while opposing abortion and gay and lesbian rights.

Pro-life advocates most closely resemble gun rights supporters in their passion and commitment. Both groups claim dramatic and dreadful consequences if their side loses. For Gun Crusaders, the loss of gun rights signals the end of frontier masculinity and the rise of the "nanny state." For pro-life crusaders, the moral fabric of our society will be torn apart by allowing what they often view as the genocidal practice of abortion. The moral fabric argument, and in some cases the claim that we will incur God's wrath for allowing this abomination, is also used by Christian Right opponents of same-sex marriage and adoption, pornography, sex education in schools, divorce, and stem cell research. This speaks to the fact that the pro-life movement is more accurately described as a key plank in the broader Christian Right movement than as a single-issue movement.[18] Losing the abortion issue may produce horrific outcomes for the country, according to pro-lifers, but these are limited to the demise of morals and spirituality. The Christian Right does not claim that a pro-choice victory will lead to the loss of gun rights and other individual rights and freedoms, or undermine U.S. foreign policy and military action. The slippery slope arguments of the Christian Right do not lead down the paths of libertarianism or neoconservatism. Gun Crusaders view their cause differently. To them, losing gun rights will undermine all conservative frontier masculinity values and any attempts to export these abroad. Confiscate guns today, and tomorrow we will be a communist country, unable to defend Christian Right, democratic, and capitalist values. For the most committed pro-gun supporters, the single issue of gun rights is the foundation of their political, cultural, and moral philosophies, and, they believe, the foundation of everything good about the United States. It is easier to understand their moral outrage against *any* form of gun control if you recognize the consequences they envision if gun rights are lost.

5

Fighting the Culture Wars

Moral outrage is a cornerstone of the culture wars, especially surrounding the big three culture war issues, "Guns, Gays, and God." Cultural combatants and critics of all stripes tend to dismiss their adversaries as naïve, hateful, dishonest, insane, and worse. Popular liberal journalist Molly Ivins once wrote,

> I do think gun nuts have a power hang-up. I don't know what is missing in their psyches that they need to feel they have [the] power to kill. But no sane society would allow this to continue. Ban the damn things. Ban them all. You want protection? Get a dog.[1]

The "gun nuts" and the "freedom-hating anti-gun terrorists," as each side sometimes calls the other, are not about to break bread to see if they can find a common ground. For die-hard NRA members, whether the topic is guns, gays, or God, the enemy in the culture war is the same. As strong conservatives, they fear that liberals are trying to ban guns, give "special rights" to women, gays, immigrants, and the poor, and coddle criminals and terrorists.

Just as with any large group, "conservatives" vary tremendously in their social and political views. The three primary threads of U.S. conservatism have been libertarianism, anticommunist militarism (succeeded by neoconservatism), and traditionalism.[2] The NRA, a large and not always uniform group itself, reflects these different conservative worldviews.

Libertarianism, with its strong constitutional and individual-rights stance, as well as its opposition to government power, meshes best with NRA gun rights politics. Both the NRA and libertarians want to keep politicians out of Americans' holsters, gun safes, and lives. The second group of conservatives, yesteryear's Cold War anticommunists and today's neoconservatives, target foreign non-democratic nations for their self-professed goals of spreading freedom to the world. Though a communist military threat faded with the breakup of the Soviet Union, NRA leaders and members still cite communism (along with fascism) when worrying about what they see as the fragile nature of freedom. Libertarians and neoconservatives both see communism/socialism/fascism as the converse of their political ideologies, because these forms of government reduce individual rights and freedoms at the hands of "big government." They see communism and socialism as equivalent to collectivism and dependence, the antithesis of frontier masculinity.

The last key strand of U.S. conservatism, traditionalism, is about the desire to maintain the status quo; or, more accurately in a rapidly changing U.S. society, return to the way things used to be. The values and beliefs of these conservatives, and arguably the NRA, cater to 1950s images of family, sexuality, and gender arrangements.[3] Religious conservatives like the Christian Right best represent this perspective. Decades of technological, cultural, and political changes in the U.S. have resulted in more relaxed gendered roles, more open discussions and displays of sex and sexuality, legalized abortion, greater separation of church and state, and so forth. All these issues are at the core of the culture war, and the battle is being led on the conservative side by the Christian Right. Communism also threatens traditionalists, because it is hostile to Christianity (and religion in general). Like libertarians and neoconservatives, traditionalists support individual rights; pull-yourself-up-by-the-bootstraps capitalism is tightly tied to the Protestant Ethic.[4] Gendered political views celebrating frontier masculinity are clearly held more frequently by men, but neither biological nor social forces lead all men or all women into a single political camp. Both men and women have led efforts to fight communism, oppose the Equal Rights Amendment, and uphold a gendered separation of spheres.[5]

At times, conservative philosophies clash: libertarians want to shrink the government and keep it out of our private lives; traditionalists want the government to ban gambling, pornography, and same-sex marriage; and neoconservatives hope to use the government and armed forces to spread democracy and engage in nation building around the world. Generally, however, different conservative groups have much more in common with one another than with liberal groups, and Republican candidates are likely to get the votes of all three conservative groups.

Just as there is no monolithic conservative or Republican, neither do NRA members all share the same political views. Highly committed Critical Mass and moderately committed Reserve members are conservatives.

They are usually libertarian in their approach to government, often neo-conservative in their support of deposing dictators abroad, and traditionalist in their disdain for feminism and gay rights. As demonstrated by their sometimes competing views on a range of thorny topics, not all NRA members see a left-wing, culture war attack lurking behind every contentious issue. Overall, however, all NRA members I interviewed align comfortably on the Right side of the political continuum, and many on the Far Right. The most committed members, the Critical Mass—Ben, Albert, Donald, Bob, Rick, Mark, Quincy, and Walter—hold more consistently and further right conservative views than the still conservative and still committed Reserve members—Craig, Ian, Pete, Irene, Helen, Gerry, Frank, Andrew, Harry, Ernie, Zach, and Nicole.

Although NRA members are not likely to talk about guns and masculinity in the same sentence, their broader political views clearly suggest that they see gun control as a threat to frontier masculinity.

Masculine Pro-Gun Logic vs. Feminine Anti-Gun Emotion

The main foes in the culture war, according to NRA members, are feminists, liberals, Democrats, and socialists, all "anti-gunners" who want to expand the government's reach into citizens' private lives. The NRA takes an all-or-nothing approach to gun rights politics; politicians who do not oppose all forms of gun control risk facing the organization's wrath. Many members also view the world in black and white, with femininity, emotions, and gun control on one side and masculinity, logic, and gun rights on the other. The NRA and the conservative movement label their culture war enemies as feminine, connecting liberal "nanny state" politics to a lack of (masculine) independence. NRA members use essentialist language that relies on supposed genetic differences to explain women's and men's differing attitudes and behaviors. They argue that gun control support comes from irrational and emotional responses to gun violence, and giving in to these emotions creates personal and national weakness. To them, gun control threatens logic, reason, independence, and masculinity. Some members fear that women voters and politicians will react emotionally not only to gun deaths and gun control but to all political issues.

NRA member Bob bemoaned the fact that being a man "used to be a thing of privilege." "Now," he told me, "you've got [women] legislators voting on emotions, CEOs hired because it's politically correct," and they're basing important decisions on feelings instead of logic. Bob thinks that men's rationality is being replaced by women's irrational behavior in government and business, which endangers gun rights and America's well-being. Members like Bob believe it is up to the NRA to counter emotional reactions to gun violence, and they generally believe the organization is doing just that. Mark claimed that the NRA "is reasonably effective in arguing from the logic side as opposed to the emotional side . . . There's enough emotion to take care of everything in the gun control deal." Irene also accuses gun control groups of focusing too much on emotion. She thinks that "The Brady [Campaign], that's what they concentrate on, the victim. They are playing with people's emotions instead of letting them make decisions based on what they've been educated to [do]." NRA members attempt to remove emotion from gun-related violence by referring to firearms as tools or instruments, claiming that guns are no different than farm implements or automobiles.

The debate over firearms, then, is cast as the emotional (feminine) gun control side that says guns kill people, especially innocent children, versus the logical (masculine) gun rights side that says firearms are inanimate tools ("Guns don't kill people. People kill people"). NRA members' claims of rationality are similar to those of hunters dismissing their critics. These men view hunting as scientific, logical, and rational ("wildlife management") and animal rights activists as "emotional, sentimental individuals, 'bleeding hearts.'"[6] Disputes about rationality and emotion are gendered, not biological absolutes. Like the men NRA members I interviewed, the women also agreed with the NRA's position that, if the general public were educated about the benefits of gun rights, the emotional pleas of gun control groups would lose their effectiveness. Nonetheless, they know that the public (and particularly women) will not react to gun violence in an emotional vacuum.

"I'm worried about soccer moms," Craig told me, "they don't think about [the gun debate] a lot. They vote, they network. The hunters are guys." He thinks "soccer moms" are overly emotional voters easily manipulated by fear-mongering gun control groups. The gun control politics of these groups is intrinsically tied to greater government control over everything, according to Mark:

The "liberals" in the Democratic Party believe in the nanny state in that they want to take care of everybody, and they can't take care of everybody if [people] run around [like] a bunch of cowboys [with] guns.

Mark takes the "nanny state" metaphor to its gendered conclusion. The government is an overbearing nanny (woman) trying to protect and control her dependents (men gun owners) by restricting their freedoms. In this way communism (dependence on government) is associated with femininity, and capitalist democracies (built on individualism) are the masculine alternative. The Founding Fathers guaranteed individual rights, first and foremost gun rights, to escape control from Britain's nanny grip and fend off future internal nanny state threats.

Feminists: Fighting Nature, Hating Men

NRA members do not like feminine men. The same can be said for their attitudes toward masculine women. Women speakers at the 2003 annual meeting reinforced the idea of traditionalist gendered behavior, even for women hunters and NRA officers, at the "Women Aiming High" session. Susan LaPierre, wife of NRA EVP Wayne LaPierre, said that her friends tease her for painting her nails on hunting trips in the African bush, but she thinks one can still be feminine and hunt. Fellow speakers Sandy Froman and Susan Howard, NRA officer and board member, respectively, talked about having to overcome the perception that guns are masculine objects and so women NRA members must be unusually aggressive. Howard said that outsiders stereotype them as "truck-driving types." The speakers talked about wanting to and actually being "treated like one of the guys," as Froman put it.[7] Women are certainly welcome to join the NRA, they point out, even serve as its president as Froman later did, without compromising their femininity. As NRA member Irene said, "I know how the [good ol' boy] system works and I've learned to work within it . . . if men want to rescue women, okay let them rescue me! It doesn't cost me anything. I'm not a feminist."

Both masculine women and feminine men threaten the gender status quo and promote feminist goals, members say, which include anti-freedom policies like gun control and group rights. When I asked Ian his opinion about the term "feminist," he answered, "lesbians." Sighing deeply, he continued, "Feminists are women who want to be like men in every which way because they can't accept that they are women." He associates sexuality (attraction to women) with gendered characteristics (masculine behavior) and assumes that women fighting against sexism are actually pursuing manhood.

Women in the military are also often thought of as overly masculine. Regardless, research has shown that many men view women soldiers as "weakening" or "polluting" combat situations.[8] One of the least committed Reserve members, Ernie, has mixed feelings on the topic:

> I think [having women in the military] makes too much of a touchy-feely military . . . [But] most women that are in combat situations are pretty tough. They're not the shrinking violet type. Maybe it's all right you know. I've read pros and cons on it.

Critical Mass member Mark disagrees, facetiously citing his sex characteristics to justify his position: "You take care of future generations, which means you take care of the females. Do I think that they are incapable? Absolutely not, but I've just got this hormone that kicks in that says women and children first and that's just the way I am." Even among members who think women have a place in the military, the vast majority do not think they belong on the battlefield. Violence is a sacred masculine realm.

Some cultural critics argue that men oppose women in the military because it leaves men with no one to defend.[9] Allowing women to be soldiers is merely one gender distress signal for many NRA members, part of a broader pattern of women leaving caretaker and nurturer roles to become breadwinners. For going against women's and men's "natural" complementary roles (either God-given or biologically based), women are blamed for the "breakdown of the family" and the resulting poor behavior and outcomes for their children.

Gerry unhappily reflected, "I'm in a generation where I have seen mothers leave home and go to work. I wish more of them could stay home with their children." He sees this breakdown leading to problems for children: "It has affected our country in a great way because the destruction of the family unit has definitely affected our youth; drugs and everything else." Another member also implied that men's presence would stabilize "morally questionable" women-led families, explaining, "There's too many one-parent households that are run by moms who are too busy out chasing the next boyfriend. Letting the kids just look after themselves" (Donald). Most NRA members dismiss feminists' efforts to blend what have generally been held up as separate women's and men's roles. These members believe feminism is a radical ideology that fosters women's selfish behavior and leads to bad moms and troubled kids.

Single mothers are pinpointed as the source of the problem, because they are taking on roles they were supposedly not meant to fill. When I asked members their view of Hillary Clinton's book, *It Takes a Village*, in which she popularized the argument that "it takes a village to raise a child," many had hostile reactions. Helen retorted, "We need stronger families, not a village, not a government to take care of us. Strong families . . . which can allow the mom to stay home and take care of the kids." Donald saw a broader left-wing conspiracy in Clinton's book, believing that this form of community-family interdependence is yet another attempt by liberals to remove personal rights and responsibilities: "Clinton's people wanted to put that ["it takes a village"] in this country. They're more communist than the Chinese."

Despite America's status as the global leader of capitalism, the most threatened NRA members, like Donald, see little difference between U.S. liberal social policies such as social security or welfare and actual communist or socialist countries. These Far-Right NRA members label any form of government assistance to the poor as "communist." Anyone promoting liberal programs is given the same treatment. Like NRA slippery slope arguments about gun control leading to confiscation, Donald and many of his fellow Gun Crusaders see any form of social welfare assistance as ushering in a full-blown welfare state.

One of the first conservative groups to equate feminists with Communists—because both are viewed as pushing for government dependence— is the John Birch Society. This Far-Right organization drew the connection by highlighting a more literal "nanny state" supported by free, state-sponsored day care for children.[10] Traditionalists believe that free national day care will result in citizens becoming dependent on the government, sapping them of their motivation to work hard and support their families. Donald also thinks that families have been eroding over the years, because we "got the liberals in power. Family values are all messed up. Got to get more conservatives in power. Gotta stop this liberal media, liberal [television] shows, you see anything on [television]." He holds traditionalist conservative family views and is outraged at the permissiveness of U.S. culture since the sexual revolution.

Some NRA members believe that social forces demand that women enter the paid labor force, even if they have no desire to do so, "because the average workingman isn't making what [he] used to make. It takes both of them now to do it. Because the cost of living has gone up so much" (Gerry). This perspective does not blame women for trying to "be like men," but the end result is the same in their eyes—women leave their "natural role" in the home, families break down, and children are harmed.

But most members *do* see feminists as the primary culprit in challenging the gender status quo. Helen declared, "I'm not a woman's libber." She disassociates herself from this group, because she sees feminists as "militant. Far-Left . . . You know, hating men [laughs]. Anti-family." Irene joins in: "I'm all for equality and stuff, but I'm not a man-hater." Another woman member, Nicole, struggles with the issue, eventually acknowledging that she is indeed a feminist, while distancing herself from what she sees as radical feminist views.

The feminists from whom NRA women distance themselves come from the most radical and probably smallest camp, held up as straw persons for anti-feminist attacks. As part of a backlash tactic against feminism, conservatives have rebranded the term to mean "man-hating radical" (think Rush Limbaugh's popularization of the term "feminazi"). As Nicole put it, "I'm not what people make us [feminists] sound [like]." Conservatives have relatively successfully denigrated the term to the point where many women who hold feminist viewpoints shun the label. Some men NRA members join their women peers in pointing out the problems posed by radical feminists, even parroting Limbaugh's famous hyperbole. When asked what he thinks about feminism, Bob replied, "A joke [laughs]. [Feminism] is an effort to give less than attractive women access to important issues in this country."

Albert spoke about how feminists attacking men relates to other threats to white men and American freedom:

> Well, it's the same, it's the same deal [as attacking whites]. It's divide and conquer, is what the whole ballgame is about. It's being sponsored by the Socialist Party and they know how to play this game real well; they've done it over and over and over, two centuries.

Here Albert links feminism, socialism, and, implicitly, civil rights, viewing these as long-standing threats to America. In his view, and in the eyes of like-minded members, feminists and other left-wing groups are attacking individual rights, freedoms, and the gender and racial status quo, whether through gun control or social programs such as affirmative action. They are waging a culture war on conservative white men, and they must be defeated.

My interviews with NRA members reveal clear-cut conservative patterns in their cultural and political views, although every topic of discussion produced some variation. NRA members' thoughts on gender inequality and feminism are no different. Some simply do not see feminism as having much impact at all, such as Pete, who brushes feminists aside because he thinks they are in the minority. Reserve member Zach does not feel threatened by feminism, because he doesn't "think it's anything special being a man . . . Do your job, raise your kid, obey the law, respect your neighbors. I'm not much on this macho shit; you might get that [from some other men]. Beating up your neighbor—I don't consider that being a man." Disagreeing with the contention of more conservative members that women are too emotional to make sound decisions in business and government, Andrew pointed out, "We have more female legislators [and CEOs] today than we ever had in our country's history. And that's only good for America." His position is closer to the nearly three-quarters of U.S. gun owners—only a tiny fraction of whom are NRA members—who do not think that "most men are better suited emotionally for politics than are most women."[11] NRA members as a group are more likely than other gun owners to worry about women's decisions being fueled by emotions.

Critical Mass member Ben objects to "Hillary Clinton and that administration" worrying more about human rights than anything else. It is notable that he refers to Bill Clinton's presidency as *Hillary* Clinton's administration. The first dual-career White House couple, Bill and Hillary became frequent targets of gendered jabs; jokes around the theme that "Hillary wears the pants" paint her as dominant and overbearing (or in some more explicit versions floating about, as a ball-busting bitch), and possibly a lesbian, and draw Bill as a hen-pecked, emasculated non-leader.[12]

Ben's comment reflects a broader anti-feminist backlash politics that criticizes women who leave their "natural" roles and forcefully take over men's jobs—in Hillary's case, one that *Bill* was elected to do. But even Ben largely agrees with a liberal feminist perspective regarding equal opportunity. "I don't have any problems [with a woman] working anywhere in a job that she wants to do. If she can do a job as good as a man, then that's fine." This version of equality is consistent with a pull-yourself-up-by-the-bootstraps philosophy. He implies, however, that men are the standard to which women should be compared.

Welfare and Unemployment: Nanny State Creep

No topic elicits more criticism from NRA members who ardently defend frontier masculinity than welfare, which, more than any other program, conjures up big government, liberals' "nanny state" threats, and especially feminists. Contemporary U.S. welfare policies are already condemned by many conservatives as the socialist/communist legacy of the New Deal, President Franklin D. Roosevelt's 1930s response to the Great Depression. Decades after this federalist interventionist expansion, Marxist feminists proposed that the government should pay moms to raise their children. Women are exploited as housewives, they argued, serving as capitalism's necessary unpaid labor so that men are free to be the breadwinners.[13] Some European socialist democracies use a similar alternative, whereby the government pays for day care, allowing moms of all income levels to work. These are the literal "nanny state" policies that conservatives cite as threats, and they arise from feminist politics challenging the patriarchal and capitalist systems that have disempowered women by limiting their choices and opportunities.

In their efforts to counter women's and other group-rights movements, conservatives and anti-feminists attempt to connect any form of social welfare to "nanny state" socialism. Feminists campaigning for welfare and the women who receive it are easy targets. NRA members dislike welfare, because they think women are getting paid (well) by the federal government to have babies and not work. Members also begrudge unemployed and impoverished single men, the most visible of the homeless, for failing to support themselves. Both single moms and homeless men are anathema to the American Ethos. Instead of being self-reliant, welfare mothers and panhandlers depend, respectively, on government support and the generosity of strangers. This is what happens, most NRA members reason, when feminists, liberals, Democrats, and socialists attack frontier masculinity.

The most conservative and committed NRA members frame welfare as a culture war attack by liberals, but most members simply view welfare as a threat to individual rights and responsibilities, not to mention their wallets. NRA Critical Mass member Mark summarized his thoughts on welfare in gendered terms: "It goes back to the nanny state. The government will do it all for you . . . I go back to personal responsibility and self sufficiency and all that." For Albert, where there's smoke, there's fire. "You know, [the Democratic Party is] pushing the big welfare thing, just like they always have, using our tax money to buy a boat." Looking beyond his boat-buying embellishment, it is important to recognize that he interprets welfare as a program that takes money out of the pockets of hard-working Americans to subsidize the comfortable lifestyles of those too lazy to work. Moreover, Albert thinks that the Democrats "continue to use [welfare], to push for that, because they can, they're just literally buying votes with our tax money." He sees a vicious cycle: Democrats raise taxes on workers, expand welfare for the unemployed and poor, and then these people vote for more Democrats, leading to another round of tax hikes, government spending, and Democratic vote-getting. For members like Albert, expanding welfare is one more step in the slippery slope toward socialism, where greater government control fosters dependence, removes freedoms and individual rights, and necessitates gun confiscation.

Many members emphasize that we cannot end welfare completely, because there are "some people out there, maybe single mothers or kids that need opportunities," and "you can't let people starve. This is not a Third World country."[14] However, most say that welfare should only be offered to those *incapable* of working because of physical or mental conditions. Having children doesn't count. Some members allow for a brief, temporary safety net for those who lose their jobs. Otherwise, they worry that welfare will become habit-forming, like a drug addiction.

Welfare dependency has "been a tremendous problem . . . I see [that] welfare has been well-meaning, but [it] has a crippling effect on recipients," Frank told me. "It takes a very strong person to get off welfare," he added. Members also compare welfare to the releasing of a virus, spreading through communities and especially families, often lasting several generations. "We do have a big problem of constant generation to generation [welfare recipients]," Libertarian and Reserve NRA member Harry said, adding,

> There is a need for [welfare]. I don't want to live in a society where people are starving in the streets, where disabled people are unable to do anything for themselves. I don't want to walk down the street and see beggars. Nobody likes that. It's not becoming of a progressive society, but then we also don't need people making a career of welfare.

"Just giving it away indiscriminately to everybody is wrong," explained Irene. Despite the lack of evidence supporting this conclusion, that welfare is a financial boon is a widespread belief among NRA members (and many other Americans as well). These attitudes are the legacy of the then Republican presidential primary candidate Ronald Reagan's "welfare queen," a racially coded and false story about a Chicago woman using dozens of fake names, addresses, and social security numbers to get rich by defrauding the welfare system.[15] Some members repeat similar and culturally familiar discourses created to undermine welfare support by framing it as something that makes recipients a bit too comfortable, if not wealthy. Mark believes that we have a responsibility not to allow anyone in this country to starve, "but then again you shouldn't eat steak." Welfare recipients should only be provided "staples, not New York Strip and stuff like that, you know," Donald adds, laughing.

Other members have even less patience. "You know, if you don't work, you don't eat. . . . [barring disasters]," Helen admonished. Ian attacked (women) whom he believes are having "more babies for more benefits." He fumes, "But, if they're having kids and they want the government to pay for them, no! You got pregnant by this turkey over here, you get the money off of him!" These conservative critics of government, more likely men, are implicitly arguing that "male taxpayers should not have to pay for other men's children."[16] The responsibility to take care of children falls on individual mothers according to American cultural attitudes. If they cannot provide proper care, they must find a way to obtain money from fathers who don't take on their responsibility. Men, and especially fathers, are rarely thought of or mentioned as intergenerational welfare dependents.

All the assumptions members make—that welfare recipients are lazy and don't work, that welfare provides financial stability or is even a boon, and that welfare is an intergenerational problem—fly in the face of the facts. To be eligible for welfare, household income must be less than half of the federal standard for poverty. In 2002 a single mother and two children could make no more than $7,510 a year to be eligible. The average welfare recipient in 1996 received a mere $1,680 a year in cash and services, reflecting the fact that most recipients are the *working* poor.[17] In terms of race and ethnicity, just under 40% of recipients are Black, followed by 31% white and 25% Latina and Latino. Poor immigrants do not have higher welfare rates than native-born recipients, and their tax contributions more than account for their benefits. One of the most glaring misconceptions about welfare recipients is that they and their children become permanently dependent on government aid. Even before the 1996 policy changes, "the vast majority of adult recipients left welfare within two years, with most leaving it within one year. Most of their daughters did not receive welfare later in life."[18]

But none of these facts get in the way of the fundamental American belief that anyone can be successful if they simply "pick themselves up by the bootstraps" and display a hard-working Ethos. This attitude spawns from a self-made man, individualistic history of American freedom, whereby social forces like deindustrialization (causing factory closings) or economic recessions (causing layoffs) are not included as reasons for unemployment. Instead, so this argument goes, people need to figure out how they got themselves into their lousy situation and how to get out of it. Andrew put it this way,

> Just because you give up on life, you decide that you can't get a job, you've been unemployed . . . But, why are you unemployed? Are you injured? Do you need a prosthesis? Do you need some training, some technical or . . . some labor training or something like that? Let's make opportunities available to these people in both the workplace and in terms of education so that the need for welfare isn't there.

This perspective focuses on individual causes of unemployment (lack of will, health, training, or education), avoids the issue of persistent structural unemployment, and denies the uncontrollable forces (from one unemployed person's standpoint) that occasionally lead unemployment rates to go up or down multiple percentage points.

Promoting welfare, most NRA members argue, threatens independence and self-reliance. The more dependent citizens become on government, the more willing they will be to relinquish their individual rights, including their gun rights. Generous welfare programs are considered a hallmark of socialism and signs of a creeping "nanny state," redistributing money from the wealthy to the poor. NRA members believe that they must guard against this threat to frontier masculinity, and, as some see it, a plank of the left-wing, culture war agenda.

Taxes: Democrats' Domain

When I asked members for their thoughts on the U.S. tax system and if their tax dollars are used appropriately, they usually complained about their money going toward liberal programs that take us further and further away from America's frontier roots. NRA members lambasted their tax dollars going to:

1. *The Arts*: "In Washington too, they give millions of dollars for crap. Endowing the arts and stuff. They then put up filthy pictures on display. There shouldn't be any endowment for the arts." (Donald)
2. *Social Security*: "Meals on wheels for alcoholics and drug addicts." (Bob)
3. *Education*: "There shouldn't be any national education department. Education should be handled by the local people." (Donald)
4. *The Unemployed*: "We shouldn't have to be taxed to pay for people that are too lazy or too spoofy [*sic*] to go out and work." (Ben)
5. *Unfair Tax System*: "The Democrats, especially, keep griping about tax cuts going to the top of the elites, but they don't realize that the elites pay all the taxes; the top wage earners." (Ernie)
6. *Foreign Aid*: "A lot of [money is wasted] on foreign aid." (Harry)

Whether they are labeled "liberal pet projects" (National Endowment for the Arts), decades-old social(ist) programs (Social Security and Welfare), federal government excesses (Federal Education and Taxes), or global relief policies (Foreign Aid), NRA members see all these programs as a façade for an underlying agenda: socialism.

Donald insisted that we should "quit giving our money away to all these Third World countries, unless we can control how they, the way they think about that, teach them our ways of thinking." Unless we can spread capitalism and the American Ethos throughout the world, then, in his eyes, we are simply subsidizing threats to freedom. Donald maintains a Cold War-era, anticommunist conservatism, fearing its newest menacing versions ("I won't buy anything from China. It's made by 5 cents, 10 cents an hour Communists"). Zach offered a more modern neoconservative view on the topic of aid. "If I'm correct, like North Korea, we're giving them economic support and they're battling us. I mean what the hell are we doing?"

Most members confine their critiques to internal U.S. expenditures. Another member, Ian, wandered off on a tangent about the Internal Revenue Service:

We're being taxed by an organization called the IRS, which is not really an American organization. . . . The IRS was never intended for the U.S.A., it was intended for the [Virgin Islands]. It was never intended for the

American people to be taxed the way they are. Okay. So, we are losing our freedom. The thing is we don't have people today who know this.

Ian's underlying complaint is not off-base for many members. They disagree with how their tax money is collected and distributed, and believe that it threatens individual rights and freedoms by compelling citizens to subsidize social programs that promote collective rather than personal responsibility.

Critical Mass and Reserve NRA members, of course, are not the average gun owners. They are highly conservative Gun Crusaders who fear liberal plans to implement gun control and confiscation, which they see as simply a prelude to the bulldozing of all individual rights and freedoms. They think frontier masculinity values are under attack by big-government, "nanny state" policies. Most of their views are more conservative than the overall U.S. gun-owning population.

Only a little more than half of all gun owners think the government is spending too much money on welfare. Americans who do not own guns apparently see even fewer welfare threats to independence, as just over one-third of them are worried about overspending. Regarding conservatives' ultimate "nanny state" fear, government "assistance for child care," about half of American gun owners believe that the United States is spending too *little* on helping kids. Two-thirds of non-gun owners agree. There is also a gap between the views of NRA members and gun owners on the topic of improving the standard of living for the poor. More than one-third of gun owners feel that it is up to individuals to take care of themselves. About one-fifth think the opposite, that "the government in Washington should do everything possible" to raise living standards, and the remaining gun owners, somewhat less than half, view it as a shared responsibility between the government and individuals.[19] These views contrast sharply with NRA members who overwhelmingly want to reel in the government.

Albert believes that his tax money is going toward "a lot of these socialist programs that they got going on in this country, socialist experimental programs and all that stuff." And just who are these socialists promoting higher taxes? "Democrats are tax spenders, we're [those in his well-paid occupation are] the ones that earn the money and pay a tax" (Ernie). Both Ernie's professional colleagues and fellow NRA members perceive Democrats reaching into taxpayers' pockets to enact social(ist) programs. These are the same Democrats, they note, that also threaten freedom by attempting to restrict and even suspend gun rights through nanny state policies. In the view of many NRA members, these anti-freedom forces are pushing for socialism along many fronts in the culture war. If gun rights are removed, they say, Americans will not be able to defend against the Left's creeping socialist agenda.

Gay Rights, Special Rights

Just as members worry about special privileges going to the poor, they also see other undeserving groups being treated differently, such as gays and lesbians. The agitators behind all so-called preferential treatment policies, they note, are the same: liberals and feminists. Traditionalist conservatives see connections between a liberal anti-gun and pro-gay feminist agenda. In the 1950s Senator Joseph McCarthy linked homosexuality and communism—"both represent gender failure."[20] Today, with the Cold War over and the legacies of liberal social movements visible everywhere, cultural conservatives worry about *internal* American threats to freedom. And the threats are many. As Madison Brigade member Randall Merriweather explained, "Today, groups lobby to keep prayer [out] of schools, to teach homosexuality in our schools, and to take guns from our homes." He fears anti-God, pro-gay, and anti-gun liberal forces.

Looking at the issue through a gendered lens helps explain NRA members' sense of threat from feminism and gay rights—both challenge frontier masculinity and the men who support and benefit from it. Just as boys and men tend to avoid the gender demeaning label of "girl" or "woman," they also steer clear of behavior that leads others to label them as "gay."[21] In fact, being gay is the most subordinated of masculinities (especially to men from older generations like NRA members), because gay men are pigeonholed as effeminate "sissies" and "pantywaists" and are thereby closely aligned with femininity and women. Proving your masculinity is largely about proving that you are *not* effeminate. In contemporary popular language, to retain your masculine identity is to avoid being called a "little bitch," "fag," or "pussy." According to many NRA members' zero-sum views whereby one group's gain is another's loss, if women, femininity, and lesbians and gays gain acceptance and status, men, masculinity, and straights are threatened.

Critical Mass NRA member Ben believes that our culture celebrates and privileges gays and lesbians, thanks to liberal group-rights activists. He doesn't mind women who work hard and succeed at whatever job they desire, but he dislikes it when they and other liberals engage in a broader gender and sexuality politics. His sense of moral outrage surfaces when discussing certain feminists and others who he thinks take these issues too far. He complained,

> They also promote homosexuality and all that stuff, most [of them] do. And that is totally against our Founding Fathers' beliefs, the Bible, and what God teaches us. For people that believe in God. Not only our belief, not only Christian belief, other religions believe the same thing . . . The liberal media, the liberal community, and the socialist people, the pro-abortionist people. They all think that [homosexuals] should be protected, and all this kind of stuff and everybody should tell everybody that they are homosexuals. Everybody should say, "well that's okay, and it's just another lifestyle. It's okay." But what makes me mad is that they promote it, they say it openly. They're *bragging* about being homosexual . . . [Gay people] are led by the pro-homosexual groups, pro-feminism groups, and all that stuff; keep agitating them that they should tell everybody what they are doing and expect to be treated differently, with kid gloves and stuff. Acting like it was something that was hereditary. It's not that. They can stop being homosexuals if they want to. With God's help for sure.

Ben's thoughts are instructive for several reasons. First, he links gay/lesbian rights with feminist and liberal groups. Second, he insists that sexuality is strictly a choice that people make, one that many conservatives attribute to cultural permissiveness and recruitment by gay and lesbian groups. Anyone dedicating themselves to God would be able to "overcome" their "abnormal" sexual desires, he says, repeating arguments made by activists in the ex-gay movement. Finally, Ben uses the same language as several conservative movements that try to recast liberal group-rights movements' battles for "equal rights" into a ploy for "special rights"—preferential treatment for gays over straights.[22]

Many fellow members, like Donald, also think that gay rights are unfair. "That's another thing that's wrong with our country," he says, "Giving them more rights than we have for heterosexuals. It's a bunch of crap." These traditionalist conservative opinions are consistent with early 1990s Christian Right ballot initiatives opposing "special rights" for gays and lesbians in Oregon and Colorado.[23]

Many NRA members, especially the highly committed Critical Mass, use Christianity to denounce gays and gay rights. "I'm not prejudiced, I don't hate gays," Ian pointed out, "it's just not normal and I don't care what they say, it's not normal. No, they don't have God on their side. No, God didn't create them that way. [Because] that would make God either confused or, you know what, but he's not." Thus being gay becomes an immoral practice and an affront to God. "You should be prayed for and try to get on the right track there," says Ben. He believes that homosexuality is an affront to God that can only be (possibly) overcome through the help of virtuous heterosexual men praying for and saving those gay men who represent failed masculinity.

Rick has an abrasive view regarding sexuality and employment discrimination. He believes that employers should be able to fire gays if their sexuality hurts the business, because, if a customer goes into a gas station to get something and the guy working behind the counter is a "male acting like a damn female," that customer is going to wonder "where's his finger been, up some guy's ass?" Rick conflates sexuality and gender, like so many people do, because he associates gay men with acting effeminate. Being gay is like being a woman to him; neither one is masculine. Because gay men are still men, they challenge the gender status quo.

Queering Gender and Sexuality

Many NRA members (and Americans) think homosexuality threatens heterosexuality, especially when it comes to marriage and children's socialization. Part of their fear is the perception that gay men are all highly effeminate, violating sex and gender norms. Queer theory challenges the privileges accorded to dominant social groups by calling into question the very existence of such groups. Forget gay men "acting like females." Queer theory questions, "What does it even mean to be gay? Or masculine?" No such absolute biological or cultural category, or person, exists. What does it mean to be 100% straight, masculine, or male? Biology no more produces such categories than does the range of human cultures, or individual expressions within these cultures. The mere *presence* of a man who self-identifies as bisexual and conforms to the most hyper-masculine behaviors upsets the status quo. Lesbian and gay activists who fight for rights in the face of inequality and discrimination are even more upsetting, because they are turning what should be the private matter of sexuality into a political issue, according to NRA members.

NRA members often distance themselves from both homosexuality and the reasons why men would have sex with other men. When I asked

Ian why he thought men "become homosexual," he says, "I'm a very heterosexual male, I don't know." Rick is stumped, too: "I'm a Christian and can't comprehend a man sleeping with another man. To me it's just gross." Most of these men's fears and hostility are directed toward gay men, who pose a stronger threat to dominant cultural versions of masculinity then lesbians do. Zach unwittingly pointed out this double standard when he talked about gay and lesbian intimacy. He admitted,

> When I think about two guys going to bed together in the sack it makes me sick. But the funny thing of it is, if I think of two good looking women together in the sack that doesn't bother me as much. I just can't imagine two men making love to each other.

Gay men making love to each other challenges how men are expected to behave, so much so that the thought of it literally makes some men ill. But two lesbians having sex is erotic and less dangerous to men's masculine identities, particularly if these women conform to hetero-normative beauty and femininity standards.

NRA members who either do not identify as strongly religious or tend to place their political beliefs above their moral beliefs are less prejudiced against gays and lesbians. Some members either self-identify as libertarians or express beliefs consistent with that ideology when discussing sexuality. In Walter's opinion,

> As long as it's not illegal, I'm happy in some cases that some of the laws have changed. That's my kind of liberal leaning, only because I have known some very, very loving gay couples, both male and female, and find it so bizarre that in some places they are considered criminals.

Even those who try to follow a live-and-let-live philosophy tend to struggle to live up to it when it comes to homosexuality, adding qualifiers to their position. Ernie offered terse acceptance, stating, "I think I'm probably tolerant of gays as long as they do their job, keep their mouths shut, go about their own business." A lot of NRA members said that they'll "tolerate" gays so long as they don't discuss their sexuality or, worse, fight for gay rights. Both threaten frontier masculinity, because they aim to validate competing versions of what it means to be a man.

"Sexual preferences I think are of a person's personal business," Gerry stated, "but they shouldn't be spread out in front of me or anybody else."

Some members' personal moral and religious anti-gay beliefs are trumped by their political philosophies, which demand freedom for all. They (reluctantly) support the same individual rights for gays and lesbians. For the most part, their views allow anyone to do what they want so long as no one else is harmed (or has to witness it). Instead of a clear-cut "your rights end where mine begin" libertarian approach, they wrestle with an awkward internal debate that half-heartedly concludes with a "your rights end where I have to see them" stance.

Cultural and political changes have made sexuality a more public, contentious issue. Craig exemplifies the mixed views of many members who have been pushed into wrestling with gay rights by these societal changes. At first he argued that "the people after the gays are a bigger problem than the gays." However, he, too, is critical of lesbian and gays:

> [I don't appreciate] their in-your-face games. They do the parades and all that kind of . . . I think that's stupid. Why don't they just do what they have to do and do it when they want to? I mean, I don't have to go out and screw my wife in the middle of Market Street to make a point.

Like many older men raised according to a frontier masculinity view from generations past, Craig believes that people can do as they please, but that does not include making their sexuality a public matter or political debate. If it is made public, members regard this as crossing the line and another warning shot in the culture war. Although he may disagree with their sexual "preferences" or even their politics, Craig said, "I know a lot of gays and they're fine people; they're nice people. They're not trying to convert you." Ernie echoed this claim, saying, "I certainly work with a lot of gay people and nobody has tried to seduce me."

Gays in the Military

Of all our discussions concerning topics of sexuality, NRA members were least threatened by gays in the military. Certainly many are worried about this, but not as much as they worry about feminist activism or boys near gay adults. Most members do not interpret gays in the military as a liberal culture war assault. Indeed, they generally do not think the issue has much impact at all. Perhaps NRA members simply will not disparage anyone in the military because of its frontier masculinity representations of hard work and the defense of American freedoms.

Critical Mass member Ben broke from his usual stance about the culture war to take a libertarian attitude: "As long as they don't bother me or bother people that don't want to be bothered, they don't do it in front of people and everything. They do it in their home, in their off time—I don't care." Ben won't fight it, but he doesn't want to witness gay intimacy. Some NRA members, particularly those with recent military experience, are more concerned about job performance than sexuality. Walter knows a high-ranking, bisexual military officer, about whom he said, "I would trust him in a heartbeat with my life." Although Quincy "[has his] issues with homosexuality," he said that "having gays in [my] unit never affected me." I asked him if he would fight with gay soldiers in a foxhole, to which he exclaimed, "Fuck yeah! You're either a good soldier or you're not." Their military experience defied gay men's stereotypes as passive and effeminate, incapable of being good soldiers.

However, keeping in mind the overall conservatism of this group, many had strong feelings about threats posed to the morale of "normal" troops, and even their safety, when gays are allowed in the military. To these members, there is no room for what they see as failed men in an institution as crucial, and masculine, as the military. Historically the military is known for "turning boys into men" and wars have served as a proving ground for many men, launching many political careers. Until recently, the military has basically been a homosocial masculine institution. But with women's expanding presence and a hotly contested public debate resulting in the "Don't ask, don't tell" sexuality policy, military dynamics have changed for the worse, some NRA members maintain. Bob does not have a problem with same-sex *civilian* marriages but thinks that the military is no place for it, given its importance and traditionally masculine nature: "A normal bread and butter guy in the military probably doesn't like gays. There's really no room for them there. They don't belong there."

Heterosexuality is a key standard of masculinity. Bob believes that those who fail to live up to it, like gay men, threaten "normal" men. Others say it is "not conducive to a strong military environment," because "the military is for breaking things and killing people and should not be used as a social experiment."[24] The military is about violence, power, and control, characteristics long dominated by straight men. If you "experiment" with this institution by admitting gays (or women), these members argue, you jeopardize the military, national defense, and therefore all American rights and freedoms.

Ian believes that armed forces personnel have the right to know the sexual preferences of those fighting beside them, for health reasons: "[If a gay] guy next to you just [got] shot and you get shot and his blood gets into you, you might as well just shoot yourself right there, you know. No, I don't think gays should be in the military." Clearly, to Ian, gays equal AIDS. If we could isolate the spread of AIDS by segregating gays, following his line of thinking, then the dangers to "normal" men would be eliminated.

Ian is not the only member who sees the presence of gays in the military as nonsensical. Albert sees it as a culture war issue:

> [Allowing gays in the military] was another one of the ploys used by the socialists that literally helped to try to degrade and demoralize our troops. And that's literally all it's about. They have absolutely no business being in the military. That's, you know, kinda like the same thing as gays wanting to be Boy Scout [Scoutmasters] . . . It makes absolutely no sense whatsoever.

Albert senses another left-wing culture war conspiracy to destabilize the armed forces and adversely affect the morale of U.S. troops so that socialists can take over the country.

According to some NRA members, socialists, that is, anti-gunners, feminists, and advocates for gay and lesbian rights, are intent on taking over the country. They have started a culture war that will lead to the destruction of individual rights and responsibilities, frontier masculinity, and ultimately freedom. Straight men have been relegated to second-class citizens, expected to stand idly by as less deserving group-rights advocates are given preferential treatment. These committed NRA members are responding to the dramatic changes that began in the latter half of the 20th Century—gun control threats, liberal group-rights movements, and challenges to men's breadwinner status.

The Race Wars

Gendered topics and language—separate roles for women and men, worries about being emasculated by the "nanny state"—are crucial to understanding NRA members' fears of liberals. Race is a similarly critical issue in explaining members' perception that they are under attack from anti-freedom forces. NRA members see both *external* and *internal* racial threats to American freedom.

The anti-freedom threats from abroad are terrorists (and no longer Communists), who cannot be reasonably classified as left-wing. But, the Gun Crusaders hold, the same internal liberal forces who promote the "nanny state" are the ones who fail to strongly defend against external terrorist threats. NRA members are not unusual in that they speak of racial and religious threats when discussing 9/11 and terrorism. The related topic of immigration bridges external and internal racial threats, whether because terrorists take advantage of our "open borders" policy or because non-terrorist immigrants choose not to assimilate and feast on free social services paid for by citizens. Threats to life, culture, or resources are all potentially hazardous to America's health. Internally, members link race to fears of crime and the dismantling of individual rights and responsibilities by group-rights movements' support for affirmative action. Members fear the worst if liberals win the culture war and take control of the country.

Here's how the Gun Crusaders see it: "Gun grabbers" and "bleeding-heart liberals" are afraid to use racial profiling to protect (white) Americans from terrorists and criminals, because the Left doesn't want to offend anyone who might be innocent. The liberals don't coddle only criminals and terrorists but also the lazy poor and unqualified minorities. And they do it by stealing hard-earned money and opportunities from middle-class white men through liberal welfare, taxation, and affirmative action programs.

The culture war, as seen in policies such as affirmative action, welfare, and same-sex civil unions and marriages, rages on against conservative, straight, white men, leading many NRA members to feel defensive about their very existence. Craig railed,

> If you don't like the damn country, get out. But don't tell me I have to say I'm Hispanic-American or Black-American or Arabian-American or something like that. Because I was born here and I choose to live here. I'm American. No more of this hyphenated business. It's bullshit.

Craig's annoyance at new, hyphenated racial and ethnic terms speaks to a broader conservative backlash against "political correctness." As cognitive linguist George Lakoff explained, "In the culture wars, the liberal attitude is called 'political correctness,' a snide term suggesting that liberals think they know what's right and are trying to impose it politically on ordinary people, who know better."[25]

Craig's angst is matched by his conservative peers, who think post-1960s racial and gender shifts threaten white men. Referring to what former NRA president Charlton Heston called the "cultural shock troops" of the Left,[26] Albert mourns,

> And they're using racism for their attempt at dividing people. Every time you have an election going on, you'll see it yourself out there. They will jump out there and say, "Well, uh, this guy, the only reason he's doing this is because he's white and," uh, you know, they all—of course—they always just pick on white folks.

The promotion of civil rights (code for threats to white men's individual rights) is a formidable threat at the highest levels of government, according to some members. Ben protested, "That's what's happening to this country today . . . They get away with anything; we can't do anything today. 'You can't do that because you're violating my civil rights' . . . It's just like being a traitor almost." Ben sees broad trends within the United States, a culture war waged by "traitors" of America—those who hate frontier masculinity and its individual rights, responsibilities, and freedoms.

Terrorism and Racial Profiling

During our conversations, NRA members spoke at length about the relationships between 9/11, terrorism, racial profiling, and threats to America. Race and ethnicity play a central part in NRA members' thoughts on these topics. The fear is palpable in several members' discussion of 9/11—"We're at war with a certain race of people, and in no way, no how, are they all bad, but my children have the right to be protected from [Muslims]." Rick's comments are somewhat contradictory because he defines the terrorist attacks (and presumably the "war on terrorism") as a race-based war, essentializing diverse racial, ethnic, and religious groups. Yet he simultaneously qualifies his statement by noting that not *all* of these people are bad.

But if the criteria for the war is being Muslim or of Arabic descent (and not, for example, being a radical fundamentalist), then they must *all* be threats. He expressed his fear in the last part of his statement which focused on his children's well-being. When Rick said "we," he implied whites as the in-group or, possibly, just all non-Muslim Americans. He made it known that there are ten million Muslims "running around" in this country, and he believes that every one of them should be given a lie-detector test. Citizenship and constitutional rights are revoked in the race wars, at least for those deemed the enemy.

If 9/11 or some comparable act was perpetrated against the United States by white, Western Europeans, race would likely fade to the background. NRA members might speak instead about the threat posed by Americans of French or German descent. We would not be "at war with a certain race of people," just as we were not at war with whites after Timothy McVeigh bombed a federal building in Oklahoma City. Why? Because, in all these situations, "we" are whites, the dominant racial group in the United States. The NRA likely has a much higher proportion of whites than the country does. Probably no less than 90% of the membership is white.[27] Just as a "normal" man isn't gay, according to NRA members, the generic person, or American, is white.

Ben offered another example of this whites-as-the-norm default assumption. "People getting on an airplane with someone [who] looks like an Arab, they're going to be thinking twice. Everybody. They're going to be wondering if they're terrorists or not," he said. "Everybody" clearly doesn't include the millions of Americans who could be targeted, nor does it count those who do not assume that all Arabs are potential terrorists. Quincy argued similarly when he said that racial profiling is "Human nature . . . I mean, think about it for a minute . . . If a Black guy with cornrows comes up to your car, pants hanging down, sagging way down . . . it changes how you feel." The "other" in these situations—Arabs and African Americans—are only others if you are not one of "them." Most Arab Americans likely do not think twice when seeing other Arab Americans board planes and most African Americans probably do not feel intimidated by their peers' hairstyles or dress, particularly when these simply reflect young, urban culture. Ben's "everybody" and Quincy's "you" are whites who fear threats posed by darker-skinned others.

NRA members are unconcerned about racial profiling, because they have not been profiled. Reserve member Harry told me, "I mean, let's face it, I mean they are profiling criminals . . . I mean, all of the terrorist acts—I don't want to sound like a racist—[have] all been committed by Muslim men between the ages of 17 and 40." Similar to their argument concerning firearms, that people should rely on common sense rather than emotions, members believe that racial profiling is the logical and correct response to terrorism and crime. Ernie mentioned watching "a press conference on

CNN and they were talking about how profiling is wrong, which I think is crazy. If the people that are blowing stuff up are Islamics [*sic*], then why not profile Islamics?"

Mark sees a connection between those opposed to racial profiling and those who highlight gun violence in support of gun control. Both, he believes, are trying to substitute emotion for logic. "I think racial profiling is a buzz word to get people excited. Another emotional approach. I say you find out who you're looking for and you look in that group . . . [that's not] racial profiling, that's picking your target and common sense and practicality." Conservatives' (masculine) logical solution is clouded by liberals' emotional (feminine) arguments. "It seems like it shouldn't be an issue. Up until we're getting an influx of blonde Canadians coming in and blowing up things," Mark continued, "I would say let's focus on where we think the threat is coming from." Of all fears and concerns of NRA members, in the years following 9/11, terrorism is the one they probably share the most with other Americans.

Because of a sense of imminent danger, NRA members feel justified in speaking their minds about issues of race, religion, and profiling. Donald related his experience and thoughts on a flight he took after 9/11, laughing throughout:

> Well, they were searching me, and this guy walks by and looks like a terrorist and they didn't motion him over to me. You don't do that. You gotta have a little common sense. I don't look like an A-rab at all. Guy walks right by and I thought, Jesus, I don't even want him on the plane with me.

He emphasized and intentionally mispronounced the two syllables in the word Arab (A-rab) to make it pejorative. The fear of the other, as well as support for profiling "them" to protect "us," comes up repeatedly. "But, the fact is 70% of the people in jail. . . are Black, 100% of the people who hijacked the airplanes are Middle Easterners. So, yeah," Frank said, "if you don't profile racially, you probably wouldn't catch anybody. They were all Islamic, so if you don't profile religiously you just eliminated a good opportunity." Looking beyond his exaggeration of the rate of imprisonment of African Americans, Frank finds logic in racial profiling because he believes it increases the odds of netting terrorists.

Craig also believes that racial profiling is a logical, beneficial response to safety concerns in a post-9/11 environment:

If you have six Arab nationals getting on [an airplane together], I think you have the right to do everything legal to find out why are they there. You're not gonna stop the next group in line because they're white. These are extraordinary circumstances. We're talking about a bunch of people who've made it their business to say that they're gonna kill all the Jews and Americans and everything else.

Although the war on terror is more real to most Americans than the culture war, NRA members feel threatened daily by both and draw parallels between the two.

NRA Reserve member Irene supports the Bush administration's post-9/11 policies, which she contrasts with liberals' naïve and ineffectual approach:

It's time that we stop digging deep, "save the world," you know [laughs]; the social workers that want to save everybody and the bleeding hearts. This is real stuff that is happening. It's bad stuff and if we don't do something to stop it then it's going to get worse.

For Gun Crusaders, the "bleeding heart liberals" who manipulate people's emotions by focusing on the victims of gun violence are the same people who are too busy trying to "save the world" to recognize an imminent danger that must be dealt with by force. They are also the same people who oppose racial profiling and expose Americans to further terrorist acts, Irene and her peers contend.

Not all members fear a global racial or religious war. Some of them raise concerns about stereotyping an entire region of people. Walter stated, "I have never felt any fear whatsoever [when I was in the Middle East] and I don't believe that all of the people [there] hate us, or hate the rest of the world." He has never sensed anything other than warm feelings for Americans from his Middle Eastern friends. But even Walter has no problem with racial profiling. Zach thinks that the U.S. government tries to be more subtle when profiling today, but he believes it is unethical, if not illegal. He is alone in his guarded criticism. NRA members, virtually all white, are willing to profile "them" to protect "us" from another terrorist attack.

Crime, Punishment, and Race

Although NRA members have strong feelings about racial profiling and terrorism, they usually don't talk about race so openly. They tend to use race-neutral, broad categories (socialists, liberals, Democrats) to classify various American threats to gun rights and other individual rights. Occasionally, however, they addressed the topic of race more directly during our interviews. The only other subject besides terrorism that elicited explicit racial comments was crime. Their perception of criminals and criminal threats to their safety reveal powerful images of racial and ethnic stereotypes.

Critical Mass member Albert remarked that "most [criminals in his area] are Hispanic, and a lot of it is drug-related and all that stuff. But you don't have any problems with law-abiding citizens and firearms. It goes back to the same elements." The frequently used NRA term "law-abiding citizens" is a code word for whites (reminiscent of "states rights" and "law and order"). The "same criminal elements" are not law-abiding citizens; according to Albert, they're Hispanic.

Politicians have long used racial code words to appeal to the fears of white voters. Most notably, the Republican Party implemented the "Southern Strategy" during the Civil Rights era to peel off Southern Democratic voters (and ex-Democratic candidates) who opposed desegregation. These Southern whites fought civil rights and federally mandated integration, claiming "states' rights" over what would now be called big-government interference. "States' rights" was one of many code words politicians used in place of (increasingly unacceptable) openly racist rhetoric. It allowed them to signal to anti-integrationist whites their shared feelings of superiority over, or at least resentment and hostility toward, African Americans. Democratic Alabama Governor George Wallace used his inaugural speech to support segregation "forever," and later literally prevented Black students from entering the University of Alabama by standing in the doorway. He ran as a pro-segregationist, Independent presidential candidate in 1968, when both he and Republican Richard Nixon campaigned using a "law and order" message, another code word appealing to white voters' fears of Black violence, stoked by urban rioting.[28]

In some ways whites' racial criminal fears persist. When I asked Rick if he lives in a high-crime area, he answered, "We got Blacks, we got drugs." He conceded, however, that he lives in a low-crime area and that the threat of crime is not a serious one for him and his family. In a wandering response to a question about the Founding Fathers, he came around to the issue of crime and armed self-defense, stating, "If three big ol' Black dudes come at you [when you're with your wife and children], you gotta be able to protect your family."

Race and crime are inseparable in his eyes. Whether it is drugs or violence, black and brown folks are criminal threats. Noting that I was interviewing him while in California, he observed that there are "lots of Mexicans, Chicanos" there and therefore lots of gangs and a significant possibility of getting "blown away." From terrorists hiding in the United States and "waiting to use WMDs" to Palestinians who "have it in their blood to kill" to African American and Chicano drug and gang presence, Rick senses many threats as a white man surrounded by what he perceives as dangerous others.

Many NRA members have obtained concealed carry licenses in response to these fears. As Frank put it, "I generally use my Second Amendment right to carry a gun in unfamiliar territory." This unfamiliar territory is counter to the "fairly safe area, fairly affluent homogeneous type neighborhood" that he lives in. He doesn't say that he lives in a white neighborhood, but the implication is clear.

NRA members' support for armed self-defense in response to crime significantly differs from all gun owners, 30% of whom think more gun restrictions will reduce violent crime by preventing criminals from getting their hands on guns. The same portion of gun owners feel the opposite, agreeing with the NRA that these restrictions will only increase crime by disarming "law-abiding citizens." The remaining 40% of gun owners are not sure which argument is true.[29]

With politicians using racial code words and local news and other media focusing on violent crime ("if it bleeds, it leads"), it is not surprising that many white Americans fear being victimized by Black or Latino offenders. As with their opinions on welfare, NRA members' perceptions do not always align with reality. Frank spoke of the police using racial profiling to help protect themselves:

> A lot of times when people are in cars [initially] you don't know what you have in terms of color or race or sexual preference or whatnot, but there are some common denominators, I think, the fact that the prisons [contain] 70% black and 30% white [inmates] is one indicator.

Frank's summary of race and prison rates reveals his misconceptions about prisoner rates and black-on-white crime. At the time of our interview, African Americans comprised roughly 45% of the state and federal prison population for those inmates serving at least one-year sentences.[30] Regarding violent crimes, whites are much more likely to be victimized by other whites than by other racial groups.[31] Frank relied on (false) statistics to avoid making explicitly racist generalizations. He attributed Black crime to social causes:

> Most people out here if they're born Black, they're born poor. And they're born [within a] lower socioeconomic family and the father is in jail . . . if they know their father [at all]. It's sort of a situation, a social situation where they're brought up in it.

The sometimes identified, sometimes implied perpetrators are poor men of color (always either African-American or Latino) in NRA members' crime scenarios. The victims are middle-class whites. NRA members discuss gender even less so than they openly address race when discussing crime, but the perpetrators are always men. Whether they are "big ol' Black dudes," gang members, or kids (boys) with missing fathers, criminals are *men*, according to NRA members.

The problems leading to high crime rates are also gendered, according to some members. They believe that societal stability is threatened not just by absent fathers but also by criminal-coddling liberal policies like discretionary sentencing. These "bleeding hearts" would rather try to help criminals deal with their own earlier victimizations then lock them up in order to protect everyone else, in the view of many NRA members. In Ben's opinion,

> The socialist people, or the ultra liberal people . . . They really think that nobody should be hurt; they should not be punished for their crimes they can't help. That's their attitude. They can't help [but commit crimes because] their mama beat them or something. Their daddy beat them when they were little or something. They think it's okay, it just happened. That's the attitude of these ultra liberal idiots, and the media fall right in that category.

Ben and his peers accuse liberal gun control advocates of undermining "law and order" and trying to remove individual responsibility by being "soft on crime." Liberals want to "wallow in the 'Victim Culture,'" Madison Brigade member Fred Haley warned.

The gendered language—the feminization of liberals (soft, bleeding-hearts, victim culture)—reinforces NRA members' sense of masculine correctness. Conservatives use logic to enforce the moral order, whereas liberals allow their emotions to affect their decision making. Gendered language also identifies the opposition, gun control supporters, who would rather confiscate guns and restrict law-abiding citizens than hold criminals responsible. For the Gun Crusaders, all the same forces are acting against individual rights and responsibilities; the shock troops of the Left's culture war against native-born white men are the same people who want to take away the guns of NRA members. Or, as Madison Brigade member Drew Ariola, expressed it, "I thank God for the NRA and all freedom-loving, patriotic Americans who do what they can to protect our Second Amendment rights from being trampled by the godless, gutless, gun-grabbing bleeding hearts in this world."

Immigration Costs and Benefits

Violent crime and immigration, legal and illegal, are topics members feel strongly about, particularly in light of 9/11. "So many thousand illegals can get here every week. How many people of those could be terrorists?" Gerry asked anxiously. Irene saw the role of immigration policies in 9/11: "I think we've been very liberal in letting people into our country. I think with such a bleeding heart, it's like, 'oh yeah, send us everybody, we'll give them asylum.' We have to take care of our people first." Even though Irene herself is the granddaughter of immigrants, she believes we should seal our borders. NRA members I interviewed criticized what they perceive to be an open-borders policy. Democratic politicians are most responsible, members claim, because lax immigration laws and enforcement during the Clinton years led to 9/11.

Critical Mass member Donald claims that the United States has been subsidizing terrorists:

> When they teach them that Koran to kill us, it's right in the Koran. Those Muslims, to me that's terrible. I mean we put up with this, the government is handing money to all these students from the Middle East over here. They should kick 'em all out; kick most of 'em out. Some of them are good ones. A lot of them I'd have kicked out.

The impact of 9/11 is clear, as members do not raise concerns about students emigrating from other parts of the world. The threat of violent terrorist acts is narrowly focused on one region, but members' anxiety about immigration extends well beyond threats of violence. Members' fears of immigration leading to more terrorism are often coupled with resentment about providing support for new immigrants (documented or otherwise) at the expense of U.S. citizens.

"You know," Albert said, "they come across the border here and they could get [welfare] money just as easy as anybody else. In fact, easier than a lot of United States citizens." Other members agree, such as Rick, commenting on Cubans immigrating to Florida, "It's payday for them to come over here," referring to government giveaways, not job opportunities. Dade County, in Florida, went bankrupt, he believes, "because all their money is going to the Cubans, because they're from a communist state," and so they expect the government to take care of them. Independence and self-sufficiency are inherently American in members' eyes. Many believe that immigrants bring with them a culture of dependence, which makes them gravitate to liberal politicians. The culture war is global for committed NRA members, whether fighting the perceived United Nations gun-ban agenda or immigration threats.

Immigration is a key component of the culture war because it threatens native values and morals, many conservatives argue, thus providing a reason for the "liberal Left" to push for increased immigration. "We are just flooded with [immigrants] . . . It's just ridiculous. They keep asking for more and more stuff," Albert argued, "and you know they have no rights, and the [American Civil Liberties Union] is hammering on every issue that they bring up." The ACLU's lack of defense of gun rights, combined with their perceived attack on white citizens' rights and status, validates NRA members' fears that this organization is run by left-wingers. In Harry's words, "I look at the ACLU and I think there's a lot of socialists involved in that and I've never seen them protect the Second Amendment rights." Even members who are sympathetic to the ACLU's ideals find a threat in the group's perceived hypocritical defense of some, but not all, civil rights. These "socialists" are defending immigrant rights on one hand and ignoring gun rights on the other.

The ACLU's positions are clear examples of hypocrisy, not unlike immigration policies, according to some members. Craig complained, "I think it's *criminal* to adapt your laws to somebody else that's coming in to be a citizen. If they want to be a citizen, if they want to do it, they should, we should make the laws stick to them." Unconsciously reflecting on the United States prior to the culture war, he asked, "Remember how it used to be? You shouldn't be given a break because you're an illegal." Craig is referring to the days prior to liberal immigration policies, when, in his view, gun control didn't exist and white men weren't under attack, when undocumented immigrants were not coddled like they are today.

When asked to discuss the economic impact that all forms of immigration have on the United States, Pete responded, "it's costing taxpayers money," because immigrants aren't supporting themselves. Countless other NRA members shared this opinion. They assume that immigrants come to the United States and either cannot find work or choose not to, instead soaking up government benefits to survive. These benefits come from taxpayer dollars, so NRA members see themselves paying for immigrants' laziness. These (racial and ethnic minority) non-citizens are surviving, even flourishing according to some members, thanks to the hard work of (white) American citizens. The unparalleled American work ethic is able to sustain not just hard-working Americans and their families but untold free-riders as well.

If not for these drains on taxpayers, Walter argued, the country would flourish: "I think a lot of our ills can be resolved and a lot of our economic issues might be resolved if we were able to stem the tide [of immigration]." Some members see immigration as a double-edged sword even when immigrants find work. Albert unhappily noted, "And they send all their money back to Mexico, and of course we have to provide these people with free medical care anytime they want it and, uh, anything else they ask for. We have to provide schooling for their kids and everything else." Here not only are hard-working Americans paying for immigrants' health and education, but these non-citizens turn around and send the American dollars they earn out of the country, further damaging the U.S. economy. Thus even immigrants with jobs threaten the tax base and, ultimately, the amount of taxes U.S. citizens have to pay.

A handful of NRA members either do not link immigration to liberal politics or do not think immigration is a problem. Displaying the former opinion, Gerry partially blames "Republicans [because they] want cheap labor and they let every damn Mexican and half of Mexico come up here." Virtually all immigration scenarios that members paint revolve around Mexican immigrants, ignoring the millions of immigrants from other parts of the world, and often labeling any Spanish-speaking immigrants as Mexican.

Some members not only disagree that immigrants are ruining the country but argue that they are actually improving the U.S. economy. Bob believes a few immigrants live off of society but that most come here to work and do the kinds of work that most Americans won't do. A few

members spoke of Mexican immigrants who attend church, are solid contributors to their communities, and work hard (some mentioned friends
who run businesses who told them that immigrants were their hardest
workers). Other members empathized with the plight of immigrants in
their native countries. "I like Mexicans, I like Mexico. I don't really feel
threatened by them. I understand why they're coming over here—it's not
for the movies and popcorn," Harry said. Speaking about other members'
dislike of Mexican immigrants, Zach pointed out, "I'll tell you, there's a
lot of people here that just hate them. But, as poor as they are in Mexico,
if we were there we would try to get into this country. They're just doing
what the rest of us would do." This is a far cry from perceiving immigrants
as lazy and seeking to reap the fruits of American citizens' labor through
taxpayer-funded social programs. But, again, this view reflects a small minority in the NRA; most members found immigrants to be threatening in
one way or another.

Another complaint about immigrants among NRA members was that
they are not exerting enough effort to assimilate. Whether they remain
isolated in their respective communities, do not learn English, or simply choose to speak their native tongue when around American citizens,
many members are bothered by their behavior. Donald complained,

> That's another thing that rankles me too; Hispanics aren't around much
> here, but I go to Florida around Miami airport, and I want to get direc-
> tions. And these idiots can't talk English in those gas stations. I'm not in
> Mexico. Doggone it that burns you up![32]

Several members strongly support the ideas offered by the English Only
movement (which Charlton Heston was involved in), with many expressing interest in the proposal to make English the official national language.
Bob calls English-only instruction in schools a "no-brainer" because, as
his fellow members says, "if [immigrants] want to communicate in this
country, they should learn English" (Ian). Irene gets right to the point:
"This is America . . . speak English."

Some members simply dislike Mexican immigrants, and others are
unhappy when immigrants choose to speak a language other than English, but still others see foreign languages as an explicit culture war threat.
Harry cited French Canadian attempts to secede from the rest of the
country as an example of what *not* having an official national language
can do to a nation. Mark agreed (using his typical over-the-top sarcasm),

"I don't think we should have thirty-five ballots in Chinese, and Mandarise, and Vietnamese, and Canadian, and Louisianan, and Byunan. It's still one country and I think that one language will keep it, will make it work better." Donald offered the most conservative position: "If they're gonna come over here, they oughta learn English. [Otherwise] they shouldn't be allowed to be a citizen." He relented somewhat, allowing them "so much time to learn English or get deported."

Affirmative Action: More Special Rights

Affirmative action policies, to NRA members, are like high and unequal tax rates or welfare programs that subsidize immigrants and the poor; they are liberal inventions that reduce individual freedoms by siphoning resources and opportunities from hard-working citizens and redistributing them to the undeserving and sometimes free-riding "welfare queens," immigrants, and people of color. Affirmative action was the only issue that did not generate disagreement among NRA members. In their view, affirmative action cuts to the heart of self-reliance and the American Ethos; it is favoritism based on race (few acknowledge the gender component) and simply a form of discrimination.

During the Reagan years, Republicans' race-neutral framing of egalitarianism gained widespread acceptance. By not explicitly addressing race, their ideas became acceptable to a broader audience. White Americans supported Civil Rights but they did not want to be the victims of "special rights." Egalitarianism and fairness meant opposing preferential treatment for women and people of color, while pushing the rhetoric of a meritocracy. Liberalism and affirmative action were equated with gender and race-based inequities, or "reverse discrimination."[33]

As a conservative white man, Mark agreed. "Affirmative action is once again discrimination. If you're [against] discrimination you can't be for affirmative action. You know, 'It's okay for me but not for you. These are the laws but I don't have to do it.' We either do it or we don't." When I asked Mark what is wrong with America today, he responded, "I'd like to see the multiculturalism go away. I'd like to see affirmative action be down to affirmative opportunity." Like many Americans, he mistakenly believes that affirmative action programs are based solely on racial quotas that demand employers hire less qualified people of color over more qualified whites. Group rights are unequal "special rights" to NRA members, threats to two fundamental hallmarks of American idealism: individualism and egalitarianism.

Nothing is more threatening to frontier masculinity than giving people jobs, raises, and other preferential treatment based solely on their race, ethnicity, or gender. Repeating the American mantra of the self-made man, Pete told me, "I don't think we should have affirmative action at all. I don't think we ever should have had it . . . It's not needed. If a guy is a different race than white, he can go as far as his skills will take him." NRA members dismiss the possibility of ongoing institutional discrimination (either racism or sexism) in a post-Civil Rights era. Whatever racial inequalities exist today, they believe, arise from individual choices and effort. Even those rare members who stand to benefit from affirmative action fear they are being singled out based solely on their race or gender. Irene's support of the American Ethos equals that of her white men peers:

> Well, you know we've got all this equal pay and equal work stuff. You've got all this affirmative action stuff. You know I want to go out there and make as much pay as they have but based on my skill, not on my gender.

Walter summed up NRA members' view of affirmative action: "I think everybody needs to stand on their own merit or fall on their face." A few members shared personal stories where they believed that coworkers benefited because of their race or gender, leaving behind the more deserving of such privileges—qualified white men. Affirmative action, therefore, threatens white men's status and resources, another attempt by the political Left to institutionalize the destruction of frontier masculinity.

Displaced and Coddled

> [These social terrorists] celebrate sex before marriage, homosexual lifestyles and any other culture other than the American culture. The language they use is tolerance and experimentation and multiculturalism. But, in fact, they wouldn't know tolerance if it kicked them in the ass. (NRA Madison Brigade member Chris Jackson)

Highly conservative and committed NRA members, like the NRA leaders, identify threats from the political Left and fear they are losing the culture war. Members who refer to "social terrorists" reveal the fear and oftentimes contempt they have for gun control and gay rights activists, "revisionist historians," affirmative action supporters, and others who challenge conservative, straight, middle-class white men's status, power, beliefs, values, and identities. NRA members simultaneously see themselves as *victims* of the liberal group-rights culture war and patriotic *heroes* defending American individual rights and freedoms.

They want to roll back liberal group-rights policies and practices and return to the frontier days of a more hands-off government. To their libertarian-leaning minds, equal rights result from the government doing *little or nothing*, interfering minimally in people's lives. To liberals, it is the government's responsibility to give everyone equal opportunities, particularly those in groups who have long been denied the same opportunities as middle-class white men. Conservatives want freedom from government coercion, which means low taxes (at the same rate for everyone) and the right of citizens to do as they please with their communities (local governance) and property (no gun control). They believe they are best qualified to judge what to do with their money and lives, and they resist being compelled by ("nanny state") authorities to wear a motorcycle helmet or not smoke in restaurants. Liberals, by contrast, see freedom from fears as a prerequisite for people to thrive. Freedom comes from protection (from second-hand smoke) and a sense of security (from gun violence), as well as equal opportunities (made available to disadvantaged groups through programs like affirmative action).[34] Of course, these are oversimplifications, not representative of all conservatives or liberals, but they fit well with Gun Crusaders' social and political views, and their conception of rival culture war factions.

Although some NRA members are only moderately conservative and others members' degree of conservatism varies by issue, as a whole they overwhelmingly lean to the political Right. Their politics arises from their usually lifelong frontier masculinity principles and a sense of threat from liberals. These (mostly) men feel "dispossessed," as if they have "lost the country," to gays, feminists, and immigrants.[35] Some refer to this phenomenon as "displaced" masculinity, whereby white, heterosexual men feel as though they are now marginalized second-class citizens to the countless "others" who have replaced them. As author Susan Faludi put it, these men feel "stiffed."[36]

Similar to the Charlton Heston-era NRA leadership, many members frame liberal causes as treasonous, anti-American attacks on freedom. They build on the groundwork laid by George Wallace and Richard Nixon, who, according to journalists Thomas Byrne Edsall and Mary Edsall, framed liberalism as, "the favoring of blacks over whites . . . illegitimacy, welfare fraud, street crime, homosexuality, anti-Americanism, as well as moral anarchy among the young."[37] The culture war is being fought by "anti-gunners," revisionists, socialists, and feminists together, according to the most conservative members I spoke with, and they must defend their gun rights, individual rights, heritage, freedoms, and, ultimately, men's hegemony. "To be right-wing means to support the state in its capacity as *enforcer* of order and to oppose the state as *distributor* of wealth and power downward and more equitably in society."[38] By this definition, most committed NRA members are right-wing. Yet there are qualitative differences in their conservatism, and, not by chance, these overlap greatly with how committed members are to the NRA and its Gun Crusade.

PART III

Committing to the NRA, Committing to the Right

6

The Politics of Commitment

"There's not a gun law that's ever been written to promote gun safety," Bob assured me. Bob is white, in his late forties, grew up in the South, attended a military school, and works in a family business involving precision diagnostics. He has been an NRA member for more than twenty years and is currently a consecutive five-year voting member. Bob has been to many NRA annual meetings and is active in the organization "financially and physically." He donates money to the NRA, writes to legislators about gun rights issues, volunteers for the NRA's political lobbying wing, participates in the NRA's Eddie Eagle program (directed at gun safety practices for young children), and is an instructor for the NRA's self-defense program. When I asked Bob why he is so active in the NRA, he responded without hesitation, "Because I believe in the Second Amendment to the Constitution."

Bob would like to see unlimited gun rights but knows that the public does not feel the same way. He is a political pragmatist and is committed to the NRA, because they are "more realistic" than other gun rights organizations: "We can't have everything we want all of the time." For example, he thinks that guns should be allowed in schools so that armed citizens can respond to campus shooters, but he concedes that this "good idea" is "bad publicly" and a "lost cause" that will not help the image of gun owners or the NRA. Bob's main criticism of the NRA is that it is too focused on "image control" and "very heavy damage control" in response to negative media depictions of the NRA as ignorant gun lovers who are unsympathetic to victims of gun violence. NRA employees' dossiers reveal a "very diverse, politically correct bunch," he told me, adding that the organization is always looking for "college-bred" people, sometimes at the expense of applicants who are more committed to gun rights. He understands the NRA's concerns about its image. "[It's] because of the press. They're at our jugular every day." Overall, Bob is a highly committed Critical Mass NRA member.

Fellow member Frank agrees with Bob that the media misrepresents gun rights supporters: "I think there's an attitude [in the media] that the NRA is a bunch of radicals." Unlike Bob, however, Frank is less invested in the NRA and gun rights, believing that the Second Amendment is "probably as important as any of them," but he is not a single-issue, gun rights voter. Frank is white, a married father of three, and grew up in the San Francisco Bay Area but lives in the South. He was in the U.S. Air Force for four years and has a bachelor's degree in marketing, but he is now a busy retiree, including volunteering as a Reserve Deputy with his local sheriff's department. He volunteers because, "I have an interest in good law enforcement and I [can] make a contribution." Frank bought his first .22 rifle at the age of twelve, and has been an annual member of the NRA, on and off, for fifteen to twenty years. In 2002 he attended his first NRA annual meeting, because a friend invited him and he likes Reno. He has been to a couple of NRA fundraising dinners, but, overall, "the NRA [for me] there's not a lot of participation." Frank sees the NRA's priorities as "the gun safety issue as well as the right to maintain your arms," and he is relatively pleased with NRA leadership. Though he believes the leadership is doing well, they could do more to "[combat] a lot of the negative views held by so many people, [that] firearms are simply an instrument of death."

"When I grew up [in the 1950s and 1960s], there wasn't as much negative sentiment about firearms as there is now," Frank said, adding, "I used to ride my bicycle up to the hills in Oakland, and I'd carry my rifle with me on my bicycle so I could go target shooting at the target range." Of course, you can't do that today, he laments. Frank has become more concerned about the loss of gun rights, as our society's views and laws have changed since his childhood. He worries about major political figures in the Democratic Party who want to register and confiscate firearms. However, he supports some gun control laws such as those that work to keep guns out of the hands of dealers selling to criminals or to "people that are deranged." Frank considers himself more an outdoor enthusiast than a gun enthusiast. He says that he is equally committed to the NRA and Wildlife Action, a group that "supports carrying arms, but [is] not a gun organization. It's more of a supporting organization and somewhat environmentally tuned. They have an educational program to teach children how to fish, how to hunt, how to shoot, how to canoe. There's a variety of activities, shooting is just one of them." Frank sees our society becoming more urbanized and culturally opposed to firearms. He worries about the loss of outdoor activities, including hunting and shooting. Because of these fears, Frank is a moderately committed Reserve NRA member.

Types of NRA Members

As my interviews indicate, clearly some NRA members are more committed to the organization than others. Similarly, members were not all of one mind on gun rights threats and whether any form of gun control should exist. Two types of members emerged during the interviews: those deeply committed to gun rights and the NRA, and those only moderately committed (see Table 6.1). The most committed members are the Critical Mass—members like Bob—who can be counted on to donate money and time to the NRA, lobby their representatives for gun rights, and vote only for gun rights candidates. The second type are the Reserves. They are still generally satisfied with the NRA and supportive of gun rights but less financially and emotionally committed to the movement and willing to accept some forms of gun control. They do not think that anyone will try to confiscate guns and eliminate individual rights and freedoms tomorrow, instead viewing this as an incremental threat over time. But if anyone ever tries to force them to register their guns, or, worse, confiscate them, these currently less committed Reserve members—members like Frank—will join the Critical Mass and make protecting gun rights their priority.

A third group of weakly committed NRA members exists, though they are not included here. They are competitive shooters forced to join the NRA to compete in sanctioned events, lifelong hunters whose sporting guns have not been the focus of gun control measures, and apolitical firearms enthusiasts who enjoy collecting firearms from decades and centuries past. The NRA is not only the go-to group for those seeking to align themselves with the largest and most potent defender of gun rights, it is also a publisher of sophisticated magazines that extensively cover everything to do with firearms—from gun history to gun politics to technical specifications to shooting competition results. If you have an interest in firearms, whether for hunting, sport shooting, collecting, or self-defense, you are likely to cross paths with the NRA. Therefore, I speculate that a third group of minimally committed NRA members exists—the Peripherals.

Peripheral members join to compete in matches, get current information on firearms, and generally become more informed about gun-related topics. They are exposed to the gun wars, but the NRA's message does not

TABLE 6.1
Typology of NRA Members

Key Measures of Commitment	Interview Data[a]		Inference
	Critical Mass	Reserves	Peripherals[b]
Membership Status?	Lifetime	Mix of annual and lifetime	Annual
Donate money to NRA?	Yes	Some yes, some no	No
Volunteer for NRA?	Yes	Mostly no	No
Vote in NRA elections?	Yes	Some yes, some no, some unsure if eligible	Not eligible, or no
Attend NRA annual meetings?	One or more times	Once, only because it was near home	No
Satisfied with the NRA?	Yes	Yes	Mixed
Dissatisfied with the NRA?	No. Or, needs to be stronger, compromise less	No. Or, a little too uncompromising, condescending	Too rigid on gun control; (or little knowledge)
Satisfied with NRA Leadership?	Yes	Yes (but don't know that much about them)	Don't know much about them
Perceive serious gun control threats?	Yes. Registration and confiscation a possibility soon or eventually	Mostly yes; some not so sure about confiscation	Mixed
Single issue voter for gun rights?	Some yes, some put gun rights second	No, with a couple exceptions	No

[a] Critical Mass and Reserve member data represent general patterns. Not everyone in the Critical Mass is a lifetime member who donates and volunteers to the organization. Overall, though, Critical Mass members are likely to be and do these, and much more so than Reserve members

[b] Peripherals are a hypothesized third group of members. All of the data in this column are based on inferences rather than interview data

resonate as strongly with them. Peripherals do not attend meetings, donate money, vote, or pay much attention to the organization or its leadership, beyond their narrow apolitical interests. Compared to non-member gun enthusiasts, the Peripherals are somewhat more committed to the NRA but are not excited about its politics. Many non-member gun owners are likely turned off by the NRA's conservative politics.

Committed NRA members are Gun Crusaders. There are also undoubtedly a fair number of Gun Crusaders who are not NRA members, because they think the NRA is too much of a political animal and too willing to compromise away some gun rights. Leaders of gun rights groups such as

Gun Owners of America, for example, often criticize the NRA for its lack of gun rights purity. As the largest and most influential gun rights social movement organization, however, the NRA enjoys the largest organized group of Gun Crusaders. Gun Crusaders have felt threatened by challenges to gun rights and frontier masculinity since the 1960s. The NRA frames multiple threats to gun rights, and presumably gun owners join the organization (at least in part) because they agree with the views and practices of the NRA.

In the course of my research, I wondered how closely aligned the leadership and membership are; in the words of sociologists Francesca Polletta and James Jasper, "Is the identity a group projects publicly the same one that its members experience?"[1] The answer is "yes" for Critical Mass members and "mostly yes, but sometimes no" for Reserve members. This answer leads to a second question: Why are some members more committed to the NRA and the defense of gun rights than others? The most committed members, the Critical Mass, give lots of their time and money to the NRA because the NRA's message resonates with them: liberals are trying to take away gun rights and other individual rights via a culture war, and only NRA members' defense of *America's First Freedom*, gun rights, can secure the future of frontier masculinity values and freedoms. This message also resonates somewhat with Reserve NRA members, but not as consistently or strongly because their gun and conservative politics are less hardcore.

The Critical Mass

Collective action needs a "Critical Mass" that does the majority of the work or provides the necessary funding or recruits to initiate a social movement. The Critical Mass is a small segment of the population that makes large contributions to the movement, whereas the majority of the population generally offers little or nothing.[2] Among the twenty NRA members I interviewed, eight provided critical contributions to the NRA through various forms of commitment (see the appendix): Ben, Albert, Donald, Bob, Rick, Mark, Quincy, and Walter. Each of these eight Critical Mass members is eligible to vote in NRA elections (they have been members for at least five consecutive years) and most of them have life memberships, including two who have committed to the highest level of membership—NRA Benefactor status. The most recent member in this group joined a decade ago, but most have belonged to the NRA for several decades, often having joined in their teenage years.

Two important issues merit consideration when assessing the length of time NRA members have been part of the organization. First, the NRA has changed dramatically since the 1977 Revolt, and many Critical Mass members joined prior to its transition to a social movement organization. Second, although membership status is probably linked to financial resources (some members cannot afford lifetime dues), the Critical Mass and Reserve members I interviewed are not divided by income. It is reasonable to assume that spending the extra money to increase membership status is a sign that these Critical Mass members are highly committed to the NRA.

Donations to the NRA distinguish which members either respond to the group's fundraising pleas or simply contribute without any organizational prompting. Almost every Critical Mass member has donated money beyond their membership dues to the NRA. For those who are well-off financially, donating money may not be much of a sacrifice. Still, it shows that these members are strongly aligned with at least some portion of the NRA's goals. Perhaps the strongest display of commitment to the NRA is volunteer work. At least half the Critical Mass members volunteer as NRA recruiters, annual meeting volunteers, or NRA course instructors for self-defense courses such as "Refuse to Be a Victim" or for firearms training courses. Of those who volunteer, most are involved in two or three NRA programs.

All Critical Mass members I interviewed are eligible to vote in NRA elections, and only one does not participate (97% of all NRA members and 90% of all eligible voters do not vote; see the appendix). Most Critical Mass members have been to at least one annual meeting somewhere in the country, and several have been to more. Just one member in this group attended a meeting only because it was near his home, something more common among Reserve members.

Another indicator of members' allegiance to the NRA is how satisfied they are with their organization and its leadership. Quincy thinks that the NRA is "probably one of the most effective grassroots organizations out there." Other Critical Mass members agree, such as Albert, who, despite what he views as too many NRA compromises on gun control legislation in the past, said, "You gotta understand, they're still the biggest organization in the country and . . . they're still doing a lot of good." Ben flatly stated, "If it hadn't been for the NRA a lot of places would not be allowed to have guns. Probably our guns would have been confiscated." Walter was pleased with LaPierre and Heston, because they have "[moved] [the NRA] towards not so much a . . . political sledge hammer, but a guiding hand towards responsible legislation." When Heston became an officer, "[I] bumped my membership up another notch to Benefactor," Walter reported. Mark thinks that the earlier NRA factional struggles are over, and now the leaders and Board of Directors are fine: "There's some of everybody. There's a few radical, or . . . a few aggressive members and there are a few . . . more moderate [members]." Like all Critical Mass members, many of whom offer their unqualified devotion, Mark is a satisfied and committed NRA member.

Still, Critical Mass members express some dissatisfaction. Among all those I interviewed, four major complaints were that the NRA is compromised in its defense of the Second Amendment, is not strong enough, is unprofessional, and is too radical. These critiques range from wanting the NRA to fight harder for gun rights to wanting the organization to be more moderate. Overall, Critical Mass members do not want the NRA to compromise and hope the organization becomes bigger and more powerful. The Critical Mass believes that the Second Amendment is under serious attack (or will be soon) and do not want the NRA to compromise on gun control. Critical Mass members are highly committed to the organization and generally only find fault with the NRA when it takes actions that may jeopardize a fundamentalist defense of the right to keep and bear arms.

One Critical Mass member critiqued the NRA for being too radical in its position on gun rights. Walter chose to distance himself from the organization when hard-liner Neal Knox had a higher organizational profile. "I did become inactive for about seven years in the early to mid-eighties because of the directions that certain people were trying to take the organization in," he told me, "and I felt that the organization was compromised and didn't have to be so hard-lined." Under the leaders of the new millennium—Heston and LaPierre—the NRA did not publicly compromise on gun rights, and yet they projected a more moderate image to most members. A few Critical Mass members complained about NRA fundraising letters. Quincy said that sometimes the NRA sends him "kinda hoaky fund-raisers," but he just throws them away.

Critical Mass members generally only critique the NRA for *not* being hard-line enough it its defense of gun rights. Albert believes that the NRA compromised too much in the mid-1990s, not standing firm enough on federal firearms legislation debates during the Clinton presidency. He said, "they compromised too much of ourselves away and I was a little upset with them at the time." Lately, however, he feels they have taken a firmer stance and this has increased his satisfaction and commitment.

Bob thinks that programs designed for women and children are evidence that the NRA is overly worried about its public image. He also shared a story of the NRA caving in to "political correctness" by hiring a woman with a degree in Far Eastern Language Studies who wasn't even an NRA member, simply to increase the staff's credentials. "I believe it hurts your organization" to have non-committed employees working for it, Bob stated. He thinks it is an "egregious error" not to screen applicants based on their gun rights views. Mark is not entirely satisfied with the NRA only because "it's not near as strong as I'd like it, not near the number of members I'd like." He wants to see the organization increase its power, and "I'd like to see them be more high profile, but at the same time the higher profile the more [of a] target they are and [then] everybody says 'Oh they're terrible, they're buying elections' and all that good stuff." Critical Mass members worry that anti-gun forces and political pressures will reduce the NRA's effectiveness.

While all members perceive threats to gun rights, there are a range of perspectives on the degree of threat and how fundamentalist a stance the NRA should take. As a whole, Critical Mass members perceive a greater threat to gun rights than less committed NRA Reserve members, and generally do not feel the NRA should concede anything to gun control proponents, whom they label "anti-gunners." Albert sees a link between threats to gun rights and threats to broader freedoms. "I try to encourage people, as many people as I can to try to get a license to carry because it sends a very clear message to the Socialist Party in this country," he says. Albert senses a strong threat to gun rights. Overall, every Critical Mass member feels as though there is the possibility of registration and confiscation of firearms in the United States, whether quite soon or due to gun control forces chipping away at gun rights over time.

To further gauge their commitment to the NRA and gun rights, I asked members if they cast their votes based solely on whether candidates support or oppose gun control. Overall, the Critical Mass place the Second Amendment as either their single or primary issue, or find that their broader politics mesh with the pro-gun stance of their ideal candidates. Charlton Heston's promise to fight to the death before allowing the government to take away his guns reflects, at least rhetorically, the ultimate sacrifice for a cause. Heston believed, like so many of his fellow Critical Mass members, that the loss of gun rights would result in the loss of all individual rights and freedoms. These highly committed NRA members see gun rights as the foundation of their political, moral, and sometimes religious views, and many of them would therefore not hesitate to use their guns to prevent losing their guns.

The Reserves

The Critical Mass provides a dedicated base of NRA and gun rights support, but other members numbering in the hundreds of thousands also contribute to the NRA's political power. Reserve members are moderately committed to the NRA but are ready to jump into action and join the Critical Mass if imminent and serious threats to gun rights appear. They do not perceive these threats now, however, which partly explains their qualified support of the NRA.

Of the twelve members I interviewed and classify as Reserves—Craig, Ian, Pete, Irene, Helen, Gerry, Frank, Andrew, Harry, Ernie, Zach, and Nicole—only four are lifetime members and none have Patron, Endowment or Benefactor status. The remaining eight join annually, and only a couple have been members for five consecutive years.

The newest Reserve members joined in the last few years (partly because they are young), but most of them have been members, on and off, for ten to twenty years and more. At times renewing their memberships and sometimes not, these Reserve members have a much weaker commitment to the organization than Critical Mass members. Of the Reserves with lifetime memberships, one increased his commitment because the NRA was offering a discount, and another simply wanted to further a personal fundraising agenda. The two senior Reserve members have been with the NRA for four decades. One joined because he wanted to buy a surplus rifle (which was offered at a heavy discount thanks to an NRA-U.S. government program). The other, Harry, reported,

> I've been an annual member for a long time and switched to a lifetime member when George [H. W.] Bush first canceled his membership after Wayne LaPierre made inappropriate comments about the [Bureau of Alcohol, Tobacco, and Firearms] being jack-booted thugs. I thought that comment was appropriate, but I'm not politically correct.

No other Reserve member increased his or her commitment in support of the NRA's uncompromising gun rights stance.

The majority of Reserves show a wavering commitment to the organization by not keeping up their memberships over the years. Ernie exemplifies this when discussing his history with the NRA:

> You know I can't remember the first time I joined. And like I said there's been times when I've lost my membership because I was traveling, moving [from] place to place and if I had to, to tell you the truth, I couldn't even take an honest guess [when I first joined].

Truly committed members, like the Critical Mass, are not only likely to have a lifetime commitment but would presumably keep their memberships and contact information current because of their devotion to the organization and gun rights.

The Reserves are also less financially committed to the NRA, though not because they have less money. Only three Reserves I interviewed contribute funds beyond their annual dues. Further, unlike Critical Mass members, not a single Reserve member does volunteer work for the NRA. Many Reserves are not eligible to vote in NRA elections, but of those who are, three said that they have voted at least once. One cannot recall if he ever voted, and another did not know he was eligible. The Reserves are less familiar with the workings of the organization, partly because they are not strongly committed to it. Reserve member attendance at NRA annual meetings is mixed. Most have been to one meeting, showing a degree of commitment, but none claim to have attended more than one meeting. More important, all but one Reserve member went to a meeting only because it was near their homes or those of family and friends, or to attend the gun show and not the organizational meetings and sessions. The one exception to this pattern made the trip only to work on a fundraising project.

Reserve members share less satisfaction and more dissatisfaction with the organization and its leadership than do the Critical Mass. Craig said that he is "not always in favor of what they're doing, but they get results." Fellow Reserve member Frank told me that he was not sure how the NRA is doing. Ernie is pleased with the NRA, but said that his judgment is based solely from a competitive shooter's standpoint—the primary reason he is a member of the organization.

Though a handful of Reserves do not offer their full support, overall this group is happy with the NRA. Pete cited both gun rights and the availability of gun ranges as reasons for his support. "If it wasn't for them," he says, "we more than likely wouldn't have the rights we have today . . . if it wasn't for the NRA it'd be tough to have a place to shoot." Ernie is also pleased with how the NRA has helped shooters.

> I thought twenty years ago that [competitive shooting] was a dying sport [but] it's still alive and it's even more alive now than it was then. That's a good thing and I think it's basically due to the NRA. It's not due to anybody else that's for sure. I give the NRA kudos for what they've done.

Gerry believes that the NRA is "very effective" because they let "the average American know that he has rights and that those rights need to be protected." Another Reserve also expressed his pleasure: "Overall I think it's a great organization" (Zach).

A relatively new member, Nicole, joined the NRA partly because of its reputation. "Obviously, I'd heard about them long before I ever got involved with them, but I really didn't follow what they were doing. But since I've been a member I've been pleased with the organization," she said. She is also satisfied with the lobbying aspects of the NRA, which she finds to be one of its primary strengths. Irene thinks the NRA is doing well:

> Their numbers are so big! They've got millions. I mean, it's like three to four million members. That carries a lot of weight. I think that they are very strong politically and I think they are very strong financially.

Andrew also feels that the NRA is powerful, mistakenly believing that membership is upwards of six million. He believes that, as an NRA member, he is part of a power base: "I think it means helping me be an activist . . . It means that I'm educated about my special interest." Though some Reserve members offer only partial support of the NRA, the group as a whole is mostly satisfied with the organization.

The Reserves also have mixed views about NRA leadership. Reserves mostly support NRA leaders, and yet there was a distinct lack of knowledge in this group compared to the Critical Mass. "Who was the movie actor?" Craig asked me, and after I name Charlton Heston, he said, "Yeah, I liked him. Certainly you could trust him." As with virtually every NRA member, the Reserves were quite satisfied with Charlton Heston's NRA presidency, but they had little to say about the person who runs the organization, Wayne LaPierre. Some, like Craig, think "LaPierre's probably doing a good job," but they were not familiar with specific actions or positions he has taken. Craig added, "You don't have any personal feelings regarding him [like you did Heston]." Some of the Reserves are more familiar with LaPierre and can discuss his individual contributions to the NRA, separating him from Heston, but the enthusiasm is generally qualified or muted. Ernie expressed a perspective typical of Reserve members: "I think that the NRA does present a fairly good image, although the media tries to see to it that it doesn't. I think that Wayne LaPierre and Charles Heston have always managed to present themselves as professional people." This is a qualitatively different response than Critical Mass members, who think NRA leaders are "charismatic and articulate," and "doing a fantastic job."

Reserve members are not strongly dissatisfied with the organization, but they have concerns that mostly differ from those of the Critical Mass. Not a single Reserve member criticized the NRA for *not* taking a strong enough stand on gun rights or for lacking political strength. The Reserves, unlike the Critical Mass, generally do not want to see the organization take hard-line stands on all gun control issues. Instead, most Reserve members criticize the NRA for their lack of professionalism and for being too radical.

Several Reserves think that the NRA should be much more active in children's firearm-safety education and outreach to younger shooters, which contrasts with Critical Mass member Bob's view that some of these programs are merely intended to improve the NRA's image. Reserve members think that the NRA does not always spend its money wisely. A few are unhappy about the NRA's fundraising tactics. Zach spoke of peers who have "quit the NRA because they were always getting phone calls for money," but said he has not had that problem. He acknowledged that "they're after money . . . but that doesn't mean you have to send them money."

The most jaded person on this topic was lifetime member Harry, who immediately began ticking off a list of complaints about NRA fundraising practices when I first met him in Reno outside the convention center where I was recruiting interview participants. And, later, when we spoke by phone for an interview, he detailed his complaints: he is unhappy about the number of mailings he receives, their packaging, their hyperbolic content and condescending tone, and how these detract from other important aspects of the organization. Here is just a small sampling of his objections:

My thing, or beef, with the NRA is all the mailings I get . . . I think they should be spending a lot of their time educating the American people. The NRA seems to treat us . . . like we're a bunch of good ol' boys that just go down the highway and shoot up road signs; [like] we're not educated. The kind of stuff I get in the mail from the NRA kind of looks like the stuff I get from Publisher's Clearing House . . . Then they send me surveys. With survey questions [like], "Do you want more gun control?" Obviously not or I wouldn't be a member of the NRA . . . I think that they are insulting my intelligence and I don't like it . . . It's like they cry wolf. It seems like every other month there is a bill before Congress to destroy the Second Amendment. I realize that it's a constant problem and a constant fight, but they are just not factual . . . That is a big problem. They turn people off. If they are going to keep members they need to not harass them with so much paperwork and scare tactics, it's just insulting the intelligence [of members] and it's really irritating when they do that.

Harry, as noted, is a lifetime member and so his commitment to the NRA, though strongly qualified, is permanent. He told me,

I look upon the NRA as a necessary evil. They are the biggest organization fighting for Second Amendment rights. And I just wish that they would have a different tact. I don't see any ads on TV. Maybe in [his state, which strongly supports gun rights] they don't need them. Maybe they are playing ads in Los Angeles and San Francisco [and I don't see them].

Though Harry believes that other gun rights organizations are fighting the good fight, in his view they pale in comparison with the NRA's size and influence. People tend to join movements that are big and rich, because they don't want to throw their money away or find themselves on the losing side of contentious politics.[3] Harry concluded, "But that's the only organization that we have. That's part of the problem . . . I'll support them because they are the bacon. But I would certainly like them to change their tactics."

Some Reserve members disagree with the NRA's no-compromise gun control positions as well as some of the organization's related views and politics. Craig flatly stated, "I see no reason to have automatic, semiautomatic firearms . . . I know there's politics in any organization, but you gotta roll over on certain stuff for the common good." Zach said that the only time he "had [a] major problem with the NRA" was when Wayne

LaPierre made the comment about "jack-booted thugs. In fact," Zach recalled, "[that] was the only time I quit." Fellow Reserve member Gerry is unsure about the direction the NRA is taking, worrying that it is becoming too radical:

> The political side, some of them are a little too right-wing for me. But I mean they do need to inform the people of their rights and that they deserve those rights. On the other hand, sometimes I think they get a little too far out there. . . . In the last four years or so I think [the NRA has] shifted to spend a lot of it on lobbying and trying to promote their own Far-Right agenda to a certain degree.

None of the more committed Critical Mass members criticized the NRA for being overly fundamentalist, whereas several Reserve members stated that the NRA should compromise on some gun control legislation, believing that not all forms of gun control legislation pose serious threats to gun rights.

Like Critical Mass members, however, most Reserve members also perceive serious threats to gun rights, although some think just the opposite. "Let's get realistic here," Gerry said. "I don't think [gun confiscation] would happen either way . . . in some ways I think the NRA paints too grim a picture." Zach stated that "[the Second Amendment] is very important. I think we need it and we should never lose it. It was put in there for a reason . . . but I don't think it's any more important than the rest of the amendments." Unlike many Critical Mass members and the NRA itself, many Reserve members view the Second Amendment as simply one more important part of the Bill of Rights, not the foundation of freedom.

Ernie shared his moderate NRA views when he discussed gun violence:

> I read both sides of the issue and somewhere in the middle lies the truth. The [Handgun Control, Inc.] people believe that having guns around leads to fifty thousand homicides a year and the NRA says there's none. There's no doubt . . . that if [a firearm is] out of the house and somebody gets pissed at the next one, that may cause a problem. But I certainly would feel, in this day and age especially, quite insecure without having something [for] defending myself.

Ernie not only thinks that NRA members should be prepared to forsake some gun rights for other issues but also that gun control advocates have some legitimate concerns: "Some gun rights I think we shouldn't have. Like these AK 47s. I see no need for those whatsoever. They're not a sporting rifle. They're out for killing." Ernie acknowledges that his views on gun rights and politics do not reflect those of the most committed members, saying that "I'm probably a more moderate member of the NRA."

Reserve members often cite their interest in guns, rather than gun politics, as their reason for joining the NRA. They originally joined the NRA not because they perceived serious threats to gun rights and wanted to align themselves with the self-proclaimed defenders of the Second Amendment but because they hunted or wanted to shoot competitively. Ian said he is a member "because I got into shooting again on a regular basis and I felt like joining the NRA." But he is not at odds with the NRA's focus on preserving gun rights: "We're losing our rights to carry arms and I, basically, I wanted to know that I could protect my own family." Andrew pointed out that the NRA regulates competitive shooting and that, to compete, shooters must join the organization just as bowlers must join a national bowling organization to compete. This is why he first joined the NRA a couple of decades ago.

> So, that's really what motivated me to join, because [back then] I wasn't as politically active or as politically knowledgeable that there was even a threat to the Second Amendment. I was just oblivious to it. I never thought that the Constitution was in jeopardy in any way.

After becoming a member, he now perceives threats to gun rights, and, more broadly, the Constitution. Members are exposed to the NRA's framings of threats to gun rights through magazines, fundraising letters, and other contacts. This often increases their commitment to the NRA and the defense of gun rights. Andrew noted, however, that many apolitical gun enthusiasts (as he was originally) are compelled to join the NRA if they want to compete in matches.

Only two Reserve members—Irene and Andrew—are single-issue, gun rights voters. Reserve members overwhelmingly feel that guns are only one of many factors that determine their vote. This is a decidedly moderate interpretation of the importance of gun rights and contrasts with the position of the NRA and most Critical Mass members that "rolling over" on the Second Amendment will ultimately lead to the end of all individual rights and freedoms.

Compared to their Reserve peers, Critical Mass members join the NRA at higher levels, have been members longer, donate money to the NRA more frequently, are much more likely to volunteer for the NRA, cast ballots more often in NRA elections, and attend annual meetings more frequently. Critical Mass members are more knowledgeable about and satisfied with both the organization and its leadership. Reserve members are much more likely to be critical of the NRA because it is too radical, whereas Critical Mass members are more likely to argue just the opposite—that the NRA needs to assert its dominance and not back down from any legislative attack on gun rights. Critical Mass members are more likely than the Reserves to perceive serious threats to gun rights and therefore make this their sole or primary issue come election time. There is a greater degree of "frame alignment" between the NRA and Critical Mass members than Reserves; that is, the NRA's message of threats to gun rights and freedom resonates more strongly with Critical Mass members.[4] Reserve members are much more likely to be willing to compromise with gun control advocates and rarely identify themselves as single-issue gun rights voters. Both Critical Mass and Reserve members are committed to the NRA, though there is a clear difference in the degree of this commitment.

Who Are the Critical Mass and the Reserves?

> But I don't agree with the NRA totally in all the issues either, or I would be a very right-wing Republican. (NRA Reserve member Gerry)

To understand why some members are more committed to the NRA and gun rights than others, we must revisit how the NRA discusses gun rights and threats to these rights. The NRA frames threats to gun rights as threats to individual rights and other broad freedoms. NRA leaders identify the Second Amendment as the foundation of freedom, that is, of conservative white men's version of freedom, or frontier masculinity. Gun rights, NRA members argue, are under siege from Democrats, socialists, feminists, and other so-called left-wing groups that desire greater government control over both firearms and other individual rights and freedoms. The NRA defends gun rights in a narrow sense, but, in a broader sense, it is defending frontier masculinity.

If the NRA's message is aimed at conservative white men, those who stand to benefit the most from NRA politics, then common sense suggests that the most committed members to the organization will share the NRA's decidedly conservative political views. Critical Mass members do just this. Less committed members like the Reserves are not as conservative but still identify with NRA messages about threats to frontier masculinity. Presumably the third and least committed group, the Peripherals, have the most moderate political views of the three NRA member types, yet still usually identify as centrist-leaning conservatives.

The most committed NRA members I interviewed, the Critical Mass, are all white men who self-identify as either conservative or Republican. Of these eight Critical Mass members, six are or were professionals or small business owners (a few are already retired), and two hold well-paying, blue-collar occupations. I did not ask how much money they make, but, as a group, they appear to be solidly middle-class with some living quite comfortably. Partly because of their older age as a group—most Critical Mass members are in their fifties, sixties, and seventies, and none is younger than forty—and the higher proportion of men in the military during previous generations, about three-fourths of these men, most of whom predate the Vietnam War-era, either served in the military or were involved in it during their education (for example, serving in the Reserve Officers' Training Corp [ROTC]).

At least half the Critical Mass displays attitudes consistent with Christian Right beliefs. Rick connected this to political parties: "We're Christians, we don't believe in abortion. The Democrats do." Donald commented that if we "put prayer back in schools and rely on the Ten Commandments, we'd be a lot better off." Ben was one of many members who considers lesbians and gays to be problematic. "I'm a Christian and can't comprehend a man sleeping with another man." The Christian Right has been a key player in the late-20th-Century resurgence of conservative politics, so finding overlap among these political-religious views and NRA members is not surprising. Overall, the Critical Mass are older, more likely to be white, more likely to be men, more religious, more aligned with Right politics, and more financially stable than both the U.S. population as a whole and NRA Reserve members.

The twelve Reserve members I interviewed differ from the Critical Mass on more than just their level of commitment to the NRA and gun rights. Three Reserve members are women—two white and one Latina—and the remaining nine are white men. Almost all Reserves self-identify as conservative or Republican, although this group also has two members who consider themselves Libertarians and one who identifies as a "labor Democrat." There are five professionals or small business owners, two well-paid blue-collar workers, two students, one sales representative, and two who identify as semi-retired. Slightly more than half have had some form of military affiliation, all of them men. Their age range, from early twenties to seventies, is much larger than that of Critical Mass members.

Somewhat less than half the Reserve members hold beliefs consistent with the Christian Right, although several criticize this branch of conservatism. Similar to the Critical Mass, a handful of Reserve members hold strong religious beliefs that likely adhere to a Christian Right philosophy. Ian is vocal about the role of religion in the United States as he cites culture war battles:

> The government has no right to come in and say that prayer has to be taken out of school, you can't mention God in the Constitution; you can't have a Constitution with the Ten Commandments stuck on the courthouse of a federal building, because of separation of church and state. The Constitution never says anything about separation of church and state. "The state will not show any respect towards an established religion." That's what it says . . . I don't like using the term "Christian Nation" anymore, because we're not. But we're still a good country.

When I asked Frank what major problems he saw facing the nation today, he offered, among others, "the lack of spiritual values." Similarly, Gerry claimed that the sources of our problems are twofold: "One is momma leaving the home, and the other is that God got replaced by the dollar bill [for] so many people. And that took us away from our basic rights and wrongs." These views are representative of a large proportion of Critical Mass and Reserve members, reflecting the overall conservatism of the NRA and its two most committed groups of members.

Other Reserve members share mixed religious views or even flatly reject the beliefs of the Christian Right. In Craig's view, "overall . . . [the Christian Right] don't impress me at all." But he went on to say: "We like to call ourselves a religious country. Why is it we can't say [laughing] 'God Bless America?'" He also supports some form of prayer in school.

Harry is the least religious of the bunch. Continuing his train of thought on his inability to grasp liberal political beliefs, he commented,

"It's just like it's hard for me to understand strong religious beliefs. I'm not a Christian . . . I find it hard [to understand] how an educated person can follow some of these beliefs." Another Reserve member, Zach, admitted that he is "not a real religious person" when it comes to abortion. He supports a woman's right to choose, arguing that, in many cases, especially for young girls, the option to abort a pregnancy is best. Still, he is undecided about the position of the Christian Right that an abortion at any stage of pregnancy is murder.

The Reserves are more likely than the general U.S. population to be men, white, middle-class, and politically right-wing, but, again, less so than among the Critical Mass. I did not ask either group to discuss their sexuality. No one mentioned same-sex partners, and, judging from their views on homosexuality and gay rights, probably all or nearly all these members would identify (at least publicly) as straight.

A key demographic distinction between NRA members and the U.S. population is regional location. Nearly 80% of Americans lived in "urban areas" in 2000.[5] NRA members are far more likely to live in rural areas, where hunting and shooting is more accessible. Firearms, especially gun violence, are a much greater concern in urban areas. "In the city the guns are killing people," Irene said. She believes that this is why so few people of color attend NRA meeting. Walter mentioned that those who grow up around firearms and view them as simply another tool have no problems with gun violence, but, "unfortunately in the inner city [a gun] becomes an equalizer."

Political Party Affiliations and Attitudes

Critical Mass members would probably be happy to discover that NRA leaders attend, speak at, and are active participants in the annual Conservative Political Action Conference, which draws speakers such as President G. W. Bush, conservative commentators like Robert Novak and Ann Coulter, and a long list of conservative organizations such as Americans for Tax Reform, the Heritage Foundation, and the Media Research Center.[6] After attending two annual meetings, analyzing NRA magazines and fundraising letters, and speaking at length with members, I find it safe to say that the NRA is a conservative organization. Jokes about liberals and hostility toward Democrats is overt at NRA meetings, whether a member off-handedly remarks that he would like to bomb the famously liberal city of Berkeley or members refer to politicians in the Democratic Party as fighting for gun control legislation.

A strange dance sometimes occurs at these gatherings. NRA leaders must play up their political neutrality as a not-for-profit organization devoted to the "nonpartisan" issue of defending gun rights, yet simultaneously they must let Critical Mass and Reserve members know that the leaders share their conservative political beliefs. In truth, gun politics are anything but nonpartisan. Republicans, especially at the federal level, typically offer nearly unqualified support for gun rights, whereas gun control proponents are virtually all Democrats. As one member explained, the country needs more conservatives in power "[because] conservatives are pro-gun" (Donald). The NRA also knows who "the bacon" is—they must appeal to conservative white men if they are to continue to maintain a sizable Critical Mass.

The six most conservative members, all belonging to the Critical Mass, are extremely Far Right in their political views. Only two of the eight Critical Mass members have more moderate beliefs, and none of the less committed Reserve members hold political views to the Far Right. Although the connection is not exact, clearly the more conservative NRA members are far more likely to be the most dedicated to the organization.

Madison Brigade member postings are not comparable to in-depth member interviews, but they reflect the same pattern of commitment and conservatism. These members responded to an NRA fundraising letter by donating money, which allowed them to create and post their thoughts on the NRA's Madison Brigade Web site. This (admittedly thin) evidence of their commitment is matched by their overall highly conservative postings and is consistent with Critical Mass interview data. Just as the most conservative members are the most committed, the less (though still) conservative members are much less likely to be highly dedicated to the NRA. Presumably the least conservative NRA members feel no commitment to the organization much at all. Individuals holding left-wing views are highly unlikely to be affiliated with the NRA.

Donald spoke happily of his lifelong commitment to conservative politics: "I voted for Goldwater in '64 and I'm proud of it [laughing, cackling]. After we saw what happened afterwards, there [were] a lot of other people who wished they did too." Quincy stated that he has been a registered Republican all his life, and upon turning eighteen, he promptly voted for Ronald Reagan in 1980. Strongly committed NRA members, like other conservatives, laud various golden years and idyllic figures of conservatism. Bob said there is "no doubt" that the 1980s was the best decade in U.S. history, because "we had the greatest President" and escaped suffering under Jimmy Carter. He cheerfully strolled down memory lane:

To see Reagan come riding in . . . and turn this country around . . . under the kind of circumstances he was facing . . . [it was] the most artful thing in the history of mankind to do what he did [while facing a Democratic Congress].

In Bob's view, Reagan ranks as the number one president in U.S. history. Another Critical Mass member, Donald, reflected on the past while bemoaning the present:

We need nationalists like we had in the 1800s; built the country, you know. Took over the Wild West. Made our country what it is, set the basis for our country. They were nationalists—America first, everybody else second. We don't have enough of that. That's by definition a Patriot—America first . . . Everybody was a nationalist then. Or the majority of them were [who were] in power. The government was pro-United States. Not a bunch of liberal pantywaists, or pansies. I kinda like Pat Buchanan's ideas. He's a pretty good nationalist. But he can't get elected [laughing]. He comes on too strong . . . So I'm kind of a nationalist. U.S. over all. Hitler used to say "Germany over all." I think that way about the [United States]. U.S. first and the rest of the world second.

Donald believes that conservatives must maintain political power to secure the freedoms he cherishes. Yet, the comparison that comes to his mind when thinking about American patriotism and nationalism is that of fascist Germany under Hitler. Donald fears liberals retaining political power, because he believes they are anti-United States and more inclined than conservative nationalists to exert greater government control over Americans.

Critical Mass members are almost all highly supportive of very conservative politicians of the past and present, with many expressing their support of President George W. Bush and his cabinet and appointments. Ben is pleased that Bush selected staunch pro-Second Amendment advocate John Ashcroft as Attorney General because, unlike his Democratic predecessor Janet Reno, "[Ashcroft] is not stupid and led by ultra-liberal idiots. That's a redundant phrase—ultra-liberals are idiots."

Mark told me, "more often than not I would be a conservative Republican, which would basically put me on the side of most either neutral or pro-gun people." "I guess I'm a pretty conservative individual," Walter acknowledged, pointing out that "many of [the political action groups I participate in] are Republican-affiliated or Libertarian-affiliated [laughing]."

One Critical Mass member recently switched parties for the first time in his life, becoming a Republican because they support gun rights and other issues he cares about. But Republicans are hurting organized labor, he said , and "I'm a union man . . . they don't protect the working people" (Rick). Feeling painted into a corner and having to decide between his workplace protections or firearms protections, Rick chose the latter, thereby reaffirming his commitment to the NRA.

NRA Reserve members are much more moderate than the Critical Mass, though still almost entirely politically Right. Pete declared, "As long as a Republican wins, I enjoy politics." Irene said she always votes Republican. Reserve members are much more cautious about stating their allegiances to conservative politics, however, particularly views of the Far Right. To Frank, a quality candidate is "conservative, concerned, a person that exhibits wisdom [in] what they do [and] what they say. A person that doesn't seem to be an extremist. A person's way of thinking, thinks [logically]." I asked Craig if he is aligned with any particular political view, to which he replied, "No, I wouldn't align myself with anybody. I'll vote for [whom] I think is the right [candidate]." Yet he admitted, "I'm registered Republican. If you're not with one of the two major parties, you have no voice."

Craig is not the only reluctant Republican among Reserve members. Ian said, "I'm kind of getting tired of both parties." He likes independent parties, but conceded, "I'm a Republican." Another member partially identifies with the G.O.P. but leaves the door open: "I'm considered a Republican, but I wouldn't be nailed to the wall on that one. If I don't like something I go the other way" (Zach). These members are clearly not as committed to Republicans or Far-Right politics as are their Critical Mass peers.

Andrew's views split between both major parties depending on the issue. He said that he is "on the fence on so many issues," but on issues such as the environment, Civil Rights, and labor, others would not hesitate to label him a Democrat. Yet his positions on spending, the Second Amendment, religion, and education show that he is "conservative all the way." Andrew wants to vote independent but thinks it's a wasted vote. But he "[doesn't] believe in the party system" and finds both parties to be somewhat extreme. But prior to the 2004 election, he planned to vote for President Bush because of his position on gun rights, along with terrorism and Iraq. Thus Andrew is a moderate but ultimately a single-issue voter along gun rights, which leads him to vote Republican most of the time. Two

Reserve members call themselves Libertarians, with one explaining that individuals holding this perspective "tend to be a little more liberal in social issues but conservative when it comes to the country and economic issues" (Harry). Overall, however, Libertarians lean toward conservatism.

Sharing a mixture of liberal and conservative views similar to Andrew, Harry stated,

> I get concerned when I look at the Right or the Left. That the right-wing people may get too radical sometimes, they remind me of the Republican Party somewhat hijacked by the Religious Right. They have good moral standards, but they also sometimes put their own beliefs above the Constitution. I look at the left side, the Democratic Party got hijacked by the socialists. There's been an argument between socialism and capitalism; it's been going on since we've started. You have to look at the balance and I think the Libertarians have that balance.

Harry and his fellow Libertarian, Nicole, who joined a Republican group at her college, both reveal much more moderate views than right-wing Critical Mass members. "We look back in history, [Joseph] McCarthy, that guy wasn't an American as far as I'm concerned," Harry commented, "his tactics were totally un-American. People have a right to express their political views whether they are communist, socialist, or whatever." Though he is legitimately worried about the United States creeping toward socialism, Harry doesn't want to violate constitutional rights by stamping out liberal opposition. Harry, like most of his Reserve peers, is conservative on most issues, but only moderately so.

Gerry is an interesting exception to the rule. He is the only member who identifies as a Democrat. "I'm a labor Democrat. I have been all my life," Gerry stated, "and when we had twelve years of Reagan and Bush [that] did hurt me. My wages went down; they've beaten my conditions and wages down [and] I was out of work more." His Critical Mass counterpart and former fellow laborer, Rick, ultimately sided with his gun rights over his worker rights in the 2000 elections. According to Gerry, this dilemma was widespread:

> What I saw in [the 2000] election was a classic example . . . I saw labor Democrats that have voted Democrat probably most of their [lives] that were totally confused because they thought, "If I vote [Republican] they're going to take away my job. If I vote [Democrat] they're going to

take away my gun." Well that is a hell of a thing to sit and try to figure . . . well, do I want my gun or do I want my job?

To a non-gun owner or non-Gun Crusader, that seems an obvious choice—you can't pay your rent or mortgage with your gun. But committed NRA members see gun rights as *America's First Freedom*, the foundation of their political philosophy and individual identity. Jobs (or unemployment) are temporary. But rights and freedoms are forever.

As Gerry conveyed, the gun debate is deeply partisan. Those supporting gun rights but not committed to conservative politics often find themselves faced with two unpleasant options. Gerry remains a Democrat, though he is a centrist politically who worries about partisan politics: "Either way, if you go too far Left or too far Right it's not good." Gerry directly addressed why he is not more committed to the NRA:

> The political side, some [in the NRA] are a little too right-wing for me. But I mean they do need to inform the people of their rights and that they deserve those rights. On the other hand sometimes I think they get a little too far out there . . . Because I do get the impression that they are very conservative, ultra right-wing in a lot of ways that I'm not. They are very careful. They try not to present that issue because if they did, all of us that were labor-oriented would drop out . . . In the last four years or so I think [the NRA has] shifted to spend a lot of [time] lobbying and trying to promote their own Far Right agenda to a certain degree. I'm not really in favor of that, but I don't necessarily think I should drop out because of it either.

Unlike Critical Mass members who are worried only about "ultra-liberal idiots," Reserve members also worry about the Far Right and largely identify as moderate conservatives.

Overall, committed NRA members are largely supportive of Far-Right politics. When Albert and I discussed the term "patriotism," he said, "A lot of people have no idea what it means to be a patriot. You got these idiots running around here with these flags on their cars and all that, but they'll vote for a Democrat at the drop of a hat." He thinks these voters are ignorant, and added, "They have no idea what these Democrats are doing to us. And they will vote for them." Albert holds strictly partisan views, condemning anything that has to do with the Democrats. Donald flatly stated, "The Democratic party platform stinks." "Get rid of the liberals and this country would be a lot better," he argued. Ben offered a radical Right take on Clinton administration Democrats:

In my opinion of Janet Reno and Bill Clinton and Hillary Clinton and Al Gore and other people in his administration—they should be arrested and be charged with treason and tried, and be convicted and executed . . . because they definitely are traitors. Every single one of them. [Why?] [Because they were] accepting money from communist China for one thing. Selling our [military] secrets to China, giving them away to China.

Ben holds some of the most extreme views on the Clinton administration, but fellow Critical Mass members are also critical of current Democrats, whom they are quick to label socialists and Communists. Drawing in the frequently cited "liberal" media, Ben complained, "The media and the anti-gunners are one [and] the same . . . They are ultra-liberals. Left-wing liberals is what they are," and he added: "If you were to do an interview with them you would see that they were all socialist for sure. And they are pro-communist." He claimed that "Fox News is as close as they get [to accurate media coverage], and even then they are liberal, too."

Other Critical Mass members frequently complain about the media, which they perceive to be among the worst offenders of liberal bias. Echoing other members' sentiments, Bob said that Fox News is "a little bit balanced" but not conservative, and because liberals head the media and educational systems, children are being indoctrinated by liberals. Chuckling, Mark answered a question regarding the media: "You mean the lackeys, the lapdogs of the Democratic Party and liberal . . . I think there's a little bit of media bias . . . I think there's a *lot* of media bias." The first and foremost victim of liberal media bias, according to these NRA members, is the Second Amendment. "I religiously read the *Wall Street Journal*," Mark said, "I read *USA Today* when I want to laugh, and I read the *New York Times* when I really want to laugh." Historian Eric Alterman has challenged the widespread conservative argument that the media is liberally biased, in part by documenting the power and influence among conservatives and liberals in all forms of media and concluding that the *perception* of a liberal media helps drive the myth, even among liberals.[7]

Regional politics are evident in many of my discussions with NRA members, as well as at NRA meetings. Members make countless references to California's liberal politics—San José is the "eye of the storm," according to a member commenting on the gun control battle at an NRA session on the media. San Francisco, however, is the object of most conservative animosity and Critical Mass members toe the party line on this issue. During interviews, I often brought up that I was living in southern California, which drew numerous comments about regional politics. Soon after a California court ruled the Pledge of Allegiance unconstitutional because of its inclusion of "God," Bob said, "You folks in San Francisco [messed up that one]." It didn't matter that I was hundreds of miles away from that city—anywhere in California was still the "Left Coast" for most members. NRA member Walter excitedly told me, "Oh, you cannot believe how involved I am in the recall [Democratic Governor] Gray Davis issue!" One Critical Mass member identified the regional differences within parties, noting, "It's mostly Republicans that take the stance we take, but there are pretty good Democrats out there. Like [Congressman and NRA Board member] John Dingell in Michigan" (Donald).

Reserve member Nicole became more aware of regional political differences when she moved from a more conservative to a more liberal area of the country and quickly realized that "the Democrats from [a liberal part of the Northeast] weren't Democrats in [the Midwest] . . . I really understood the meaning then of the Southern Democrat." Though she recognizes how much more liberal her fellow Northeasterners are, as one of the least conservative participants in this research, she has no unkind words for these liberals. Her Reserve peers do not hold overtly hostile views of Democrats, although they are generally conservative and mostly disagree with Democratic policies. "Democrats are tax spenders, [higher-income individuals like myself are] the ones that earn the money and pay a tax," commented Ernie, who is wedded much more to his wallet than to party politics. "If the stock market would go back up," he said, "I would vote for the goddamn Devil himself." Harry simply does not fathom Democrats, admitting, "It is hard for me to understand political liberals." His fears, like many of his moderate colleagues, are bipartisan: "I don't know which is worse . . . religious fanaticism or socialism. I fear them both myself. I think freedom-loving people must be vigilant to both possibilities of control." Gerry agreed: "There are some Democrats that should go because they are so ultra-left and they would take everything away from you. There are also some Republicans that would take away other rights, too." Reserve members are not die-hard Republicans or conservatives, so they do not inherently view all left-leaning politics with contempt.

Gun Owners and Gun Crusaders

NRA members, both Critical Mass and Reserves, are more conservative than both the non-gun owning general population and gun owners, according to General Social Survey data.[8] More than one-quarter of American gun owners identify as Democrats or strong Democrats. No Critical Mass or Reserve NRA members would self-identify as either. Only one Reserve member would describe himself as Democratic-leaning (but basically independent), compared to another nearly 10% of U.S. gun owners who do. Just less than 50% of all gun owners are "leaning" toward "strongly" Republican. Another 15% of U.S. gun owners identify as up-the-middle independents. Non-owners are even more likely to be Democrats. These data demonstrate that the general gun owner population leans much more toward the Democratic view compared to NRA Critical Mass and Reserve members.

On a separate question gauging respondents' political orientation, only 5% of gun owners label themselves as "extremely conservative." About 40% of gun owners are in the next two conservative groups (combined) and the dead center "moderate" category. The remaining gun owners, less than 20%, identify as anywhere from slightly liberal to extremely liberal. Like party identification patterns, non-gun owners are more liberal and less conservative than gun owners, with 30% falling into the liberal categories. Similar to party identification data, no Critical Mass or Reserve NRA members are liberals, and many in the Critical Mass would likely self-identify as extremely conservative. Perhaps the most revealing data are about presidential elections. Major NRA gun control nemesis and 2000 Democratic presidential candidate Al Gore collected 30% of U.S. gun owners' votes (and 50% of non-owners). Even among the less committed Reserve NRA members, it is difficult to imagine even one or two of them voting for Gore.

Gun politics and political parties are inseparable. NRA members' varying commitment to gun rights and conservative politics reflects the close connection between the two. For the most committed NRA members, their fears of gun control, registration, and confiscation mesh well with their broader Far-Right conservative views and commitments. These Critical Mass members are highly dedicated to the NRA and gun rights and also to right-wing politics. NRA Reserve members are less committed to the NRA, gun rights, and conservative politics but still supportive of all three. The gun politics of NRA members from these two groups inform and correspond with their broader moral politics.

7

Right and Far-Right Moral Politics

NRA Critical Mass member Bob and Reserve member Frank are differently committed not only to the organization and gun rights but also to conservatism. Bob is a highly committed member of a quarter century who donates money to and volunteers for the NRA. Frank is a moderately committed member who has attended NRA fundraising dinners on a couple of occasions but describes himself as not a very active member. There are also distinguishable differences in their politics, yet both are NRA members and conservatives. Bob and Frank generally hold different views on contentious political issues such as terrorism, racial profiling, same-sex marriage, and taxes. At times, however, their views converge, reflecting their shared status as conservatives. Overall, highly committed Critical Mass member Bob leans much further to the Right than Frank.

Talking terrorism and racial profiling, Bob thinks it is "perfectly appropriate" to question a Middle Eastern man instead of a "little old lady" before they get on a plane. We have used racial profiling before he argues, citing Japanese internment camps during World War II, which he describes as "perfectly just." Frank also sees racial profiling as useful in fighting crime.

Bob is also highly conservative on gender and sexuality issues. He supports restrictions on women's jobs in the military and applauds the military's "Don't Ask, Don't Tell" policy, preventing openly gay individuals from serving. He is displeased with the changes to gender arrangements brought on by World War II and feminism, arguing that these are "detrimental" to society and families. He also finds fault with same-sex marriage and same sex-couples adopting children, and worries about the negative effects these may have. Bob expresses his strong support for constitutional rights and allowing everyone (including gays and lesbians) to do as they please in the same conversation where he derisively refers to gay adoption as a form of "indoctrination." Frank shares similar views regarding sexuality but differs regarding gender. Frank sees no reason to exclude women from the military: "I can't think of many jobs they shouldn't do." On the other hand, he feels differently about gays and lesbians, arguing that homosexuality is immoral and same-sex marriages should not be legalized.

With respect to taxes, Bob and Frank revealed their different conservative orientations. Before I even ask Frank directly about his views on taxes, he brings up the issue in our discussion of patriotism, telling me that paying taxes is part of his patriotic duty because it contributes to a stronger and healthier country. Bob, on the other hand, has a libertarian conservative view of taxes—he hates them, at least at the federal level. Federal taxes should only be collected to protect our borders, protect our overseas interests, and keep peace and harmony between states, Bob argued. He voiced his displeasure at the federal government's involvement in public education and is dumbfounded that Social Security exists. Like the regulation of firearms, Bob sees the government's involvement in regulating education or addressing poverty as beyond its scope as outlined in the Constitution.

Critical Mass members support aggressive policies against nations and enemies deemed hostile, including practices that violate current national and international laws. These members worry that the United States is soft on terrorism, its immigration policies are lax and ineffectual, and opposition to racial profiling embarrasses and endangers the country. Although Reserve members sometimes align with Critical Mass members, they generally hold moderately conservative, even liberal centrist positions, on contentious social and political issues. In short, a strong relationship exists between a Gun Crusader's commitment to the NRA and gun rights, and the extent to which his or her politics lean toward the Far Right (see Table 7.1).

Critical Mass and many Reserve members also believe that Americans are losing their moral compass. These NRA members point to divorce rates, threats to "traditional families" posed by feminists and gay couples, policies allowing women and gays in the military, and people's reliance on welfare (at the expense of others working and paying taxes to support these programs). They see American becoming soft, weak, feminine, and liberal, moving further and further away from frontier masculinity values. If Democrats obtain power, these NRA members argue, the country will become weaker politically, militarily, economically, and morally; cowardly liberals will coddle criminals by focusing on gun control instead of harsh

TABLE 7.1
NRA Member Social-Political Views

	Critical Mass	Reserves
Issues with broad consensus		
Political Affiliation	Conservative and/or Republican; Democrats and liberals are primary threats to guns and freedom	
Feminists	Militant "man-haters" pushing for big government programs; strongly opposed	
Welfare	Fosters dependence on government; welfare-to-work policies help people to become independent	
Affirmative Action	Discriminatory at worst, not needed at best; anyone willing to work hard can get ahead	
Issues with moderate consensus		
Racial Profiling	Looking at terrorists and criminals, of course you need to racially profile	Most say it's needed for law enforcement; some say it's been used to discriminate
Illegal Immigration	A serious problem; it drains taxpayers and threatens the economy; our "open borders" policy lets in terrorists	A serious problem, though some see these immigrants as hard workers, taking jobs Americans won't
Gay and Lesbian Rights	Homosexuality is immoral, wrong; don't allow openly gay people in the military	Mixed views on homosexuality and gays in the military; it's a free country, but keep it to yourself/don't flaunt it
Issues of disagreement		
Taxes	Liberals and Democrats create unfair tax policies; wealthier, hard-working Americans have to subsidize lazy, poor people	Some support for a flat tax and concerns about waste; some can't think of any programs to cut
Patriotism	A sense of nationalism, defending conservative American values, supporting the military	Love of country, respect for the Constitution; questioning the government and voicing opposition as needed

sentencing, indulge terrorists and foreign enemies by failing to use our military might, foster immorality by treating immigrants and gays and lesbians with kid gloves, and generally embrace the group-rights, "nanny state" values of feminists and socialists. Gun rights preserve and enforce not only individual rights and freedoms but also frontier masculinity values and morals.

War and Terrorism

I interviewed NRA members beginning in the summer of 2002, after the United States initiated a war against Afghanistan in response to the 9/11 attacks. My last interview took place more than a year later, many months after the United States invaded Iraq in March 2003. NRA members mostly supported President Bush's initial responses to the 9/11 terrorist attacks, but discernable differences were apparent between Critical Mass and Reserve members on various anti-terrorism means and goals.

Critical Mass member Donald said this about the "war on terrorism": "We gotta get tougher, tougher intelligence networks, tougher CIA, tough like the second World War—like the old SS." More than half a year before the Iraq War began, Mark expressed support for the Bush administration's aggression against Iraq, arguing shortly after 9/11,

> Iraq should be a parking lot by now, and I'm not that, quite that brutal . . . I just would have liked to have seen [President Bush] be more aggressive in the Philippines for starters. I'd like him to strong-arm Saudi Arabia. I would like to see him on September 11 actually bomb downtown Baghdad just for fun, but then again I'm a redneck. I'll fly the plane.

As with nearly all his responses, Mark offers a dash of tongue-in-cheek. But his Far-Right politics are evident in a range of issues, and his joking manner should not be misread as a distancing from his brand of conservatism.

Shortly before I spoke with Donald, the then accused and later convicted 9/11 plot member Zacharias Moussaoui was ordered by the courts to be examined by a psychiatrist. Incredulous, Donald commented, "I don't think he needs a psychiatrist. I think he needs to be sentenced to death and taken out back to a firing squad like what happened during the Civil War . . . Anybody who had anything to do with that 9/11 should be sentenced to death." He thinks these "executions should be carried out . . . swiftly. Use a firing squad and they'll change their way." He does not recognize that terrorists willing to commit suicide will not be deterred by the threat of capital punishment. Donald's thoughts reflect a typical conservative Strict Father Morality worldview of the state's role as enforcer of the social order.[1]

Ben goes even further than his fellow highly conservative Critical Mass peers, offering a pair of radical responses to 9/11 and terrorism. First, he offers a blueprint for dealing with al Qaeda leader and 9/11 planner Osama bin Laden:

> And I'm not the only one that would have been behind [President Bush] if he said, "Okay, either you turn over bin Laden and all those people or one city [in Afghanistan] would be vaporized by a nuclear weapon." And if they didn't do it within a certain time, vaporize the city. With a tactical nuclear weapon. And if they didn't [turn] him in, do one more. And then after that let it be known if anyone ever drops a . . . does anything, kills any of our citizens, any terrorist ever kills any of our citizens again, wherever that person is, from that city in that country will be vaporized. Then we wouldn't have terrorism anymore.

Regarding how we should deal with terrorism at home, Ben said,

> Execute them . . . publicly . . . I think it should be more than just putting them to sleep. I think it should be hanging or a firing squad—one or the other . . . Those people should have to suffer. A little bit anyway . . . People relate to pain.

It is not clear if Ben thinks that adding a dose of suffering to executions will deter future terrorists or simply serve as a form of increased retribution for the crimes committed. However, his support for public executions certainly speaks to his broader philosophy of deterrence through punishment, a philosophy that arises from frontier masculinity. Public executions conjure up images of nineteenth-century outlaws in nooses, about to face the harsh reality of frontier justice. With individual rights come individual responsibilities.

NRA member Rick warns that the Palestinian government cannot control its people because they've been killing for thousands of years. Therefore, he supports greater government scrutiny of all Muslims. "I wouldn't appreciate a lie detector test," Rick says, "but I was born here. The government knows everything about me." Critical Mass members' fear of brown-skinned "Others" terrorizing whites motivates them to withdraw constitutional rights for some citizens.

Albert's stance is somewhat less radical in response to terrorism: "The justice department . . . or even President Bush, by executive order, and I think that's what it's gonna take, executive order to do it, to start filtering, getting these people out of here." Albert believes we should "send them back to their countries and let them come back at a later date once we get everybody straightened out here." Having a "cooling-off period" is less extreme than the approaches of other Critical Mass members, but still it would appear radical to those immigrants who are suddenly deported. Albert's support for a "straightening-out" process is code for protecting U.S. citizens (especially whites) from foreign, threatening Others who are branded potential terrorist immigrants. They are guilty until proven innocent.

Reserve NRA members are generally supportive of actual U.S. responses to 9/11, but their comments are mild compared to the harsh punishments Critical Mass members concoct. Reserve member Craig agrees with Albert, stating, "I don't see anything wrong with pulling visas, telling potential terrorists, 'We're going to protect ourselves. We're not going to make it easy for you.'" Nicole feels that "a military response was in order" after 9/11. Her perspective is in line with most Americans shortly after 9/11 who overwhelmingly supported the U.S. bombing of Afghanistan and President Bush's War on Terror.[2] I spoke with Ian after the United States invaded Iraq, and he recalled the (G.H.) Bush-led Iraq war of the previous decade, saying about the younger Bush, "I don't want to speak against President Bush. Personally, they should have been dealt with before, when we were first there. They should have gone in when they were first there and dealt with it; 9/11 may never have happened if we did that . . . I think he's doing good." Ian's conflation of Iraq and 9/11 is common, especially among conservatives and in the immediate years after 9/11, when the Bush administration often implied connections between Saddam Hussein and the 9/11 terrorists.

Overall, the less committed NRA Reserve members display strong support for G. W. Bush and his handling of the war on terrorism and Iraq. "I think he's been doing exactly what he should have done," Pete says, "I'm for him 100%." Irene speaks to the general public sentiment immediately after 9/11, noting, "I think that people have the attitude that, 'This is my President and I'm going to stand behind him, because this is America and this is patriotism. That if he says it's okay, then it must be okay.'" Most students of the framers of the Constitution would disagree wholeheartedly with blind loyalty to political leaders, particularly in times of war. Irene is probably in touch with public opinion, however, judging from President Bush's 90% approval ratings immediately after 9/11.[3]

Most NRA members, Critical Mass or Reserve, support Bush for reasons other than those Irene expressed. They simply agree with his policies and actions, and as conservatives they would likely have no difficulty criticizing a Democratic president taking different actions in the same situation. Gerry, talking about Bush and the war on terrorism, said, "So far I think he's done pretty damn good with it . . . [Secretary of Defense Donald] Rumsfeld and the rest of them have done a hell of a good job so far." Andrew offered his thoughts on President Bush's military actions post-9/11:

> I think he's handling them very well. I think he's a lot gutsier than I think a lot of previous presidents we've had . . . I'm very, very proud of how he approached the Saddam Hussein deal. I was a little disappointed that it took so long to get there, but I think in a political climate [we're in today], I think, that time was necessary . . . But, I'm pleased because if you look back at World War II, if somebody, if some either British or American president had taken the kind of actions against Adolf Hitler that this guy has taken against Saddam Hussein, millions of lives would have been saved.

Andrew supports President Bush's image of being a tough guy, labeling him "gutsier" than his predecessors and rewarding Bush's frontier masculinity approach to foreign policy. Bush's "you're either with us or against us" and "wanted dead or alive" approaches supported his well-crafted image as the cowboy president, a throwback to the frontier of yesteryear when justice was delivered with righteous violence.

Most Reserve members support this cowboy image and these policies, whereas Democrats of all stripes quickly retreated from their post-9/11 support of Bush. Ernie, a moderate Reserve member, disagreed with his peers: "I don't think Bush has the answers, I don't think [Democratic Senate leader] Tom Daschle has the answers either."

The Critical Mass, not surprisingly, are also supportive of Bush's post-9/11 actions. Quincy gives the president a "nine out of ten" on his handling of the military responses in Afghanistan and Iraq. Walter was upset at the criticism leveled at Bush, particularly as time passed and Iraqi weapons of mass destruction were not found: "I'm concerned about all the [Bush] bashing going on. I have faith that the information that we got was accurate and true, and that eventually these horrible weapons or the residue from them are going to be [found]."

Critical Mass members were unlikely to criticize the president for his responses to 9/11, and if they did voice any concerns, they believe he erred on the side of caution and has not taken a tough enough stand.

At least one-third of the Reserve members voiced displeasure with Bush's policy of preemptive war, reflecting their qualified level of commitment to right-wing politics which in turn mirrors their qualified commitment to the NRA. Gerry pointed out the euphemisms so casually thrown about since 9/11, noting the constitutional requirements for declaring war: "Our Congress has not declared war on anybody, so when we say 'war on terrorism' it's no different than [the] war on drugs or anything else. It's a play on words." He shared his concerns:

> And of course right now with this war on terrorism we're watching very carefully, we're watching some rights being infringed here for the sake of this or that. So [threats to freedom] can come from either side [Democrats or Republicans] . . . But we're having to deal with this terrorism thing and we've lost some freedoms and a life we'll never see again because of it . . . A lot of things; now we're going to be checked a lot more, our movements are going to be checked a lot more. And who knows where we're headed?

Gerry, a moderate conservative, is critical of *anyone*, whether conservative or liberal, who infringes on constitutional rights and freedoms. This resembles Harry's Libertarian perspective: "You know we all got mad when somebody bombed our country, but what are we trying to protect, if not the Constitution and our way of life, our justice?"

Another Libertarian Reserve member, Nicole, also finds fault in some of G. W. Bush's domestic responses to 9/11: "In terms of homeland kind of stuff, I'm not quite his biggest fan . . . [this] stuff really conflicts with what I believe in terms of personal liberty." She does not think Bush's approach will be effective and will in fact have detrimental effects on individual rights. Harry, unhappy with encroachments on civil liberties, also doesn't want the United States to be involved in international affairs to the extent it has been historically and currently is, and he links our involvement overseas to terrorism at home:

> What happened on September 11, I'm not saying, some people say, "Well, we deserved it." No, we didn't deserve it at all. But certainly some of our foreign policy may have helped some madman pick us as a target . . . But I also think that we ought to have a foreign policy where we're not meddling in other countries' affairs.

Notably, two days after 9/11, it was Christian Conservative leaders Jerry Falwell and Pat Robertson who blamed American policies for 9/11, but for very different reasons than those supposedly suggested by liberals, namely, blowback against U.S. imperialism. "God continues to lift the curtain and allow the enemies of America to give us probably what we deserve," Falwell said, and added:

> The abortionists have got to bear some burden for this because God will not be mocked. And when we destroy 40 million little innocent babies, we make God mad. I really believe that the pagans, and the abortionists, and the feminists, and the gays and the lesbians who are actively trying to make that an alternative lifestyle, the ACLU, People for the American Way—all of them who have tried to secularize America—I point the finger in their face and say, "You helped this happen."

In response, Robertson said, "I totally concur."[4] Right-wing Christian ideology, in its most extreme form, blames liberal practices and policies for the 9/11 attacks, whereas the NRA and its members argue that anti-frontier masculinity, "soft-on-crime" liberal policies on gun control and terrorism are at fault.

The most outspoken Bush critic among the NRA members I interviewed is, not surprisingly, also one of the least conservative members. Zach sees the Iraq war as "shaky. . . It's pretty obvious all these weapons of mass destructions aren't there. That was the tool to get the war done." In other comments Zach offers critiques consistent with liberals and progressives: "And did we do this to save the people or to get the oil? Oil has . . . always been our big concern even though they don't talk about that." As to whether Bush or Rumsfeld might have intentionally misled us into war, he said, "I think that could very well be true. From what I've seen they definitely didn't tell the truth. They told us what they wanted us to believe." Parroting critiques raised by the political Left, NRA Reserve member Zach wants to find out more about Iraqi civilian casualties: "And the thousands and thousands of people that were killed, Iraqis, civilians, I mean that's a terrible toll. And you know, I'd like to know how they feel." Still, although believing the Bush administration may have lied, in the end Zach revealed his centrist conservative optimism about the U.S. leadership: "I would support [the war] if I knew there [were] weapons there. I mean . . . Hussein's been known to use them on his own people at times, so we had a good argument, maybe he had them." Resignedly he added,

"You know, it's a big country. Maybe they're there and they haven't found them yet." Clearly Reserve member Zach's views contrast sharply with the "bomb downtown Baghdad" stance of Critical Mass members, reflecting the strong disparities between these two NRA groups.

Racial Profiling

Racial profiling is tightly connected to recent debates about terrorism and immigration post-9/11, and NRA members' broad support for profiling is unsurprising given that they are predominantly white. The one Latina NRA member I interviewed, Irene, said, "I swear I only saw one Black man in that whole NRA convention the whole time I was there." The most committed NRA members have no problem supporting a policy that does not negatively affect them.

Critical Mass member Bob, reflecting his Far-Right politics, cited the World War II internment camps in the United States as an argument *in favor* of racial profiling. Neither Bob nor any other Critical Mass member ever mentioned white terrorists such as Timothy McVeigh or the Unabomber or raised the issue of profiling when the perpetrators of actual terrorist acts are white. In Donald's view, "You probably should racial profile because all of these terrorists are of Arabic descent. You have to figure what goes for the whole majority of the people, you maybe have to step on a few toes." When asked his opinion, Ben reacted angrily:

> We didn't do that, they did that. They caused it to happen. There should be no such thing as racial profiling. There should be no issue there. If a person looks like somebody [who is thought to be a terrorist], check him out. Everybody should be checked out if they're suspicious.

Because the targets of racial profiling are strictly younger men of Arabic descent, "everybody" is a small fraction of the more than one million people residing in the United States who claim some Arabic ancestry, almost none of whom are NRA members.[5]

"I wouldn't mind if anyone asked me, if they thought I looked like, or might have acted like somebody. I wouldn't mind them asking me because I have nothing to hide," Ben told me, adding, "they must have something to hide or they wouldn't have been complaining." As someone who probably never had to submit to extended searches and questioning because of his racial or ethnic identity, Ben suspects that those who complain about such targeting must be guilty of a crime, ignoring their feelings of having been violated, intimidated, or stripped of their constitutional rights.

We know that Ben, like his peers, are angry at the very idea of having to relinquish their right to own and carry a gun, but they do not identify with the violation of civil rights through racial profiling. It is simply not in their experience, because, of course, they have never been profiled like their American counterparts—whether Arab-Americans today or Japanese-Americans during World War II.

Walter, the least conservative Critical Mass member, argued that the Middle East is "not an area of evil people," but this belief does not translate into his opposition to racial profiling. He even offered the following domestic profile: "I see a guy wearing baggies hanging down below his butt with a doo-rag on his head and oversized [sneakers] that aren't tied and all, I could be pretty darn sure that he is probably affiliated with some street organization." Walter's profile for urban gang members mostly matches contemporary young urban dress (that crosses racial boundaries), and leads to non-gang members experiencing racial profiling firsthand. "I don't have a real problem with profiling," Walter added, and actually I know for a fact that in law enforcement profiling has been used for many years." Most NRA members, not unlike most Americans in the months and even years after 9/11, are fearful of terrorist attacks, and it is this fear that drives their moral and political views.

The racial profiling views of some Reserve NRA members are as conservative as those of their Far-Right Critical Mass peers. Craig, arguably the most conservative of this less committed and more moderate bunch, continues Walter's theme regarding urban dress and gang members:

> They know perfectly well that if you're in a Black neighborhood, or a Hispanic neighborhood, or whatever kind of a neighborhood you're in, drugs are going on, drive-by shootings are going on. If you happen to see a guy going down the street in baggy pants, with four other young guys, or peering out of the top of a car—you know, the kind where they just barely put their head over the windshield . . . the reason they get low in the seat is because they don't wanna get shot.

That Craig equates Black and Hispanic neighborhoods with drugs, violent crime, and gangs aligns with his lack of moral qualms with respect to racial profiling. Regarding 9/11, he added: "People from those countries that are living over here or are citizens now, they gotta make the extra effort to show they are from this country. If they're not, the hell with them." Despite the NRA rhetoric about guarding the Constitution and individual rights, sentiments such as these show that NRA members are far more interested in defending against their fears and guarding their own rights as white citizens. On the surface, frontier masculinity espouses equal rights and opportunities for all; in truth, however, it has always ignored group disadvantages and used conservative white men as the default group to which all others are compared.

"If everybody that hijacked the plane is an Arab," Gerry pointed out, "better start looking for Arabs." But like most of his moderate Reserve member peers, he does not want to see racial profiling go "too far." He cautioned,

> I mean, granted you just don't want to go around and hurt innocent people either . . . because there a lot of Arabs that are very good citizens in this country. But we've got to use a little common sense here.

Andrew also has mixed views on the topic, stating that "we've been doing racial profiling for the last two hundred years" across all aspects of society (law enforcement, business, and government), so he does not view the current practices as "unique or outstanding." "I mean, we've always done it," he argues, "in some cases . . . very destructively, in some cases . . . very constructively."

Andrew immediately reverts to his more moderate conservatism, reciting language rooted in individual rights and freedoms: "Now, we've also done things by racial profiling to not allow people of color or race or religion some of the accesses of some of the freedoms that we have. Now, that's a whole different thing. That's a violation of civil rights." Andrew is one of the extremely rare NRA members to use the politically progressive term "people of color" to note common experiences of racism by groups who prefer not to be collectively identified based on what they are not—such as "non-white"—or based on their subordinate status—such as "minority." He is also among the few who occasionally identify with those who are profiled. While talking about 9/11, the discussion brought him around to police profiling of Black motorists, popularly known as "Driving While Black":

> To the extent that this racial profiling starts infringing on civil rights then I have a problem with it . . . I haven't seen that yet. [Yet] if you're a Black

guy driving through [a wealthy white neighborhood] and you get pulled over, and you weren't speeding and they want to see your I.D., it's a pretty good chance that Black guy is going to say, "What do you mean you don't see it? I see it every day. I'm profiled every day."

In Harry's opinion, "I guess in some respects profiling works, but it is bad and I know people in this country, Black Americans who have been profiled because they might have been driving an expensive car that some cop thought might not be his. That's wrong, without a question it's wrong." Irene believes that racial profiling is "just another form of discrimination" and is no better or worse than before, it is just that "we finally put a name to it." These NRA members maintain what is arguably a purer view of frontier masculinity, at least on the topic of profiling. They support individual rights and responsibilities, and they don't want to see these jeopardized simply based on an individual's racial or ethnic group.

Ian criticizes his Critical Mass peer, Bob, who thinks that forcing innocent Japanese-Americans into World War II internment camps was justified. In Ian's view, this is an example of racial profiling going too far: "It wasn't the Japanese Americans here who [were attacking us]. It was the Japanese country itself that did it, you know." Nicole also offers qualified critiques of racial profiling: "And I feel like there's a larger kind of art/science of profiling, many different aspects of people. It can be a good thing, but not racial profiling for the sake of your race." Although Harry recognizes the discrimination that African Americans have experienced because of racial profiling, he still thinks that it has its place in post-9/11 America: "but if they are carrying a foreign passport and they're in our country, I think they have a right to be scrutinized. I mean they have rights through our Constitution, but still they are visitors here and I think we have a right to take a second look at them." Reserve members offer more qualified support of the practice of racial profiling as a group, and are much more likely to criticize it if race is used as the only factor in profiling. These members are also more likely to point out cases where it should be considered discrimination. Critical Mass members are more right-wing, and their politics (and demographic characteristics) make them much more likely to support racial profiling.

The more conservative members are also more likely to wander into the realm of racist generalizations. I spoke with Albert about crime and he has the following thoughts on how it plays out in his part of the country:

And I don't know if you've noticed this or not, but in the newspapers here, like in [my] area, every time, most of the time of the year, [when there's] a shooting that takes place, you look at surnames of 'em, I think you'll find the same types of surnames in your part of the country there, too [in southern California].

Albert dances around his beliefs about crime—that Chicanos are the main perpetrators, and thus the main threats as well. He does not want to come out and identify any group, for fear of being considered overtly racist, but when I press him to be specific, he relents and identifies them as "Hispanics."

Reserve NRA members are more likely to identify racism as a problem, similar to their concerns about some uses of racial profiling. Andrew told me, "I am kind of concerned about a national attitude that has prejudice against people of Middle Eastern descent." He believes that society, rather than the government, fosters this attitude. "It's primarily a conservative society," Andrew added, "which is taking action against, actually developing attitudes around people of Middle Eastern decent which I think is, which is again a violation of civil rights."

As a Latina, Irene notices that "racism [in the Midwest] is a little bit subtle. People don't talk to you." She believes that multiculturalism in schools would lead to "less [of a] tendency to discriminate because you're teaching them everybody's equal. That everybody's different but that's okay." For most members with a frontier masculinity worldview, multiculturalism is an affront to the philosophy that everyone should be treated as individuals. Harry is another exception to the rule on this issue. He supports acculturation rather than assimilation, claiming that multiculturalism is "very healthy for our society." Even his less conservative attitude eventually finds its roots in a frontier masculinity perspective: "I'm totally in favor of interracial marriages. Eventually," he projects, "everyone will be the same color. No, I don't have any problem with that. It's good for our society." For Harry, multiculturalism will eventually result in a single people with no competing group identities. This contrasts with Critical Mass member Mark, who thinks that multiculturalism is "self-imposed segregation." Reserve members demonstrate more moderate views on this topic and stray from NRA rhetoric decrying "politically correct revisionists," a phrase used in postings by Madison Brigade members.

NRA members with less right-wing views on all issues, especially those dealing with race, are less committed to the organization. Why? Because the NRA's implied views on race and politics appeal to a large, active base of members committed to a conservative, white men's reactionary politics—the Critical Mass. These members offer harsh responses to 9/11, aiming to shut down immigration and punish terrorists with actions not practiced by other Western industrialized societies. They are Far Right, conservative, white men who identify with the NRA's commitment to defend not only gun rights but all individual rights and freedoms aligned with white men's establishment of frontier masculinity. Just as NRA leadership denigrate the supposed lack of utilization of racial profiling (such as in U.S. airports, where increased inspections have impacted even travelers who are not of Arabic or Middle Eastern descent), Critical Mass members are dumbfounded that the government does not strictly focus on immigrants with similar backgrounds to the 9/11 terrorists.

In these Gun Crusaders' eyes, members of certain groups shouldn't be granted "special" rights or privileges because everyone should be evaluated and sink or swim based on their individual characteristics. However, hardcore Gun Crusaders are comfortable shelving their individual rights and treatment philosophy, telling members from those same certain groups that they will have to give up some of their rights at times because of their group affiliation. Less conservative NRA members are more likely to express concern over racial profiling, worrying that their country is in some way engaging in discrimination.

Gendered Views on Gays, Marriage, and Adoption

NRA members are no different than anyone else in that they see the world in part through gendered lenses. Their attitudes and beliefs reflect their life experiences; their interest in firearms is often rooted in childhood experiences which are in turn rooted in family history and regional location. Similarly, their politics are shaped in many ways by the fact that they are white men who grew up and live in more rural and conservative areas of the country. These demographic characteristics, much like genetic characteristics, are not absolute determinants of individual attitudes or behaviors, but they do play a major role in the politics of NRA members.

That Critical Mass members are less diverse than Reserve members is not surprising, as the former adhere to a more reactionary right-wing interpretation of social change. Reserve members do not agree with NRA rhetoric to the extent that Critical Mass members do. They feel less endangered by progressive changes and are less inclined to defend frontier masculinity, though still more inclined to do so than the overall U.S. population, which is much less conservative.

NRA members are a lot more conservative than the general population as well as all gun owners on many contentious political and cultural issues, but sexuality does not appear to be one of them. Over half of American non-gun owners and nearly two-thirds of gun owners think that "sexual relations between two adults of the same sex" is always wrong.[6] NRA members find gay sexuality problematic as well, but many couldn't care less what happens behind closed doors.

Same-sex marriage is a source of ongoing contentious public debate, and NRA members are no exception to the strong feelings voiced on this topic. Critical Mass members, many of whom likely identify with the Christian Right, largely oppose same-sex marriage. Only one Critical Mass member, Bob, offers a non-religious and constitutionally consistent position of "[letting] people do what they want to do" and respecting their individual rights, so long as it does not bother anyone else. Still, he is not a proponent of gay and lesbian rights. Donald contends that same-sex marriage is "completely wrong." Allowing gay couples to marry reduces heterosexual men's control over what society deems to be gender-appropriate behavior.[7] Further, a fundamental aspect of asserting masculinity for men is proving they are *not* gay. Frontier masculinity is implicitly heterosexual.

Reserve members are much more likely to support lesbian and gay rights—based on a broader philosophy of individual rights—as well as same-sex marriage. Nicole offered her support: "A lot of those arguments [against same-sex marriage] suddenly don't stand, so really I think I've taken on more of the view of supporting gay marriage, understanding that it's a big controversy . . . but it's a hard issue." Many members struggle with their support, because their traditionalist views firmly oppose same-sex love and attraction at the same time that their views of individual rights support personal freedoms.

Nicole's fellow Reserve member Frank voices the opposite opinion, relying strictly on his belief that gays and lesbians are acting immorally. He thinks that same-sex marriages are "a contradiction in terms." Pete goes much further, stating, "I don't think you should let gays be anywhere." Only a few members support same-sex marriage, and even these individuals tend to struggle with gays and lesbians enjoying equal rights. Some opponents of same-sex marriage argue that this will confer "special" benefits to lesbians and gays, a strategy that conservatives frequently use to stave off changes to the status quo and to counter challenges to frontier masculinity. By preventing gays and lesbians from obtaining equal rights, heterosexuals protect their monopoly of the many economic and social privileges of state-recognized marriage.

Gendered Views on Welfare, Taxes, and the Ethos

Like same-sex marriage, many NRA members believe that welfare recipients are receiving special benefits and taxpayers are footing the bill. Giving "special" benefits to anyone, but particularly gays and lesbians or the poor, goes against NRA members' beliefs in individual rights and responsibilities. To many Gun Crusaders, welfare programs foster dependence on the state. When I asked Critical Mass member Ben for his thoughts on welfare recipients, he replied,

> They just don't want to [work]. They're too lazy, or the government will just give them money. They don't work. There are so many socialist programs that so many people can tap into that they don't have to work. They figured it out—that they don't have to do this . . . the government will give them this [money].

Ben blames socialists for encouraging dependence and attacking the American Ethos. Just as the pioneers were self-reliant as they "conquered" the West—with firearms in hand—every worker today should be able to persevere and obtain the American Dream. Those who don't make it simply have not tried hard enough, according to the frontier masculinity philosophy of these NRA members. To them, welfare recipients are lazy and dependent, no questions asked.

"I don't recall anybody starving in this country, and nor should they," Mark said. In reality, even before the economic meltdown and recession beginning late 2008, 7.7 million adults and 3.4 million children lived in households with "very low food security," and who, many times during the course of a year, do not eat enough owing to insufficient resources.[8] Many NRA Members also seem unaware of the 14 million people whose household income is less than half the federal poverty level, 5 million of whom are children younger than eighteen years of age.[9] Mark offered his opinion:

> Temporary [welfare] is fine. There is nothing that says everybody is gonna be doing well for their whole life . . . And how do you force them

out of it? Slowly and painfully, because it's going to be. And you're going to be accused of being heartless, cold, and cruel. Well, maybe you are for a while. You know, small dogs and small kids, once in a while you spank them, but they learn.

This Critical Mass member assumes that those on welfare, who are mostly the *working* poor and minors not old enough to work, must be trained like pets or children. His metaphor regarding spanking "small dogs and kids" implies that welfare recipients are not capable adults, and will only respond to threats and punishment. As discussed in chapter 5, the foundations for this argument—that most welfare recipients are lazy, do not work, stay on welfare for countless years, and enjoy a comfortable lifestyle thanks to government assistance—are simply not based in fact. But facts matter little among these members whose views are created and confirmed by conservative, and indeed popular, symbolic representations of lazy, leeching, welfare queens.

Fellow Critical Mass member Donald also has no patience for welfare recipients: "Put them to work, and if they don't take a job they don't get welfare [laughing]." He suggests altering the food stamp program to force recipients to only buy specially marked packages, so they "will get embarrassed and wouldn't want to spend food stamps." Underlying such arguments against welfare is that those receiving aid have it too easy, while the rest of us have to work hard just to make it easy for them.

NRA Reserve members tend to agree with the sentiments of the Critical Mass, but the Reserves are not as uncompromising on this issue as their highly committed counterparts. Helen declared, "I don't believe in handouts," claiming that the welfare reform policies are a major effort in getting people back to work instead of relying on the government for their livelihood. "Well we need welfare," Pete remarked, "We need to help people that can't help themselves; people that are down and out. Everybody needs some help sometimes, but I think we've got too much welfare." Irene's view was similarly mixed:

I think welfare is good, but it's not for everyone. I think if you put people on welfare and you say, "I'm going to help you get on your feet for the next two years, but during that two years you have to work," I think that's good.

These Reserve members are less upset with and threatened by welfare, though they are still supportive of restrictions on welfare eligibility. Not one of them thought that the pre-1996 reform system of welfare was a good one.

"You got to have some people out there," Gerry stated, "maybe single mothers or kids that need opportunities. And some of those programs to give them opportunities if they'll take them, but on the other side of the coin, if they don't take them, give them so long and boot them out of it." Like other conservatives, he would be happy to repeal benefits from those who do not try hard enough to get off welfare. To these members, not temporarily helping out those in need and helping them out for too long a time are both immoral, for they become discouraged from helping themselves. Zach thinks that people "get used to being fed," so he supports the reform. "Welfare is necessary for a lot of people. You can't let them starve, especially when we're a country of plenty," he stated, "but it gets out of hand." None of the members criticize welfare reform policies or consider growing unemployment and the lack of living wage jobs.

Nicole acknowledges the struggle that the working poor face, dismissing myths about how easy it is to get off welfare and how easy it is for recipients to remain on welfare. She elaborated:

> And so it's something that I've always kind of been surrounded by but I'm not a big fan of it. And I feel like for the most part private groups can do a better job than government can, cause I know it's really hard to look at a family and see parents who are working two to three jobs apiece, and whenever they go in and apply for something they're making just a few dollars over the cut off, and you know, at the same time, they still very much need help.

Conservative rhetoric that bashes any form of welfare and other so-called socialist agendas does not resonate with less conservative Reserve NRA members like Nicole. She holds more moderate views about welfare reform, reflecting her more moderate commitment to conservatism and the NRA. Defending a frontier masculinity view that everyone must be entirely self-reliant is less of a concern for the slightly more diverse and significantly less conservative Reserve NRA members.

NRA members see obvious connections between welfare and taxes. In short, they believe that their hard-earned dollars are unfairly collected and unfairly redistributed to undeserving groups and for liberal social agendas. Critical Mass members offer a laundry list of "socialist" programs on which they feel their tax dollars are being wasted, for example, welfare, foreign aid, the arts, affirmative action, and social security. Many are also unhappy with the IRS because of the different percentages people are supposed to pay based on their income levels. Donald said, "I think the income tax should be made fair. There should be a flat tax." As a group, Critical Mass members are comfortable financially, as are most Reserve Members. The Reserves, as moderate conservatives, are also dissatisfied with the tax system, but they rarely cite "socialist agendas" as the source of the problem.

Reserve member Ian likes flat tax proposals, saying, "That's a very good idea. Everybody pays 10%. No matter what your income is you pay 10%. If you're like Howard Hughes, Rockefeller, Getty, you pay 10%." Ian's 10% figure would not come near meeting the government's budget and is thus well below the figure typically offered by proponents of the flat tax. Nevertheless his sentiment aligns with that of other NRA members and frontier masculinity. What matters most is to treat everyone the same right now, not the disproportionate impact a flat tax would have on the working poor or inequality owing to past or current experiences of discrimination.

Those members with higher incomes are more likely to express grievances with the tax system because they are paying higher percentages. Reserve member Ernie commented, "I pay more in taxes every year than most people . . . I think a flat tax like [Steve] Forbes proposed, I think would be a very fair thing." The flat tax argument has gained steam, not coincidentally, after group rights' movements challenged institutional racism, sexism, and class discrimination in the latter half of the 20th Century. White taxpayers have taken their cue from Republican leaders, who claim that progressive taxation is a form of discrimination at best and socialism at worst, and the main beneficiaries of this system are "minorities" who are being given special preferences.[10]

As on virtually all topics we discussed, Reserve NRA members have mixed conservative views on taxes. Ernie once again reveals his moderate beliefs by thinking through the issue out loud and slowly moving away from his original reactionary conservative stance. "I don't know. I don't want to pay more taxes," he said, "but I certainly don't want to cut a lot of the programs. . . . Defense certainly needs to have its money. The Medicare system needs its money. I don't know what to cut back; I don't think there is any place to cut back. I wouldn't be in favor of cutting money anyway."

Reserve members are more likely to recognize the benefits they receive from paying taxes, as opposed to the greater tendency of more conservative Critical Mass members to point out where others benefit. "I think the government basically does a really good job," stated NRA Reserve member Frank about the collection and distribution of tax money. This is a far cry from the right-wing views that some Critical Mass members relay about what they perceive to be socialist conspiracies to steal from the rich and give to the (lazy) poor. Moderate Reserve member Zach dismissed talk of socialist conspiracies when taxes increase: "And they talk about raising [local taxes] a penny . . . and people go and they want to revolt. Well someone's got to pay for police, fire protection, the parks, the highways, so I don't see a problem in that." Irene, too, does not see a socialist conspiracy: "I think [taxes are] probably going where they need to go. We do have to fund, help cancer people that can't afford it, Medicare and Medicaid. We have to fund people that need welfare. We do have to have roads."

"Typical Americans" or "Gun Nuts"?

NRA members are not "typical Americans" either demographically or politically but are overwhelmingly white men and conservative compared to the following Census Bureau data regarding the U.S. population: approximately 51% women, 12% African-American, 13% Latina/o, and a Congress that has roughly averaged an equal voting split between Democrats and Republicans since the 2000 elections.[11] On the other hand, depictions of NRA members as "gun nuts" or "radicals" are not only ambiguous but are also misleading; the membership is not comprised primarily by right-wing militia members or reclusive survivalists who do not pay taxes. Committed NRA members are conservatives, from the Far Right to just right-of-center moderates. Critics of the NRA often assign demeaning labels to members like the Critical Mass because of their uncompromising views on gun rights as well as their broader right-wing politics.

The term "radical," however, implies operating out of mainstream debates. It would be patently false to assume that the NRA or its members reside outside standard contentious political debates. The gun rights and political views of Reserve members, though still clearly conservative, lean closer to the American center. These members are more likely to distance themselves from the NRA argument that "all gun control leads to gun confiscation," and they even occasionally attempt to distance themselves from what they perceive to be radicals within the organization.

Overall, however, members would never call for widespread gun control measures, nor are significant liberal or progressive public voices ever heard in the NRA. Some slightly left-of-center gun owners may comprise a portion of the hands-off Peripheral members, but they do not influence the organization's politics. The reason the organization leans significantly to the right is because gun rights is a conservative issue in a deeply partisan and contentious debate. Any individuals or groups taking extreme sides (either entirely opposed or in favor of any form of gun control or gun confiscation) in this debate simply cannot be considered nonpartisan or representatives of "middle America."

NRA framings occasionally claim that the organization is a nonpartisan group comprised of Americans from every background. Yet the NRA is generally not shy about expressing quite partisan, conservative views. The organization is well aware that its members, particularly the most committed members, are conservatives. The NRA has also helped create, and benefits from, the strong connections between gun rights and the Republican Party. Despite evidence showing that the NRA membership is overwhelmingly made up of conservative white men, most members like to repeat the NRA line that they represent the American population. They see themselves as an open group, liable to appeal to anyone.

"The NRA is made up of ordinary people," Craig declared, in an attempt to create distance from media references to NRA members as "rednecks" or "gun nuts." Or, as Bob put it, "We're not like [what] Chuck Schumer said, a bunch of rednecks running around with rifle racks and beer." Zach agreed: "I don't think there's a typical member. I think it's all races, all ages, all walks [of] life . . . It's just, the NRA appeals to a lot of people . . . I don't think it's all shooters and hunters." Walter thinks the NRA needs to "[prove] to the public that people [who] believe in the Second Amendment come from every walk of life and are not a bunch of rednecks and gun nuts; that we have come from every educational background, from every religious group." Although the NRA may represent the U.S. population in terms of education and economic characteristics, it is entirely unrepresentative with regard to race and ethnicity, sex and gender, religion, and age.

I asked Helen to describe a typical NRA member, and she replied: "Just a typical person. Probably holds a job, middle-income level. Could be hunters, could be anybody. They're like a typical American." Regarding the politics of NRA members, she added: "I don't think they're too far Left. I don't think they're too far Right. I think they represent middle

America very well." Frank also claimed that "[NRA members are] pretty much middle America. Sensible people. They're not radicals. [They] care for their families and homes. They care for their firearms that they have to have. They want to keep them."

Charlton Heston has done more for the NRA's public image than any other figure in the organization's history. Heston's star power and association with traditional American values helped propel the organization to its strongest position financially and politically. NRA members gladly point out how Heston helped to counter stereotypes about the organization and its members. Reserve member Pete said:

> I think [Heston] definitely helped the organization. He's such a famous person and such a good person. People know him, they know his reputation and they know he wouldn't be joining or representing any group of people that are not above board.

Mark stated, "I think Heston has done a great job in personalizing—you know, [showing that] everybody's not a gun nut. I think the membership has gone up, what, a million since he became president," adding, "[Heston's] high profile, he's articulate, he embodies what everybody wants to be I guess." Moreover, Mark thinks that Heston has sent the organization down a path of future success, and he wants the NRA to continue to recruit NRA leaders who are "high-profile, individual, Charlton Heston-type, Mr. Everyman kind of deal." Irene also was pleased with Heston, particularly because he served as a good spokesman for the NRA. Like many members, she does not distinguish between his on-screen and off-screen personas, stating, "I'm just thinking that if Moses tells me I could carry a gun, hey, it must be okay."

Andrew thinks that NRA members would have voted for Heston for a fifth term as president had he not had to step down for health reasons:

> It's kind of a shame that we had to lose Charlton Heston, because I think he did more for this organization than any president that's been there since I've been there. He's just an incredible patriot, incredibly passionate, and we were very lucky as an organization to have such a leader.

Virtually no members knew the name of Heston's successor, 1st Vice President Kayne Robinson. Zach said of him, "Well, let's hope he does at least as good a job, but all that Heston had going for him—he was a well-known actor, and he was popular, and I'm sure he gained a lot of publicity, good publicity for the NRA. I'm sure he did them a lot of good." It is worth noting that Zach refers to the NRA as "them" rather than "we," probably reflecting his more moderate political views and his status as one of the least-committed NRA members I interviewed.

Charlton Heston's presence led members who are less politically conservative and less committed to feel better about belonging to the NRA and probably encouraged many members to become more committed to the organization. Nevertheless, many NRA members are well aware of member stereotypes (sometimes propagating these themselves) and had much to say about them. Ben dismissed the notion that NRA members only care about gun rights:

> NRA members are not like that. That's not what most NRA members, or most people that I know who are NRA members, or that I get to be members—they are interested in the whole issue of the country. The patriotism of this country. If the candidates are not patriots, true patriots, most NRA members don't vote for them.

Moderate conservative Reserve member Zach thinks that radical individuals do exist within the organization, but he believes they are a minority: "I've met some of [them] and they put me in the mind of this jack-booted thugs state; they're damn near separatist but of course I have no idea what percentage [of the membership they are]. Hopefully it's small. But there are radicals." Unsure about my own gun politics and broader political views, he said to me, "You're not one of them I hope."

Reserve member Ernie distinguished between himself and his fellow members, contending that he is "Probably better educated. That helps me know that there are two sides to every story. And I think that's a basic difference. I'm not saying that the people I shoot with are dumb, because a lot of them are very skilled at what they do." He finished his thought by attributing his differences with other NRA members to region, saying, "I'm a Yankee; I shoot down in the South. Yankees are a little more moderate." Harry declared,

> [The NRA needs] to get members that are educated, professional people. That's what they need to go after. Those are the people that are going to read this stuff and actually do the voting and talk to other people. You don't need to get a bunch of redneck yahoos.

Reserve members especially identify with Charlton Heston and supported his campaign to improve the NRA's public image because they want to distance themselves from real or perceived "radicals" and "rednecks" within the organization.

Some NRA members recognize the overall conservative politics of the group. Ernie stated, "Well some of them are a little more redneck than I am, but most of them are Republican thinking. I think practically 100% of them." He also said that they are "hard-working, honest folk" who aren't surviving because of free rides. Here Ernie labels NRA members as conservative and lauds their behavior based on the conservative philosophy of frontier masculinity. Critical Mass member Donald agreed that this is no liberal bunch, stating,

> They're a lot of independent-minded folks for the most part, conservative. Yeah, they're pretty nice people. Basically most of the people you run into are pretty nice folks, you know. Not too many idiots. There's a few, but mostly down-to-earth Americans like we used to have a hundred years ago in this country I think [laughing]; a declining breed.

Donald taps into images of men on the frontier—independent, conservative, grounded—when thinking about today's NRA members. Some members appreciate the NRA's occasional claims of nonpartisanship, but most (and especially the most committed) would agree that the membership is overwhelmingly conservative.

NRA members fear outsiders labeling and perceiving gun rights defenders as extremists, or worse, that the label accurately describes some members. Frank expressed his concern: "I think there's an attitude that the NRA is a bunch of radicals." Ernie also worries about extremist groups, concerned about possible NRA involvement with militias:

> I certainly hope that they are not tied to the NRA. Because they are radical organizations. When I think of militias I think of Neo-Nazis and that's wrong . . . the people that go out playing with tin cans with their assault rifles, dressed up in camouflage fatigues, I think that does more to give our image a bad name than anything else.

NRA members mostly distance themselves from right-wing extremists who are apt to engage in violence (such as Timothy McVeigh and his bombing of a federal building in Oklahoma City), even if they share similar grievances (such as government agents' illegal actions against gun owners at Ruby Ridge). Instead, NRA members prefer to think of themselves as typical Americans, patriots fighting for constitutional rights. They promote a moral politics rooted in the values of frontier masculinity that ultimately arise from a conservative worldview.

8

The Ties That Bind

The gun rights movement, like any other, formed and became effective for a number of reasons. The NRA has been particularly successful since the late 1990s, because it began to systematically frame threats to gun rights as threats to all individual rights and freedoms, and therefore to a conservative frontier masculinity. NRA frames aligned with and helped shape the concerns of like-minded gun rights supporters, leading these Gun Crusaders to dedicate much of their time and money to the NRA and the fight against gun control. Framing strategies are not the only reason why social movements emerge and succeed. Political opportunities can generate support and lead to meaningful change. A new president who supports gun rights or a famous and widely respected figure willing to be the public face of a movement may increase people's participation, as they sense an opportunity to create positive change.

Similarly political threats often lead people to mobilize and bring about change. Widespread calls for gun control after a major gun violence episode or impending gun control legislation may motivate people to join or increase their commitment to a movement. Although the political climate (opportunities or threats) may be ripe and a large number of potential movement activists may share the same ideology and beliefs, movements generally require organization and social networks to succeed. Social movement organizations, like the NRA on behalf of the gun rights movement, can mobilize resources, notably time and money, and thereby coordinate potential supporters into a more unified force. Of course, frames, opportunities, and threats overlap. Opportunities and threats are not absolutes but rather are framed and perceived by leaders and supporters. The creation and effective use of the frame "gun rights" is rooted in both the shared cultural language of the 1960s cycle of protest (Civil Rights, Women's Rights, and so on) and a broader American emphasis on rights and freedoms. The amount and use of resources a movement can mobilize also greatly impact the political opportunities or threats it faces, and therefore the movement's success.[1]

Officially the NRA is nonpartisan. Unofficially it is a sledgehammer for conservative causes and Republican politicians. The National Rifle Association is the leading conservative social movement organization fighting not just the gun war but the culture wars. No other organization comes close to the NRA's powerful combination of membership numbers, revenue, political power, the ability to mobilize its members, and lack of strong opposition. Broadly speaking, the Christian Right is a bigger conservative force, but it has many voices addressing a number of issues through an array of organizations. The gun rights movement, and, more accurately, the entire gun control/gun rights debate, is dominated by the NRA. Despite its official status as a nonpartisan organization, the reason the NRA dominates the gun debate is *because* of its partisanship. The NRA's conservative discourse and frames as well as its members' conservative politics are, by now, self-evident. The organization's right-wing credentials are also bolstered by its economic and political ties to conservatives and Republicans. Now more than ever the NRA's political donations go to conservative groups and politicians, its members' votes go to conservative candidates, its officers and directors are embedded in the conservative movement, its meetings welcome and celebrate conservative voices, and the organization aligns itself with Republican candidates and the Republican Party itself.

Follow the Money

The NRA brings in a lot of money from its millions of members and supporters, both in membership dues and donations. The organization's total income peaked at more than $200 million during Charlton Heston's NRA presidency and the end of the Clinton-Gore and beginning of the George W. Bush political eras.[2] A little less than 10% of NRA revenue is spent directly by the NRA's lobbying arm, the NRA Institute for Legislative Action, with many millions more spent on supporting lobbying activities through member communication and advertising. The NRA also raises millions of dollars from its members for its political action committee (PAC), the NRA Political Victory Fund. Most of those millions of dollars go to Republican candidates and organizations. In theory, a candidate from any party may support gun rights, and a gun rights organization may support any candidate that supports its agenda. In reality, however, since the 1960s and especially since the late 1990s, the gun debate has taken on an increasingly partisan tone. Today Republicans overwhelmingly oppose gun control and reap the rewards of gun rights support, mostly from the NRA.

For many years two political action committees have been the leading gun rights donors: the NRA and Gun Owners of America. A close look at where gun rights groups send their dollars speaks to the partisan nature of the gun debate. The percentage of gun rights PAC dollars going to Republicans has been in the high 80s and low 90s since the 1996 election cycle, peaking at 94% in 2002. In 1990 and 1992 the figures were only 65% and 64%, respectively. Gun rights dollars were largely going to Republicans then, but today they are almost exclusively ending up in Republicans' hands. In fact, excluding groups that are explicitly aligned with the party itself (such as the Republican National Committee), gun rights PACs are the most Republican-partisan of the top eighty industries dating back to 2000.[3]

Gun rights PACs contributed more than $20 million to political candidates and parties between 1990 and the end of September 2008, including about $4 million for the 2000 election cycle, highlighted by the battle for the presidency between Democrat Al Gore and NRA-backed Republican George W. Bush. In terms of dollars donated, these figures are modest compared to other industries. For example, "lawyers/law firms" topped all donors at nearly $1 billion during this period (they lean "strongly Democratic"). The biggest "strongly Republican" donor was the oil and gas industry at more than $225 million.[4] What distinguishes gun rights groups from these other industries is their heavy Republican partisanship and a multimillion-member grassroots army that recruits voters and goes to the polls.

As the leading gun rights group, the NRA and its Political Victory Fund PAC reflect the trend in the gun rights industry. As an individual PAC, the NRA's power and influence is clear compared to individual PACs in other industries. For example, lawyers and law firms contributed more than $180 million during the 2004 cycle, but the top PAC in this industry was the Association of Trial Lawyers of America, which donated about $2.2 million to federal candidates and spent roughly $6.5 million.[5] Exxon Mobil topped the oil and gas PACs in 2004, with less than $1 million in contributions.[6] As shown in Figure 8.1, the NRA received a little over $1 million in donations for the same cycle, with 85% of the candidate money going to Republicans. NRA PAC expenditures, $12.8 million in 2004, are twice that of the Trial Lawyers PAC.[7]

If the NRA's PAC donated only about $1 million to federal candidates and parties, where did the other millions of dollars go? Much of the money went toward "independent expenditures." Whereas a law firm will

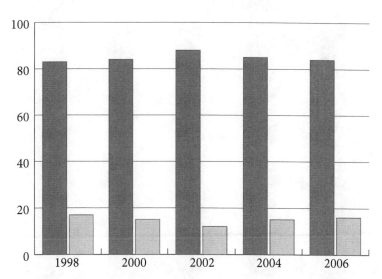

FIGURE 8.1
NRA PAC Contributions to Federal Candidates

All data are from the Center for Responsive Politics' Web site, opensecrets.org

bundle their lawyers' large donations and send these to a candidate or a party, the NRA is much more likely to spend the money itself rather than forwarding it to candidates and parties. Independent expenditures include money spent on behalf of candidates but not given directly to them, such as renting a billboard sign or airing a television advertisement endorsing John McCain or opposing Barack Obama for president.[8] Thus the NRA donated just over $1 million directly to federal candidates in 2004, but the organization spent more than $7 million on independent expenditures. Of this $7 million, $5 million went to ads *supporting* Republican candidates and nearly $2 million went to ads *opposing* Democratic candidates. The NRA's PAC spent only $21,461 supporting Democrats and not a single dollar opposing Republicans during this cycle. In other words, 99.7% of the NRA's 2004 independent expenditures helped Republican candidates. During the 2000 cycle, the NRA spent an even smaller amount helping Democratic candidates: $2,056 ($42 of which were used to oppose Republicans rather than support Democrats). Conversely, Republicans enjoyed nearly $6.5 million of the NRA's independent expenditures, or 99.97% (see Figure 8.2).[9]

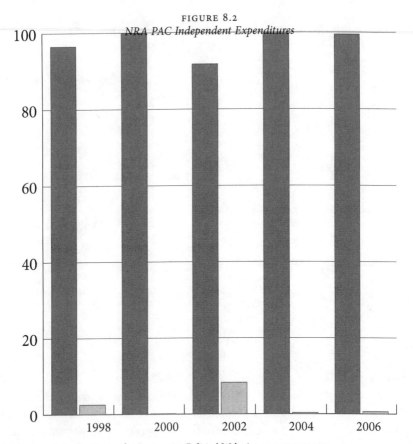

FIGURE 8.2
NRA PAC Independent Expenditures

All data are from the Center for Responsive Politics' Web site, opensecrets.org

Adding the roughly $1 million for federal candidates and parties and $7 million for independent expenditures, we still only account for approximately $8 million of the $12.8 million the NRA's PAC spent on the 2004 elections. About $3 million of the remaining money went to postage, printing, mailings, and advertisements costs.[10] With four million members, the NRA spends a considerable amount on internal communications, alerting its members to gun rights supporters and opponents running for office.[11] In addition to costs associated with any operation of this size (banking, supplies, etc.), the NRA also donates money to other PACs as well as to state and local politicians. In 2004, among the five-figure contributions of the Political Victory Fund were the following:

$80,000 to the Republican Governor's Association

$50,000 each to the Republican Leadership Council and the 2004 Joint State Victory Committee (Republican-supporting)

$30,000 each to the Florida Republican Party, the National Republican Congressional Committee, the National Republican Senatorial Committee, and the Republican National Committee

$25,000 to the Republican State Leadership Committee

$15,000 to both the (Republican) Dominion Leadership Trust PAC and the Illinois Republican State Senate Committee

$10,000 each to the Georgia Republican Party, the (Republican) Leadership PAC, and the (Republican) Senate Majority 2004 PAC.

The only five-figure donation to Democrats was a $10,000 contribution to the Democratic Party of Georgia.

For the five election cycles between 1998 and 2006, the NRA's PAC has been outside the top-ten list in total expenditures for all PACs only once, coming in at fourteenth in 2006 and eighth, fifth, second, and fifth during the earlier four cycles. The NRA Political Victory Fund has also been in the top ten among all PACs in independent expenditures during these cycles. More important, it has been *the* top Republican-leaning PAC for every one of these cycles. Partial data for 2008 suggest that these trends continued. Although the NRA Political Victory Fund did not contribute the most money to Republican candidates directly, its independent expenditures ensures its status as the most important single PAC for the Republican Party.[12] As if this was not enough to solidify its status as a Republican bedrock, the NRA spends millions more that it does not have to report to the Federal Election Commission (FEC), such as issue ads, including a reported $20 million for the 2000 election cycle.[13]

Considering these numbers, clearly the NRA has largely shed any pretense of nonpartisanship. Although not every dollar is spent to support Republicans, most are, and this pattern markedly began during the 2000 election. The Bush-Gore contest was a key election year for the gun debate, evidenced by the NRA Political Victory Fund's ranking second in total expenditures of any PAC, and fourth among all direct contributions to Republican candidates.[14]

American Handgunner writer Cameron Hopkins argued,

Previously, the NRA had backed candidates from either party who had a strong pro-gun record. This time the NRA opened its coffers primarily to the Republican Party. NRA spent $25 million during the fall campaign, including $17 million through ILA [Institute for Legislative Action], and $1.5 million directly to the Republican Party. Such largesse was not missed by Republican organizers who now regard the NRA as the single most powerful vote-getter for the party.[15]

Indeed, other than the NRA's record-setting spending during the 2000 elections, their spending in 2004 and 2006 (nonpresidential election cycles) looks the same.[16] Overwhelmingly, the NRA's Political Victory Fund PAC gives money directly to Republican candidates and Republican PACs, spends its own money on behalf of Republican candidates or in opposition to Democratic ones, and spends a lot of money informing its members which (mostly Republican) candidates support gun rights and which (mostly Democratic) candidates support gun control. The NRA's record-setting spending in 2000 signaled that it was willing to put its faith in the Republican Party. This move was largely a response to eight years of Bill Clinton's support for gun control measures and the threat of another four or eight years of Al Gore posing the same problem for the NRA.

The NRA's Institute for Legislative Action director, Chris W. Cox, brags on the NRA Web site that during the 2004 elections the NRA was responsible for 6.5 million endorsement postcards and letters, 4.6 million endorsement newspaper poly-bags, 4 million John Kerry "That dog don't hunt" fliers (Figure 8.3), 2.4 million endorsement phone calls, 1.6 million bumper stickers, 28,000 television ads, 20,000 radio ads, 1,700 newspaper ads, and 510 billboards, with much of these targeting key battleground states such as Ohio.[17] "That dog don't hunt" flyers and billboards were Cox's idea, the result of his 2004 election strategy brainstorming for the NRA. Anticipating the Democrats trying to recruit gun-owning voters, Cox scribbled down the hunting metaphor and embellished it by adding a dog that literally does not hunt—a French Poodle with a pink ribbon—to suggest that Democrats are as likely to be pro-gun as a French Poodle is to hunt.[18] Notably Vermont governor Howard Dean could have won the Democratic nomination, which would have doomed Cox's idea because the NRA backed Dean for governor and gave him "A" ratings.[19] Regardless of who the Democrat nominee was going to be, the NRA would be backing incumbent Republican President George W. Bush in his reelection campaign.

When Democratic primary voters eventually picked John Kerry, the stars had aligned for Cox and the NRA. Conservative anti-Kerry forces

That dog don't hunt.

John Kerry says he supports sportsmen's rights. But his record says something else.

- 👎 **John Kerry voted for Ted Kennedy's amendment to outlaw** most ammunition used by deer hunters.[1]

- 👎 **John Kerry supports higher taxes on** firearms and ammunition.[2]

- 👎 **John Kerry voted in favor of banning** semi-automatic firearms, including many firearms favored by sportsmen.[3]

- 👎 **John Kerry voted to allow** big city politicians to sue the American firearms industry and hold legitimate firearms manufacturers and dealers responsible for the acts of criminals.[4]

- 👎 **John Kerry voted to close** off hundreds of thousands of acres to hunters.[5]

- 👎 **John Kerry voted to commend Rosie O'Donnell's** Million Mom March, an organization calling for gun owner licensing, gun registration, and other radical restrictions on law-abiding gun owners.[6]

- 👎 **With a 20-year record of voting against** sportsmen's rights, it's no wonder John Kerry has been called a "hero" by the Humane Society of the United States, an extremist group that wants to outlaw hunting in America.[7]

If John Kerry wins, **you lose.**

NRA-POLITICAL VICTORY FUND
11250 Waples Mill Road • Fairfax, Virginia 22030 • www.NRAPVF.org • Chris W. Cox, Chairman

VOTE FREEDOM FIRST

[1]Voted for Kennedy Amendment to S.1805 (3/2/2004). [2]On CNN "Late Edition" (11/7/1993) Kerry said "I think you ought to tax all ammunition more, personally. I think you ought to tax guns." [3]Nine separate votes for gun ban legislation. Most recently, Kerry voted to amend S.1805 to include the Feinstein amendment to reauthorize the Clinton gun ban for ten years (3/2/2004). [4]Voted to amend S.1805 to include gun ban legislation, effectively killing lawsuit reform legislation. [5]Voted against Wallop Amendment to S.21 (8/25/1994). [6]Voted for Daschle Amendment to S.2521 (5/17/2000). [7]Humane Society of the United States (not the American Humane Society), which wants to ban all sport hunting in America, called Kerry a "hero" for his anti-hunting record (see www.HSUS.org).

PAID FOR BY NRA POLITICAL VICTORY FUND WWW.NRAPVF.ORG AND NOT AUTHORIZED BY ANY CANDIDATE OR CANDIDATE'S COMMITTEE

Figure 8.3. A 2004 election advertisement warns that Democratic presidential candidate John Kerry is a threat to gun rights and, implicitly to frontier masculinity. NRA Political Victory Fund, http://www.nrapvf.org/media/pdf/doghunt.htm.

invested their resources in framing Kerry as a bit too "French"—code for elitist, arrogant, and effeminate. There was a particularly strong anti-French sentiment at the time, created and reinforced by conservatives upset with France for opposing the Iraq War.[20] Secretary of Defense Donald Rumsfeld famously dismissed France (and Germany) as "Old Europe" to marginalize their antiwar efforts at the UN prior to the U.S. invasion of Iraq.[21] A couple of months later, in early 2003, Republicans Bob Ney and Walter Jones spearheaded a change at the House of Representatives cafeterias—French fries were officially renamed "freedom fries" and French toast became "freedom toast" as a symbolic rebuke of French antiwar efforts.[22]

The NRA's message to gun owners: a pink-bowed French Poodle "don't hunt" and a (pinko) "French" Democrat won't fight. Kerry's distinguished combat service record was not enough to prevent him from being painted by conservatives as not masculine, an indecisive "flip-flopper" incapable of strong and swift action. The NRA's sizable efforts to cast Kerry as dishonest and a wimp demonstrates their ongoing efforts to become the most important Republican-backing group in the country, spending millions of dollars and turning out millions of voters.

Like PAC contributions to candidates and parties or internal communication costs targeting members or employees, independent expenditures such as the NRA's anti-Kerry ads must be reported to the FEC. The NRA and other organizations can also run issue ads that do not explicitly endorse or oppose any candidate, and the law does *not* require this money to be reported. For example, the other NRA, the National Restaurant Association may run newspaper ads opposing an increase in the minimum wage, or the Human Rights Campaign may create and air a television ad opposing a state ballot measure banning same-sex marriage. Similarly the NRA runs ads opposing state or federal gun control legislation. Of course, political candidates may simultaneously run ads that share their views on these issues, enabling voters to see, for example, that the NRA wants you to support gun rights and John McCain says that he will not sign any gun control legislation as president. Therefore, McCain must be the NRA's candidate.

The NRA's Political Victory Fund PAC made the "Heavy Hitters" list of the "100 biggest givers in American politics since 1989," sponsored by the Center for Responsive Politics.[23] The NRA ranked thirty-fourth with more than $16 million in contributions to federal candidates and party committees, 82% of which went to Republicans. This made the NRA the third biggest "Strongly Republican" donor—70% plus of donations having gone to Republicans—among all PACs, as well as the only one in the top fifty that gave more than 80% of its money to Republicans. The NRA trails only the Altria Group (formerly Philip Morris, the leading tobacco producer) and the National Beer Wholesalers Association among strongly Republican donors, but, in reality, the NRA is far more valuable to Republicans than the other two. Whereas the NRA has spent millions of dollars in independent expenditures since 1998 to promote Republican candidates, the Altria Group had no independent expenditures and the Beer PAC only spent six figures one time—to back the Colorado Senate run of Coors Brewing Company chairman Pete Coors.[24]

Much more important, the tobacco and beer PACs do not have a multimillion-member grassroots army behind them, ready and willing to get out the vote and vote themselves for Republican (pro-gun) candidates. Politicians from both parties are well aware of the importance of the gun debate for voters. The importance of the gun vote for Republicans is well documented, dating back to at least the 1994 Republican takeover of the House of Representatives, a year gun owners comprised one-third of all votes for Republican congressional candidates.[25] The NRA frames gun rights as a conservative culture war issue that is threatened by left-wing big government, gun control politicians. In response, NRA members send the organization millions of dollars to help swing elections in favor of gun rights supporters. Their money takes them far, but the NRA's army of voters makes them the unmatched conservative culture war force for the Republican Party.

Ties to Congress

Partly because of the millions of dollars the NRA gives to and spends on behalf of political candidates and the number of their members that vote and contact their representatives about gun rights, the NRA wields a great deal of power on Capitol Hill. A 2001 survey by *Fortune* magazine crowned the NRA's lobbying wing the most powerful in Washington.[26] Although the NRA frames any form of gun control legislation as a slippery slope threat down the path to gun registration and eventual confiscation, no such serious legislative threats to gun rights exist. It doesn't hurt the NRA's cause that at least eleven sitting members of Congress have served on the NRA board of directors since guns became a culture war issue. Prior to the 2008 elections, current NRA board members include Senator

Larry Craig (R-ID) and House of Representatives members Don Young (R-AK) and Dan Boren (D-OK). Although a fair number of Democrats have been on the NRA board over the years, they tend to be conservative Democrats from Republican-leaning states and districts, such as Georgia Democrat Zell Miller.

The NRA's rank as the most powerful lobby is once again a reflection of the group's influence at the polls much more so than its economic might. Thanks to millions of printed NRA magazines and instant communications through faxes, e-mail, and Web sites, the NRA's Institute for Legislative Action (NRA-ILA) can alert members to gun bills and generate a flood of calls and mail to any politician's office. NRA-ILA has spent about $18 million on lobbying between 1998 and September 2008.[27] That, of course, is a respectable figure, but, by contrast, some of the biggest spenders during this period include the U.S. Chamber of Commerce at $427 million, the American Medical Association ($195 million), General Electric ($178 million), and the American Association of Retired Persons ($148 million).[28]

Similarly, the amount that the gun rights industry spends on lobbying pales in comparison with those of other industries. The top slot during this period was the pharmaceutical industry, spending a stunning $1.5 billion, and joined by other billion-dollar spenders in the insurance industry and the electrical utilities industry.[29] The NRA, and its four million members, get a lot more bang for their fewer bucks. Gun rights groups have spent about $50 million on lobbying since 1998 (fellow gun rights group Gun Owners of America often outspends the NRA on lobbying), whereas gun control groups only spent a little over $8 million.[30] For the 2000 election, Firearms/Guns/Ammunition lobbies had the 65th most lobbyists out of 76 issue areas. The 114 lobbyists in this area worked for 46 clients, including gun rights groups like the NRA, gun control groups, and firearms industry groups. By contrast, the 1,400 groups lobbying on taxation/internal revenue code matters employed nearly 3,000 lobbyists.[31] Given that the NRA is merely one group among many in an issue area ranking in the bottom ten, it seems almost incomprehensible that the NRA lobby could ever be ranked highly, let alone be considered the most powerful of all. In naming the NRA the most powerful lobby, *Fortune* magazine implicitly explains why the NRA's lobbying wing is so powerful:

> Nothing inspires zealotry like a threat, and few people feel more threatened than gun owners, more and more of whom are finding comfort in

the NRA. It has 4.3 million members, up one million since last year, and two million since 1998. Its budget increased from $180 million to $200 million last year, including $35 million for political campaigns. The money supports a state-of-the-art lobbying machine with its own national news-cast, one million precinct-level political organizers, and an in-house tele-marketing department. The NRA's pre-election rallies in 25 cities last year drew 5,000 to 9,000 people each—often more than [Democratic Presi-dential candidate] Gore drew.[32]

Big business may have deeper pockets, but the NRA's big stick is its four million members, many of whom will vote solely or primarily based on a candidate's views on guns.

Among its many political activities, the NRA publishes voter guides in its magazines. Only one member I interviewed expressly admitted only using NRA voter guides at the ballot box. But given NRA members' status as high-information voters—particularly regarding candidates' views on guns—I imagine that NRA voter guides merely serve as confirmation to many Gun Crusaders. As one NRA voter laughingly pointed out, NRA candidates are virtually all Republicans, so gun rights supporters can sim-ply vote the party line. Though the partisan split on gun control is not quite so simple, the pattern is strong.

Looking at 2008 NRA Political Victory Fund ratings for members of Congress, the NRA assigned ratings of "A-" or higher to 177 Republicans but awarded that rating to only 57 Democrats. The vast majority of strong gun rights supporters in Congress are Republicans, though some Demo-crats are on their side. Completing this partisan picture of the gun debate are the candidates who favor gun control and receive "F" ratings from the NRA. In 2008, 144 Democrats were given failing grades versus only 3 Re-publicans.[33] Adding to these numbers, the congressional support for gun rights over gun control reduces the likelihood of gun control legislation passing. It is important to emphasize that this situation occurred during a cycle when Democrats regained control of both the Senate and the House, although President Bush's potential use of the veto could serve as another NRA-backed obstacle to gun control legislation.

Several months before the 2008 elections, the Democratic primary race had come down to two candidates: Barack Obama spent little time dis-cussing gun control, whereas Hillary Clinton tried to appeal to gun own-ers by citing her childhood shooting experiences. Their Republican coun-terpart, John McCain, spoke at the 2008 NRA annual meetings in the hope of mending fences after having criticized and clashed with the NRA in the past.[34] After Obama secured the Democratic nomination, guns continued to receive little attention for the rest of the campaign. By 2008, the NRA and other Gun Crusaders have taught politicians enough lessons at the polls to make most gun control supporters avoid or downplay their views on the issue.

Clinton-Bush Gun Laws

Presidents Bill Clinton and George W. Bush signed into law several gun-related bills from 1993 to 2008, four of which I discuss here. Bill Clinton signed the Brady Handgun Violence Prevention Act (the Brady Bill) in 1993.[35] The bill's roots lay in an assassination attempt on Ronald Reagan more than a decade earlier, when his press secretary, Jim Brady, was shot and partially paralyzed. Sarah Brady, Jim's wife, became a champion of gun control, eventually chairing Handgun Control, Inc., later renamed the Brady Campaign to Prevent Gun Violence.[36] The House version of the Brady Bill was introduced by gun control supporter and eventual New York senator Charles Schumer, and was "to provide for a waiting period before the purchase of a handgun, and for the establishment of a national instant criminal background check system to be contacted by firearms dealers before the transfer of any firearm." Of the 435 members of the House of Representatives, 155 signed on as cosponsors of the legislation. In the end, Democrats voted 182 to 70 in favor of the bill, and Republicans opposed it by a vote of 116 to 56. In the Senate the bill passed 63 to 36, with 16 Republicans voting in favor and 8 Democrats voting against the gun control legislation.[37]

A year later, and shortly before congressional elections, Clinton signed the Violent Crime Control and Law Enforcement Act of 1994. Included in this enormous bill was the Federal Assault Weapons Ban, which outlawed civilian sales of certain assault style weapons that had been produced after the ban. The bill was introduced in the House by Democrat Jack Brooks of Texas, a lifelong NRA member who opposed the ban but backed the broad bill despite the ban's inclusion. As a result, Brooks became an NRA target in the 1994 elections. In the House two Democrats co-sponsored the legislation; Democrats supported it roughly three to one, and Republicans opposed it by a similar ratio. In the Senate only two Democrats opposed the legislation, and just six Republicans supported it.[38]

Two months later Republicans took back control of the House for the first time in forty years. Jack Brooks was among the many Democrats to lose his seat to a pro-gun Republican challenger. President Clinton summed up the 1994 elections in his autobiography:

The NRA had a great night. They beat both Speaker Tom Foley and Jack Brooks, two of the ablest members of Congress, who had warned me this would happen. Foley was the first Speaker to be defeated in more than a century. Jack Brooks had supported the NRA for years and had led the fight against the assault weapons ban in the House, but as chairman of the Judiciary Committee he had voted for the overall crime bill even after the ban was put into it. The NRA was an unforgiving master: one strike and you're out. The gun lobby claimed to have defeated nineteen of the twenty-four members on its hit list. They did at least that much damage and could rightly claim to have made [Newt] Gingrich the House Speaker.[39]

Although Clinton exaggerated the NRA's electoral strength at times, scholarly research showed that the NRA played an important role in the 1994 Republican takeover of the House.[40] After many years locking horns with Bill Clinton, some NRA members displayed their feelings on bumper stickers such as "Charlton Heston Is My President." The NRA struggled with factional battles, financial concerns, and a consequent drop in membership in the next few years, but by the time Charlton Heston became the NRA's public face in 1997, the organization was well on its way to becoming a Republican-backing political force.

The NRA's new power was on full display during the 2000 presidential elections. The organization helped end the Democratic gun control, Clinton-Gore combo and reaped the reward of a strongly pro-gun president in George W. Bush. During the campaign season, NRA Vice President Kayne Robinson told a gathering of NRA members that "gun rights advocates would have 'unbelievably friendly relations' with a Bush White House . . . 'if we win, we'll have a Supreme Court that will back us to the hilt. If we win, we'll have a president . . . where we work out of their office.'" [41] The gun debate tables had indeed turned in the NRA's favor. When the assault weapons ban was set to expire in 2004 owing to a ten-year sunset provision, the NRA scored a major symbolic victory. President Bush had indicated that he would sign an extension, but he never pressured congressional leaders to bring the bill before him and the Republican-led Congress gladly let the ban expire.[42]

George W. Bush signed two significant gun-related laws, and both had the NRA's support. The first was the Protection of Lawful Commerce in Arms Act, "a bill to prohibit civil liability actions from being brought or continued against manufacturers, distributors, dealers, or importers of firearms or ammunition for damages, injunctive or other relief resulting from the misuse of their products by others."[43] The bill was an effort to end lawsuits against manufacturers that held them liable for gun violence. These lawsuits, the NRA argued, could be used to bankrupt the firearms industry and were a backdoor gun control scheme.[44] The bill was introduced in the Senate by Republican Larry Craig, an NRA board member, and was sponsored by sixty-one cosponsors eventually passing with a 65 to 31 vote. Fourteen Democratic senators supported the NRA-backed bill, and two Republicans opposed it. When introduced by a Republican in the House, along with 257 co-sponsors, it passed by a vote of 283 to 144. Republicans voted for the bill by 223 to 4, and Democrats opposed it by 140 to 59. President Bush signed the bill into law in 2005. The Republicans, with little support and significant opposition from Democrats, delivered legislation for the gun industry and the NRA.

In 2007 gun control became a major issue once again. A mass shooting at Virginia Tech University resulted in thirty-two deaths. The shooter, student Seung Hui Cho, should not have been allowed to purchase handguns because of his history of mental illness. However, the National Instant Criminal Background Check System (NICS), used to do background checks on gun buyers at the time of purchase, suffered from poor record keeping in some cases, and Cho was not flagged when purchasing the firearms. Having retaken both chambers of Congress by 2006, Democrats were intent on strengthening the NICS system. Senior Democrats and the NRA engaged in "sensitive talks" to do just this, with the NRA negotiating key concessions, including preventing the federal government from charging background check fees to either sellers or buyers and creating a petition process for people to be removed from the database if they have only minor infractions. Democrat Representative John Dingell (MI), a former NRA board member, led the talks. The NRA has long argued that it supports only "law-abiding" gun owners, so as long as the government does not retain gun purchase data, the NRA will not oppose the denial of gun purchases for certain convicted criminals, fugitives, persons with certain mental illnesses, and others deemed unfit for gun ownership.[45]

Gun Owners of America (GOA) opposed the bill and continued its on-going critique of the NRA as too quick to compromise. GOA argued that despite claims to the contrary, the bill would continue to prevent many military veterans from regaining their gun rights after losing these because of mental health issues. GOA was also unhappy that the compromises on the bill still satisfied Representative Carolyn McCarthy (D-NY), who came to Congress to push for gun control after her husband was one of six homicide victims and nineteen wounded in a shooting spree on the Long Island Railroad in 1993.[46]

McCarthy had been pushing to strengthen the NICS system for some time. The NRA-backed compromise bill, the NICS Improvement Amendments Act of 2007, was brought by McCarthy in the House along with fourteen Democratic and three Republican cosponsors. It passed by unanimous consent in both chambers and was signed into law by President Bush in January 2008.[47] After the worst single shooter killing spree in U.S. history, and with Democrats controlling both the Senate and the House, congressional leaders still went to the NRA to receive their blessing (and give the NRA several concessions) on a narrow piece of gun control legislation largely meant to fix inadequacies in earlier legislation. As other scholars have pointed out, Congress has had little effect on gun owning or gun crime, instead passing legislation that merely fiddles at the periphery.[48]

No national or congressional debate about gun registration and confiscations followed the Virginia Tech tragedy. Given that Republicans are firmly in the NRA's camp and many Democrats also consistently oppose gun control, that the NRA supports (mostly Republican) pro-gun candidates with millions of dollars, that NRA board members serve in Congress, that gun control organizations are weak, and that a powerful NRA lobby walks the halls of Congress to remind politicians of their enormous and active gun rights army, several conclusions can be drawn: even before the U.S. Supreme Court decision overturning Washington's handgun ban on Second Amendment grounds, restrictive federal gun control legislation appeared highly unlikely, gun registration was a non-starter, and gun confiscation was unfathomable. The NRA's 2008 presidential candidate lost, but two of the other three branches of government remain firmly in the corner of gun rights. The NRA has embedded itself with the conservative movement and the Republican Party, thus ensuring a seat at the table and a chorus of loud congressional voices whenever gun legislation appears.

Movement Conservatives

The conservative wing of the Republican Party has gained increasing sway since their candidate, Barry Goldwater, won the party's nomination (but was later defeated by President Lyndon Johnson) in 1964. Since the 1990s, gun owners have increasingly become a reliable vote for Republicans and a trusted force for the conservative movement. Among the most dedicated political party members are the delegates who vote at the parties' national conventions, typically only symbolically casting their votes as a representative for their states' earlier primaries and caucuses. Whereas 50% of 2008 Democratic delegates in Denver self-identified as moderates, 72% of the GOP delegates in Minneapolis identified as conservatives. Roughly one-third of the Republican delegates identified as evangelicals, 60% reported that they have a firearm in their household, and one out of four claimed they were NRA members. NRA membership rates among 2008 Republican National Committee delegates were almost 50% higher than in 2000. On the other hand, only 3% of Democratic delegates self-identified as NRA members.[49] Conservatives have taken control of the Republican Party, and right at or near the top of the most important and influential groups among conservatives are the NRA's Gun Crusaders.

In 2009, along with conservative organizations such as Concerned Women for America, Human Events, the National Taxpayers Union, and the Young America's Foundation, the National Rifle Association cosponsored the Conservative Political Action Conference.[50] CPAC is a gathering of thousands of current and future leaders of the conservative movement, hosted each year by the American Conservative Union. The ACU is committed "to a market economy, the doctrine of original intent of the framers of the Constitution, traditional moral values, and a strong national defense," identifying itself as "the nation's oldest and largest conservative grassroots lobbying organization."[51] It was formed shortly after Republican Barry Goldwater lost to President Johnson in 1964. Today the ACU has about a million members, publishes a widely used congressional rating of conservatism, and hosts the annual CPAC gathering in Washington, D.C.[52] Everyone who is anyone in the conservative movement makes an appearance at CPAC. In 2008 alone, CPAC speakers included President Bush, Vice President Cheney, former House Speaker Newt Gingrich, and the then remaining 2008 Republican presidential candidates John McCain, Mike Huckabee, Mitt Romney, and Ron Paul. Ronald Reagan spoke at CPAC a dozen times, both before and throughout his presidency.[53]

For many years, NRA leaders Charlton Heston, Wayne LaPierre, Kayne Robinson (a former chairman of the Republican Party of Iowa), Sandy Froman, and John Sigler have attended and spoken at CPAC. NRA Executive Vice President LaPierre is on the ACU's board of directors. Likewise, ACU chairman David A. Keene has been on the NRA's board of directors and was elected 2nd Vice President of the NRA in 2007. If tradition holds, he will move up the ladder in the following years, taking over as NRA President in 2011. President of Americans for Tax Reform, Grover Norquist, sits on both the ACU and NRA boards, further linking the NRA to the conservative movement.

Like the ACU's Keen, Norquist is a major player in the conservative movement. Norquist's involvement included leading the National College Republicans and the National Taxpayers Union before forming Americans for Tax Reform (ATR). In response to President Reagan's request, Norquist founded ATR in 1985. He's been a key figure in President George W. Bush's tax cut policies.[54] Norquist is deeply anti-tax and anti-big government, once famously telling an interviewer on national radio, "I don't want to abolish government. I simply want to reduce it to the size where I can drag it into the bathroom and drown it in the bathtub."[55]

A couple of years later, in another National Public Radio interview, Norquist drew an analogy between the Holocaust and the U.S. government not abolishing the estate tax (or, as Norquist calls it, the "death tax"). He reasoned that both are cases of the majority allowing the government to do something to the minority—genocide against religious and other minority groups in the former case and, in the latter, heavily taxing estates worth more than $2 million that are passed down upon someone's death. Norquist explained, "I mean, that's the morality of the Holocaust. 'Well, it's only a small percentage,' you know. 'I mean, it's not you, it's somebody else.'" When the interviewer, Terry Gross, somewhat incredulously questioned if he just compared the estate tax to the Holocaust, he replied:

No, the morality that says it's okay to do something to a group because they're a small percentage of the population is the morality that says that the Holocaust is okay because they didn't target everybody, just a small percentage. "What are you worried about? It's not you. It's not you. It's them." And arguing that it's okay to loot some group because it's *them*, or kill some group because it's *them* and because it's a small number, has no place in a democratic society that treats people equally. The government's going to do something to or for us, it should treat us all equally.[56]

Though Norquist has made a couple of media blunders, his importance to the conservative movement is widely recognized. Among his many ties to the Republican Party, he helped write the Republican Contract with America, ushering in a significant conservative and Republican victory in the 1994 congressional elections.[57] Soon after Democrat Bill Clinton took office, Norquist began holding a weekly meeting of conservatives in Washington. The Wednesday meetings include representatives from conservative think tanks, lobbying groups, and organizations addressing a full range of interests, including gun rights, tax opposition, property rights, school vouchers, religious conservatives, and small business owners. "Norquist calls it a 'leave us alone' coalition, divided on some individual issues but united by a desire to limit the size and power of government. 'As long as the Christians don't steal anyone's guns, the anti-tax activists don't violate anyone's property rights, the property owners don't interfere with the home-schoolers, the home-schoolers don't want to regulate the small businessmen and the gun owners agree not to throw condoms at the Christians' kids, then we can all work together,' he says."[58] The meetings are also attended by the staffs of Republican politicians.

Two years before he ran for president, and throughout his presidency, George W. Bush sent a representative to the Wednesday meetings. Vice President Cheney also sent a representative. The heart of the conservative movement and the base of the Republican Party—gun rights crusaders, anti-tax activists, and the Christian Right—attends these meetings, so leading Republicans send representatives to keep a pulse on the movement and generate support. There are clear benefits for the movement as well. For example, all three U.S. delegates sent by the Bush administration to the 2006 United Nations Conference on Small Arms are "strong NRA supporters," which comes as no surprise given that two of them—former governor James Gilmore, III (R-VA) and American Conservative Union chairman David Keene—are NRA board members.[59]

Norquist is an important member of the NRA board and the conservative movement, but he is primarily known for his anti-tax rather than anti-gun control agenda. The figure most closely associated with gun rights since the late 1990s remains Charlton Heston. Like other NRA leaders, Heston was involved in a number of conservative movement causes, most of which he addressed in his culture war speeches just prior to and after joining the NRA board of directors. Heston's political activism shifted Right after his support for Civil Rights decades ago. He campaigned for Ronald Reagan and both Bush presidents, was a major voice in the anti-labor union "right to work" movement, gave the introduction to an anti-abortion film, and served as an advisory board member for Accuracy in Media, a conservative media watchdog group, and as a board member for U.S. English—a social movement organization dedicated to making English the official language of the United States.[60] Heston, like the NRA, embedded himself in the conservative movement and Republican Party by waging a conservative culture war against liberals and Democrats. No liberal culture war forces serve on the NRA's board or lead the organization as executives and officers. The Gun Crusaders are movement conservatives.

A look at the NRA's members' banquet keynote speakers further illustrates the organization's connections with conservatives/Republicans. Prior to the NRA's politicization and internal coup in 1977, their honored guests were almost uniformly military leaders. Today the lineup is filled mostly with conservative political voices. The keynote speakers at the NRA's annual meeting Members' Banquet, dating back to 2000, included the following: conservative media figure and newly minted lifetime NRA member Glenn Beck (who admitted, "Let's be honest. I don't know my butt from my elbow when it comes to guns."),[61] George W. Bush-appointed U.S. Representative to the United Nations John Bolton (deeply involved in many Republican administrations and conservative groups like the American Enterprise Institute), retired army general Tommy Franks, former Republican House majority leader Tom Delay, Vice President Dick Cheney, Florida Republican Governor Jeb Bush, conservative Democratic Senator Zell Miller, Bush administration Interior Secretary Gale Norton, and then Oklahoma Republican Congressman J.C. Watts. The only Democrat in the bunch, Zell Miller, went on to support Republican presidential candidate Bush in 2004, even speaking at the Republican National Convention, and was elected to the NRA board of directors.

Gale Norton, speaking at the 2001 NRA meetings, was the first U.S. administration official to do so since President Ronald Reagan in 1983. She thanked NRA members for helping put George W. Bush in the White House.[62] Despite his nonpolitical credentials, General Franks was well versed in NRA political rhetoric, telling the crowd in 2006, "You folks, NRA, are patriots and intellectually gifted. You know the difference between criminals and citizens. You are the people who applaud those men and women who serve in our Armed Forces and law enforcement, who are not ashamed to say, 'One country under God.'"[63] The NRA said Bolton's 2007 remarks were "a sobering speech from [the] former U.S.

Ambassador to the United Nations, [outlining] how dangerously close our gun rights came to being decided by an international body."[64]

In his speech, Bolton highlighted the threats to international gun rights:

> The fact is that within the United States, on this issue and many others, these leftist groups could not prevail in a fair democratic contest. They find that in political environment after political environment their views are not the majority's views. So through the mechanism of what they call civil society, these nongovernmental organizations change the dimension of the problem from an issue of national policy to make it a matter of international policy, where they're going to have, in effect, a second bite at the apple they couldn't win in the American political context. They try to reargue it in the U.N. or other international organizations where they have a lot more supporters.[65]

The key to defending against a global gun ban, according to Bolton, is the American people, who must fight to prevent the loss of their sovereignty, and ultimately freedoms and democracy, to international forces.

The political inclinations and activities of the NRA leadership, including executive staff, officers, and directors, provide further evidence of the NRA's overall politics. In addition to members of Congress and people in the conservative movement, the NRA board of directors includes former governors (Republicans Joe Foss of South Dakota and James Gilmore III of Virginia), conservatives and Republicans who unsuccessfully ran for national, state, and local offices, gun industry executives (Steven Hornady of Hornady Manufacturing Company), academics, entertainment stars (actor Tom Selleck, rocker Ted Nugent, basketball star Karl Malone, and country singer Louise Mandrell), and notable figures such as *Soldier of Fortune* magazine founder Robert Brown and Lt. Col. Oliver North of Iran-Contra scandal fame.

Political donations by more than 150 NRA board members, officers, and executive leaders from the last decade demonstrate the heavily Republican bent of the NRA leadership, similar to the organization's donations.[66] The large donations of $500 and above to political candidates and organizations (such as national and state parties) from 1990 to 2008 testify to the fact that NRA leaders overwhelmingly support conservatives and Republicans.[67] NRA leaders made 547 large donations to conservatives and Republicans during this period, totaling more than $610,000.

Among NRA executive leadership, Institute for Legislative Action director James Jay Baker gave nearly $50,000 to the Right and about one-tenth of that amount to liberals and Democrats. Longtime Vice President and later NRA President Sandy Froman gave her entire $15,000 donation to conservatives and Republicans. Her predecessor and Charlton Heston's successor as NRA President, Kayne Robinson, also gave his whole contribution of nearly $10,000 to conservatives and Republicans. Neither Heston nor NRA Executive Vice President Wayne LaPierre made many large donations, but none of them went to liberals or Democrats. As a group, NRA leaders made 175 large donations to liberal and Democratic candidates and groups, totaling over $160,000. One NRA board members, J. D. Williams, donated nearly $70,000 to both sides, accounting for nearly half of the NRA leaders' donations to liberals and Democrats. In sum, NRA leaders gave more than three times as many large donations at a rate of more than 3.7 times the number of dollars to Republicans and conservatives compared to the amounts they gave to Democrats and liberals.

The NRA embeds itself within the conservative movement by using its vast resources to elect pro-gun Republicans to federal, state, and local offices, by electing Republican politicians and conservative leaders to the NRA's board of directors, and by participating in other conservative movement causes and organizations. This strategy is a response to the entangling of attacks on frontier masculinity by Democrats, first and foremost in the form of gun control but also through other culture war issues. This has resulted in the NRA facing little to no serious threats to gun control because Republican (and Democratic) candidates know that the NRA has a large and active base of support ready to swing an election in favor or opposition to a candidate. The Gun Crusaders have drawn clear alliances in the culture wars.

Epilogue
Tomorrow's NRA

The National Rifle Association and the gun rights movement both benefited from a modest storm of high-profile (yet unlikely and moderate) gun control threats in 2000, and a clearing of the skies soon after. There was an active, though decreasingly effective, federal gun control agenda during the Clinton years. The possibility of a 2000 election victory for Democrat Al Gore meant more threats of gun control. Even the usually anemic gun control groups seemed to have some momentum on their side. The Columbine school shootings were still fresh in Americans' minds, and months before the election the Million Mom March drew hundreds of thousands of gun control supporters to a rally in Washington. Staring down these opponents, the NRA and their new charismatic leader, Charlton Heston, warned gun owners of dramatic and permanent losses of gun rights. The NRA of this period fine-tuned its rhetoric, skillfully and repeatedly connecting threats to gun rights with threats to all individual rights and freedoms through a culture war.

The combination of threats to gun rights and the NRA's fanning of the flames resulted in a flood of new members and cash to the organization. In the end, the threats were abated, transformed instead into NRA victories and the promise of future opportunities to pass gun rights legislation. Bush beat Gore, gun control groups lost momentum, gun rights legislation abounded in state and federal legislatures, and NRA coffers overflowed. But success often breeds complacency. For an organization that thrives on actual and perceived threats to gun rights, and one that has faced few of any consequence since the 2000 elections, a fear-free forecast is not necessarily a sunny one. The NRA has likely peaked.

Several short- and long-term trends are working against the organization. After Charlton Heston stepped down because of illness and later died, NRA presidents have been a succession of publicly anonymous long-time Gun Crusaders. With gun control off the federal agenda and the 2008 Heller decision finally providing the NRA with a Supreme Court ruling confirming their individual-rights view of the Second Amendment, gun owners' fears have shrunk. Guns were rarely discussed during the 2008 presidential primary and election season. The Democrats fielded a candidate not known for his gun control agenda, and the Republicans a candidate who had clashed with the NRA in the past, leaving little hope of rallying the NRA base, whether for reasons of fear or excitement. After the 1994, 2000, and 2004 Republican victories, the Democratic Party seems content to avoid the topic of gun control, much less make it an election issue. The lack of an imposing gun control movement adds to the likelihood of apathy by gun rights backers. By all accounts, NRA membership bled out several hundred thousand shortly after the 2000 Bush victory over Gore. The long-term trends are probably worse for the organization, with increasing urbanization, a decreasing gun culture, and an older NRA membership that may be difficult to replace.

Still, the NRA is not about to wilt away. It brought in $165 million in revenue in 2006 (although it has been spending even more to press its agenda).[1] The 2008 annual meetings in Louisville, Kentucky, drew more than sixty-six thousand attendees.[2] The loss of hundreds of thousands of members was still only a small dent for a four-million-member organization. And those that leave are likely the least committed Peripheral members who sign up for a year or two, perhaps because they admired Charlton Heston, and then fail to renew. Early indications are that the membership losses were temporary, as levels again rose after Heston's health forced him to step down.[3] The Gun Crusaders aren't going anywhere. They will continue to speak loudly and carry a big stick.

Browsing through 2007 and 2008 issues of the NRA's political magazine, *America's First Freedom*, it appeared that the NRA briefly embraced the political opportunities of the Bush years and framed itself as a victor more often than it had done previously. Threat framing also appeared to have somewhat declined. But as the 2008 election season cranked up, so did the NRA. In his speech at the 2008 NRA annual meetings, EVP Wayne LaPierre kept up the NRA's now familiar fear tactics, warning, "The Second Amendment is facing a perfect storm. In fact, the worst I've seen in thirty years."[4]

In the summer of 2008 the NRA announced that it would spend $40 million on the fall elections, including $15 million directed at painting Illinois Senator and Democratic presidential candidate Barack Obama as a threat to gun rights. Even though the NRA recently won the Supreme

Figure E.1. An angry Barack Obama, then the Democratic Party's presidential nominee, aims to destroy gun rights by appointing Supreme Court Justices that oppose an individual's right to own and bear arms, according to this NRA article. *America's First Freedom,* October 2008, 2.

Court Heller case, affirming an individual right to bear arms, they used the closely divided result of the decision to cast Obama as a threat to gun rights (see Figure E.1).[5] An angry and defiant Obama—the mirror opposite of the even-keeled, calm-under-fire persona he projects (probably consciously so)—is shown pounding away at the Heller decision. If Supreme Court Justices retire, the NRA warns, an Obama victory could lead to Heller dissenters replacing justices in favor of the decision, thereby easily flipping the 5-4 ruling. Once again the implication is clear: electing liberal Democrats will lead not only to legislative but also judicial attacks on gun rights, and ultimately all individual rights and freedoms.

As always, much of the NRA's 2008 expenditures went toward informing and mobilizing current members. NRA members reportedly vote at an astounding rate of 95%, adding to the electoral power that comes with their size.[6] A December 2007 poll found that "twenty-seven percent of all likely voters said they would be more likely to support a candidate who was endorsed by the [NRA]." The NRA's endorsement of presidential candidates is more valuable to voters than an endorsement by the AFL-CIO union, the National Right-to-Life, former President Bill Clinton, then-President G. W. Bush, and even Oprah Winfrey.[7] A 2005 poll found that 18% of respondents viewed the NRA very favorably and another 42% favorably. Only 19% had an unfavorable view, and 15% a very unfavorable opinion of the NRA.[8] The depth and breadth of NRA support is not about to vanish.

Despite NRA opposition, the stars were aligned for Obama and the Democrats in 2008. Arizona senator and Republican presidential candidate John McCain was unable to overcome President Bush's high disapproval ratings, widespread home foreclosures, an economic meltdown, and a strong sense by voters that the country was on the wrong track. McCain's V.P. pick—lifetime NRA member, widely discussed moose hunter, and Alaska governor Sarah Palin—belatedly breathed life into the Republican ticket and shored up support for McCain among Gun Crusaders and conservatives. Palin appealed to the Right largely because of her symbolic representation of and efforts to reignite a conservative culture war. Immediately after she was announced as McCain's running mate, arch-conservative radio host Rush Limbaugh summarized his and millions of his listeners' feelings: "Sarah Palin: babies, guns, Jesus. Hot damn!"[9]

As the economic crisis grew and Obama's lead in the polls expanded, Palin and McCain extended their culture war attacks. They referred to his tax plan, if not Obama himself, as socialist. Fears of "big government" liberals redistributing tax dollars to the poor and stripping citizens of gun rights have worked well in the past, and may do so again in future presidential elections. In 2008, however, "babies, guns, Jesus," and even "socialism," were trumped by many Americans' concerns that the United States was staring down another Great Depression.[10] They voted for the candidate whose economic plan was furthest from the unpopular outgoing president, despite McCain and Palin deriding it as socialist.

The Republican ticket did not have a big enough base or win enough independents in 2008, but their culture war message continued to resonate with conservatives. As the Republican Party licks its wounds, questions arise as to its future. It has relied on the support of Gun Crusaders and the Christian Right as it ran and won on culture war issues, but this has resulted in the party shifting too far to the Right for many voters. Will these conservative culture war forces support a moderate candidate who has compromised or even opposed some of their causes but can appeal to enough voters in the center? Or will conservative cultural warriors abandon moderate candidates and reduce the Republican base enough to make it similarly unable to win national elections? There are other possibilities for Republicans, but immediately after the 2008 elections their prospects look grim and the party appears to be on the verge of a power struggle. As for the NRA and its base of supporters, the NRA's framing of Obama (and a Democratic Party that will control the Congress) as a threat to gun rights seemed to resonate with Gun Crusaders. Shortly after the election, gun sales rose sharply.[11]

Frontier Masculinity (Without the Frontier)

The American frontier has been closed for generations, yet its influence persists. Americans continue to own firearms and hunt in large numbers, and frontier images continue to be woven into the nation's cultural fabric, highlighted by frequent appearances in politics, advertising, and the media. Just as candidates and companies often engulf themselves in a sea of red, white, and blue, they also use frontier rhetoric and symbols to pitch themselves and their products. Listening to contemporary speeches and ads, at times it seems as though the frontier never closed.

In a long line of presidents that campaigned and governed against a frontier masculinity backdrop, George W. Bush best represents the power and limitations of that narrative. U.S. presidents, "leaders of the free world" as we prefer to call them, can frame freedom in various ways, but one highly resonant version promotes individual rights and lack of government interference in people's lives. Although Teddy Roosevelt and Ronald Reagan appropriated frontier images and rhetoric to boost their candidacies, they also spent a lot of time carrying guns on horseback and living a cowboy lifestyle, whether in real life or on the silver screen. They were able to craft images of themselves as self-made men, heroes of the frontier who could have just as easily been any hard-working American next door.

During Bush's campaign and much of his early presidency, many Americans identified with him as a person. They sympathized with his widely covered language blunders, shared his "with us or against us" dichotomous views of the world, and responded to his small-town Texas charm (although his Crawford ranch was only purchased in 1999, with some claiming it was an election ploy). In a likeability poll that could only appear during a presidential election season, independent voters said that they would rather drink a beer with Bush than with 2004 Democratic candidate John Kerry.[12] Bush's conservative politics and years in Texas (as a child, and later as a businessman and governor) gave him legitimacy as an "everyman" despite his wealthy background and attendance at elite preparatory schools, and then Yale and Harvard.

Regardless of whether this image was constructed to appeal to American voters or is simply his actual personality on display, Bush's frontier masculinity approach resonated with a wide audience. His projection as an ordinary American helped remove the barriers and social distance between voters and the world's most powerful politician. Although it is difficult to separate Bush's actual self from the characterizations of it created for political gain, one thing is clear—he is not a cowboy. He and his advisers skillfully appropriated some of this gun populism/frontier masculinity, offering a perspective on individual rights and freedoms that resonated with NRA members, most conservatives, as well as many other Americans.

Like any gunslinger, Bush was occasionally too quick on the trigger. He saw his popularity plummet toward the end of his second term, weighed down by his decision to invade and later maintain a major military presence in Iraq. During a period of heightened attacks on U.S. soldiers, Bush was widely criticized for his cowboy-laced threat to the attackers, telling them, "There are some who feel like the conditions are such that they can attack us [in Iraq]. My answer is, bring 'em on."[13]

In a later effort to ward off calls for Secretary of Defense Donald Rumsfeld to resign based on his poor handling of the Iraq conflict, Bush continued to assert his go-it-alone style: "I hear the voices, and I read the front page, and I know the speculation. But I'm the decider, and I decide what is best."[14] Bush has stuck to his guns on many issues, but this cowboy approach has transformed him from a popular figure known for choosing his own path into an isolated leader both outside and within his country's borders. Not every historical moment calls for frontier masculinity politics. As the response to Bush in his second term has shown, an unpopular war and a weak economy easily trump any likeability factor or leadership characteristics informed by frontier masculinity. More often than not, however, political candidates who can pull it off will benefit from drawing on frontier imagery.

Advertisements for everything from rural excursions to decidedly suburban products are another popular venue for frontier masculinity. Just as American men like Teddy Roosevelt feared the feminizing influence of city life, and escaped out West, today's highly urbanized population seeks out a frontier experience in the "Great Outdoors." About 80% of Americans live in what the U.S. Census defines as urban (non-rural) areas.[15] Just as their frontier predecessors did before them, millions of Americans today go hunting. Admittedly rural residents are much more likely to hunt, but many urban dwellers also pursue this outdoor experience reminiscent of earlier times (some, however, rely on "canned hunts" where sometimes exotic animals are fenced in and customers pay to bag a trophy kill).

For those who are not up for a kill, plenty of dude ranches offer frontier experiences for the whole family, including shooting and horseback instruction, cattle drives, and even river rafting, all while enjoying a stay in a lodge complete with hot tub, sauna, and massage services.[16] Suburban and urban residents have also chosen to jump onto steel horses in search of freedom and a feeling of independence, driving motorcycle sales to sustained levels of roughly one million per year since 2002.[17]

Some escapist options are available without actually leaving the suburbs for those who are less inclined to shoulder a rifle or jump on a Harley-Davidson. The automobile industry enjoyed years of an explosive sales growth of Sport Utility Vehicles (SUVs), marketing these almost uniformly as outdoor adventure vehicles—even though most would never leave pavement and many would require a tow truck if they did. Ford alone offered up SUVs named the Escape, Explorer, Expedition, and Excursion, competing with the Pathfinder, Trailblazer, Forester, Tracker, and Mountaineer. A pick-up truck finally discarded the thinly veiled metaphor and claimed the name that all others hinted at: the "Frontier."

Even minivans, which have found SUVs to be a serious competitor for family vehicles, have names associated with escaping to the frontier—Venture, Quest, Safari, Uplander, and the Montana. I suspect that no one driving a minivan would compare it to a frontier experience, and yet the advertising strategies persist, served up as antidotes to a mundane suburban existence. An early television advertisement for the Pontiac Montana minivan featured cowboys on horseback jumping into the moving vehicle somewhere on a dirt road out West (in an apparent escape attempt from, one can only assume, a bank robbery). The key feature pitched in this ad was sliding doors on both sides of the minivan. Presumably this feature appeals more to parents loading and unloading small kids, rather than real escape artists like Billy the Kid.

The frontier and frontier masculinity values such as independence, freedom, and self-reliance remain key features of our culture. Politicians, companies, and media—such as the still successful genre of Westerns, including *3:10 to Yuma* and 2007 Academy Award Best Picture *No Country For Old Men*—use these images to sell themselves and their products, and not just to conservative white men, although they likely respond more strongly to this narrative than other groups do. The NRA frames frontier masculinity as an ideology, a way of life, with gun rights keeping the United States and its religion of freedom afloat despite stormy waters.

Gun Crusaders' deep commitment to gun rights and frontier masculinity speaks to the NRA's current and future ability to remain a potent political force. It is an impressive feat considering all the trends working against them. While the U.S. population continues to grow, the number of hunters is on the decline, slipping from 14 million to roughly 12.5 million adults during the ten-year period ending in 2006. This is partly a result of *who* goes hunting. Over 90% of hunters are men and 96% are white—neither group is on the verge of extinction, but white men represent a decreasing percentage of the population.[18] The number of gun owners is also declining because of the declining rural population. Only about one-third of U.S. homes have a gun in them, and nothing suggests that the trend downward will reverse.[19] As Americans become less likely to own guns and hunt, the NRA *should* find itself increasingly marginalized and outnumbered. Yet their power and influence endures, and I believe that it will for a long time.

The Future of Gun Politics

Prior to a 2007 Democratic presidential candidate debate sponsored by CNN/YouTube, Americans were invited to submit video questions. One Michigan resident asked the Democrats, "To all the candidates, tell me your position on gun control, as myself and other Americans really want to know if our babies are safe." He then picked up a large military-style rifle outlawed under the since expired 1994 Federal Assault Weapons Ban, stating, "This is my baby." In response, then Democratic candidate and Delaware Senator Joe Biden said, "I'll tell you what, if that is his baby, he needs help."[20] That Michigan gun owner no doubt feels the same about Biden's support for gun control, and perhaps the Democratic Party as a whole.

Gun Crusaders have a love affair with individual rights and freedoms, if not guns themselves. Politicians who chide them for it are attacking not just a private possession but a symbol of everything these gun rights advocates believe in and pledge to defend. To understand the NRA's success in the gun debate, consider the meaning guns have for both sides and ask yourself, "Which side will mobilize more supporters, especially deeply committed ones willing to spend their time and money fighting for their cause?"

Gun control supporters enter the fray because they are upset, arguing that people, especially children, are being shot and killed, and that violent crimes are occurring because of the wide availability of guns. Gun rights supporters join the fight because they are afraid, arguing that their con-stitutional rights are under attack, that liberals are imposing a socialist "nanny state," consciously trying to destroy the American values of indi-vidual rights, responsibilities, and freedoms. Attacks on gun rights are the ultimate left-wing culture war threat to the Gun Crusaders, who feel as if they are being displaced by a society that has fewer clear-cut role expecta-tions and is turning more urban and diverse.

The NRA has joined forces with the conservative movement and the Republican Party to wage a right-wing culture war. The NRA's 2008 presi-dential candidate endorsement of former NRA critic and political op-ponent, John McCain, reveals the extent to which the organization has cast its lot with the Republican Party (conservative voters, Gun Crusaders among them probably, were less supportive of him until he chose Palin).[21] Only seven years earlier, McCain graced the cover of the NRA's *America's First Freedom* magazine next to a caption, asking, "John McCain, What Are You Thinking?" Based on his campaign finance reform bill and sup-port for closing what was known as the "gun show loophole" (which had connections to the gun control group Americans for Gun Safety), the NRA sadly noted that McCain "has now become one of the premier flag carriers for the enemies of the Second Amendment."[22]

McCain did his best to reassure the NRA that he was on their side when he ran for president again in 2008. Having an "R" after his name, selecting lifetime NRA member Palin for the ticket, and running against a Democrat whom the NRA deemed a serious threat to gun rights was enough. McCain's past clashes with the organization did not cause it to detour from its increasingly deep NRA-GOP connections.

Having embedded itself within a movement and a political party, and being an important vote-getter and source of income for the Right, the NRA knows it has shored up its activist base of support for years and decades to come. The real threat to the NRA is not gun control—which only serves as a wake-up call for Gun Crusaders. The true threat to the

NRA's future is the possibility that the gun debate and culture wars will subside. Despite Obama's sweeping victory in the face of culture war attacks launched by the McCain-Palin ticket, it is too soon to tell whether the electorate has culture war fatigue.

The NRA has ridden and helped build a wave of conservative backlash against liberal group-rights movements, which had some success pushing collectivist agendas in the second half of the 20th Century. The obstacles the NRA faces, such as demographic shifts that will likely chip away at their base of support, will largely be offset by the continued resonance of frontier masculinity in American culture, a core group of committed Gun Crusaders unwilling to yield any turf in the gun debate or the culture wars, and the NRA's close connections with the conservative movement and the Republican Party. So long as gun rights and frontier masculinity continue to be threatened—or the NRA can frame these threats, and in a way that resonates with the fears and desires of conservative white men— Gun Crusaders will dominate the gun debate and be the linchpin of the Right.

Appendix

Studying the NRA

Becoming a Member

Some readers who directly experienced or grew up in areas frequently affected by gun violence may argue that I have missed the point by paying relatively little attention to these tragedies. Likewise, other readers who grew up hunting and share the NRA's gun rights politics may contend that I am an outsider and therefore cannot begin to understand the gun culture. Although I do not believe that researchers can be entirely objective about the people and groups we study—my experiences affect my views like any other person or researcher—I do believe that we can minimize biases that may result from our experiences. To conduct a more balanced critical analysis of the NRA, I joined the organization at the start of this project in 2001. Becoming an NRA member enabled me to interact with and interview other members *as a fellow member*, negating much of the well-documented NRA member suspicion of academics, reporters, and other outsiders.[1] I believe that my interview data provide an insider's account of the NRA, which is complemented by my own outsider background.

Joining the NRA also enabled me to gain access to current organizational materials, such as magazines and fundraising letters, and to attend NRA annual meetings. I chose to study the organization and its leaders without informing NRA officials of my study, relying instead on their materials and speeches. I particularly wanted to study NRA members, because they have been largely neglected in the research literature.

I designed a study that would examine the NRA within a socio-historical context, analyzing their changing rhetoric, ideology, and politics over time. Although the NRA dates to 1871, this book examines the organization beginning in 1940 and continuing into the new millennium.

The NRA underwent a political coup and dramatic political shift in 1977. This research examines continuities and changes within the NRA several decades before and after the NRA's 1977 transformation into the dominant gun rights social movement organization. I employed three primary research methods: analysis of official NRA documents and rhetoric, ethnographic fieldwork, and in-depth interviews.

Official Materials

The first methodology consisted of analyzing the enormous amount of information the NRA and its leadership produces. Shortly after joining the NRA in the summer of 2001, I began receiving fundraising letters and the monthly magazine of my choice. I passed on the *American Rifleman*, a firearms-focused magazine for all kinds of gun enthusiasts, and the *American Hunter*, which covers all hunting-related topics. Instead, I selected *America's First Freedom* because it is the most political of the NRA publications and therefore the most relevant to my research. The NRA has a thorough Web site, publishes multiple member magazines (one dating back to the early 1900s), produces videos, and sends regular electronic and paper mailings to its members. In addition to analyzing these materials, I also examined leadership interviews, books, and speeches, primarily by Executive Vice President Wayne LaPierre and President Charlton Heston. I use these data (most of the information is widely available) to study the organization's ideology, framing strategies, and general rhetoric and politics. The data reveal the projected priorities of the NRA, as well as the extent of objective and perceived threats to gun rights over time.

Like the study of any social process, the identification of transformational periods in NRA organizational history is itself an exercise in social construction. I divided a sixty-year window into two key periods: 1945 to mid-1977, and late-1977 to 2004. The first period begins when guns were not a contentious political issue and ends after a roughly fifteen-year period of gun control threats, when the NRA's largely apolitical Old Guard leadership were thrown out and replaced by hard-line, gun rights defenders. The second period marks the beginning of the NRA as an SMO dedicated to defending gun rights and concludes as Charlton Heston's term as NRA President ends. I focus on how the NRA frames gun rights and threats to these, especially the similarities and differences that appear in NRA rhetoric during these two periods.

From 1945 to 1960, guns and gun control were not topics of strong debate, within or outside the NRA. Therefore I only use data from every five years during this period to get a sense of how (non)political NRA magazines were then. As broader threats to frontier masculinity (highlighted by liberal group-rights movements) emerged in conjunction with increased threats to gun rights in the early 1960s (political assassinations and accompanying support for gun control), the organization's focus on gun rights increased, and thus I use data for every year from 1960 through 1980. Although the NRA revolt took place in 1977, and I use it to separate NRA historical periods, I use annual data through 1980 to provide a detailed analysis of the years immediately following this dramatic organizational shift.

After establishing a new organizational identity as the nation's key guardian of the Second Amendment in the late 1970s, the NRA neither experienced nor constructed threats to gun rights from Ronald Reagan's presidential victory in 1980 through George H. W. Bush's presidency. I examine data in five-year increments during the period from 1980 to 1995 (the 1990 *American Rifleman* could not be obtained and was substituted with the 1991 volume). The organization again undertook significant changes around 1998, with new leadership in the form of NRA President Charlton Heston, and several significant changes (a shift in organizational ideology, a wider strategic framing process, and so on) signaling the level of threats to gun rights seen in the 1960s. I again use annual data beginning with the Heston years (1998–2004) to thoroughly assess this second period of dramatic change in NRA framing strategies, most evident in their expanded construction and use of collective action frames.

Data for 1945–1977 consist solely of the official NRA magazine, the *American Rifleman.* Data for 1977–2004 were obtained from several sources. First, I analyzed the primary NRA publication covering gun politics (first the *American Rifleman* and later the *American Guardian,* which was renamed *America's First Freedom*). For the last five years, I also incorporated publicly available data from the NRA leadership, including published books and speeches made by Executive Vice President Wayne LaPierre, President Charlton Heston, and NRA-ILA Executive Director James Jay Baker, as well as speeches from other NRA officers and Baker's successor, Chris Cox. In addition, I used data from fundraising letters authored by LaPierre, Baker, and Cox, which I began receiving after I joined the organization in 2001. Finally, I incorporated field note data I collected while attending sessions and listening to leaders' speeches at the 2002 annual meetings in Reno, Nevada, and the 2003 annual meetings in Orlando, Florida.

Some might wonder whether these different kinds of data affect the results, especially given that the NRA magazine data from the first period may be directed at a more general, public audience than private fundraising letters. This could lead to significant differences in how the NRA frames threats to gun rights, as the general public or all gun owners are a much different target audience than paying NRA members. However, I also incorporated data from leaders' public speeches and published books for the second period, most of which for Charlton Heston focus on what he considered to be a liberal culture war and represent his most controversial comments. The styles of rhetoric in Heston's and LaPierre's public and private offerings do not appear to be qualitatively different. Therefore, much of the material I used to assess NRA discourse from the earlier and later periods were unlikely to be targeted to different audiences.

Using a modified grounded theory method and employing a contextual constructionist framework, I coded NRA magazines, letters, and speeches to note existing patterns throughout the materials.[2] I did an initial coding, identifying general categories of issues addressed within the materials. Some examples of these categories are politics, freedom, and threats. I then used a focused coding technique to provide a more detailed breakdown of my initial coding and official organizational and leadership discourse. On this pass through the documents, I further categorized the initial codes into subgroups, such as anti-/pro-Democrat or Republican, the Second Amendment as the foundation of freedom, and anti-big government. Systematically coding, recoding, and analyzing the data ensures that researchers can identify important patterns within the data, regardless of what they expect to find.

Data for chapter 8 on the NRA's political and economic ties came from official NRA documents and elsewhere. NRA materials included magazine listings of elected board members, official annual reports of the officers (distributed at the annual meetings), publicly available IRS 990 forms summarizing the organization's finances, and NRA Political Action Committee and officer/board member political donation data and NRA lobbying expenditures (compiled by the Center for Responsive Politics and published on their Web site, www.opensecrets.org). I also use a variety of official Web sites (e.g., those of other organizations in which NRA board members are involved) and secondary sources to document NRA leaders' political connections.

Observing Leaders and Members

My second primary research method was ethnographic fieldwork. I attended the NRA annual meetings in April 2002 (Reno, Nevada) and 2003 (Orlando, Florida), where I listened to speeches, took notes, casually talked to fellow members, attended breakout sessions and board of directors meetings, and generally observed the identity and politics that the NRA projected to the approximately forty thousand weekend participants that attended each gathering. To avoid attention or being perceived as a member of the media, I took notes discretely at NRA events. At larger events, it was easier to write brief notes in my pocket notepad without being noticed. At smaller events or simply walking around the meeting halls I avoided writing observations down until I found a more isolated location. This led to spending much more time in bathroom stalls than I had anticipated.

Given the size and top-down nature of the NRA gatherings, where members mostly just listened to speakers and applauded, I had little influence on the data I gathered. Unlike joining a small group and influencing its behavior because of frequent interaction, I was a participant-observer of a group that largely relegated me to the role of observer. I did interact with members in the halls, outside the convention centers, in hotels, on buses, and occasionally at the smaller sessions, but I intentionally tried to minimize the extent to which my presence or conversation would alter members' thoughts or behavior. In general, I attempted to be as agreeable as possible when I spoke with others.

From my attendance and interactions at these settings I got a general sense of member demographics for more committed members, the different forms of speech and framings that leadership offer in different settings (for example, a well-planned opening ceremony vs. the impromptu atmosphere of a board meeting), as well as how the membership reacts to leadership speeches. Finally, I attended several sessions with lower-ranking leadership and individuals sympathetic to the NRA's cause. Such sessions further revealed the broader politics of the organization and those drawn to the NRA.

In addition to attending these two annual meetings, I went to a May 2002 NRA-sponsored, self-defense course in San Diego County, California, which the NRA calls "Refuse to Be a Victim" (RTBAV). I also occasionally went shooting at a small, nearby indoor gun range, although the size and layout prevented me from gathering much data. Soon after deciding to study the NRA, I frequently noticed NRA and pro-gun bumper stickers while driving around and often found myself in conversations with friends and acquaintances who shared strong feelings on guns from a range of perspectives. Like other scholars immersed in large projects, at times it was difficult to tell where my research ended and my personal life began.

Interviewing Members

The third primary research method I used was open-ended, in-depth, semi-structured interviews. Previous research on the NRA has mostly relied upon analysis of NRA speeches and documents, sometimes coupled with observation. Neither of these has produced much data regarding the interests and concerns of members. Although I collected some data on NRA members through participant-observation at the two annual NRA meetings, in-depth interviews with members were my main source of information. NRA leaders and members view academics and the media as biased against firearms. Because they do not believe that their side of the debate is fairly covered, they are understandably leery of interviews. I knew this would be an obstacle beforehand. To relieve them of their fears, I approached members by framing my study in a nonthreatening way, using language most NRA members did not interpret as anti-NRA or pro-gun control.

At the Reno meeting, the large convention center had a main entrance with a heavy pedestrian traffic flow, including NRA leadership and staff. I did not want NRA staff or leadership to know about my research so that I could pursue it without interference (I also let members know that to obtain objective results concerning members' thoughts on relevant issues, I did not want to notify the leadership about my study; and that this research was not funded by the NRA). I positioned myself at the edge of a large parking lot in front of the Reno convention center, beyond the view of the main entrance and along the path between a major hotel (the only one nearby as well as virtually the only source of nearby food, excluding the limited convention center offerings) and the convention center. Virtually all pedestrian traffic passed by me, and I stood at this location for a few hours soliciting interview participants. In Orlando the following year, the layout was quite different. The convention center is enormous, housing several large conventions simultaneously, with the NRA using one wing of the center. Most members were bused in from what seemed like all the local hotels, and dropped off curbside in front of the convention center. In Reno I was able to approach members walking toward and away from the meetings, but in Orlando I mostly spoke with members standing directly in front of the convention center (smoking cigarettes, eating lunch, or waiting for buses). I approached members over the course of a couple days at the Orlando meetings.

At both locations, I had a clipboard and sign-up sheets so members could provide contact information for follow-up interviews. I asked them if they would be interested in talking about "some important concerns for NRA members," "threats to gun rights," "the Founding Fathers," "freedom," and similar phrasings. When I was chastised by a woman after I mistakenly mentioned gun control (rather than gun *rights*) my suspicions were confirmed. Her comment reinforced my concern that most members would not speak with me if I appeared to support gun control, and this helped me to sharpen my approach to them. I told them that I was an NRA member planning to write a book that focused on members' thoughts on gun rights and related issues, noting that some books were supportive and others critical of the NRA but that most of them ignored the membership.

On the few occasions when I stopped or spoke with couples, it was always the men who spoke to me and provided contact information. This was particularly true in Reno, which seemed to have fewer women attendees overall and even fewer who came without husbands or boyfriends. A few times I was able to convince these women to include their contact information but most declined, stating that, compared to their husbands, they were less involved or less knowledgeable about the issues.

The Reno and Orlando attendees were different in many respects, which likely led to different interview participants. The Orlando crowd had a higher proportion of women, although both meetings were overwhelmingly attended by men. There was also a visible minority of women without men at the Orlando meetings (small groups of women mostly), which was not the case in Reno. Both meetings were attended almost exclusively by white supporters, with only a handful of people of color at the forty-thousand-member gatherings. The Reno attendees had a great number of men wearing NRA shooter caps, a larger contingent of individuals in camouflage military fatigues, and, not unlike myself, were often not particularly concerned about how their clothes matched. The Orlando attendees, on the other hand, were more of a collared shirt and khakis crowd, with fewer members sporting tattoos, long facial hair, and big belt buckles. Both meetings had a small but observable number of individuals in formal business attire, probably mostly NRA staff and firearms exhibitors. Regardless of their outward appearances, I did not recognize any differences between Reno and Orlando in terms of how members responded to my soliciting their participation, nor in the tendency of some members to begin sharing their thoughts on these topics immediately after hearing my pitch (even though I was only trying to obtain their contact information to speak with them later).

I let members know that I would be calling them shortly after the meetings to talk over the phone, that I was not trying to sell them anything, and that I would not be using their real names in anything published. I chose not to pass out consent statements at this stage because they had only agreed to provide me with contact information. The majority of members I tried to speak with either just kept on walking past me (in Reno) or said they were not interested. Some asked for more details and listened to my plans for writing a book, however they were mostly a skeptical bunch that sometimes even asked for my member identification card and further evidence of pro-gun/NRA feelings. I danced back and forth between conveying to them that I was intently concerned about their thoughts on threats to the Second Amendment and gun rights, and that I was going to be objective (not "anti-gun") because I am a researcher and (with apologies to journalists) not a "biased journalist."

I framed my research in a manner that led many members to believe that I was sympathetic to their cause, but I did not lie to them simply to obtain their contact information for the study. Admittedly, this was a difficult balance. In the end, I believe my research is more accurate because members largely (and accurately) trusted that I would not alter their words or views. I assume that journalists or others who are labeled outsiders or hostile to the NRA would have received much more guarded responses to my questions, if any at all, and, as a result, less accurate data.

Shortly after returning from the meetings, I entered all contact information into a word processing program and assigned alphanumeric codes to each participant to initiate the process of confidentiality. I then mailed a contact letter to those who provided addresses so that they would remember me when I gave them a call. All but four participants agreed to be digitally audio-recorded. One said he did not want to be recorded because he was in some litigation (a divorce, according to "the soon-to-be former Mrs. [member's last name]") and the others were just not comfortable with their voices being captured. I took notes on these four, attempting to write down exact quotes whenever possible but mostly paraphrasing their responses. Prior to beginning each interview, I obtained verbal consent from the participants, digitally recording this consent for all but the four who declined to be recorded.

I used an interview guide to maintain a degree of consistency across interviews, but the questions I asked were open-ended and the style was conversational, often letting members wander onto various topics of their choice. I asked them questions and gave them open-ended prompts ("tell me about your first experiences with guns") about their gun and personal backgrounds (shooting history, careers, and political interests). I also asked and had members discuss their thoughts on the NRA, gun rights and gun control, and the Constitution. Finally, I raised a number of controversial and contentious topics for them to discuss (terrorism, immigration, welfare, feminism, homosexuality, and so forth), mostly just stating the topic and letting them take it in whatever direction they chose, then asking follow-up questions based on their comments. Immediately after the four interviews that were not digitally recorded, I typed up a clean version of my notes to ensure the accuracy of these data. The digitally recorded interviews were later transcribed, some by me but most by a paid undergraduate research assistant, and I checked each transcript for accuracy after they were completed.

I also used a snowball sample, building on my initial set of interviews. Eight of the twenty member interviews were with participants from the Reno meetings. I was able to snowball two more interviews from this group, totaling ten interviews via the Reno meetings. I interviewed one member face-to-face, because he is the father of a friend of one of my own friends, and lived within driving distance. I obtained another participant by e-mailing her after hearing about her campus firearms-related college organization in the news. Finally, I obtained eight more participants from the Orlando meetings.[3]

Because this research is exploratory and no systematic data on membership is publicly available, I cannot state with any certainty that I obtained a representative sample of the membership, nor was this explicitly the goal. My sample and this book focus on those most committed to the NRA, whether dedicated members or organizational leaders. Nevertheless, I did intentionally attempt to obtain a mix of NRA members by actively pursuing interviews with women, despite their small numbers, and making a greater effort to snowball when a member provided unique data or seemed to challenge my emerging membership categories (described in detail in chapter 6). I was also fortunate because some participants at both gatherings only attended because the meetings were local, whereas others had traveled many miles to attend. This partly reflects the varying levels of organizational commitment within my sample. The twenty members I interviewed live in ten different states from all regions of the country. Seventeen of the interview participants are men and three are women. They are mostly middle-aged and older and I believe that all, with one exception, are white, although I did not formally ask for their age, race, or ethnicity.

One source of data I used in conjunction with member interviews arose from a fundraising strategy the NRA established shortly after I joined, called the "Madison Brigade."[4] To join, members gave money and in return were given a certain number of words (based on the size of their donation) to post on the Madison Brigade Web site. Members were asked to share their thoughts on freedom via inspiration by James Madison. The fund-raiser was originally framed as a way to counter "revisionist" historians attempting to write the Founding Fathers and Second Amendment rights out of history. Part of the message on the Web site reads,

> By joining the James Madison Brigade, you will have the opportunity to record your thoughts on the freedoms you cherish most as an American. Via this interactive website, your thoughts and commentary will be preserved alongside those of men like Madison, Jefferson, and Washington for future generations to review and contemplate.[5]

However, the mailing was sent out just before 9/11, and the postings mostly consist of responses to this tragic event. I used these quotes along with interview data to examine the political attitudes of NRA members and their responses to leadership framings.

I again used a grounded theory method to analyze the interview data. Some of the initial codes I used include commitment to the NRA, freedom, and, most frequently, sense of threat. Initially I attempted to develop Blumerian "sensitizing concepts" regarding these issues to allow for theoretical sampling and find negative cases, such as highly committed members who are not politically conservative or highly conservative members who are not very committed or active within the organization.[6]

I then used focused coding to provide a more detailed breakdown of my sensitizing concepts and the participants' statements. Examples of these codes include membership status and satisfaction with NRA, individual rights as freedom, and threats by terrorists or feminists. I placed quotations into a spreadsheet organized by topic. Thus I gathered all member quotes on each particular topic (roughly fifty topics, for example, anti-gun, same-sex marriages, and welfare) and placed these topical quotes in a single column. I incorporated Madison Brigade postings here as well, as I did the same initial coding of a large sample of relevant postings I copied and pasted from the Web site. I then did a focused coding and placed these members' statements in the same spreadsheet, separating interview and Madison Brigade member statements by several rows, but leaving them in the same relevant columns by topic. As I created chapter outlines and began writing, I again copied and pasted member quotes, this time into my word processing program, and began organizing the quotes along continuums. For example, arranging members' comments in order from fully supportive of NRA leadership to mixed support to highly critical, from extremely threatened by "anti-gunners" to not perceiving a serious threat to gun rights, and so forth. This is an imprecise undertaking, but there are clear qualitative differences along the continuums, as I describe in this book. By the time I was intensively writing up the findings of the interview data, I was extremely close to my data, having poured over my coding multiple times and repeatedly having read and arranged participants' statements.

Prior to submitting drafts to any readers I replaced the alphanumeric member codes used to denote members and their quotes in my spreadsheets with pseudonyms. I assigned pseudonyms to each participant and Madison Brigade poster by opening up a phone book and picking first and last names at random, sometimes mixing and matching different names to create new ones. In short, the names used are entirely made up and arise from no logical naming process. I have taken steps where appropriate to conceal the identities of participants as much as possible. For example, I avoid using unique identifying markers, such as where members live, their jobs, and other distinguishing characteristics.

Measuring Members' Commitment

I determined NRA commitment to the organization and the defense of gun rights by examining each member I interviewed on the following items: (1) NRA membership status; (2) length of NRA membership;

(3) monetary donations to the NRA; (4) participation in NRA volunteer work; (5) voting practices in NRA elections; (6) attendance at NRA annual meetings; (7) level of satisfaction with the NRA and its leadership; (8) any sources of dissatisfaction with the NRA; (9) sense of threat to gun rights; and (10) whether they identify as gun rights, single-issue voters. Given this book's focus on the NRA, I weigh the first eight items more heavily.

The first six commitment items involve members' self-reported involvement with the NRA. First, NRA members must select a membership level, or status, when they join the organization. At the time of my interviews, membership levels for adults included Annual, five-year consecutive Annual, Life, Endowment, Patron, or Benefactor. The Annual membership ($35) is the same as the five-year consecutive membership, with the latter making the member eligible to vote in NRA elections. Discounts are provided to those who sign up for multiple years at one time. A lifetime membership cost $750 (half as much for seniors or disabled veterans), compared to higher status lifetime memberships including Endowment ($1,500), Patron ($2,500), and Benefactor ($4,000) status.[7]

The third item, monetary donations, refers to members contributing funds beyond their membership dues to various causes within the organization—lobbying, education, and so forth—often prompted by NRA fundraising letters. I did not ask for exact figures, but I did get a sense of how often and why members donated. Next, I asked members about any volunteer work they do for the organization, which ranges from serving as NRA-certified firearms instructors (teaching courses on firearms basics, range safety, and personal protection, for example) to recruiting NRA members (both at and away from the annual meeting) to working with the NRA Institute for Legislative Action (NRA-ILA) or volunteering for the NRA's Eddie Eagle gun safety program for children.

I also asked eligible members if they vote in NRA elections. According to NRA election data, of the roughly 1.3 million eligible voting members (lifetime or five-year consecutive members), approximately 9–10% of them had cast ballots in NRA elections in 2001 and 2002.[8] Thus roughly 3% of *all* members cast ballots in NRA elections. The 1.3 million eligible voters are approximately one-third of all NRA members, meaning two out of three members are not eligible to vote. My interview participants are virtually the mirror opposite. Roughly two out of three of them are eligible to vote in NRA elections, reflecting my interest in and this book's focus on who drives the NRA. The sixth measure of commitment simply identifies how many times each member attended an NRA national meeting, held at different U.S. locations each year. I also asked members how satisfied they are with the organization and its leadership, particularly Executive Vice President Wayne LaPierre and President Charlton Heston, as well as why they are or are not satisfied with the NRA.

The final two items examine members' commitment to gun rights in general, rather than the NRA itself. During interviews, members conveyed their sense of threat to gun rights, with some believing that registration and confiscation was a near certainty and others not feeling particularly concerned about these threats anytime soon. As I discuss in chapter 4, I also asked members if they were single-issue voters regarding gun rights. These last two items are included as measures of commitment, because the NRA dominates the anti-gun control movement, even if they are not the only or most uncompromising of the gun rights groups. If members perceive serious threats to gun rights, they are highly likely to join the NRA. Further, as a single-issue group, the NRA puts out a voter guide that enables members to cast their ballots based solely on NRA recommendations for who is the "pro-gun" candidate.[9] See chapter 6 for NRA member categorizations and related discussion.

Notes

PREFACE

1. Scott A Melzer, "Gender, Work, and Intimate Violence: Men's Occupational Violence Spillover and Compensatory Violence," *Journal of Marriage and Family* 64 (2002): 820–832 (Correction, *Journal of Marriage and Family* 65 [2003]: 273). For more on compensatory masculinity, see Jan E. Stets, "Job Autonomy and Control over One's Spouse: A Compensatory Process," *Journal of Health and Social Behavior* 36 (1995): 244–258; Karen D. Pyke, "Class-based Masculinities: The Interdependence of Gender, Class, and Interpersonal Power," *Gender & Society* 10 (1996): 527–549; and Michael P. Johnson and Kathleen J. Ferraro, "Research on Domestic Violence in the 1990s: Making Distinctions," *Journal of Marriage and Family* 62 (2000): 948–963.

INTRODUCTION

1. Michael Bellesiles, *Arming America: The Origins of a National Gun Culture*, 1st ed. (New York: Knopf, 2000).

2. Wayne LaPierre, "2002 NRA Annual Meeting Speech," May 3, 2002 (retrieved June 30, 2008, from http://nraila.org/news/archives/speeches.aspx).

3. These quotes are taken from NRA member Floyd. More information about Floyd appears in chapter 1.

4. James Davison Hunter, *Culture Wars: The Struggle to Define America* (New York: Basic Books, 1991), 150.

5. Charlton Heston, "Opening Comments at the NRA Annual Meeting of Members," May 20, 2000 (retrieved July 1, 2002, from http://www.nrahq.org/transcripts/index.asp).

6. Motion Picture Associates, *The Ten Commandments*, Cecil B. DeMille, Director, 1956.

7. National Rifle Association, "The Reagan in You," narrated by Charlton Heston, *A Patriot at the Podium: The Public Life of NRA President Charlton Heston* (an NRA film, 2003).

8. Charlton Heston, "Speech to the Opening Session of the Arizona State Legislature," January 8, 2000 (retrieved July 1, 2002, from http://www.nrahq.org/transcripts/index.asp).

9. Paramount Pictures, *Will Penny*, Tom Gries, Director, 1968.

10. Charlton Heston, "Speech to the British Columbia Wildlife Federation," March 11, 2000 (retrieved July 1, 2002, from http://www.nrahq.org/transcripts/index.asp).

11. Quoted in Osha Gray Davidson, *Under Fire: The NRA and the Battle for Gun Control* (Iowa City: University of Iowa Press, 1998), 44, 213.

12. Frontier masculinity is the hegemonic masculinity of an earlier American period, although many of its characteristics continue to be associated with contemporary idealized versions of American manhood. R. W. Connell, author of *Gender and Power* (Stanford, Calif.: Stanford University Press, 1987) and *Masculinities* (Berkeley: University of California Press, 1995), coined the term "hegemonic masculinity," arguing that it is an ascendant or culturally dominant version of masculinity, always constructed in relation to various subordinated masculinities as well as women and femininities. Hegemonic masculinity is the measuring stick to which all men are held, yet it exists more as an ideal type than an empirical reality. It is composed of achieved characteristics (married, formally educated, successful) and ascribed characteristics (white, above-average height), instantaneously preventing large numbers of men from ever approaching this elevated status. Because it is a culturally embedded phenomenon, hegemonic masculinity is a contextual, time- and space-specific concept and is thus always open for change. It pervades social institutions and cultural representations. Connell explains, "Most of the time, defense of the patriarchal order does not require an explicit masculinity politics . . . the routine maintenance of these institutions will normally do the job" (*Masculinities*, 212). Hegemony means dominance so that, typically, those currently in power are somehow aligned with hegemonic masculinity and simply need to maintain the status quo.

13. For additional discussion of frontier masculinity, see R. W. Connell, "The Big Picture: Masculinities in Recent World History," *Theory and Society* 22 (1993): 597–623; Michael S. Kimmel, *Manhood in America* (New York: Free Press, 1996); Sine Anahita and Tamara L. Mix, "Retrofitting Frontier Masculinity for Alaska's War against Wolves," *Gender & Society* 20 (June 2006): 332–353.

14. Sara Diamond, *Spiritual Warfare: The Politics of the Christian Right* (Boston: South End Press, 1989); Michael Messner, *Politics of Masculinity* (Thousand Oaks, Calif.: Sage, 1997); Scott Coltrane, "Marketing the Marriage 'Solution': Misplaced Simplicity in the Politics of Fatherhood. 2001 Presidential Address to the Pacific Sociological Association," *Sociological Perspectives* 44 (2001): 387–418, esp. 390–391.

15. See chapter 6 for a more detailed discussion of different types of NRA members.

16. See the appendix. A 1976 internal NRA survey with an 11% response rate revealed that nearly half the members cited protecting gun rights as "the most important single reason" why they first joined the NRA. Anonymous, "Membership Drive, Survey Help NRA," *American Rifleman*, May 1976, 50.

17. U.S. Fish & Wildlife Service, National Survey of Fishing, Hunting, and Wildlife-Associated Recreation (retrieved June 1, 2008, from http://federalasst.fws.gov/surveys/surveys.html).

18. Author's notes from Robinson's and LaPierre's reports to the NRA Board, April 28, 2003.

19. E. J. Dionne Jr. and Michael Cromartie, eds., *Is There a Culture War? A Dialogue on Values and American Public Life* (Washington, D.C.: Pew Research Center, Brookings Institution Press, 2006).

CHAPTER 1. FRONTIER MASCULINITY, AMERICA'S "GUN CULTURE," AND THE NRA

1. This figure is based on the number of women who report that they have a gun in their home and that it personally belongs to them. General Social Survey (GSS), 1980, 1990, 2000, and 2006, variables *owngun, rowngun*. GSS data are available for analysis on the Survey Documentation and Analysis Web site of the University of California, Berkeley (http://sda.berkeley.edu/archive.htm). GSS reference: James Allan Davis and Tom W. Smith, General Social Surveys, 1972–2006 [machine-readable data file]: Principal Investigator, James A. Davis; Director and Co-Principal Investigator, Tom W. Smith; and Co-Principal Investigator, Peter V. Marsden; sponsored by the National Science Foundation. Chicago: National Opinion Research Center [producer]; Storrs, CT: The Roper Center for Public Opinion Research, University of Connecticut [distributor], 2007.

2. Supreme Court of the United States, *District of Columbia et al. vs. Heller*, decided June 26, 2008 (retrieved June 30, 2008, from http://www.supremecourtus.gov/opinions/07pdf/07-290.pdf); Robert Barnes, "Justices Reject D.C. Ban on Handgun Ownership," *Washington Post*, June 27, 2008 (retrieved June 30, 2008, from http://www.washingtonpost.com/wp-dyn/content/article/2008/06/26/AR2008062600615.html).

3. Quoted in William R. Tonso, *Guns and Society: The Social and Existential Roots of the American Attachment to Firearms* (Washington, D.C.: University Press of America, 1982), 287–288.

4. Wayne LaPierre, *Guns, Freedom, and Terrorism* (Nashville, Tenn.: WND Books, 2003), 196.

5. Robert Brannon, "The Male Sex Role, and What It's Done for Us Lately," in *The Forty-Nine Percent Majority: The Male Sex Role*, ed. Deborah S. David and Robert Brannon, 1–40 (Reading, Mass.: Addison Wesley, 1976), quote at 5.

6. R. W. Connell, *Masculinities* (Berkeley: University of California Press, 1995), 212.

7. Richard Hofstadter, "America as a Gun Culture," *American Heritage* (October 1970): 3–11, 82–85, quote at 7.

8. Gregg Lee Carter, *The Gun Control Movement* (New York: Twayne, 1997).

9. David B. Kopel, *The Samurai, the Mountie, and the Cowboy: Should America Adopt the Gun Controls of Other Democracies?* (Buffalo, N.Y.: Prometheus Books, 1992); J. L. Malcolm, *To Keep and Bear Arms: The Origins of an Anglo-American Right* (Cambridge, Mass.: Harvard University Press, 1994).

10. Carl Bakal, *The Right to Bear Arms* (New York: McGraw-Hill, 1966), 84.

11. Hofstadter, "America as a Gun Culture," 82; John Mitchell, "God, Guns and Guts Made America Free," *American Heritage* (February 1978): 4–17.

12. James William Gibson, *Warrior Dreams: Paramilitary Culture in Post-Vietnam America* (New York: Hill and Wang, 1994).

13. Michael S. Kimmel, *Manhood in America* (New York: Free Press, 1996), 20.

14. Ibid.

15. Michael Messner, *Politics of Masculinity* (Thousand Oaks, Calif.: Sage, 1997).

16. Kimmel, *Manhood*, 53.

17. Maxine Baca Zinn, "Family, Feminism, and Race in America," *Gender and Society* 4 (1990): 68–82, esp. 76–77; Myra Marx Ferree, "Beyond Separate Spheres-Feminism and Family Research," *Journal of Marriage and the Family* 52 (1990): 866–884.

18. For a summary of scholarship in this area, see Randolph Roth, "Counting Guns: What Social Science Historians Know and Could Learn about Gun Ownership, Gun Culture, and Gun Violence in the United States," *Social Science History* 26 (2002): 699–708. For competing views on these issues, see Malcolm, *To Keep and Bear Arms*; Kopel, *The Samurai, the Mountie, and the Cowboy*; Tonso, *Guns and Society*; Mitchell, "God, Guns and Guts"; James B. Trefethen, *Americans and Their Guns: The National Rifle Association Story through Nearly a Century of Service to the Nation* (Harrisburg, Pa.: Stackpole Books, 1967); Hofstadter, "America as a Gun Culture"; Richard Slotkin, *Gunfighter Nation: The Myth of the Frontier in 20th Century America* (Norman: University of Oklahoma Press, 1998); Robert J. Spitzer, *The Politics of Gun Control* (Chatham, N.J.: Chatham House, 1995); Gary Kleck, *Point Blank: Guns and Violence in America* (Edison, N.J.: Aldine Transaction, 2005).

19. Roth, "Counting Guns," 703.

20. Spitzer, *Politics of Gun Control*, 9, 12.

21. Slotkin, *Gunfighter Nation*, 4.

22. Spitzer, *Politics of Gun Control*.

23. Alexander DeConde, *Gun Violence in America: the Struggle for Control* (Boston: Northeastern University Press, 2001).

24. Slotkin, *Gunfighter Nation*, 4.

25. Ibid., DeConde, *Gun Violence in America*.

26. Slotkin, *Gunfighter Nation*, 379–380.

27. DeConde, *Gun Violence in America*.

28. Spitzer, *Politics of Gun Control*, 11.

29. DeConde, *Gun Violence in America*.

30. Slotkin, *Gunfighter Nation.*

31. Carter, *Gun Control Movement*, 46.

32. Roth, "Counting Guns," 706.

33. Hofstadter, "America as a Gun Culture," 82.

34. Roth, "Counting Guns," 706.

35. Kimmel, *Manhood.*

36. Carter, *The Gun Control Movement*, 25.

37. Hofstadter, "America as a Gun Culture," 84.

38. Kimmel, *Manhood*, 79, 89.

39. The sexist language, marks*man*ship, has no contemporary gender-neutral substitute, reflecting how firearms were dominated by men in the past and continue to be today.

40. James B Trefethen, *Americans and Their Guns: the National Rifle Association Story through Nearly a Century of Service to the Nation* (Harrisburg, Pa.: Stackpole Books, 1967).

41. Kimmel, *Manhood*, 182.

42. Ibid.

43. Trefethen, *Americans and Their Guns.*

44. Ibid.

45. Davidson, *Under Fire.*

46. Ibid., 29, 30, 34, 35.

47. Ibid., passim.

48. Joseph Tartaro, *Revolt at Cincinnati* (Buffalo, N.Y.: Hawkeye, 1981).

49. Davidson, *Under Fire*, 36.

50. Ibid., 31, 32.

51. Reports about NRA membership levels since the late 1990s are contradictory. For example, NRA leaders either cited the general figure of 4 million, or specifically 4.3 million, at the 2002 and 2003 annual meetings. However, the NRA Membership Division reported 3.7 million members in 2002, and a December 2003 *New York Times* article reported that membership had fallen to 3.4 million. The NRA has been accused of inflating its membership levels by continuing to count annual members who do not renew their membership and by not identifying and removing deceased lifetime members who have already paid all their dues. The 2006 peak membership level of 4.4 million, again coming from the Membership Division, seems high. Charlton Heston had long since stepped down as NRA President by that time, federal gun control threats were nonexistent during the G. W. Bush administration, and NRA membership revenue declined 10% between 2004 and 2006 according to the NRA's IRS Form 990 (on file with the author). Membership levels may have increased at the same time that revenue declined if many lifetime members who joined in the past had paid all their dues and new members were largely joining at the much cheaper annual rate. Ultimately I rely on official membership levels provided by the organization. See Stephanie Strom,

"High Price of Victory Breaks Gun Lobby's Budget," *New York Times*, December 22, 2003, A5; Kelly Patterson and Matthew Singer, "Targeting Success: The Enduring Power of the NRA," in *Interest Group Politics*, 7th ed., ed. Allan J. Cigler and Burdett A. Loomis, 37–64 (Washington, D.C.: CQ Press, 2006).

52. Jack Anderson, *Inside the NRA: Armed and Dangerous* (Beverly Hills, Calif.: Dove Books, 1996).

53. Edward F. Leddy, *Magnum Force Lobby: the National Rifle Association Fights Gun Control* (Lanham, Md.: University Press of America, 1987).

54. Trefethen, *Americans and Their Guns,* 292.

55. Davidson, *Under Fire.*

56. Anderson, *Inside the NRA.*

57. Davidson, *Under Fire.*

58. Gun Control Timeline, U.S. Government Information/Resources (retrieved April 28, 2004, from http://usgovinfo.about.com/library/weekly/aa092699.htm).

59. Davidson, *Under Fire*; Gun Control Timeline.

60. LaPierre has a master's degree in American government and politics from Boston College (*American Rifleman*, June 1991, 58).

61. Davidson, *Under Fire*, 295.

62. Gibson, *Warrior Dreams*, 255.

63. Davidson, *Under Fire*, 307.

64. Leddy, *Magnum Force Lobby*, 29.

65. Slotkin, *Gunfighter Nation*, 658.

66. Quoted in Kimmel, *Manhood*, 253.

CHAPTER 2. WHY A GUN MOVEMENT?

1. Charlton Heston, *The Courage to Be Free* (Kansas City: Saudade, 2000), 4.

2. Ibid., 5.

3. Ibid., 39.

4. Ibid., 46.

5. Ibid., 54.

6. Ibid., 5–6.

7. Ibid., 6–7.

8. CNN, "America Votes 2006: Key Ballot Measures" (retrieved November 14, 2008, from http://www.cnn.com/ELECTION/2006/pages/results/ballot.measures/); CNN, "Election Center 2008: Ballot Measures" (retrieved November 14, 2008, from http://www.cnn.com/ELECTION/2008/results/ballot.measures/).

9. Michael S. Kimmel, *Manhood in America* (New York: Free Press, 1996).

10. These have been referred to as the two crises in masculinity or crises in the gender order. See R. W. Connell, *Masculinities* (Berkeley: University of California Press, 1995); and Kimmel, *Manhood.*

11. Shoon Lio, Scott Melzer, and Ellen Reese, "Constructing Threat and Appropriating 'Civil Rights': Rhetorical Strategies of Gun Rights and English Only Leaders," *Symbolic Interaction* 31 (2008): 5–31.

12. Clarence Y. H. Lo, "Countermovements and Conservative Movements in the Contemporary U.S.," *Annual Review of Sociology* 8 (1982): 107–134, quote at 108.

13. Darren K. Carlson, "Americans Softening on Tougher Gun Laws," in *The Gallup Poll: Public Opinion 2004*, ed. Alec M. Gallup and Frank Newport, 472–473 (Lanham, Md.: Rowman & Littlefield, 2006).

14. Lio, Melzer, and Reese, "Constructing Threat."

15. Quotes from, respectively, Seymour Martin Lipset and Earl Raab, *The Politics of Unreason: Right-Wing Extremism in America, 1790–1977*, 2nd ed. (Chicago: University of Chicago Press, 1978), 428; Susan Marshall, "In Defense of Separate Spheres: Class and Status Politics in the Antisuffrage Movement," *Social Forces* 65 (1986): 327–351, quote at 359; and Joseph R. Gusfield, *Symbolic Crusade: Status Politics and the American Temperance Movement* (Urbana: University of Illinois Press, 1976), 4.

16. Gusfield, *Symbolic Crusade*, 25; George Lakoff, *Moral Politics: How Liberals and Conservatives Think*, 2nd ed. (Chicago: University of Chicago Press, 2002), 170.

17. Gusfield, *Symbolic Crusade*; Donileen R. Loseke, "Constructing Conditions: People, Morality, and Emotions: Expanding the Agenda of Constructionism," in *Constructivist Controversies: Issues in Social Problems Theory*, ed. Gale Miller and James Holstein, 207–216 (New York: Aldine de Gruyter, 1993); Barry Glassner, *The Culture of Fear: Why Americans are Afraid of the Wrong Things* (New York: Basic Books, 1999); Lakoff, *Moral Politics*.

18. Michael Messner, *Politics of Masculinity* (Thousand Oaks, Calif.: Sage, 1997).

19. Quoted in Kimmel, *Manhood*, 182; from Theodore Roosevelt, *Autobiography* (New York: Scribner's, 1913), 76.

20. Kimmel, *Manhood*.

21. Michael S. Kimmel, "The Contemporary 'Crisis' of Masculinity in Historical Perspective," in *The Making of Masculinities*, ed. Harry Brod, 143–149 (Boston: Allen and Unwin, 1987).

22. California Newsreel, *Race: The Power of an Illusion*, Vol. 3, *The House We Live In*; produced by Llewellyn M. Smith (2003).

23. Michael Omi and Howard Winant, *Racial Formation in the United States: From the 1960s to the 1990s*, 2nd ed. (New York: Routledge, 1994).

24. Kimmel, *Manhood*, 95.

25. Kimmel, "Crisis," 146.

26. Cited in Robert H. MacDonald, *Sons of the Empire: The Frontier and the Boy Scout Movement, 1890–1918* (Toronto: University of Toronto Press, 1993), 142.

27. Jeffrey P. Hantover, "The Boy Scouts and the Validation of Masculinity," *Journal of Social Issues* 34 (1978): 184–195.

28. Helen Lefkowitz-Horowitz, *Campus Life: Undergraduate Cultures from the End of the Eighteenth Century to the Present* (New York: Knopf, 1987); Mary Ann Clawson, *Constructing Brotherhood: Class, Gender, and Fraternalism* (Princeton, N.J.: Princeton University Press, 1989); Michael A. Messner, *Power at Play: Sports and the Problem of Masculinity* (Boston: Beacon, 1992).

29. Kimmel, "Crisis"; Hantover, "Scouts."

30. Peter G. Filene, *Him/Her/Self: Gender Identities in Modern America*, 3rd ed. (Baltimore, Md.: Johns Hopkins University Press, 1998).

31. Messner, *Politics*.

32. Susan Faludi, *Stiffed: The Betrayal of the American Man* (New York: William Morrow, 1999).

33. Connell, *Masculinities*; Messner, *Politics*.

34. James William Gibson, *Warrior Dreams: Paramilitary Culture in Post-Vietnam America* (New York: Hill and Wang, 1994).

35. Faludi, *Stiffed*.

36. Barbara Ehrenreich, *The Hearts of Men* (New York: Anchor Books, 1983), 42.

37. Ibid., 51.

38. Betty Friedan, *The Feminine Mystique* (New York: Norton, 1963).

39. Ehrenreich, *Hearts of Men*, 144–145.

40. Ibid.

41. Messner, *Politics*, 44.

42. Richard Doyle, *The Rape of the Male* (Poor Richard's Press, 1976); excerpts from Richard Doyle, *Save the Males* (Lulu.com, 2006) are available at his Web site, http://www.mensdefense.org/. Quoted from http://www.mensdefense.org/BookSummary.htm (retrieved June 24, 2008).

43. Doyle, *Save the Males*; quoted from http://www.mensdefense.org/STM_Book/RapeOfTheMale.htm (retrieved June 24, 2008).

44. Doyle, *Save the Males*; quoted from http://www.mensdefense.org/STM_Book/RapeAbuseClaims.htm (retrieved June 24, 2008).

45. Warren Farrell, *The Myth of Male Power* (New York: Berkeley Trade, 2001); quotes from Steven J. Svoboda, "An Interview with Warren Farrell," Menweb, 1997 (retrieved June 24, 2008, from http://www.menweb.org/svofarre.htm).

46. Kimmel, *Manhood*.

47. Quoted in Messner, *Politics*, 32.

48. Messner, *Politics*.

49. Faludi, *Stiffed*.

50. Susan Jeffords, *The Remasculinization of America: Gender and the Vietnam War* (Bloomington: Indiana University Press, 1990).

51. This is in contrast to a military culture that was, for whatever reasons, unable to win the war in Vietnam (Gibson, *Warrior Dreams*).

52. Ibid.

53. Ibid.

54. Citing Thomas Byrne Edsall and Mary D. Edsall, *Chain Reaction: The Impact of Race, Rights, and Taxes on American Politics* (New York: Norton, 1991), 4; quoted in Lio, Melzer, and Reese, "Constructing Threat," 18.

55. James Davison Hunter, "Reflections on the Culture War Hypothesis," in *The American Culture Wars: Current Contests and Future Prospects*, ed. James L. Nolan Jr., 243–256 (Charlottesville: University Press of Virginia, 1996), 245.

56. George Lakoff, *Whose Freedom? The Battle over America's Most Important Idea* (New York: Farrar, Straus and Giroux, 2006), 3.

57. Jeffrey R. Dudas, "In the Name of Equal Rights: 'Special' Rights and the Politics of Resentment in Post-Civil Rights America," *Law & Society Review* 39 (2005): 723–757.

58. Alan Wolfe, "The Culture War That Never Came," in *Is There a Culture War? A Dialogue on Values and American Public Life*, ed. E. J. Dionne Jr. and Michael Cromartie, 41–73 (Washington, D.C.: Pew Research Center, Brookings Institution Press, 2006), quote at 56.

59. I would like to thank Michael Kimmel for providing this conceptualization of the NRA's contradictory masculinity.

60. For example, see Morris P. Fiorina, with Samuel J. Abrams and Jeremy C. Pope, *Culture War? The Myth of a Polarized America* (New York: Pearson, 2005).

61. Fiorina, with Abrams and Pope, *Culture War?* 5. For more on this debate, see James L. Nolan Jr., ed., *The American Culture Wars: Current Contests and Future Prospects* (Charlottesville: University Press of Virginia, 1996); Rhys Williams, ed., *Culture Wars in American Politics* (New York: Aldine de Gruyter, 1997); Hunter, *Culture Wars*; James Davison Hunter and Alan Wolfe, *Is There a Culture War? A Dialogue on Values and American Public Life* (Washington, D.C.: Brookings Institution Press, 2006).

62. Hunter, *Culture Wars*, 31.

63. Fiorina, with Abrams and Pope, *Culture War?* 28, 78.

64. James L. Nolan Jr., "Preface," in *The American Culture Wars: Current Contests and Future Prospects*, ed. James L. Nolan Jr., ix–xvi (Charlottesville: University Press of Virginia, 1996).

65. For an extended discussion among scholars and journalists with varying views on whether a culture war exists, see The Pew Forum on Religion and Public Life, "Is There a Culture War?" Faith Angle Conference, May 23, 2006 (retrieved April 25, 2008, from http://pewforum.org/events/?EventID=112).

66. I borrow loosely from McAdam, Tarrow, and Tilly's (2001) dynamic model to explain why the NRA emerged when it did as the key social movement organization in the gun rights debate. They argue that their framework applies to contention in any system of institutionalized power as long as a member (collective actors whose interests are routinely taken into account in decision-making

processes) and a challenger (collective actors without access) are present. They contend that this broad approach is necessary, because several related fields examining contentious politics (revolutions, social movements, and war) have become too narrow and ignore one another's contributions. McAdam et al. also strive to "challenge the boundary between institutionalized and noninstitutionalized politics" (6). Their model, like many other political process models, still seems biased regarding the expectation that movements engage in noninstitutionalized (and new) forms of protest, which further reveals a general bias toward groups trying to *create* rather than *prevent* social change. Although the NRA was not necessarily institutionalized prior to its 1977 transformation, it likely has become more of a member (i.e., an institutionalized actor, especially in terms of lobbying activities) than a challenger (i.e., outside actor attempting to challenge member politics) over the last twenty years, particularly as national politics have become increasingly conservative. I contend that critical events may spark contentious politics and that collective action may be "new" for the actors (who may be new to the contentious issue as well) or for the contentious issue, but the collective action does not have to be innovative or noninstitutional in form. Thus expanding political opportunities (for gun control groups because of political assassinations) or new threats (to gun rights posed by an emerging gun control movement) are by-products of state actors' (new) collective action regarding firearms (e.g., legislation that eventually became the Gun Control Act of 1968). Gun control forces parlayed legislative opportunities into a broad coalition (the National Coalition to Ban Handguns), while the fundamentalists within the NRA used threats to gun rights to further their Second Amendment agenda by establishing the NRA Institute for Legislative Action. From here, NRA framing strategies diversified and were directed at broader audiences (e.g., citizens who are not NRA members and do not own firearms) in an attempt to let politicians, the media, and NRA members know that the Second Amendment and guns are part of our culture and heritage and that we should be enforcing the current gun laws more strictly (lock up the criminals) rather than creating new restrictive legislation against "honest law-abiding citizens." See Doug McAdam, Sidney G. Tarrow, and Charles Tilly, *Dynamics of Contention* (New York: Cambridge University Press, 2001).

67. David S. Meyer and Suzanne Staggenborg, "Movements, Countermovements, and the Structure of Political Opportunity," *American Journal of Sociology* 101 (1996): 1628–1660.

68. I refrain from referring to the budding gun control groups and forces of this era as a gun control movement based on Kristin Goss's persuasive argument that, although the 1960s were ripe for a gun control movement to launch, the fledgling groups never quite reached the level of a social movement (and continue to fall short of this label as of this writing). See Kristin A. Goss, *Disarmed: The Missing Movement for Gun Control in America* (Princeton, N.J.: Princeton University Press, 2006).

69. Kristin Luker, *Abortion and the Politics of Motherhood* (Berkeley: University of California Press, 1984), 218.

70. Doug McAdam, *Political Process and the Development of Black Insurgency, 1930–1970,* 2nd ed. (Chicago: University of Chicago Press, 1999).

71. Goss, *Disarmed.*

72. William A. Gamson and David S. Meyer, "Framing Political Opportunity," in *Comparative Perspectives on Social Movements: Political Opportunities, Mobilizing Structures, and Cultural Framings,* ed. Doug McAdam, John D. McCarthy, and Mayer N. Zald, 275–290 (Cambridge: Cambridge University Press, 1996).

73. Sara Diamond, *Spiritual Warfare: The Politics of the Christian Right* (Boston: South End, 1989).

74. Connell, *Masculinities,* 212.

75. *American Rifleman,* May 1955, 36; *American Rifleman,* June 1965, insert; Josh Sugarmann, *National Rifle Association: Money, Firepower & Fear,* 1st ed. (Washington, D.C.: National Press Books, 1992); Davidson, *Under Fire;* Wilson H. Phillips Jr. "Report of the Treasurer to the Annual Meeting of Members," in the minutes of the Annual Meeting of Members, National Rifle Association of America, May 19, 2001 (on file with the author).

76. U.S. Fish & Wildlife Service, "2006 National Survey of Fishing, Hunting, and Wildlife-Associated Recreation" (retrieved June 1, 2008, from http://wsfrprograms.fws.gov/Subpages/NationalSurvey/nat_survey2006_final.pdf).

77. General Social Survey variable *owngun;* See chap. 1 n. 1.

78. The only sociological interpretation of the National Rifle Association as a social movement (organization) is a sympathetic and rather uncritical dissertation by NRA lifetime member Edward Leddy. Greg Lee Carter discusses the NRA as an SMO only in the context of his analysis of the gun control movement, occasionally discussing the anti–gun control movement led by the NRA. The analysis Leddy offers of social movements is brief and is only partly supported by the literature. He argues that the NRA is a reaction to new class (technical workers) dominance and the phasing out of traditional notions of masculinity. He does point out, however, that the increasing politicization of the NRA around the internal 1977 Revolt led to a change in the structure of the organization, and thus social movement organizations may emerge from other organizational forms. Leddy refers to the NRA prior to the Revolt as a mass-membership organization, but after 1977 he erroneously labels it a social movement instead of a social movement organization. Leddy offers the following reason for doing so: ambiguity and strain due to assassinations, gun control debates, and legislation proposals led to widespread anxiety; the source of this strain was identified: anti-gun politicians, media, a budding gun control movement; and, a solution was proposed, namely, the uncompromising defense of gun rights. Unlike Leddy, I explicitly link the social movement literature to the NRA by identifying it as the key social movement organization participating in the gun rights movement. See

Edward F Leddy, *Magnum Force Lobby: The National Rifle Association Fights Gun Control* (Lanham, Md.: University Press of America, 1987); Gregg Lee Carter, *The Gun Control Movement* (New York: Twayne, 1997).

79. John D. McCarthy and Mayer N. Zald, "Resource Mobilization and Social Movements: A Partial Theory," *American Journal of Sociology* 82 (1977): 1212–1241.

80. Davidson, *Under Fire*; Jeffrey H. Birnbaum, "Fat and Happy in D.C.," *Fortune*, May 28, 2001 (retrieved May 28, 2008, from http://money.cnn.com/magazines/fortune/fortune_archive/2001/05/28/303880/index.htm).

81. See www.nra.org.

82. For example, a couple of small rural towns have passed laws *requiring* all residents to own a firearm (although, to my knowledge, these laws have not been enforced); or, more commonly, these groups push for concealed carry laws.

83. John R. Lott, *More Guns, Less Crime*, 2d ed. (Chicago: University of Chicago Press, 2000).

84. Similar to Sidney Tarrow's definition of SMOs, the NRA is oriented toward public authorities. Tarrow notes that "contentious politics emerges in response to political opportunities and constraints, with participants responding to a variety of incentives. . . . Building on these opportunities, and using known repertoires of action, people with limited resources can act contentiously." Further, if their actions are rooted in social networks and "draw on consensual and action-oriented cultural frames, they can sustain these actions in conflict with powerful opponents" and this marks the presence of a social movement. Tarrow, though, using the movement-related organizational typology put forth by Kriesi (1996), would likely argue that the NRA is not an SMO because, similar to public interest groups, it primarily has an indirect mode of participation by constituents. The gun rights movement can also be considered a unique case of transgressive contention because of its rare use of innovative forms of collective action. Sidney Tarrow, *Power in Movements, 2nd ed.* (Cambridge: Cambridge University Press, 1998), 10. Also see McAdam, Tarrow, and Tilly, *Dynamics*; Hanspeter Kriesi, "The Organizational Structure of New Social Movements in a Political Context," in *Comparative Perspectives on Social Movements: Political Opportunities, Mobilizing Structures, and Cultural Framings*, ed. Doug McAdam, John McCarthy, and Mayer Zald, 152–184 (Cambridge: Cambridge University Press, 1996).

85. McAdam, *Political Process*.

86. Heston, *Courage*, 66.

87. Wolfe, "The Culture War," 53, 54.

88. Heston, *Courage*, 56.

CHAPTER 3. FRAMING THREATS TO GUN RIGHTS

1. The National Rifle Association, *A Torch with No Flame: A Second Amendment Message for the Generations* (an NRA Film, 1996).

2. Charlton Heston, "Armed with Pride," in *The Courage to Be Free*, 182–190 (Kansas City: Saudade, 2000), 184.

3. Shoon Lio, Scott Melzer, and Ellen Reese, "Constructing Threat and Appropriating 'Civil Rights': Rhetorical Strategies of Gun Rights and English Only Leaders," *Symbolic Interaction* 31 (2008): 5–31, quote at 8.

4. For an example of threat-driven mobilization, see Kenneth T. Andrews, "Movement-countermovement Dynamics and the Emergence of New Institutions: The Case of 'White Flight' Schools in Mississippi," *Social Forces* 80 (2002): 911–936.

5. Noakes and Johnston's (2005) review of the framing literature reveals overlapping terms and debates about frame resonance. They suggest moving away from terms such as "frame credibility," "frame relevance," and "experiential commensurability," to simply examining the various processes related to frame makers and receivers, and the frame itself (12). See John A. Noakes and Hank Johnston, "Frames of Protest: A Road Map to a Perspective," in *Frames of Protest*, ed. Hank Johnston and John A. Noakes, 1–29 (Lanham, Md.: Rowman & Littlefield, 2005).

6. Murray J. Edelman, *The Symbolic Uses of Politics* (Urbana: University of Illinois Press, 1964), 172.

7. Clarence Y. H. Lo, "Countermovements and Conservative Movements in the Contemporary U.S.," *Annual Review of Sociology* 8 (1982): 107–134, quote at 108.

8. Lio, Melzer, and Reese, "Constructing Threat," 8–9; See Barry Glassner, *The Culture of Fear: Why Americans Are Afraid of the Wrong Things* (New York: Basic Books, 1999); David L. Altheide, *Creating Fear: News and the Construction of Crisis* (New York: Aldine de Gruyter, 2002); Frank Furedi, *Culture of Fear: Risk-Taking and the Morality of Low Expectations* (London: Continuum International, 2002); David L. Altheide, "Notes towards a Politics of Fear," *Journal of Crime, Conflict, and the Media* 1 (2003): 37–54.

9. Nella Van Dyke and Sarah A. Soule, "Structural Social Change and the Mobilizing Effect of Threat: Explaining Levels of Patriot and Militia Organizing in the United States," *Social Problems* 49 (2002): 497–520, quote at 498.

10. Erving Goffman, *Frame Analysis: An Essay on the Organization of Experience* (New York: Harper and Row, 1974).

11. John H. Evans, "Multi-organizational Fields and Social Movement Organization Frame Content: The Religious Pro-choice Movement," *Sociological Inquiry* 67 (1997): 451–469.

12. Robert D. Benford and David A. Snow, "Framing Processes and Social Movements: An Overview," *Annual Review of Sociology* 26 (2000): 611–639, quote at 614; Yet CAFs are subject to more or less flexibility depending upon the rigidity of their organizational ideologies. See Ellen Reese and Garnett Newcombe, "Income Rights, Mother's Rights, or Workers' Rights? Collective Action Frames,

Organizational Ideologies, and the American Welfare Rights Movement," *Social Problems* 50 (2003): 294–318.

13. David A. Snow and Robert D. Benford, "Ideology, Frame Resonance and Participant Mobilization," *International Social Movement Research* 1 (1988): 197–217.

14. David A. Snow and Pamela E. Oliver, "Social Movements and Collective Behavior," in *Sociological Perspectives on Social Psychology*, ed. Karen S. Cook, Gary Alan Fine, and James S. House, 571–599 (Boston: Allyn and Bacon, 1995).

15. Anonymous, "The NRA Board of Directors," *America's First Freedom*, July 2008, 56.

16. Anonymous, *American Rifleman*, May 1945, 15.

17. Anonymous, "Look Who Oppose Civilian Marksmanship," *American Rifleman*, August 1967, 38–41.

18. Ashley Halsey Jr., "Communism versus Gun Ownership," *American Rifleman*, August 1970, 16; Walter J. Howe, "Consent of the Governed," *American Rifleman*, July 1961, 16.

19. Anonymous, *American Rifleman*, April 1961, 31.

20. Walter J. Howe, "Fundamentals of Independence," *American Rifleman*, July 1962, 16.

21. James E. Serven, "Why Americans Own, Shoot, and Collect Guns," *American Rifleman*, April 1963, 12.

22. Chris Lydle, "Teaching Women Defensive Pistol Shooting," *American Rifleman*, May 1967, 31.

23. John M. Schooley, "An Address by the Retiring President," *American Rifleman*, May 1963, 27–28.

24. Ashley Halsey Jr., "Black Panthers and Blind Kittens," *American Rifleman*, September 1970, 20.

25. Anonymous, *American Rifleman*, February 1978, 16.

26. *American Rifleman*, September 1976, 25; May 1991, 15.

27. Wendy Provost, *American Rifleman*, January/February 1995.

28. Wayne R. LaPierre, "Speech to the National Rifle Association Annual Meeting," May 20, 2000 (retrieved November 1, 2002, from http://www.nra.org/speeches.aspx?sid=38).

29. M. Bahati Kuumba, *Gender and Social Movements* (Walnut Creek, Calif.: Altamira, 2001), 19.

30. Charlton Heston, "Free Thought and Freedom," Brandeis University, March 28, 2000 (retrieved November 1, 2002, from http://www.nra.org/speeches.aspx?sid=38).

31. Wayne R. LaPierre, "Speech to the Conservative Political Action Conference," January 20, 2000 (http://www.nrahq.org/transcripts/cpac0202.asp); his description of terrorists was repeated nearly verbatim at the 2002 NRA annual members meeting.

32. Charlton Heston, "Winning the Cultural War," February 16, 1999 (retrieved November 1, 2002, from http://www.nra.org/speeches.aspx?sid=38).

33. Mitch Berbrier, "'Half the Battle': Cultural Resonance, Framing Processes, and Ethnic Affectations in Contemporary White Separatist Rhetoric," *Social Problems* 45 (1998): 431–450.

34. Heston, "Free Thought."

35. Wayne LaPierre, *Guns, Freedom, and Terrorism* (Nashville, Tenn.: WND Books, 2003), 198.

36. Charlton Heston, "Speech to the Opening Session of the Arizona State Legislature," January 8, 2000 (retrieved November 1, 2002, from http://www.nra.org/speeches.aspx?sid=38).

37. Anonymous, "NRA Member Guide," *American Rifleman,* March 1991, 3.

38. An exhaustive summary of these laws would take up too much space here. There are many exceptions to the brief summary I provide. For additional information, see National Rifle Association, "Federal Firearms Laws," Institute for Legislative Action (retrieved July 1, 2008, from http://www.nraila.org/GunLaws/Federal/Read.aspx?id=63); William J. Vizzard, *Shots in the Dark: The Policy, Politics, and Symbolism of Gun Control* (Lanham, Md.: Rowman & Littlefield, 2000); Jon S. Vernick and Lisa M. Hepburn, "State and Federal Gun Laws: Trends for 1970–1999," in *Evaluating Gun Policy: Effects on Crime and Violence,* ed. Jens Ludwig and Philip J. Cook, 345–411 (Washington, D.C.: Brookings Institution Press, 2003); Robert J. Spitzer, *The Politics of Gun Control,* 3rd ed. (Washington, D.C.: CQ Press, 2004); Kristin A. Goss, *Disarmed: The Missing Movement for Gun Control in America* (Princeton, N.J.: Princeton University Press, 2006).

39. Harry L. Wilson, *Guns, Gun Control, and Elections: The Politics and Policy of Firearms* (Lanham, Md.: Rowman & Littlefield, 2007), 104.

40. Vizzard, *Shots in the Dark,* 97.

41. Ibid., 102.

42. Quoted in ibid., 110.

43. Goss, *Disarmed*; Vizzard, *Shots in the Dark.*

44. Goss, *Disarmed,* 44.

45. Spitzer, *Politics of Gun Control,* 131.

46. Goss, *Disarmed,* Appendix A, Figure A.2, 203.

47. Vizzard, *Shots in the Dark.*

48. Goss, *Disarmed,* 5.

49. Quoted in Peter H. Stone, "Showing Holes: The Once-Mighty NRA Is Wounded, but Still Dangerous," *Mother Jones,* January 1, 1994, 39.

50. Kelly Patterson and Matthew Singer, "Targeting Success: The Power of the NRA," in *Interest Group Politics,* 7th ed., ed. Allan J. Cigler and Burdette A. Loomis, 37–64 (Washington, D.C.: CQ Press, 2006).

51. Goss, *Disarmed,* 164, 18, 175.

52. Quoted in Richard Feldman, *Ricochet: Confessions of a Gun Lobbyist* (Hoboken, N.J.: John Wiley, 2008), 165.

53. Some prudence is necessary in describing the NRA during this period. Competing factions and increasing threats make the organization increasingly resemble an SMO as the end of this period approaches. Prior to the 1960s, the organization was rarely concerned with threats to, or their role in, the defense of the Second Amendment.

54. C. B. Lister, "The Backdoor Approach," *American Rifleman*, November 1945, 5.

55. C. B. Lister, "Dangerous Minority," *American Rifleman*, May 1950, 10.

56. Merritt A. Edson, "Education vs. Legislation," *American Rifleman*, March 1955, 17.

57. Franklin Orth, "Build NRA," *American Rifleman*, March 1960, 13.

58. Anonymous, *American Rifleman*, August 1960, 112.

59. Walter J. Howe, "Consent of the Governed," *American Rifleman*, July 1961, 16.

60. Anonymous, *American Rifleman*, May 1960, 21–22.

61. Walter J. Howe, "Logic and Reason," *American Rifleman*, February 1962, 14.

62. Anonymous, *American Rifleman*, May 1962, 49; Anonymous, *American Rifleman*, June 1962.

63. Schooley, "An Address."

64. Walter J. Howe, "Realistic Firearms Control," *American Rifleman*, January 1964, 14.

65. Walter J. Howe, "United We Stand," *American Rifleman*, January 1965, 16–17; idem, "Mail-Order Gun Control," *American Rifleman*, March 1965, 16.

66. Walter J. Howe, *American Rifleman*, January 1966, 14.

67. Franklin Orth, "NRA Thrives on Adversity," *American Rifleman*, January 1968, 15; emphasis added.

68. Ashley Halsey Jr., "The Latest Twist in Anti-Gun Propaganda," *American Rifleman*, December 1968, 17; idem, "Can Three Assassins Kill a Civil Right?" *American Rifleman*, July 1968, 16–17.

69. Anonymous, *American Rifleman*, February 1970, 14.

70. Anonymous, "Concerned NRA Members Redirect Their Association," *American Rifleman*, July 1977, 16.

71. Anonymous, *American Rifleman*, July 1977, 4.

72. In addition to my own research revealing this pattern at the time, a sympathetic NRA member and scholar also found this to be the case. See Edward F. Leddy, *Magnum Force Lobby: the National Rifle Association Fights Gun Control* (Lanham, Md.: University Press of America, 1987).

73. Harlon Carter, "This Is Your NRA," *American Rifleman*, March 1978, 60–61.

74. Feldman, *Ricochet.*

75. BATF has recently seen its responsibilities and name change to include explosives. It is now called BATFE.

76. *American Rifleman,* July 1978, 78–80.

77. The NRA ultimately lost the support of both these presidents because of the NRA stance in response to the Brady Bill after the assassination attempt on Reagan, and, for Bush, inflammatory NRA comments about BATF.

78. Harlon B. Carter, "Here We Stand," *American Rifleman,* April 1985, 7.

79. Institute for Legislative Action, "HCI Launches Anti-Gun Media Blitz," *American Rifleman,* July 1985, 50.

80. Wayne R. LaPierre, "Assault in Congress Puts Your Rights at Risk," *American Rifleman,* July 1991, 20–21.

81. James Jay Baker, "'First Step' Brady Bill Leads to Semi-Auto Ban and More," *American Rifleman*, August 1991, 54.

82. Wayne R. LaPierre, "Standing Guard," *American Rifleman,* December 1991, 7.

83. Author's field notes from Robinson's report to the NRA Board of Directors, April 28, 2003.

84. Anonymous, "Gore's Supreme Surprise," *America's First Freedom*, July 2000, 60–61.

85. Anonymous, "Unsafe in Any Hands: Why America Needs to Ban Handguns," Violence Policy Center (retrieved November 16, 2008, from http://www.vpc.org/studies/unsafe.htm).

86. Anonymous, "The 'F' Troop," *America's First Freedom*, September 2002, 2.

87. James O. E. Norell, "AMA Takes New Anti-Gun Offensive: Doctoring the Second Amendment," *America's First Freedom*, August 2001, 36–39, quote at 39.

88. Wayne LaPierre, *Guns, Freedom, and Terrorism* (Nashville, Tenn.: WND Books, 2003), 206.

89. Spitzer, *Politics of Gun Control,* 107.

90. Wayne R. LaPierre, Mailing to NRA Members, January 11, 2002 (on file with author).

91. Ibid., February 25, 2002 (on file with the author).

92. James Jay Baker, Mailing to NRA Members, February 8, 2002 (on file with author).

93. Ibid., March 25, 2002 (on file with author).

94. Chris W. Cox, Mailing to NRA Members, July 5, 2002 (on file with author).

95. Baker, Mailing to NRA Members, March 25, 2002.

96. Ibid., April 15, 2002 (on file with the author).

97. Author's field notes from LaPierre's report to the NRA Board of Directors, April 29, 2002.

98. Ibid., April 28, 2003.

99. LaPierre, "Speech to the CPAC."

100. Tom Zucco, "Annual NRA Convention: Guns, Pros and Cons," *St. Petersburg Times*, April 26, 2003, 1B.

101. David S. Meyer and Suzanne Staggenborg, "Movements, Countermovements, and the Structure of Political Opportunity," *American Journal of Sociology* 101 (1996): 1628–1660.

102. Anonymous, *American Rifleman*, October 1980, 38.

103. Karen Mehall, "Letter from the Editor," *America's First Freedom*, June 2000, 6.

104. Heston, "Winning the Cultural War."

105. Heston, "Free Thought."

106. Heston, *Courage*, 129, 131.

107. Kayne B. Robinson, "First Vice President's Speech to the NRA Annual Meeting of the Members," April 26, 2003 (author's field notes).

108. Wayne R. LaPierre, Mailing to NRA Members, August 2001 (on file with author).

109. NRA, *A Torch with No Flame*.

110. Lio, Melzer, and Reese, "Constructing Threat," 24.

111. Ibid.

112. Wayne R. LaPierre, "Frightened, or Free?" January 2002 (retrieved January 30, 2002, from http://www.nra.org/speeches.aspx?sid=38).

113. Charlton Heston, "Political Disobedience," June 24, 1999 (retrieved January 30, 2002, from http://www.nra.org/speeches.aspx?sid=38).

114. Sandy Froman, "Women Aiming High," Session at the 2003 NRA annual meetings, April 25, 2003 (author's field notes) (retrieved June 30, 2002, from http://www.nra.org/speeches.aspx?sid=38).

115. Wayne R. LaPierre, "Standing Guard," *American Rifleman*, March 1995, 7.

116. Charlton Heston, "Truth and Consequences," April 16, 1999 (retrieved June 30, 2002, from http://www.nra.org/speeches.aspx?sid=38).

117. Lio, Melzer, and Reese, "Construction Threat."

118. Wayne LaPierre and James Jay Baker, *Shooting Straight: Telling the Truth about Guns in America* (Washington, D.C.: Regnery, 2002), 177; Froman, "Women Aiming High."

119. Charlton Heston, "Conservative Challenge for a New Millennium," Remarks before the Conservative Political Action Conference, January 1999, 209–213, in idem, *The Courage to Be Free* (Kansas City: Saudade, 2000), 211.

120. Heston, "Political Disobedience."

121. Thomas R. Rochon, *Culture Moves: Ideas, Activism, and Changing Values* (Princeton, N.J.: Princeton University Press, 1998), 55.

122. Joan Burbick, *Gun Show Nation* (New York: The New Press, 2006), 88–89.

123. Lio, Melzer, and Reese, 11.

124. Charlton Heston, "From the President," *America's First Freedom*, June 2000, 10.

125. Robinson, "First Vice President's Speech."

126. LaPierre, Mailing to NRA Members, August 2001.

127. Charlton Heston, "Opening Remarks to NRA Members," May 20, 2000 (retrieved November 1, 2002, from http://www.nra.org/speeches.aspx?sid=38).

128. Thomas Byrne Edsall and Mary D. Edsall, *Chain Reaction: The Impact of Race, Rights, and Taxes on American Politics* (New York: Norton, 1991), 4.

129. LaPierre, Report to the NRA Board, April 29, 2002.

130. Cox, Mailing to NRA Members, July 5, 2002.

131. LaPierre, Mailing to NRA Members, February 25, 2002.

132. Wayne R. LaPierre, Mailing to NRA Members, April 8, 2002 (on file with author).

133. Kayne B. Robinson, "You Are at War," *America's First Freedom*, November 2002, 30–33, 62.

134. Heston, *Courage*, 111, 129, 140.

135. LaPierre and Baker, *Shooting Straight*, 14.

136. Wayne R. LaPierre, Mailing to NRA Members, October 1, 2001 (on file with author).

137. Bert Klandermans, "The Social Construction of Protest and Multiorganizational Fields," in *Frontiers in Social Movement Theory*, ed. Aldon D. Morris and Carol McClurg Mueller, 77–103 (New Haven, Conn.: Yale University Press, 1992), 97.

138. Feldman, *Ricochet*, 184.

139. Aldon D. Morris, "Political Consciousness and Collective Action," in Morris and McClurg, *Social Movement Theory*, 363.

140. Gerald Marwell and Pamela Oliver, *The Critical Mass in Collective Action: A Micro-Social Theory* (New York: Cambridge University Press, 1993).

141. Pamela Oliver, Gerald Marwell, and Ruy Teixeira, "A Theory of the Critical Mass, I: Interdependence, Group Heterogeneity, and the Production of Collective Action," *American Journal of Sociology* 91 (1985): 522–556.

CHAPTER 4. UNDER ATTACK

1. NRA members I interviewed are assigned only first names, whereas I identify Madison Brigade members with first and last names.

2. Robert J. Spitzer, *The Politics of Gun Control*, 3rd ed. (Washington, D.C.: CQ Press, 2004), 84.

3. Quotes from NRA Madison Brigade members are available at: http://www.madisonbrigade.com/brigade.htm

4. General Social Survey data, 2000, 2002, 2004. Gun owners are those who report that a gun in their house personally belongs to them (variable: *rowngun*).

Non-owners are those who report no guns in their homes (variable: *owngun*). The two gun control variables cited here are *gunlaw* and *hgunlaw* (the latter was not introduced until the 2004 survey). See chap. 1 n. 1.

5. Joan Burbick, *Gun Show Nation* (New York: New Press, 2006), 61–62.

6. Anonymous NRA spokesperson quoted in Peter Harry Brown and Daniel G. Abel, *Outgunned: Up Against the NRA* (New York: Free Press, 2003), 207, 215–216.

7. Jerome L. Himmelstein, *To the Right: the Transformation of American Conservatism* (Berkeley: University of California Press, 1990).

8. Katarzyna Celinska, "Individualism and Collectivism in America: The Case of Gun Ownership and Attitudes toward Gun Control," *Sociological Perspectives* 50 (2007): 229–247, quote at 234.

9. Sara Diamond, *Roads to Dominion: Right-Wing Movements and Political Power in the United States* (New York: Guilford, 1995), 246.

10. This now commonly used expression (even found on belt buckles) comes from John Mitchell, "God, Guns and Guts Made America Free," *American Heritage*, February 1978, 4–17.

11. More work is needed on the role of religion in NRA politics. Specifically, further research should shed more light on the connections between members' religious preferences and religiosity, and how these inform (or are informed by) their gun views.

12. Maureen McNeil, "Making and Not Making the Difference: The Gender Politics of Thatcherism," in *Off-Centre: Feminism and Cultural Studies*, ed. Sarah Franklin, Celia Lury, and Jackie Stacey, 221–240 (London: HarperCollins, 1991), 226.

13. George Lakoff, *Moral Politics: How Liberals and Conservatives Think*, 2nd ed. (Chicago: University of Chicago Press, 2002), 153–154.

14. Lakoff also emphasizes the similarities of conservative viewpoints, even when some conservative positions are diametrically opposed; however, no conservative groups oppose gun rights. For example, Libertarians and the Christian Right have contrasting views on gambling and drug use. The former do not think the government should regulate morality, whereas the latter believe that gambling and drugs should be outlawed because they are immoral. Lakoff reconciles this difference by arguing that Libertarians take the conservative view that government interference should be minimal, that we should be self-reliant and individually responsible for our actions. The Christian Right, Lakoff argues, takes the different but still conservative view that immoral acts must not go unpunished by tough fathers—or, in this case, governments. The outcome, supporting or opposing government regulation of gambling or drug use, is different for these two groups, but, according to Lakoff, each uses a conservative Strict Father Morality. Linguist Geoffrey Nunberg (*Talking Right* [New York: Public Affairs, 2006]) contends that Lakoff is trying to explain a historically specific phenomenon by using a model that claims to explain multigenerational phenomena. In Nunberg's view, anti-abortion, pro-gun rights, and anti-tax issues currently are linked together

under conservatism, but political alliances shift and one or more of these issues could become uncoupled from conservatism. The varying views of NRA members on the seriousness of gun rights threats are a key indicator of whether they see gun control and culture war forces as inseparable.

15. Lakoff, *Moral Politics*, 13.

16. As a cognitive scientist, Lakoff's lens is focused on internal processes to explain human attitudes and behavior. Similarly, as a sociologist, I tend to emphasize social forces outside individuals. There is actually some overlap between the two approaches, but I believe that the sources of Lakoff's internal processes and metaphors lie ultimately with social, cultural, and political arrangements. Although I thoroughly agree with his analysis of the differences between conservatives and liberals, it is important to recognize that these are not universal categories. People who grew up in other cultures (e.g., with no government or where government is not centered on two political parties) and in different times will not be constrained in their moral political thoughts by Lakoff's metaphor; that is, not everyone sees the world through the lens of Strict Father Morality versus Nurturant Parent Morality. Metaphors and language are rooted in cultures, and cultures vary. Although Lakoff claims not to offer a universal model of political thought, as a cognitive scientist he brushes over possible cross-cultural implications of his model; for instance, he mentions, in passing, that Strict Father metaphors exist "in diverse cultures around the world," but then he refers to the "peculiarly American version of the Strict Father family model" (100). Lakoff seems to imply that liberals and conservatives are born rather than made. Like most sociologists, I argue that human behavior and thought are ultimately mediated by culture, time, location, and situation. Although my focus in this book is on the effects of U.S. history, particularly on the ideology of Gun Crusaders in the last several decades, even this analysis of NRA politics could be extended into the social forces that ultimately led to modern circumstances. A historian might concentrate on the deeper histories of European religion and culture, democracies, and capitalism that are the foundation of the United States.

17. Spitzer, *Politics of Gun Control*, 85.

18. I do not mean to imply that all opponents of abortion are members of the Christian Right. Many individuals with non-Christian religious beliefs or even none at all want abortion to be outlawed. However, the pro-life *movement* is dominated by individuals who are embedded in the Christian Right.

CHAPTER 5. FIGHTING THE CULTURE WARS

1. Molly Ivins, "You Want Protection? Get a Dog," *Creators Syndicate*, republished October 20, 1997 (retrieved July 5, 2008, from http://www.chron.com/content/chronicle/editorial/97/10/29/ivins.html).

2. These are broad categories, but they cover most conservative politics. See Sara Diamond, *Roads to Dominion: Right-Wing Movements and Political Power in the United States* (New York: Guilford, 1995), 7.

3. Most of these images reflect a mythologized construction of family, sexuality, and gender arrangements during this period, glossing over enormous diversity in all three areas. For a detailed analysis, see Stephanie Coontz, *The Way We Never Were: American Families and the Nostalgia Trap*, 2nd ed. (New York: Basic Books, 2000).

4. For more on the Protestant Ethic, see Max Weber, *The Protestant Ethic and the Spirit of Capitalism* (New York: Routledge, 2001 [1904]).

5. Barbara Ehrenreich, *The Hearts of Men* (New York: Anchor Books, 1983); Glen Jeansonne, *Women of the Far Right: The Mother's Movement and World War II* (Chicago: University of Chicago Press, 1996).

6. Rachel L. Einwohner, "Gender, Class, and Social Movement Outcomes: Identity and Effectiveness in Two Animal Rights Campaigns," *Gender & Society* 13 (1999): 56–76, quote at 66.

7. Sandy Froman, Susan Howard, and Susan LaPierre, "Women Aiming High," Session at 2003 NRA Annual Meeting, April 25, 2003 (author's field notes).

8. David H. J. Morgan, "Theater of War: Combat, the Military, and Masculinities," in *Theorizing Masculinities*, ed. Harry Brod and Michael Kaufman, 165–182 (Thousand Oaks, Calif.: Sage, 1994).

9. Ehrenreich, *Hearts of Men*.

10. Ibid.

11. General Social Survey, 2000, 2002, and 2004, variable *fepoly*. See chap. 1 n. 1.

12. Hillary Clinton's 2008 Democratic presidential candidate campaign rekindled much of the anti-feminist backlash from her earlier White House days. For example, Republican political consultant Roger Stone created an anti-Hillary 527 group called Citizens United Not Timid. To ensure their acronym comes to mind, they use a logo that clearly mimics a woman's groin. A Minnesota company sold the "Hillary Nutcracker," a not-so-subtle novelty item that referenced men's fears of castration by powerful women such as Hillary. The nine-inch Hillary figure/kitchen utensil wears a pantsuit and has stainless steel thighs that are used, literally, to crush nuts.

13. For a summary of different feminisms, see Judith Lorber, *Gender Inequality: Feminist Theories and Politics*, 3rd ed. (Los Angeles: Roxbury, 2005).

14. Author interviews with Gerry and Ernie, respectively.

15. Kenneth Neubeck, *Welfare Racism: Playing the Race Card against America's Poor* (New York: Routledge, 2001), 127.

16. Jeffrey R. Dudas, "In the Name of Equal Rights: 'Special' Rights, and the Politics of Resentment in Post-Civil Rights America," *Law & Society Review* 39 (2005): 723–757, quote at 731.

17. Sharon Hays, *Flat Broke with Children: Women in the Age of Welfare Reform* (New York: Oxford University Press, 2003), 7, 8, 11.

18. Ellen R. Reese, *Backlash against Welfare Mothers, Past and Present* (Berkeley: University of California Press, 2005), 28.

19. General Social Survey, 2000, 2002, and 2004, variables *natfare, natchld, and helppoor*. See chap. 1 n. 1.

20. Michael S. Kimmel, *Manhood in America* (New York: Free Press, 1996), 236.

21. Connell, *Masculinities*.

22. Dudas, "In the Name," 724.

23. Diamond, *Roads to Dominion*, 253.

24. Author interviews with Helen and Donald, respectively.

25. George Lakoff, *Whose Freedom? The Battle over America's Most Important Idea* (New York: Farrar, Straus and Giroux, 2006), 134.

26. Charlton Heston, "Speech to the Free Congress Foundation's 20th Anniversary Gala," December 7, 1997 (retrieved November 1, 2002, from http://www.vpc.org/nrainfo/speech.html).

27. No organizational race/ethnicity data are available, but after analyzing NRA magazines and spending multiple days at two national meetings attended by eighty thousand members, and being able to count the number of people of color on two hands at both meetings, I am confident of this figure. It is likely even on the conservative side.

28. Thomas Byrne Edsall and Mary D. Edsall, *Chain Reaction: The Impact of Race, Rights, and Taxes on American Politics* (New York: Norton, 1991); Dan T. Carter, *From George Wallace to Newt Gingrich: Race in the Conservative Counterrevolution, 1963–1994* (Baton Rouge: Louisiana State University Press, 1996).

29. General Social Survey, 2004, variable *hguncrim*. See chap. 1 n. 1.

30. U.S. Department of Justice, "Prisoners in 2002," Bureau of Justice Statistics (retrieved May 13, 2004, from http://www.ojp.usdoj.gov/bjs/pub/pdf/p02.pdf).

31. U.S. Department of Justice, "Criminal Victimization in the United States—Statistical Tables Index," Bureau of Justice Statistics (retrieved July 8, 2008, from http://www.ojp.usdoj.gov/bjs/abstract/cvus/single_offender_victimizations694.htm).

32. At the Miami airport, the Spanish-speaking population is more likely to descend from Cuba, Puerto Rico, and other countries closer to South Florida than from Mexico.

33. Edsall and Edsall, *Chain Reaction*, 145, 14.

34. Lakoff, *Whose Freedom?* 73–76, 103–105; Sawer, "Gender, Metaphor, and the State," 124.

35. Martin Durham, *The Christian Right, the Far Right, and the Boundaries of American Conservatism* (Manchester, U.K.: Manchester University Press, 2000), 170.

36. Susan Faludi, *Stiffed: The Betrayal of the American Man* (New York: William Morrow, 1999).

37. Edsall and Edsall, *Chain Reaction*, 10.

38. Diamond, *Roads to Dominion*, 9.

CHAPTER 6. THE POLITICS OF COMMITMENT

1. Francesca Polletta and James M. Jasper, "Collective Identity and Social Movements," *Annual Review of Sociology* 27 (2001): 283–305, quote at 285.

2. Pamela Oliver, Gerald Marwell, and Ruy Teixeira, "A Theory of the Critical Mass, I: Interdependence, Group Heterogeneity, and the Production of Collective Action," *American Journal of Sociology* 91 (1985): 522–556.

3. Gerald Marwell and Pamela Oliver, *The Critical Mass in Collective Action: A Micro-Social Theory* (New York: Cambridge University Press, 1993).

4. For a discussion of frame alignment, see David A. Snow, E. Burke Rochford Jr., Steven K. Worden, and Robert D. Benford, "Frame Alignment Processes, Micromobilization, and Movement Participation," *American Sociological Review* 51 (1986): 464–481, quote at 464.

5. U.S. Bureau of the Census, "Urban and Rural, 2000," (retrieved May 13, 2004, from http://factfinder.census.gov/servlet/DTTable?_bm=y&-geo_id=01000US&-ds_name=DEC_2000_SF4_U&-_lang=en&-state=dt&-format=&-mt_name=DEC_2000_SF4_U_PCT002).

6. Other participants include well-known conservatives such as Vice President Dick Cheney, Lt. Col. Oliver North, Phyllis Schlafly, and David Horowitz. For more information, see http://www.cpac.org/.

7. Eric Alterman, *What Liberal Media? The Truth about Bias and the News* (New York: Basic Books, 2003).

8. General Social Survey, 2000, 2002, and 2004, variables *partyid, polviews, and presoo*. See chap. 1 n. 1.

CHAPTER 7. RIGHT AND FAR-RIGHT MORAL POLITICS

1. George Lakoff, *Moral Politics: How Liberals and Conservatives Think*, 2nd ed. (Chicago: University of Chicago Press, 2002).

2. Humphrey Taylor, "Confidence in Government's Handling of War on Terrorism," *Harris Poll #58*, November 24, 2001 (retrieved May 13, 2004, from http://www.harrisinteractive.com/harris_poll/index.asp?PID=269).

3. Jeffrey M Jones, "Bush's High Approval Ratings among Most Sustained for Presidents," Gallup Poll, November 7, 2001 (retrieved May 13, 2004, from http://www.gallup.com/poll/5032/Bushs-High-Approval-Ratings-Among-Most-Sustained-Presidents.aspx).

4. John F. Harris, "God Gave U.S. 'What We Deserve,' Falwell Says," September 14, 2001 (retrieved April 11, 2008, from http://www.washingtonpost.com/ac2/wp-dyn/A28620-2001Sep14); YouTube, "Falwell and Robertson on The 700 Club after 9/11" (retrieved April 11, 2008, from http://www.youtube.com/watch?v=H-CAcdta_8I).

5. U.S. Census Bureau, "Profile of Selected Social Characteristics, 2000," (retrieved May 13, 2004, from http://factfinder.census.gov/servlet/QTTable?_bm=y&-geo_id=D&-qr_name=DEC_2000_SF3_U_DP2&-ds_name=D&-_lang=en&-redoLog=false).

6. General Social Survey data from the years 2000, 2002, and 2004, variable *homosex*. See chap. 1 n. 1.

7. Erving Goffman, *Stigma: Notes on the Management of Spoiled Identity* (Englewood Cliffs, N.J.: Prentice Hall, 1963); R. W. Connell, *Masculinities* (Berkeley: University of California Press, 1995).

8. U.S. Department of Agriculture, Economic Research Service, "Food Security in the United States, 2006" (retrieved May 12, 2008, from http://www.ers.usda.gov/Briefing/FoodSecurity/); United States Department of Agriculture, Economic Research Service, "Food Security in the United States: Conditions and Trends, 2006" (retrieved May 12, 2008, from http://www.ers.usda.gov/Briefing/FoodSecurity/trends.htm).

9. Bernadette D. Proctor and Joseph Dalaker, "Poverty in the United States, 2002," U.S. Census Bureau (retrieved May 8, 2004, from http://www.census.gov/prod/2003pubs/p60-222.pdf).

10. Thomas Byrne Edsall and Mary D. Edsall, *Chain Reaction: The Impact of Race, Rights, and Taxes on American Politics* (New York: Norton, 1991).

11. U.S. Census Bureau, "Sex by Age, 2000" (retrieved May 13, 2004, from http://factfinder.census.gov/servlet/DTTable?_bm=y&-geo_id=01000US&-ds_name=DEC_2000_SF3_U&-_lang=en&-redoLog=false&-mt_name=DEC_2000_SF3_U_P008&-_sse=on); U.S. Census Bureau, "Race and Hispanic or Latino, 2000" (retrieved May 13, 2004, from http://factfinder.census.gov/servlet/QTTable?_bm=y&-geo_id=01000US&-qr_name=DEC_2000_SF1_U_QTP3&-ds_name=DEC_2000_SF1_U&-_lang=en&-redoLog=false&-_sse=on).

CHAPTER 8. THE TIES THAT BIND

1. David A. Snow and Robert D. Benford, "Master Frames and Cycles of Protest," in *Frontiers in Social Movement Theory,* ed. Aldon D. Morris and Carol McClurg Mueller, 133–155 (New Haven, Conn.: Yale University Press, 1992); Doug McAdam, Sidney G. Tarrow, and Charles Tilly, *Dynamics of Contention* (New York: Cambridge University Press, 2001).

2. Wilson H. Phillips Jr. "Report of the Treasurer to the Annual Meeting of Members," in the minutes of the Annual Meeting of Members, National Rifle Association of America, May 19, 2001 (on file with the author), 37–38; Better Business Bureau Wise Giving Report for the National Rifle Association, 2004 (retrieved May 26, 2008, from http://charityreports.bbb.org/public/Report. aspx?CharityID=1420).

3. Much of this chapter's data on the NRA's and other gun rights PACs and lobbying activities are available through the Web site of the Center for Responsive Politics, opensecrets.org, which documents money in politics. All 2008 election cycle data reflect Federal Election Commission data only through the end of the third quarter, September 30, 2008. Fourth quarter 2008 data had not been released as of this writing. Data are "based on contributions of $200 or more from PACs and individuals to federal candidates and from PAC, soft money and individual donors to political parties, as reported to the Federal Election Commission. While election cycles are shown in tables as 1996, 1998, 2000, and so on, they actually represent two-year periods. For example, the 2002 election cycle runs from January 1, 2001 to December 31, 2002. Soft money contributions to the national parties were not publicly disclosed until the 1991–92 election cycle, and were banned by the Bipartisan Campaign Finance Reform Act following the 2002 elections" (Center for Responsive Politics, "Most Heavily Partisan Industries" [retrieved November 15, 2008, from http://www.opensecrets.org/bigpicture/partisans.php?cycle=2006]; and idem, "Gun Rights: Long-term Contribution Trends" [retrieved November 15, 2008, from http://www.opensecrets.org/industries/indus.php?ind=Q13]).

4. Center for Responsive Politics, "Top Industries" (retrieved November 15, 2008, from http://www.opensecrets.org/bigpicture/industries.php?cycle=All);

5. Center for Responsive Politics, "Lawyers/Law Firms: Top Contributors to Federal Candidates and Parties" (retrieved May 28, 2008, from http://www.opensecrets.org/industries/contrib.php?ind=K01&cycle=2004); idem, "Association of Trial Lawyers of America: 2004 PAC Summary Data" (retrieved May 28, 2008, from http://www.opensecrets.org/pacs/lookup2.php?strID=C00024521&cycle=2004).

6. Center for Responsive Politics, "Oil & Gas: Top Contributors to Federal Candidates and Parties" (retrieved May 28, 2008, from http://www.opensecrets.org/industries/contrib.php?ind=E01&cycle=2004).

7. Center for Responsive Politics, "National Rifle Association: 2004 PAC Summary Data" (retrieved May 28, 2008, from http://www.opensecrets.org/pacs/lookup2.php?cycle=2004&strID=C00053553).

8. Center for Responsive Politics: "Independent expenditures are ads that expressly advocate the election or defeat of specific candidates and are aimed at the electorate as a whole. Under federal rules, these expenditures must be made completely independent of the candidates, with no coordination, and they can

only be made by the organization's PAC" (retrieved November 15, 2008, from http://www.opensecrets.org/bigpicture/whatis_pop.php).

9. Center for Responsive Politics, "National Rifle Association: 2004 PAC Summary Data" (retrieved May 28, 2008, from http://www.opensecrets.org/pacs/lookup2.php?cycle=2004&strID=C00053553); idem, "National Rifle Association: 2006 PAC Summary Data" (retrieved May 28, 2008, from http://www.opensecrets.org/pacs/lookup2.php?strID=C00053553&cycle=2006).

10. Center for Responsive Politics, "National Rifle Association: 2004 PAC Summary Data" (retrieved May 28, 2008, from http://www.opensecrets.org/pacs/lookup2.php?cycle=2004&strID=C00053553).

11. Center for Responsive Politics: "Internal communication costs are internal political messages generally aimed only at the members of a union or organization, or company executives. These may be coordinated with the candidates and can be paid for directly from the organization's treasury" (retrieved November 15, 2008, from http://www.opensecrets.org/bigpicture/whatis_pop.php).

12. This excludes party committees. Center for Responsive Politics, "Top 20 PACs by Total Expenditures, 2005–2006 [2003–2004; 2001–2002, 1999–2000; 1997–1998]" (retrieved May 28, 2008, from http://www.opensecrets.org/pacs/top-pacs.php?cycle=2006&Type=E&filter=P).

13. Center for Responsive Politics, "National Rifle Association: Summary" (retrieved May 28, 2008, from http://www.opensecrets.org/orgs/summary.php?id=D000000082).

14. Center for Responsive Politics, "Top 20 PAC by Total Expenditures, 1999–2000" (retrieved May 28, 2008, from http://www.opensecrets.org/bigpicture/toppacs.php?Type=C&party=R&cycle=2000); idem, "Top 20 PAC Contributors to Federal Candidates, 1999–2000: Republicans" (retrieved May 28, 2008, from http://www.opensecrets.org/bigpicture/toppacs.php?cycle=2000&Type=E).

15. Cameron Hopkins, "A New NRA," *American Handgunner*, July 2001 (retrieved May 28, 2008, from http://findarticles.com/p/articles/mi_m0BTT/is_153_25/ai_75211999).

16. Center for Responsive Politics, "National Rifle Association: 2000 PAC Summary Data" (retrieved May 28, 2008, from http://www.opensecrets.org/pacs/lookup2.php?strID=C00053553&cycle=2000); idem, "National Rifle Association: 2006 PAC Summary Data" (retrieved May 28, 2008, from http://www.opensecrets.org/pacs/lookup2.php?strID=C00053553&cycle=2006).

17. Chris W. Cox, "Your Tools for Victory: Victory Report, Election 2004" (retrieved May 28, 2008, from http://www.nraila.org/issues/Articles/Read.aspx?ID=154).

18. John J. Miller, "High Caliber Advocacy: How the NRA Won the Fight over Gun Rights," *National Review*, January 28, 2005 (retrieved May 30, 2008, from http://article.nationalreview.com/?q=OWVhYTcoMDBkYmMyNGU3OGMwMjIzN2E4ZWQxYTNmNzQ=).

19. Annenberg Political Fact Check, "Liberal Group Attacks Dean on Gun Control," Factcheck.org, December 9, 2003 (retrieved May 30, 2008, from (retrieved May 30, 2008, from http://www.factcheck.org/liberal_group_attacks_dean_on_gun_control.html).

20. Anna Cornelia Fahey, "French and Feminine: Hegemonic Masculinity and the Emasculation of John Kerry in the 2004 Presidential Race," *Critical Studies in Media Communication* 24 (2007): 132–150.

21. Anonymous, "Outrage at 'Old Europe' Remarks," BBC News, January 23, 2003 (retrieved May 30, 2008, from http://news.bbc.co.uk/2/hi/europe/2687403.stm).

22. Sean Loughlin, "House Cafeterias Change Names for 'French' Fries and 'French' Toast," CNN.com, March 12, 2003 (retrieved May 30, 2008, from http://www.cnn.com/2003/ALLPOLITICS/03/11/sprj.irq.fries/).

23. All 2008 election cycle data reflect Federal Election Commission data only through the end of the third quarter, September 30, 2008; Center for Responsive Politics, "Top All-Time Donors, 1989–2008" (retrieved May 28, 2008, from http://www.opensecrets.org/orgs/list.php?order=A).

24. Center for Responsive Politics, "Altria Group PAC Summary Data" (retrieved May 28, 2008, from http://www.opensecrets.org/pacs/lookup2.php?strID=C00089136); idem, "National Beer Wholesalers Association Independent Expenditures" (retrieved May 28, 2008, from http://www.opensecrets.org/pacs/indexpend.php?cmte=C00144766&cycle=2004).

25. Martin Durham, *The Christian Right, the Far Right and the Boundaries of American Conservatism* (Manchester, UK: Manchester University Press, 2000).

26. Jeffrey H. Birnbaum, "Fat and Happy in D.C.," *Fortune*, May 28, 2001 (retrieved May 28, 2008, from http://money.cnn.com/magazines/fortune/fortune_archive/2001/05/28/303880/index.htm).

27. Center for Responsive Politics, "Lobbying: National Rifle Association" (retrieved May 28, 2008, from http://www.opensecrets.org/lobby/clientsum.php?lname=National+Rifle+Assn&year=2008).

28. Center for Responsive Politics, "Lobbying: Top Spenders" (retrieved November 15, 2008, from http://www.opensecrets.org/lobby/top.php?indexType=s).

29. Center for Responsive Politics, "Lobbying: Top Industries" (retrieved November 15, 2008, from http://www.opensecrets.org/lobby/top.php?indexType=i).

30. Center for Responsive Politics, "Lobbying: Ideology/Single Issue [1998–2008]" (retrieved November 15, 2008, from http://www.opensecrets.org/lobby/indus.php?year=2008&lname=Q).

31. Center for Responsive Politics, "Lobbying: Influence Inc. 2000, Top Issue Areas" (retrieved May 28, 2008, from http://www.opensecrets.org/lobby/lobby00/issueareas.php).

32. Birnbaum, "Fat and Happy."

33. Project Vote Smart, "National Rifle Association, 2006" (retrieved November 10, 2008, from http://www.votesmart.org/issue_rating_detail.php?r_id=4229).

34. Peter Hamby, "Clinton Touts Her Experience with Guns," CNN Political Ticker, April 12, 2008 (retrieved May 30, 2008, from http://politicalticker.blogs.cnn.com/2008/04/12/clinton-touts-her-experience-with-guns/); Anonymous, "McCain Courts Gun Owners at NRA," Associated Press, May 16, 2008 (retrieved May 30, 2008, from http://www.cbsnews.com/stories/2008/05/16/politics/main4103429.shtml).

35. The Library of Congress, retrieved May 23, 2008 (http://thomas.loc.gov/).

36. Brady Campaign to Prevent Gun Violence, "About the Brady Campaign" (retrieved May 30, 2008, from http://www.bradycampaign.org/about/history.php).

37. Library of Congress.

38. Ibid.

39. Bill Clinton, *My Life* (New York: Knopf, 2004), 629–630. Cited in Wikipedia, "National Rifle Association" (retrieved May 29, 2008, from http://en.wikipedia.org/wiki/National_Rifle_Association#1994).

40. Christopher Kenny, Michael McBurnett, and David Bordua, "The Impact of Political Interests in the 1994 and 1996 Congressional Elections: The Role of the National Rifle Association," *British Journal of Political Science* 32 (2004): 331–344.

41. Alicia Montgomery, "Politics 2000: Trail Mix," *Salon* (retrieved May 26, 2008, from http://archive.salon.com/politics2000/feature/2000/05/04/trail_mix/index.html).

42. Jill Lawrence, "Federal Ban on Assault Weapons Expires," *USA Today*, September 12, 2004 (retrieved May 30, 2008, from http://www.usatoday.com/news/washington/2004-09-12-weapons-ban_x.htm).

43. Library of Congress.

44. David Firestone, "Gun Lobby Begins Concerted Attacks on Cities' Lawsuits," *New York Times*, February 9, 1999 (retrieved May 30, 2008, from http://query.nytimes.com/gst/fullpage.html?res=9A0CE2DC133BF93AA35751C0A96F958260).

45. Jonathan Weisman, "Democrats, NRA Reach Deal on Background-Check Bill," *Washington Post*, June 10, 2007, A02.

46. Gun Owners of America, "Compromisers on Capitol Hill Reviving Brady Expansion Again," June 12, 2007 (retrieved May 30, 2008, from http://www.gunowners.org/a061207.htm).

47. Library of Congress.

48. Harry L. Wilson, *Guns, Gun Control, and Elections: The Politics and Policy of Firearms* (Lanham, Md.: Rowman & Littlefield, 2007), 104.

49. CBS News/*New York Times* Poll, "The 2004 Republican Delegates," August 28, 2004 (retrieved May 15, 2008, from http://www.cbsnews.com/stories/2004/08/28/opinion/polls/main639203.shtml); CBS News/New York Times Poll, "2008 Republican Delegates: Who Are They?" August 31, 2008 (retrieved May 16, 2008, from http://www.cbsnews.com/htdocs/pdf/RNCDelegates_who_are_they.pdf).

50. Conservative Political Action Conference, "CPAC 2009 Cosponsors" (retrieved June 2, 2008, from http://www.cpac.org/sponsors.html).

51. American Conservative Union, "About ACU" (retrieved June 2, 2008, from http://www.conservative.org/about/default.asp).

52. David A. Keene, "Four Decades of Leadership," American Conservative Union, May 2, 2004 (retrieved June 2, 2008, from http://www.conservative.org/columnists/keene/040502dk.asp).

53. The American Conservative Union, "CPAC 2008 Speeches" (retrieved June 2, 2008, from http://www.conservative.org/pressroom/2008/080220_CPAC-speeches.asp); idem, "Ronald Reagan's CPAC Speeches" (retrieved June 2, 2008, from http://www.conservative.org/pressroom/reagan/reagan.asp).

54. Americans for Tax Reform, "About Grover G. Norquist" (retrieved June 2, 2008, from http://www.atr.org/home/about/ggnbio.html); idem, "About Us" (retrieved June 2, 2008, from http://www.atr.org/home/about/index.html).

55. Mara Liasson, *National Public Radio*, "Morning Edition," May 25, 2001 (retrieved May 25, 2008, from http://www.npr.org/templates/story/story.php?storyId=1123439).

56. Terry Gross, National Public Radio, "Fresh Air," October 2, 2003 (retrieved May 21, 2008, from http://www.npr.org/templates/story/story.php?storyId=1452983).

57. Ibid.; Media Transparency, "Personal Profile: Grover G. Norquist" (retrieved June 2, 2008, from http://www.mediatransparency.org/personprofile.php?personID=52).

58. Susan Page, "Norquist's Power High, Profile Low," *USA Today*, June 1, 2001 (retrieved June 1, 2008, from http://www.usatoday.com/news/washington/2001-06-01-grover.htm).

59. Center for Defense Information, "Power of NRA Showcased in U.S. Delegation to Small Arms Conference," June 26, 2006 (retrieved May 16, 2008, from http://www.cdi.org/program/document.cfm?DocumentID=3561&StartRow=11&ListRows=10&&Orderby=D.DateLastUpdated&ProgramID=23&typeID=(4,5)&from_page=relateditems.cfm).

60. Emilie Raymond, *From My Cold Dead Hands: Charlton Heston and American Politics* (Lexington: University Press of Kentucky, 2006); Internet Movie Database, "Biography for Charlton Heston" (retrieved June 2, 2008, from http://www.imdb.com/name/nm0000032/bio).

61. Angie Fenton, "TV/Radio Host a New NRA Member," *The Courier-Journal*, May 18, 2008 (retrieved June 2, 2008, from http://www.courier-journal.com/apps/pbcs.dll/article?AID=/20080518/NEWS01/805180503).

62. Mike Miller, Reuters, "Cabinet Member Thanks NRA for Helping Bush Win White House," *San Diego Union-Tribune*, May 21, 2001, A5.

63. National Rifle Association, "2006 NRA Annual Meeting and Exhibits: Freedom's 2nd Army Takes Milwaukee" (retrieved June 2, 2008, from http://www.nraam.org/pastmeetings/2006_pastmeeting.asp).

64. National Rifle Association, "2007 NRA Annual Meeting and Exhibits: Gateway to Freedom" (retrieved June 2, 2008, from http://www.nraam.org/past-meetings/default.asp).

65. Ibid.

66. NRA board members serve three-year terms and may continuously run for reelection. I have gathered 155 names of NRA board members, officers, and executive leadership to examine their political histories and connections as well as their political donations. Admittedly this is an imprecise undertaking. Although the NRA lists its various boards of directors in its magazines, the names of these individuals are often not unique, thus making it difficult to identify some board members with full confidence. For the vast majority of NRA leaders, enough information is available to confirm their identities (e.g., in candidate biographies). There is nothing to suggest that the few NRA leaders whose information is unobtainable would bias the current results in one direction or another.

67. Data included through May 26, 2008. Donor data available at the Web site of the Center for Responsive Politics (http://www.opensecrets.org/indivs/index.php).

EPILOGUE. TOMORROW'S NRA

1. IRS Form 990, on file with the author.

2. *America's First Freedom*, July 2008, 16.

3. Kelly Patterson and Matthew Singer, "Targeting Success: The Enduring Power of the NRA," in *Interest Group Politics*, 7th ed., ed. Allan J. Cigler and Burdett A. Loomis, 37–64 (Washington, D.C.: CQ Press, 2006).

4. Wayne LaPierre, "Remarks at the 137th Annual Meeting of Members," National Rifle Association, May 17, 2008 (retrieved June 26, 2008, from http://www.nraila.org/News/Read/Speeches.aspx?ID=57).

5. Jonathan Martin, "NRA Plans $40M Fall Blitz Targeting Obama," *The Politico*, June 30, 2008 (retrieved June 30, 2008, from http://www.politico.com/news/stories/0608/11452.html).

6. Cummings, "Why the NRA Gets Its Way," *The Politico*, April 18, 2007 (retrieved June 30, 2008, from http://www.cbsnews.com/stories/2007/04/18/politics/politico/main2698141.shtml).

7. Associated Television News, December 18, 2007 (retrieved May 16, 2008, from http://www.prnewswire.com/cgi-bin/stories.pl?ACCT=104&STORY=/www/story/12-18-2007/0004724878&EDATE).

8. Lydia Saad, "NRA Viewed Favorably by Most Americans," Gallup News Service, April 15, 2005 (retrieved May 28, 2008, from http://www.gallup.com/poll/15868/NRA-Viewed-Favorably-Most-Americans.aspx).

9. The Rush Limbaugh Show, "Sarah Palin: Babies, Guns, Jesus," August 29, 2008 (retrieved November 12, 2008, from http://www.rushlimbaugh.com/home/daily/site_082908/content/01125111.guest.html).

10. Thomas Frank has written on what many Democrats see as working-class and poor voters casting ballots against their economic self-interest, responding to Republicans' culture war messages instead of what Democrats see as their better economic programs for the working poor. Thomas Frank, *What's the Matter with Kansas? How Conservatives Won the Heart of America* (New York: Metropolitan Books, 2004).

11. Kevin Bohn, "Gun Sales Surge after Obama Election," CNN.com, November 11, 2008 (retrieved November 12, 2008, from http://www.cnn.com/2008/CRIME/11/11/obama.gun.sales/index.html).

12. Richard Benedetto, "Who's More Likable, Bush or Kerry?" *USA Today*, September 17, 2004 (retrieved June 9, 2008, from http://www.usatoday.com/news/opinion/columnist/benedetto/2004-09-17-benedetto_x.htm).

13. Sean Loughlin, "Bush Warns Militants Who Attack U.S. Troops in Iraq," CNN.com, July 3, 2003 (retrieved June 9, 2008, from http://www.cnn.com/2003/ALLPOLITICS/07/02/sprj.nitop.bush/).

14. CNN.com, "Bush: 'I'm The Decider' On Rumsfeld," CNN.com, April 18, 2006 (retrieved June 9, 2008, from http://www.cnn.com/2006/POLITICS/04/18/rumsfeld/).

15. U.S. Census Bureau, "United States—Urban/Rural and Inside/Outside Metropolitan Area, 2000," (retrieved June 9, 2008, from http://factfinder.census.gov/servlet/GCTSubjectShowTablesServlet?_lang=en&_ts=231078635104).

16. For example, see The Dude Ranchers' Association Web site, http://www.duderanch.org/ranches.cfm.

17. Paul Wyche, "Gasoline Prices Push Scooter, Motorcycle, Mid-Size Cars," *The Saginaw News*, May 5, 2008 (retrieved June 10, 2008, from http://www.mlive.com/business/index.ssf/2008/05/post.html); WebBikeWorld, "U.S. Motorcycle Sales, 1992–2007" (retrieved June 10, 2008, from http://www.webbikeworld.com/Motorcycle-news/blog/).

18. U.S. Fish & Wildlife Service, "2006 National Survey of Fishing, Hunting, and Wildlife-Associated Recreation" (retrieved June 9, 2008, from http://wsfrprograms.fws.gov/Subpages/NationalSurvey/nat_survey2006_final.pdf); U.S. Census Bureau, "Table 1a. Projected Population of the United States, by Race and

Hispanic Origin: 2000 to 2050," (retrieved June 10, 2008, from http://www.census.gov/ipc/www/usinterimproj/).

19. General Social Survey 2006, variable *owngun*. See chap. 1 n. 1.

20. CNN/YouTube Democratic Debate, July 23, 2007 at the Citadel in South Carolina. Transcript available at Council on Foreign Relations, "Democratic Debate Transcript," July 23, 2007 (retrieved June 11, 2008, from http://www.cfr.org/publication/13876/democratic_debate_transcript_cnnyoutube.html).

21. The Pew Research Center for the People & the Press, "McCain Gains on Issues, But Stalls as Candidate of Change," September 18, 2008 (retrieved November 14, 2008, from http://people-press.org/report/450/presidential-race-remains-even).

22. James Bovard, "What's Happened to John McCain?" *America's First Freedom*, July 2001, 29–33.

APPENDIX. STUDYING THE NRA

1. Jack Anderson, *Inside the NRA: Armed and Dangerous* (Beverly Hills, Calif.: Dove Books, 1996); Osha Gray Davidson, *Under Fire: The NRA and the Battle for Gun Control* (Iowa City: University of Iowa Press, 1998); Joan Burbick, *Gun Show Nation* (New York: New Press, 2006).

2. Barney G. Glaser and Anselm L. Strauss, *The Discovery of Grounded Theory* (Chicago: Aldine, 1967); Kathy Charmaz, "The Grounded Theory Method: An Explication and Interpretation," in *Contemporary Field Research: A Collection of Readings,* ed. R. M. Emerson, 109–126 (Boston: Little, Brown, 1983); Kathy Charmaz, "'Discovering' Chronic Illness: Using Grounded Theory," *Sociology of Health and Illness* 30 (1990): 1161–1172; Shoon Lio, Scott Melzer, and Ellen Reese, "Constructing Threat and Appropriating 'Civil Rights': Rhetorical Strategies of Gun Rights and English Only Leaders," *Symbolic Interaction* 31 (2008): 5–31.

3. I interviewed one other woman who is not an NRA member (instead involved with a different Second Amendment organization), but only used this to facilitate my broader understanding of the issues. I do not include data from her interview here.

4. Wayne R. LaPierre, Mailing to National Rifle Association Members, August 2001 (on file with the author).

5. See http://www.madisonbrigade.com/brigade.htm.

6. Herbert Blumer, *Symbolic Interactionism* (Englewood Cliffs, N.J.: Prentice Hall, 1969), 147.

7. Over the years, the NRA has run specials on their memberships, spurring some of the members I interviewed to join or increase their membership level. I asked members how long they have been in the organization and if their

membership status has changed during that period. This allowed me to identify members who have come and gone, as well as discover why their membership statuses changed.

8. National Rifle Association, "Minutes of the Annual Meeting of Members," May 19, 2001 (on file with the author); National Rifle Association, "Minutes of the Annual Meeting of Members," April 27, 2002 (on file with the author).

9. As other gun rights groups such as Gun Owners of America have argued, the NRA has a reputation for supporting incumbent candidates whom they have previously supported, even if the challenger is *more* supportive of gun rights (that is, grades are higher on gun rights voting records). Critics argue that the NRA backs incumbents in these situations because incumbents are more likely to win elections and this bolsters NRA claims about its candidates' success rates.

Index

About the Author

SCOTT MELZER is Assistant Professor of Sociology in the Department of Anthropology and Sociology at Albion College.